THE GRAND FLEET 1914–19

Fourth Battle Squadron of the Grand Fleet at sea, 1916. (Author's collection)

THE GRAND FLEET 1914-19

THE ROYAL NAVY IN THE FIRST WORLD WAR

DANIEL G. RIDLEY-KITTS MBE

FOREWORD BY STEPHEN PAYNE OBE RDI FRINA FREng

In memory of

Leading Stoker Simeon Kitts 306264 (Dev)
HMS *Monmouth*
Sunk at Coronel 1 November 1914

Stoker 1st Class Robert F. Kitts K25413 (Dev)
HMS *Indefatigable*
Sunk at Jutland 31 May 1916

And to all those of all nations who gave their lives
at sea in the Great War 1914–18

All ship illustrations and maps drawn by Daniel G. Ridley-Kitts.

First published 2013
by Spellmount, an imprint of

The History Press
The Mill, Brimscombe Port
Stroud, Gloucestershire, GL5 2QG
www.thehistorypress.co.uk

British Library Cataloguing in Publication Data.
A catalogue record for this book is available from the British Library.

ISBN 978 0 7524 8873 8

Typesetting and origination by The History Press
Printed in Great Britain

CONTENTS

FOREWORD

During the period between 1914 and 1919, the Royal Navy reached its zenith in terms of powerful, technologically advanced battleships, battle-cruisers and other vessels.

Collectively the disposition was simply termed the Grand Fleet.

Amassed just in time to counter the threat from Kaiser Wilhelm's High Seas Fleet, the Grand Fleet was the bastion of empire and ultimately ensured Britain's victory in the First World War. Daniel Ridley-Kitts' book *The Grand Fleet 1914–19* superbly describes how First Sea Lord Jacky Fisher outwitted his protagonists to build the fleet and the technology that made the ships the envy of the world.

Superb illustrations compliment the informative text to provide the reader with the complete story, making this a thoroughly recommended addition to any enthusiast's library.

Stephen M. Payne OBE RDI FRINA FREng

Past President of the Royal Institution of Naval Architects

From RMS *Queen Mary 2* at sea, North Atlantic, 6 October 2012

ACKNOWLEDGEMENTS

As a boy growing up during the Second World War, I, like many other children, followed the course of the war through the pages of the *Daily Mirror*, where our 8th Army were forever giving Rommel a bloody nose, or our fighter boys were downing the Luftwaffe in astronomical numbers, whilst Bomber Command were night after night meting out just punishment to the Reich. The Royal Navy seemed to appear less often in the papers, but when they did, invariably it was to announce some naval victory, such as the sinking of the *Graf Spee*, the *Bismarck* or the Italian fleet at Taranto, and made all the more exciting by seeing these events represented on *Pathé News* at the cinema.

Through these media and reading *The Wonder Book of the Navy* I soon became familiar with our great battleships, aircraft carriers, cruisers, destroyers and submarines, so that by the age of ten the lore and ethos of the Royal Navy was firmly inculcated in my mind.

My own father had served as a cabin boy in the Merchant Navy in the closing stages of the Great War, sharing with other seamen the perils of the U-boat war, and had a great fund of thrilling naval exploits that he recounted to my brothers and I that excited my curiosity in that earlier sea war.

Accordingly, my initial acknowledgements must go to all those who, through their work, aroused my interest in all things naval long ago.

More recently, as this book was being put together, I have to thank, initially, my wife Christine for putting up with my papers and reference works spread over the dining room table for the last eighteen months. I would also like to thank Peter Lindsley of CBM Publishing Services, Cromer, Norfolk for his assistance with the preparation of some of the photographs. I am also indebted to Stephen Payne, the naval architect responsible for designing the liner RMS *Queen Mary 2*, for contributing the foreword. Also, a special word of thanks to Chrissy McMorris for commissioning my efforts in the first place, and latterly to Paul Baillie-Lane for his assistance in sourcing additional photo images, and to Rebecca Newton for her meticulous editing of the text. And finally to the various friends who have offered encouragement along the way.

1

THE VICTORIAN NAVY

On 26 June 1897, on the occasion of Queen Victoria's Diamond Jubilee, the sparkling waters of Spithead were alive with bustling activity with four lines, each stretching 5 miles in length, of great warships drawn up in review order at anchor under a cloudless sky.

The Prince of Wales, representing the queen, sailed between the long columns of warships aboard the Royal Yacht HMY *Victoria and Albert* as each in turn fired a twenty-one-gun salute.

The assembled fleet comprised more than 150 ships, including twenty-two battleships, the most powerful warships of their day, dressed overall with flags and resplendent in their Victorian paint scheme of black hulls, red boot topping, white superstructure, and buff masts and funnels.

The port line was led by the fleet flagship HMS *Renown* of the *Royal Sovereign* class, mounting four 13.5in guns and displacing 14,000 tons, together with the even more modern units of the *Majestic* class of similar displacement, but with better armour protection and armed with the new 12in 46-ton wire wound weapons, which gave greater penetrating power and accuracy together with a higher rate of fire.

Also present were more than forty cruisers, including the new first-class cruisers HMS *Powerful* and HMS *Terrible,* each of 14,600 tons and 100ft longer than the battleships, whose purpose was to protect merchant trade and hunt down would be commerce raiders.

Along with these giant vessels were the smaller second- and third-class protected cruisers, the maids of all work to carry the flag to all oceans of the world, the successors of the frigates of Nelson's day.

Among the smaller craft were twenty torpedo boats, the precursors to the later destroyers whose dashing exploits became legendary in two World Wars in the next century.

The inclusion of the submarine in the ranks of the Royal Navy was still three years away on that sunny afternoon, but the portent of change that all too soon would radically alter the structure of the service, its training and the design of the ships themselves was represented by the uninvited presence of Charles Parsons' revolutionary steam-turbine propelled launch *Turbinia*, which, to the chagrin of the assembled high-ranking officers, raced up and down the lines at 30 knots in a demonstration of the superiority of this method of propulsion, while the naval steam pinnaces ineffectively tried to intercept this vision from the future.

This overwhelming display of naval might represented the high-water mark of empire and Great Britain's predominance as master of the oceans of the world.

Since the Battle of Trafalgar almost one hundred years before, the Royal Navy had been the undisputed master of the waves. The British fleet was the sure shield that protected British trade and the Empire, and it was no empty boast, as stated in the Articles of War drawn up during the Dutch wars, that, 'It is upon the Navy, under the good Providence of God, that the safety, honour and welfare of this realm do chiefly depend.'

The rattle of the anchor chain through the hawse pipe as a cruiser anchored in some foreign roadstead under the White Ensign was all that was necessary to project the awesome power of Great Britain, evoking awe and envy in equal measure, and regarded as guarantee of the Pax Britannica that protected our extensive overseas maritime trade, ensuring that our merchantmen could ply the oceans of the world in perfect safety.

During this period British supremacy at sea was unassailable. The following table demonstrates the comparative strengths in battleships of the great powers in 1897:

Great Britain	France	Italy	Russia	Germany	U.S.A.	Japan
Built - Bldg	Built - Bldg	Built - Bldg	Built - Bldg	Built - Bldg	Built - Bldg	Built - Bldg
24 - 10	13 - 5	8 - 2	6 - 5	4 - 2	3 - 6	2 - 2

It will be seen from the table that only France anywhere near approached Great Britain in terms of battleship numbers. In the forty years since the Crimean War Great Britain had not been involved in a major European war, although conflict of colonial interests with France during the Scramble for Africa from the 1870s onward cast that country in the role of a potential future enemy. British military and naval defence strategy were therefore oriented towards this possibility.

As early as 1858, the launching of the 5,600-ton steam-powered ironclad *Gloire* and three later sister ships caused great concern to the Lords of the Admiralty, who controlled a fleet of 'Wooden Walls' that had hardly evolved since Nelson's time. The immediate response by a hastily convened parliamentary committee was to recommend that, as an interim measure, several of the latest three-deckers should be cut down to two decks and converted to 'razee' steam frigates, sheathed over with iron plating.

On further consideration, this was seen to be an inadequate panic response to the situation, and wiser counsels at that Admiralty reflecting on this expansion of French naval power requested revolutionary designs of armoured steam-powered ships from the Royal Dockyards and no fewer than twelve private shipyards.

Following the results of the competition, the Naval estimates for 1858 set aside £252,000 for the construction of two large iron-framed armoured frigates. The first of these, HMS *Warrior,* was laid down at the Thames Ironworks at Blackwall in May 1859 and launched in December 1859, joining the Channel Fleet in October 1861, with her sister HMS *Black Prince* built on the Clyde a year later. In rapid succession, a further fourteen armoured frigates came down the ways between then and 1864.

At a stroke, the French attempt to steal a march over the Royal Navy had been effectively trumped, and faced with this overwhelming display of powerful warships ranged against them, the French Government decided that coming to some form of an understanding with their rival naval power offered a better solution than an arms race, and almost immediately there was a general improvement in Anglo-French relations.

Because of the abrupt change from wood to all-iron construction, new armoured frigates such as HMS *Royal Oak*, HMS *Prince Consort* and the *Caledonia* had a composite wood and iron construction in order to use up the vast stocks of timber stored in the Royal Dockyards.

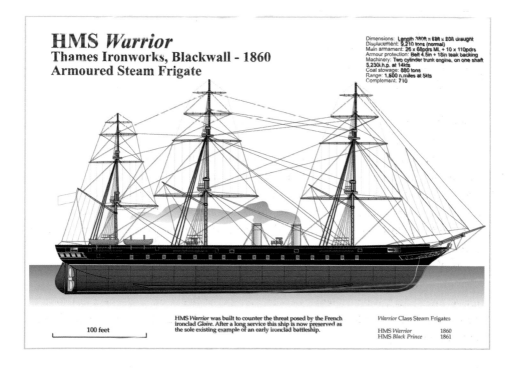

HMS *Warrior*
Thames Ironworks, Blackwall - 1860
Armoured Steam Frigate

Dimensions: Length 380ft x 58ft x 26ft draught
Displacement: 9,210 tons (normal)
Main armament: 26 x 68pdrs ML + 10 x 110pdrs
Armour protection: Belt 4.5in + 18in teak backing
Machinery: Two cylinder trunk engine, on one shaft
5,230 h.p. at 14kts
Coal stowage: 880 tons
Range: 1,800 n.miles at 5kts
Complement: 710

100 feet

HMS *Warrior* was built to counter the threat posed by the French ironclad *Gloire*. After a long service this ship is now preserved as the sole existing example of an early ironclad battleship.

Warrior Class Steam Frigates

HMS *Warrior*   1860
HMS *Black Prince*   1861

The *Warrior* herself, although iron framed and clad, also benefited from a backing of 14in of teak, and was further protected along the waterline by twelve coal bunkers arranged on the outboard side of the two boiler rooms.

The *Gloire* was demonstrably a converted wooden three-decker that had been cut down to two decks and with iron plating fixed to her sides.

The *Warrior*, on the other hand, was revolutionary in design, having been built from the keel up, incorporating a more powerful armament, armour protection and propulsion system than her French rival.

Her displacement of 9,000 tons was almost twice that of the French ship and she was 367ft on the waterline, mounting originally a battery of 26 × 68pdr muzzle-loading smooth-bore cannon together with 10 × 110pdr breech-loading rifled Armstrong guns, and 4 × 70pdr breech-loading bow and stern chasers, disposed on the upper and lower gun decks in broadside fashion and protected by the 1,200 tons of armour in the ship's sides.

Her machinery comprised a powerful two-cylinder horizontal trunk engine of 5,200hp built by John Penn and Co. at a cost of £79,400. Fed by steam from her two boiler rooms, this gave her a speed of 14 knots, with sufficient coal stowage for steaming 5,000 miles. Her three masts carried 36,000 sq. ft of canvas, plus an additional 18,000 sq. ft if studding sails were set, and with her screw lifted out of the water, with a favourable wind this press of canvas was capable of driving her at 12 knots on sail alone.

Warrior and *Black Prince* were formidable vessels that completely outperformed the French ironclads in every respect and it was not for nothing that they were referred to as the 'Black Snakes' of the Channel.

In subsequent ships the mounting of an ever more powerful armament in the broadside battery arrangement required ever longer ships, such as the 400ft-long *Minotaur* from the Thames Ironworks at Blackwall, and it became evident that this disposition of guns was no longer tenable due to the increasing weight of armour needed to cover the large areas on the sides of these long ships.

During the American Civil War the appearance of the Federal armoured turret ship USS *Monitor* directed attention towards the revolving turret-mounted gun, which coincided with the development of larger and improved breech-loading guns. The revolving turret offered not only the advantage of being able to bring guns to bear on a target independent of the heading of the ship but also concentrated the main armour around the guns and their magazines in a more satisfactory manner.

Over the following years a range of largely experimental turret ships were built with varying degrees of success, including HMS *Devastation* and her sister HMS *Thunderer* of 1873. These were the first British warships to dispense with a sailing rig, successfully relying solely on steam power and having a range of 5,000 miles.

An accident occurred in one of the *Thunderer's* turrets in January 1879 due to the accidental double charging of one of the 38-ton muzzle-loading guns, which caused it to burst, killing and wounding most of the turret crew.

This incident highlighted the inherent danger when two barrels were discharged simultaneously and, if an unexpected hang-fire went undetected, it could then be double loaded with a charge leading to an explosion. This dangerous set of circumstances was to be repeated a number of times in various ships over the years and eventually encouraged the general changeover to breech-loading guns as the main armament.

A little before this accident in 1876 another naval scare materialised in the Mediterranean with the launching by Italy of two very heavily armed warships, the *Duilio* and *Dandolo*.

Designed by the talented naval architect Benedetto Brin, these ships displaced 12,000 tons and mounted four huge 100-ton 17.7in rifled muzzle loaders, built by the British armaments manufacturer Armstrong Whitworth, mounted in two armoured barbettes under a light spar deck amidships.

Despite their massive size, the rate of fire from these weapons was painfully slow as they could only be reloaded from a single fore and aft position, with the guns being depressed below the armoured deck where a hydraulic rammer loaded the charges and shells. From there the gun was then raised into firing position and trained on the target, the whole process of firing a salvo taking from 10 to 15 minutes.

In this design the vitals of the ship, engines, magazines, turrets and control positions were contained in a central armoured citadel, comprised of 50cm thick plate backed by 20in of oak planking, leaving the ends of the vessel unprotected, but subdivided into numerous watertight compartments to counter flooding in case of damage during action.

The appearance of these ships carrying what were at that time the biggest naval guns in the Mediterranean required an immediate reply from the Admiralty, which took the form of HMS *Inflexible*, designed by Sir William White. This was a rather hurried and unsatisfactory response, built following the same layout as the Italian ships but carrying four smaller 81-ton 16in guns.

The *Inflexible* had the distinction of being the first ship in the Royal Navy to be equipped with electric lighting and in July 1882 took part in the bombardment of Alexandria during the Urabi revolt, where she fired eighty-one shells, again with a slow rate of fire of one salvo every 10 minutes. Despite receiving some minor damage, she managed to silence the Egyptian shore batteries.

At the time, the Italian ships represented such a threat to British naval supremacy in the Mediterranean – being superior in power to any vessel of the fleet and outgunning the shore batteries at British Mediterranean bases – that immediate action was called for.

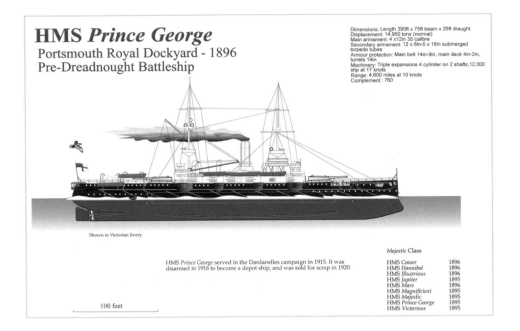

HMS *Prince George*
Portsmouth Royal Dockyard - 1896
Pre-Dreadnought Battleship

Dimensions: Length 390ft x 75ft beam x 26ft draught
Displacement: 14,950 tons (normal)
Main armament: 4 x12in 35 calibre
Secondary armament: 12 x 6in-5 x 18in submerged torpedo tubes
Armour protection: Main belt 14in-9in, main deck 4in-2in, turrets 14in
Machinery: Triple expansions 4 cylinder on 2 shafts,12,000 shp at 17 knots
Range: 4,600 miles at 10 knots
Complement : 760

Shown in Victorian livery

HMS *Prince George* served in the Dardanelles campaign in 1915. It was disarmed in 1916 to become a depot ship, and was sold for scrap in 1920.

Majestic Class

HMS *Cæsar*	1896
HMS *Hannibal*	1896
HMS *Illustrious*	1896
HMS *Jupiter*	1895
HMS *Mars*	1896
HMS *Magnificent*	1895
HMS *Majestic*	1895
HMS *Prince George*	1895
HMS *Victorious*	1895

100 feet

In response, the Government ordered four of the 100-ton Armstrong guns, two of which were installed at Gibraltar and two at Malta, to protect the naval bases there and to restore the status quo.

In the years that followed, the Royal Navy experimented with an assortment of battleship designs, employing differing layouts of armament and armour protection in the search for the optimum type of ship to fulfil their needs.

Perhaps the most notable of these were the *Admiral* class of 1885, mounting four 13.5in breech-loading guns in unprotected barbettes fore and aft, which pointed the way towards a standard layout that more nearly represented the vessels present at the Diamond Jubilee review.

A few anomalous designs were still to be built, such as the *Victoria* and HMS *Sans Pareil* of 1887, a curious layout with two 110-ton 16.25in breech-loaders mounted in a single huge turret forward, with a smaller 10in gun at the stern, plus twelve 6in guns disposed around the citadel on a 10,500-ton low freeboard hull that made working the guns difficult in heavy weather.

As with the earlier ships, the rate of fire of these guns was very slow, with battle practice being made at a range of around only 4,000 to 5,000yd, the distance between ships in which it was considered future actions would take place. In such actions against similarly armed ships the low rate of fire would render them ineffectual weapons of war, and one can speculate that their main use in time of war would have been to reduce coastal forts and batteries rather than fighting in the line of battle, much like the *Inflexible* did. As was the fashion in ship design of the period, the *Victoria* also carried a sharp ram bow, which at that time was seen by

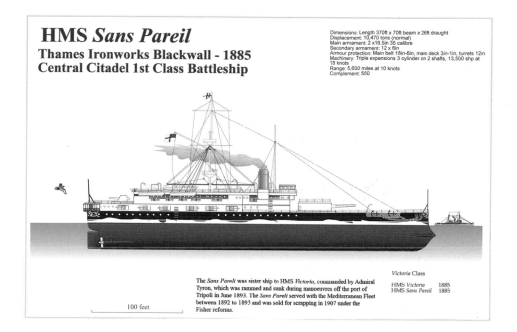

HMS *Sans Pareil*
Thames Ironworks Blackwall - 1885
Central Citadel 1st Class Battleship

Dimensions: Length 370ft x 70ft beam x 26ft draught
Displacement: 10,470 tons (normal)
Main armament: 2 x16.5in 35 calibre
Secondary armament: 12 x 6in
Armour protection: Main belt 18in-6in, main deck 3in-1in, turrets 12in
Machinery: Triple expansions 3 cylinder on 2 shafts, 13,500 shp at 18 knots
Range: 5,600 miles at 10 knots
Complement: 550

The *Sans Pareli* was sister ship to HMS *Victoria*, commanded by Admiral Tyron, which was rammed and sunk during manoeuvres off the port of Tripoli in June 1893. The *Sans Pareli* served with the Mediterranean Fleet between 1892 to 1895 and was sold for scrapping in 1907 under the Fisher reforms.

100 feet

Victoria Class

HMS *Victoria*	1885
HMS *Sans Pareli*	1885

naval strategists to be a viable weapon in the close-range actions envisaged by the Lords of the Admiralty.

The *Victoria* herself achieved notoriety when on manoeuvres in the Mediterranean off the coast of the Lebanon on 22 June 1893 she was lost in an altogether avoidable accident.

The *Victoria* was part of a fleet of eight battleships and five cruisers that were cruising in two lines six cables (1,200yd) apart coming into Tripoli Bay, when they were ordered by the Commander, Vice-Admiral Tyron, leading the starboard division aboard the flagship *Victoria*, to turn inward through 180°.

TRYON

Admiral Markham, leading the port division aboard HMS *Camperdown* and parallel to the flagship, knowing the turning radius of both ships required 3.5 cables (700yd) to complete the manoeuvre, questioned the order by flag signal, but was again ordered by Tyron to execute the order.

As both ships turned inward it became clear to Markham that a collision was inevitable and, despite reversing the engines in a desperate attempt to avoid disaster, the 10,000-ton battleship struck the *Victoria* on her starboard bow, with the *Camperdown*'s ram ripping a huge hole below the waterline.

As the ships drifted apart, the watertight doors in *Victoria* were closed in an attempt to save her as she began to head for shallower water, but within 12 minutes of the collision the ship suddenly rolled over to starboard and, with her screws still turning, plunged bow first to the bottom, taking more than half her crew with her, including Vice-Admiral Tyron. The *Camperdown*, also badly damaged, managed to limp into port safely. While the reasoning behind Vice-Admiral Tyron's actions is difficult to understand, as he was well known as an able tactician, it is recorded that a survivor heard him say 'It was all my fault' on the bridge as the vessel slipped beneath the waves.

In 2001 the wreck of the *Victoria*, which had eluded those looking for it with side-scan sonar, was discovered some 5 miles off the port of Tripoli and showed why it was such an elusive target, as it was standing vertically in the silt of the seabed at a depth of 490ft.

The great weight of the guns had caused the ship to plummet vertically downward causing 100ft of the bow to be buried in the mud up to the bridge structure.

The hull is in excellent condition, thanks to the thickness of armour plate, and is likely to survive for several centuries as one of the few wrecks in the world to have ended up in this unusual position.

One of the survivors of the disaster was Commander John Jellicoe, who was to become Admiral of the Grand Fleet in 1914.

Sometime before this unfortunate incident, the British position relative to France in the number of battleships in the battle fleet, although seemingly satisfactory, still gave cause for concern. In 1889 Britain had sixteen first-class and seventeen second-class battleships, while France had twelve first-class and seventeen second-class.

Other navies were at this time beginning to expand, particularly the USA and Italy, while the German Navy was still essentially a coast defence force and did not at this time figure in the Admiralty's concerns. British cruiser squadrons were twice the number of their French counterparts.

While on the surface Great Britain seemed to be in an unchallengeable position, the spectre of France forming an alliance with some other foreign power, most of whom were at that time modernising and expanding their fleets, caused disquiet at the Admiralty and in Parliament and encouraged the 'Two Powers' doctrine, whereby it was decreed that the Royal Navy should at all times be sufficiently strong in first-line warships to be able to take on and vanquish the combination of any two foreign navies in a possible naval alliance against Great Britain.

The result of parliamentary deliberations under Disraeli's ministry resulted in the 1889 Naval Defence Act and the unprecedented expenditure of millions of pounds for the immediate construction of eight first-class battleships of the *Royal Sovereign* class plus two second-class battleships (HMS *Centurion* and *Barfleur*) and the laying down of sixty modern cruisers.

Under these measures, by 1894 the battle-fleet was being augmented by the battleships HMS *Nile* and HMS *Trafalgar* that were already under construction prior to the Act, and now contained twenty-six first-class battleships against France's fifteen. Against the ninety-two modern cruisers that the Royal Navy could field, the French Navy could only range nineteen.

Developments In Steam Propulsion and Naval Gunnery

Some mention should now be made of the mechanical innovations that took place from the 1850s onward in ship design, particularly in the area of propulsion.

The change from sail to steam in the Royal Navy during the 1870s saw the rapid technological development of propulsive machinery with ever more powerful steam engines being built to answer the designers' call for greater speed, economy of operation and the more efficient use of coal in terms of reducing consumption.

The Scotch Tube or 'cylindrical boiler' was typical of the installation employed in the earlier steam ships.

In this design, a series of 36in-diameter tubes carried the heat from the furnace through the water-filled boiler, this method necessarily taking longer to heat the water due to the comparatively small heated surface area of the tubes relative to the large volume of cold water to be heated.

However, thanks to their typically heavy outer shells, it was possible with this form of boiler to achieve pressures of up to 150lb per square inch, this being far in excess of the earlier shell rectangular boilers of the 1850s and 1860s where pressures of between only 20–30lb per sq. in were common.

For the new *Royal Sovereign* class of 1892–94 a new and much more fuel-efficient type of water-tube boiler was introduced, where the boiler contained tightly packed, small-diameter water-filled tubes that passed directly through the furnace, heating the water more rapidly and efficiently, being both lighter and requiring less maintenance. The ability of these water-tube boilers to raise steam more rapidly than the earlier types was of course a great advantage to warships in particular.

The machinery powered by these boilers also developed rapidly over this period. For example, the screw engine of Brunel's SS *Great Eastern* of 1854 produced only some 1,000ihp, while the *Warrior* of 1860, as previously mentioned, had engines of 5,000ihp.

Succeeding classes had ever more powerful engines. HMS *Royal Sovereign*'s triple expansion engines were 9,000hp and powered these ships at 15.5 knots, or under forced draught to 11,000hp at 16.5 knots, with sufficient coal stowage for 5,000 miles. In the triple expansion engine the initial steam pressure was re-used by being passed in sequence through three (in some cases four) cylinders of increasing diameter, thereby achieving a more efficient use of the power available, which in turn reduced coal consumption and therefore increased their range markedly over earlier types of engines.

Until the end of the nineteenth century and beyond, the reciprocating triple expansion engine became the standard marine prime mover for merchant ships and warships alike, until it in turn was superseded by the steam turbine of Charles Parsons.

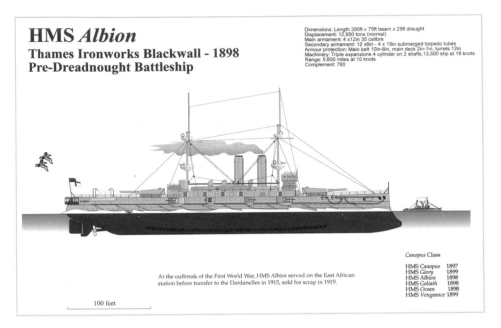

HMS *Albion*

Thames Ironworks Blackwall - 1898
Pre-Dreadnought Battleship

Dimensions: Length 390ft x 75ft beam x 25ft draught
Displacement: 12,950 tons (normal)
Main armament: 4 x12in 35 calibre
Secondary armament: 12 x6in - 4 x 18in submerged torpedo tubes
Armour protection: Main belt 10in-6in, main deck 2in-1in, turrets 12in
Machinery: Triple expansions 4 cylinder on 2 shafts,13,500 shp at 18 knots
Range: 5,600 miles at 10 knots
Complement: 760

At the outbreak of the First World War, HMS *Albion* served on the East African station before transfer to the Dardanelles in 1915, sold for scrap in 1919.

Canopus Class

HMS *Canopus*	1897
HMS *Glory*	1899
HMS *Albion*	1898
HMS *Goliath*	1898
HMS *Ocean*	1898
HMS *Vengeance*	1899

100 feet

The advent of the steam turbine revolutionised propulsive machinery and marked the next advance in the development of the fast battleship.

Initially, the steam turbine was trialled in the smaller torpedo gunboats and quickly won adherents to the steam-turbine cause. Their almost vibration-free performance, with the whirring blades humming within their neatly enclosed, gleaming white-painted casings, projected an air of power and ordered modernity compared to the manic gyrations of the reciprocating engines, whose crank shafts, pistons and gear wheels shook the deck as they thundered round in a continuous shower of flying oil, bilge water, and escaping steam.

Many of the early torpedo–boat destroyers, as they were known, built in the late 1890s and equipped with direct-drive turbines, had three propellers on each shaft and could achieve 30 knots on 7,000hp.

In 1904 the Cunard Company laid down two huge 32,000-ton liners, RMS *Lusitania* and RMS *Mauretania*, both powered by the new steam turbine engines. Originally conceived to be fitted with triple expansion reciprocating engines, the bold move by the company to employ turbines in such large ships was fully justified and both ships proved themselves on the North Atlantic service to be both fast and popular with passengers, with the *Mauretania* taking the Blue Riband from the Germans in 1909, a record she held for twenty-three years.

By 1904 the Admiralty had already ordered the first turbine-powered cruiser *Amethyst* to join the fleet and within two years was laying down the first of the turbine battleships, HMS *Dreadnought*.

The *Royal Sovereign* class represented the first standardised type of battleship after a long period of experimentation with the disposition of armament, first with the broadside battery, the central citadel box, the revolving turret, served by muzzle-loading cannon, then the open barbette and finally the armoured turret with breech-loading guns. The Royal Sovereigns displaced 15,500 tons and were 380ft in length with a beam of 75ft and armed with four 13.5in breech-loaders in two open barbettes positioned either end of the main superstructure.

These vessels were designed by the able naval architect Sir William White, whose influence on capital ship construction in the Royal Navy was to extend into the new century with succeeding classes of highly efficient ships coming down the ways.

The following *Majestic* class was characterised by twin funnels set side by side, while the later *Canopus* class of 1900 had two funnels in the fore and aft positions.

By 1900, British battleship squadrons presented a uniform appearance, with some thirty-two ships, ranging in displacement from 14,000 to 16,500 tons each, mounting four 12in guns as main armament disposed fore and aft of the main superstructure and capable of steaming at 17 to 18 knots. This uniformity of design allowed their fleets to operate with greater cohesion and efficiency than those foreign navies whose vessels were a mixture of various designs.

The *Lord Nelson* and HMS *Agamemnon* were both laid down in 1905 and represented the last examples of the pre-dreadnought battleship to join the fleet; splendid ships though they were, they were rendered obsolete before they were completed by the advent of the *Dreadnought*, launched in the following year, which was to radically change the navies of all nations and how the war at sea would now be fought.

2

LESSONS FROM THE EAST

Before Europe plunged itself into the carnage of the Great War, two wars on the other side of the world at the end of the nineteenth century were to influence naval tactics and the design of capital ships. The first was fought between Japan and China and the second, a few years later, between Japan and Russia in the Far East.

In this period of great change and technological advance, new principles for conducting war at sea were being experimented with that were to result in incorrect interpretations and conclusions being put on the outcome of the various engagements by naval strategists and observers in both Europe and the United States. These would have misleading effects on the design of the next generation of warships, particularly in Great Britain.

The forced opening of Japan to trade was led by an American squadron under Commodore Perry in 1852. After initial resistance, a trade agreement, the Treaty of Kanagawa, was signed that ended Japan's isolation, bringing them into the modern world.

Realising that their centuries-old way of life was to change irrevocably, the Japanese pragmatically adopted many of the western ways, integrating into the financial and political establishments of the western world. In particular, they embraced the rapid industrialisation of their country to build a modern society, while managing to maintain their unique Japanese culture. Recognising the need under these changed conditions of international involvement for the establishment of a navy, initially as a coastal defence force and later as a deep-water fleet, the Japanese turned first to French and German firms to supply the required ships, building a fleet that compared favourably with the generally similar collection of varied warships possessed by the other naval power in the Far East, China.

By 1894 the Japanese had instituted the centralised Meiji Restoration under an Emperor, as befitted an emerging modern state. This form of government replaced the earlier rule by the Shogun warlords.

The Japanese had for many years based the organisation, training and development of its fleet on that of the Royal Navy, as a pattern representing the greatest naval power on earth. They eagerly absorbed the ethos of that service to serve their own ends.

Britain supplied technical advisors to Japan to train their officers and men in all aspects of seamanship, tactics and weapon training and development. Japanese officers were trained in Great Britain, working in the shipyards where they could study the latest techniques in warship construction, and enrolled in British naval colleges, adopting the Royal Navy's organisational systems, uniform and even its customs.

Thanks to the tutelage of British instructors, the Imperial Japanese Navy soon acquired a highly dedicated cadre of officers and men skilled in the arts of seamanship and gunnery unsurpassed by any other navy in the Far East. Additionally in this period the Japanese Government were ordering major warships from British yards.

The Chinese under the Qing Dynasty, on the other hand, were plagued by the demands of foreign powers, namely Great Britain, France and other European powers, who, during the 1840s and 1860s, had used force and persuasion to open a China weakened by natural disaster, famine and internal civil wars (the Taiping Rebellion in the 1850s and 60s was the bloodiest civil war in history with an estimated 30 million dead). Unrestricted foreign trade through a number of treaty ports compelled that country to become more closely involved with other foreign governments and with their policies and politics.

One potentially positive feature of this widening of Chinese international relations was the establishment of a modern navy, essential to protect her interests, which should have increased her international standing; in fact it had the opposite effect.

The Qing Government did not have a standing army and had to rely on tribal groupings to aid the central government forces on a regional basis. These tribal groupings often failed to provide support in time of trial. The most reliable fighting force was the Beiyang Army, composed mostly of Anhwei (Han) and Huai (Muslim) soldiers.

The corresponding Beiyang Fleet, established in 1888, was by comparison initially well equipped, with modern ships built in France and Germany, and symbolised a new and powerful China.

However, corruption among all levels of officials was widespread, with the wholesale embezzling of funds destined to maintain the navy being widespread among court and Admiralty officials in all departments and rendering the effective management of the service impossible. For instance, in 1895 30 million taels of silver earmarked for the construction of new battleships were diverted by the Dowager Empress Tzu-Hsi, who effectively ran the country and was the last absolute monarch, to reconstruct and enlarge the Summer Palace in Beijing.

This form of mismanagement and corruption spread rapidly through all departments of the Imperial Navy to the extent that even the supply of ammunition to the ships stopped in 1891, as funds were stolen by corrupt officials.

As time went on the ships' fighting efficiency and condition deteriorated rapidly. In the case of one ship, even its guns were removed and sold to a local warlord. Poor levels of maintenance rendered ships almost useless as fighting units, while discipline and morale amongst the crews rapidly fell to an unacceptable level.

Against this background, Japanese expansion into Korea in 1894 provoked a war between the two countries, in which the Japanese Army soon asserted its superiority over the Chinese troops, entering Seoul in July 1884 and expelling the Chinese troops from most of the peninsula.

At sea, after a series of small naval actions in which the Japanese triumphed, a major engagement between the two fleets took place off the mouth of the Yalu River in September 1894.

The Chinese fleet consisted of two battleships, four large cruisers and assorted torpedo boats, while ranged against them the Japanese had a fleet of twelve modern warships. At this stage the Japanese did not have the financial resources to purchase modern battleships but instead adopted the French 'Jeune École' school, which propounded the theory of employing smaller and faster armoured cruisers that could outmanoeuvre and bring a rapid concentration of fire onto heavier, slower-firing enemy battleships, negating the advantage of their greater gun power.

During the battle the Japanese fleet comprehensively defeated the Chinese fleet, sinking eight out of ten of the Chinese ships.

The outcome of the battle caused foreign naval observers to draw the conclusion that lighter and faster ships could successfully fight battleships, a misconception that was to adversely affect tactical thinking and design in varying degrees for some years to come.

In the course of the battle the Chinese Beiyang fleet disposed in line-abreast, opening fire ineffectually at the then great range of 6,000yd, while the faster Japanese warships passed diagonally across their front, closing the range to 3,000yd, where the combined rapid fire of their lighter weapons was used with terrible effect.

As no major naval action had taken place since the Battle of Navarino in 1827, a major problem facing naval strategists at this time was that when the Turkish fleet was defeated by the combined British, French and Russian fleets, they had no experience of battle in the light of the innovative technical developments that had taken place in the intervening years.

Japan, now established as a major naval power and with an expansionist foreign policy, began to build up her fleet with modern battleships, ordered from British shipyards in increasing numbers.

While Japan had been heavily involved in military and naval operations in Korea against the Chinese since the 1890s, the corresponding Russian expansion in

Manchuria and the acquisition of the port of Vladivostok in 1860, together with the later extension of the Trans-Siberian Railway, served to increase tension between the two countries, with numerous border incidents taking place over the years leading up to the twentieth century.

Finally, in February 1904, without a declaration of war, Japanese naval forces attacked the Russian fleet anchorage of Port Arthur on the Liaodong Peninsula at night with torpedo boats.

This attack resulted in two Russian battleships and a cruiser being sunk in the harbour and the remaining ships being trapped by the rapidly advancing artillery of the Japanese Army.

Over the next few months the Russians suffered a series of military defeats and eventually all the Russian ships in Port Arthur were sunk by shore-based artillery fire.

Prior to this disaster, efforts were made to reinforce the Russian Pacific fleet by sending almost the whole of the Baltic Fleet halfway round the world on a trip of 18,000 miles that took 8 months to accomplish.

The fleet, now renamed the 'Russian Second Pacific Squadron', under Admiral Rozhestvensky – a capable commander, but hampered by the quality of ships at his disposal and the poor discipline of the crews – sailed from the naval base at Kronshtadt. This motley collection of ships was unsuited to working together in line of battle due to its mixed armament and inability to manoeuvre effectively as a unit.

While passing down the North Sea in October 1904, the jumpy Russian gunners opened fire at night on British fishing boats, under the impression that they were Japanese torpedo boats. This event, in which several British fishermen were killed and wounded, became known as 'the Battle of Dogger Bank', and caused a diplomatic incident, resulting in an indemnity to be demanded of the Russian Government and the Russian ships being escorted as far as Gibraltar by warships of the Royal Navy.

By the time the Russian fleet finally reached the Far East, Port Arthur had already fallen, so Admiral Rozhestvensky elected to pass through the Straits of Tsushima to reach the only other free Russian port of Vladivostok.

However, the Japanese Admiral Togo, leading a fleet of four fast battleships, six armoured cruisers and other smaller craft, crossed Rozhestvensky's 'T', the classic manoeuvre in which a line of battleships cuts across the line of advance of an enemy fleet, thereby bringing a devastating barrage of fire to fall on the enemy van.

A feature of battle was the extreme range at which the Russians initially opened fire, at some 7,500yd with their heavy 12in and 10in guns, which were capable of only around two rounds per minute.

Admiral Togo calculated that his ships were in little danger of being hit at this range and accordingly turned toward the Russian ships to close the range passing diagonally across their front.

The Russian secondary armament scored the first hits but, as the range closed rapidly to 5,000yd, the superior Japanese gunnery and rate of fire had its effect. Rozhestvensky tried to close the range to improve the chances of obtaining hits with his main and secondary armaments, at the same time turning to starboard to avoid having his 'T' crossed.

The two fleets continued on parallel courses to the north-east at a range of 5,500yd, with the Japanese pounding the Russian ships to which they could only make an ineffective reply.

The Japanese battleships – the flagship *Mikasa* and the *Shikishima* – fired on the Russian battleship *Suvorov*, their shells bursting with terrible effect. Soon the other battleships, *Alexander III*, *Osliabia* and *Borodino*, were heavily engaged and by early evening all four were sunk, with the remaining main unit *Orel* being badly damaged and captured, together with the rest of the fleet that had not either been sunk or had escaped to neutral ports.

One of the features of the battle from which later spurious conclusions were drawn was the inclusion of four armoured cruisers in Admiral Togo's battle line. While the four battleships (15,000 tons) were armed with four relatively slow-firing heavy 12in guns, the armoured cruisers (9,000 tons) carried mixed batteries varying from 10in to 8in, together with up to fourteen 6in quick-firers.

Additionally, these ships had adequate armour protection for the period, and were capable of steaming at over 21 knots, which was considerably faster than the Russian battleships, and could also deliver a telling weight of shot against the Russian ships.

The armoured cruisers' 8in guns could deliver five 250lb shells per minute and the 6in guns eight 100lb shells in the same time.

It was the most comprehensive defeat of one fleet by another, and a modern one at that, since Nelson's victory at Trafalgar almost one hundred years before. The effect of the defeat of a major European nation by an Asiatic power was not lost on the chancelleries of Europe and gave cause for concern at the Admiralty that its Far Eastern protégé had grown into such a powerful sea power in so short a time.

While these events were being played out in the Far East, the results were being analysed by naval strategists in Europe and the United States. The enormous 7,000yd range, as it was then seen, at which both fleets opened fire and the mixed calibre of the armament, posed a whole new set of problems to the tacticians. The fact that both sides failed to register hits at extreme range, only hitting their targets when the range closed to around 4,000yd, was not recognised as a failure, but rather encouraged naval observers to predict that future battles would be fought at these extreme ranges, which, although a correct observation, would need a complete change of tactics and equipment to implement.

At these ranges the existing fast-burning propellant powders produced irregular rates of burn that militated against achieving an accurate fall of shot. Also it was impossible to differentiate between the shell splashes of the mixed-calibre weapons together with the slow rate of fire of say a 12in gun (one shell every 2 minutes), that enabled a target to turn away between salvoes, making the gunlayer's task almost impossible in calculating the 'rate of change' of a target and correcting their aim.

Prior to the Battle of Tsushima, the Admiralty, in the shape of the gunnery expert Captain Percy Scott, was studying the problems of improving the accuracy of gunnery at extreme range and the tracking of a target.

The introduction of large-grain, slower-burning propellant charges greatly improved the accuracy of the fall of shot while eliminating the tendency for the shell to tumble towards the end of flight and keep on target.

The introduction of long-based optical range finders went some way to allowing a more accurate assessment of the enemy's range and position, and in battle practice the percentage of hits recorded to number of rounds fired improved from 31 per cent in 1895 to 71 per cent in 1905.

An important innovation introduced by Captain Scott was the director fire control system, an early analogue computer device that could predict the course and position of the target and accurately direct the fall of shot, while allowing for adjustment of the range and deflection to keep subsequent salvoes on target.

One of the false conclusions drawn from the Japanese victory was the belief that armoured cruisers with their lighter, quick-firing weapons could take on and defeat battleships in line of battle.

This misconception to a degree influenced Britain's Admiral 'Jacky' Fisher, then First Sea Lord, who was already planning a class of fast, heavily armed but lightly protected cruisers that were to become the battle-cruisers. These were shown to be a flawed concept when three were lost at the Battle of Jutland, together with three of the earlier armoured cruisers.

Naval architects fought a continuing struggle against the increasing penetrating power of ever more powerful guns and the need to provide adequate armour, protection that could only be achieved at the expense of an increasing weight penalty that had to be balanced against the requirements of speed, gun power and displacement.

The early wrought-iron armour of the *Warrior* was soon replaced by compound armour, which consisted of iron sheets faced with steel, forming a sort of composite sandwich. Effective though this arrangement was initially, soon the increasing power of the new breech-loading guns required a more resistant form of armour. In the *Majestic* class battleships of 1895 it was replaced by Harvey case-hardened steel plate within a 9in-thick main belt.

This armour originated in the USA and was manufactured by the Carnegie Steel works. The hardening process involved sandwiching carbon between two steel plates at high temperature in the furnace for an extended time before quenching in water to surface-harden the plates.

At the time, this armour gave protection from a 12in shell fired from 4,000yd. The Harvey, case-hardened armour of steel plates in a 9in-thick belt, 16ft in depth had the equivalent resistance of the 18in composite armour of the earlier classes.

A little later, the German firm of Krupp introduced a hardened steel plate of nickel steel from 1in to 12in thickness that broke up all projectiles fired in test firings. Following this success, British shipbuilders employed nickel steel armour in subsequent battleships.

From the 1860s, advances in metallurgy and precision mechanical engineering enabled guns to be manufactured, employing such advances as breech loading (perfected by Armstrong), together with the interrupted screw thread (a device developed by the French that closed the breech with a one-third turn) and the advent of rifling that imparted spin stability to the shell in flight. All of these advances contributed to the advent of the modern long-range naval gun.

Naval guns were constructed as a series of forged tubes of differing diameters that were heated and shrunk to fit over each other, with the area around the breech – where pressures of up to 200,000lb per square inch would be experienced – being reinforced by multiple layers of tubes in that area.

The bore of the innermost 'A' tube was machined internally, with a series of spiral grooves or 'lands' (typically one and a half turns of the barrel length) that engaged the driving bands on the base of the shells to impart spin stability to the projectile. The 'wire wound weapon' was a further method of reinforcement against the tremendous pressures exerted in the breech chamber when the gun was fired. This consisted of winding the outer surface of the innermost rifled 'A' tube with up to 120 miles of a steel wire ribbon, over which the second 'B' tube was then shrunk on to. This process not only strengthened the tube against the detonation of the propellant charge but also increased the accuracy of the gun.

The standard British naval gun, as mounted in the battleship HMS *Albion* of 1899, was the 12in Mk IX 40 calibre weapon. It could fire a 850lb armour-piercing shell at a muzzle velocity of 2,480fps, for a distance of 15,000yd at 14° elevation and could penetrate 12in of Harvey or Krupp hardened steel plate at 3,500yd.

The later Mk X 45 calibre 12in gun of 1906 could fire a shell of similar weight, but with an increased muzzle velocity of 2,700fps to a range of 25,000yd at 30° elevation. This model of gun, with minor modification, remained in use until 1945.

In the *Albion*, 300 to 400 shells were stored in the shell rooms and magazines for each gun, where three main types of shell were in use – common, armour piercing and high explosive. These were filled either with powder or the newer Lyddite.

The shells and projectile charge were brought up from the magazine and handling room by the mechanical shell hoists into the turret where the shell was rammed into the breech, followed by the cordite charge, which, in British ships, consisted of a bundle of tightly packed, extruded cordite sticks bound together by tape and enclosed in a silk cloth bag forming the cartridge.

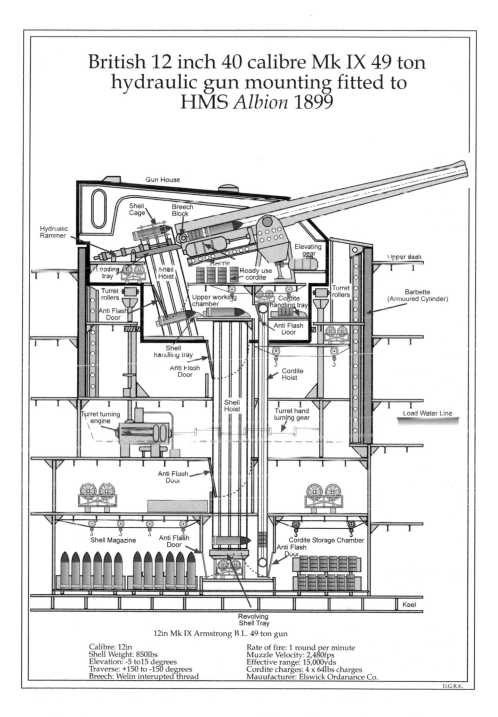

British 12 inch 40 calibre Mk IX 49 ton hydraulic gun mounting fitted to HMS *Albion* 1899

12in Mk IX Armstrong B.L. 49 ton gun

Calibre: 12in
Shell Weight: 850lbs
Elevation: -5 to15 degrees
Traverse: +150 to -150 degrees
Breech: Welin interupted thread

Rate of fire: 1 round per minute
Muzzle Velocity: 2,480fps
Effective range: 15,000yds
Cordite charges: 4 x 64lbs charges
Mauufacturer: Elswick Ordanance Co.

D.G.R.K.

This seemingly Heath-Robinson arrangement was standard practice throughout the time these large calibre guns remained in service with the Royal Navy, although all smaller calibre weapons had brass cartridge cases with the shell attached as a single unit.

It is noteworthy that from the outset the Imperial German Navy chose to employ sealed brass cartridge cases for all calibres of gun, including their 11in (280mm) main armament guns, which was to give them greater protection from flash fires if a turret was hit, unlike the British ships where a hit on a turret could send tongues of flame down the ammunition hoists into the handling rooms and magazines, setting off the exposed charges with fatal results.

The main weapon fitted as secondary armament to battleships and mounted on destroyers in the 1900s was the 4in Mk1 quick-firer, which fired a 31lb projectile at a muzzle velocity of 2,600fps for 13,700yd at a rate of ten shells per minute. Later Dreadnought battleships had their secondary armament upgraded to the Mk IX 6in QF gun, which at an elevation of 15° could throw a 100lb shell a distance of 13,500yd, with a maximum rate of fire of six rounds a minute. This weapon was also favoured as main armament for the new generation of Dreadnought light cruisers, such as the HMS *Arethusa* and later wartime classes.

A weapon that was to have increasing importance over the years in naval arsenals was the locomotive torpedo, as it was originally known, first proposed by an Austrian naval officer, Captain Lupus, and developed by the British engineer Robert Whitehead at his factory in Fiume on the Adriatic in the 1860s.

Early versions of the torpedo were of limited range and were so slow that they could be outrun by the attacked ship steering away from the track in the opposite direction, but by 1893 a torpedo establishment had been set up at HMS *Vernon* in Portsmouth to develop the weapon for the Royal Navy. By 1906 torpedoes of the Whitehead design, powered by a compressed air piston engine carrying a warhead of gun-cotton and pressure-firing pistol, had a range of over 1,000yd and could travel at a predetermined depth below the surface at up to 35 knots, with a reasonable degree of accuracy steered by gyroscopic control.

A further improvement in performance was the provisoin of greater power and range. This was acheived by heating the air in the compressed air reservoir, either by burning paraffin or discharging a shot-gun cartridge internally to substantially raise the air temperature.

Torpedoes were initially installed in battleships in submerged beam and bow tubes, for defence. At the same time, torpedo boats – small, fast, light craft – were being developed, whose function it was to attack larger vessels.

These torpedo boats were in turn countered by the introduction of the torpedo boat destroyers, which were much larger and more heavily armed ships that eventually took over the duties of the torpedo boat and became known simply as the destroyer, and which usually included a heavy torpedo armament.

The effectiveness of torpedo boats and destroyers was shown in the First World War when Italian motor torpedo boats attacked and sank the modern Austro-Hungarian dreadnought *Szent Istvan* with two torpedoes off the Dalmatian coast in 1918.

The torpedo was also to become the main weapon of the submarine, which the British introduced into the Navy in 1900, with the Germans following suit in 1908.

During the First World War Germany employed her U-boats in pursuing the *Guerre de Course* of commerce raiding. This was to prove so effective that at one stage during 1917 Britain's merchant shipping losses were so heavy that it was in danger of starvation.

So by 1904 great changes were taking place in the way the war at sea would be fought in future conflicts, with the introduction of the steam turbine and the development of the long-range naval gun, submarine and torpedo.

3

THE COMING OF THE DREADNOUGHT

Towards the end of the nineteenth century the British preoccupation with France as its natural enemy was challenged by the emergence of the Imperial German Empire as a growing naval power.

As the century drew to a close, the political, economic and colonial ambitions of Imperial Germany increasingly came into conflict with the interests of Great Britain and France. As a rapidly developing industrial power, Germany felt constrained in its efforts to find markets for the manufactured goods it produced in ever increasing quantities and the expansion of its trading networks, due to the near monopoly enjoyed by Britain, France and latterly the United States.

Until the 1890s, although Germany had one of the largest standing armies in Europe, its navy was little more than a coastal defence force. This was to change under the influence of the autocratic Kaiser Wilhelm II, a man brilliant in many aspects of governing his country but dangerously unbalanced in others. It transpired that he was a mercurial and deluded figure who set his country on the path of world domination, making him in his time as great a danger to world peace as Hitler was to prove half a century later.

Wilhelm had a great admiration for his grandmother's navy; however this was tinged with an almost childish envy that made him resolve to build a navy of his own that would rival the Royal Navy.

He had a fascination with warships and personally took a hand in the design of the various classes of ship he deemed necessary for his projected fleet, where, despite his dilettante approach to naval architecture, his observations and suggestions were in line with accepted practice.

His recently retired Chancellor, Otto von Bismarck, had moulded the modern Germany from a collection of principalities and loosely associated Germanic states into a powerful nation under Prussian domination. He had planned an ordered, modern and industrialised state while conducting a careful foreign policy designed to maintain the balance of power that ensured the peace in Europe after the Franco-Prussian war of 1870.

Bismarck had protected the frontiers of this powerful European state against its neighbours and potential enemies with the establishment of a large standing army, as he saw that any conflict would and should only take place within continental Europe.

The Franco-Prussian War of 1870 had secured Germany's place as the dominant player in European affairs and a series of military alliances with the Austro-Hungarian Empire, and latterly Italy, reinforced her position at the international conference tables, while her ever-expanding industrial development promised burgeoning markets for her products.

Bismarck had always counselled against entering into any form of naval rivalry with Great Britain and directed German foreign policy to avoid clashes of interest with what was then the world's greatest naval power. However, now freed from the old Chancellor's restraining hand, the Kaiser could indulge in his personal ambition of the development of a navy that would be equal to that of the Royal Navy in power and prestige.

With the appointment of Admiral Alfred von Tirpitz as State Secretary for the Imperial Navy in 1898, the Kaiser had an enthusiastic supporter for his own views on naval expansion and at once began building a fleet, the 'Heimatflotte' (Home Fleet), that could rival the Royal Navy. Tirpitz envisaged he would achieve a two-thirds parity with the Royal Navy that would seriously impinge on Britain's command of the seas in Germany's favour.

His rationale was that with a large and powerful German fleet, the 'Fleet in Being' sitting across the North Sea would by its presence – even if it did not put to sea – tie down the battleships of the 'Grand Fleet', rendering them largely ineffectual. It would also allow squadrons of armoured cruisers and fast armed merchant cruisers, converted from liners, to roam the world's trade routes, attacking British mercantile trade, with the probability of not having to fight more powerful ships than themselves during a cruise.

The first German Naval Defence Act of 1898 was seen as a direct challenge to the Royal Navy, with the creation of the High Seas Fleet under the impetus of the Kaiser leaving the Lords of the Admiralty in no doubt that at some time in the not too distant future the two fleets would inevitably meet in combat, as relations between the two governments deteriorated.

Great Britain's response was to accelerate the building of battleships and other warships, with no less than thirty pre-dreadnought battleships going down the ways between 1900 and 1907, at an enormous cost, in order to maintain the lead over Germany.

Great Britain suffered political isolation and unpopularity as a result of its scorched earth policies against the Boer farmers during the South African War (1899–1902), which included the incarceration of women and children in 'concentration camps', where, due more to mismanagement than direct cruelty, many died from cholera and malnutrition, causing Great Britain's standing in world opinion to sink to an all-time low. By these measures, Britain had alienated the majority of other European powers; therefore, the British Government urgently sought to form political and military alliances with Continental powers and with Japan in the East in order to counter German naval and military expansion.

The most important of these new alliances was the Entente Cordiale of April 1904 between Great Britain and France, which brought an end to centuries of rivalry and warfare between the two countries. These negotiations for military and naval co-operation had been under discussion for some years by succeeding governments, but much of the success for achieving agreement was down to King Edward VII, who, independently of the government, made the first informal approaches and latterly became an immensely popular figure among the French. He did much to smooth the way to secure the desired result.

A similar agreement, the Anglo-Japanese Naval Alliance of 1902, was particularly useful to the Royal Navy's Far Eastern commitments. Under the conditions of the agreement, with the Imperial Japanese Navy acting as an intermediary in looking after its interests, Britain was able to withdraw a large proportion of its cruiser squadrons nearer to home waters.

So, by the early 1900s Europe was divided into a series of complicated military alliances, with Great Britain, France and Russia forming the Triple Alliance of 1907 and Germany, Austria-Hungary and, initially, Italy forming the Central Powers. The stage was set for war.

At the Admiralty, the new First Sea Lord, Sir John Fisher, was overseeing a revolution in the running of the Royal Navy. This officer, who had begun his career during the Crimean War aboard a wooden three-decker, seen action in the Second Opium War (1860) and devised an early armoured train for reconnaissance in the Anglo-Egyptian War of 1882, was a talented officer and able strategist who strongly supported the modernising changes in naval tactics that were becoming evident at the end of the nineteenth century, often against the general view of the Admiralty and his brother officers.

Fisher was an early proponent of the introduction of the submarine into the fleet along with the torpedo, and as Third Sea Lord and Controller of the Navy between 1892 and 1897 he pressed for the introduction of the torpedo boat destroyer to protect capital ships from this form of underwater attack.

Fisher had earlier encouraged the development and use of the more efficient water-tube boiler in ships of the fleet, with the first installation being made in the gunboat *Sharpshooter* in 1894. However, his efforts to have them generally adopted were frustrated by assertions of vested interests and they became the subject of a parliamentary enquiry before they were eventually adopted as standard.

On Trafalgar Day 1902, Admiral Sir John Fisher became First Sea Lord and began immediately to introduce the reforms that he had long planned for the Royal Navy. The first of these, which was designed to bring the Royal Navy into the twentieth century, was to revise the educational system for officers at Dartmouth and Osborne naval colleges, with greater emphasis on the technical aspects of training that reflected the advances in engineering, gunnery, navigation and strategy that were daily becoming more evident.

At the same time, he improved the lot of the common sailor with better conditions of service and introduced the daily issue of fresh baked bread, consigning hard tack to history.

Between 1900 and 1904, the implementation of the German Naval Defence Act of 1898 caused the British naval estimates to double to £50,000,000 – almost £5.4 billion at present-day values. This sum represented more than half the total defence budget for that period, with the money being spent on the building of twenty-two pre-dreadnought battleships, twenty-one large armoured cruisers, eleven protected cruisers, sixty destroyers, eighteen submarines, as well as a range of other craft.

Social historians have speculated that, despite Britain's great wealth at a time of notable social inequality, the many social ills that plagued society in the early years of the twentieth century (bad housing, poor health provision, poor and dangerous working conditions in factories and mines, lack of educational opportunities and so on) could have been cured and the lot of the average British subject improved if even only a small proportion of this money had been diverted.

On the other hand, many industries such as coal mining, steel production, shipbuilding and associated engineering businesses were to benefit greatly from the expanded naval armament programmes in those years, with an accelerated rate of employment among the working populations in the centres of shipbuilding activity. The rate of employment in the shipbuilding industry increased by over 50 per cent between 1903 to 1906, with corresponding increases in employment for associated engineering trades providing good regular wages to large sections of the working-classes, often for the first time in their lives. (Thames Ironworks shipyard at Blackwall, one of several yards on the River Thames, employed 3,000 workers alone at this period.)

So it could be concluded that amongst the boilermakers, platers and riveters of Canning Town, Tyneside, Clydebank, Belfast, Plymouth, Barrow and Chatham the expansive naval policy was met with approval.

As First Sea Lord, Fisher had inherited a vast fleet of disparate ships, each designed for disparate purposes. Recognising that many of these ships were totally unfit for the modernised navy, he immediately resolved to reduce their numbers, on the grounds of economy, scrapping those ships that, in his own words, could 'neither fight nor run away'. One hundred and sixty ships were removed from the navy list in a few short years and their crews were redistributed to more modern vessels.

By these measures, Fisher initially managed to reduce the naval estimates for 1905 by £3.5 million and effected savings in real terms for the years 1906–07, after which the next intensive dreadnought building programme once again dictated ever increasing expenditure.

He also organised the concentration of the battleship units of the fleet to home waters, divided into two commands by 1904 as the Atlantic Fleet and the Channel Fleet, leaving the cruiser squadrons to carry on the work of trade protection and showing the flag in distant seas. Furthermore, he reorganised the manning of ships in the reserve fleet, while the main fleets were at instant readiness to be deployed in an emergency.

The advent of the all large-calibre gun ship had for some time been seen to be an inevitable development, with salvo firing at long range, offering the most effective solution to engage an enemy before he could inflict damage in return. Fisher had been planning a ship such as this for some time, with the help of a committee that included the naval architect Sir Philip Watts and the future Commander of the Grand Fleet, Captain John Jellicoe.

Drawing on the results of the recent Battle of Tsushima, their deliberations led to the design of a new type of battleship: the Dreadnought. Such a vessel had already been proposed by the Italian naval architect Vittorio Cuniberti, who, in Brassey's *Naval Annual* for 1903, had suggested a ship not so very different from the eventual Dreadnought, describing it as being the 'perfect design of battleship for the Royal Navy for its future needs'. Cuniberti proposed a ship of 17,000 tons mounting twelve 12in guns in super-firing turrets, driven by reciprocating engines to give 25 knots.

No doubt Cuniberti's design at least convinced Fisher of the correctness of his own vision of what constituted the ideal battleship in a new age, and he pressed ahead with all due facility to bring the Dreadnought into being.

The 1904 design committee recognised the tactical advantages of higher speed that would allow the new ship to choose the range and the ability to manoeuvre into the optimum position to engage an enemy vessel to advantage. This revolutionary vessel was to be armed with ten 12in guns and driven through the water by the power of four Parsons steam turbines of a combined 23,000hp at 21 knots. Considering the early stage of development of this form of propulsion and the disappointing results that some other nations were to initially experience as they attempted to introduce turbines in their own ships, the choice of installing steam turbines was itself a gamble

One feature of the design that was not repeated was the carrying of the transverse bulkheads up to the main deck level without interconnecting watertight doors, in order to achieve greater watertight integrity. This arrangement created difficulties of communication between different parts of the ship, as all movements between the compartments had to be made at main deck level.

Five thousand tons of armour was included in the design, with an 11in-thick belt, 1.5in to the main deck (that was largely to remain at this thickness in succeeding ships) and 11in armour to the turrets and turret trunks.

The paradox was that by building the *Dreadnought* all other battleships, including those of the Royal Navy, would be rendered immediately obsolete.

Dreadnought's main armament of ten 12in B/L 45 calibre Mark X guns were mounted in five turrets, arranged with three on the centreline and two wing turrets firing a 850lb projectile, with a velocity of 2,735fps, giving a range of 17,900yd at 13.5° elevation or 20,400yd at 16° elevation.

The whole *raison d'être* for the *Dreadnought* concept was to be able to engage an enemy at great range, operating from a zone of immunity from enemy fire, to hit first and hit hard before the enemy could effectively reply.

It had been shown in trials that accurate fire at long range was possible using a central fire-control system that was being developed by Sir Percy Scott and others. They had established that heavier calibre weapons when discharged in the salvo-firing method ensured accurate ranging, where the combined fall of similar shell splashes allowed the range to be quickly established and altered to straddle the target.

Admiral Fisher was very conscious of the new threat posed to the battle line of a fleet by the torpedo; a weapon that he himself had championed. This dictated the necessity of long-range fire to protect the main units from being closed to action by torpedo boats, which could cause the battle line to turn away from the torpedo tracks and lose contact with the enemy, as occurred on two occasions to the British fleet at Jutland.

Other countries were already on the verge of taking the step of building ships that adhered to Fisher's vision. Following lessons learned at Tsushima, the Japanese were studying designs for similar all big gun ships and in May 1905 had laid down two battleships, the *Aki* and the *Satsuma*, armed with four 12in guns and twelve 10in guns, capable of 20 knots.

These 'intermediate' dreadnoughts were fine designs but, due to the ruinous costs of the war against Russia, they took almost six years to complete, by which time they were outmoded. They did, however, point the way to the new generation of battleships.

Meanwhile, in the United States similar views prevailed and two ships had already been designed that incorporated many of the principles that Fisher was advocating. The *Michigan* and the *South Carolina* had been designed before the *Dreadnought* and laid down in 1906, but not completed until after the *Dreadnought* was launched. These vessels mounted eight 12in guns in superimposed turrets on the centre line, a more advanced layout than the single *en echelon* arrangement of the British ships, and an arrangement that would not be adopted by the British until the launch of the *Neptune* in 1909.

At this period an act of Congress restricted the tonnage of US battleships to 17,000 tons on the grounds of economy, which severely constrained the American naval architects in their desire to build the most efficient ships that incorporated all the conflicting requirements relative to armour protection, armament, speed and range. The Americans also experienced severe problems in the development of turbine propulsion machinery for their warships, failing to achieve the same high quality of engineering that were to be found in Great Britain and Germany at the time.

Accordingly, due to this failure, the two new battleships were retro-engined with the older reciprocating machinery, which limited their top speed to give only 18 knots; although, by making a virtue out of necessity this was considered to be acceptable to the Admirals, as the new ships could now keep station with older units of the fleet and vice versa.

Meanwhile, at Portsmouth feverish activity had been taking place and now that the decision had been taken there was no going back; speed of construction for the *Dreadnought* and her successors was of the essence if Great Britain was to maintain her pre-eminent position in the oceans of the world.

The keel plate for *Dreadnought* was laid on 2 October 1905, and by drawing on the large stores of stockpiled materials in the Royal Dockyards it was only 4 months later, in February 1906, that the completed hull slid down the ways.

The hectic rate of construction continued, with Admiral Fisher ordering the diversion of equipment from other projects, including appropriating the 12in gun turrets from the intermediate dreadnoughts *Lord Nelson* and *Agamemnon* then being built; it could take up to two years to manufacture similar turrets at an armament works under normal circumstances.

By these extreme measures the *Dreadnought* was completed on 3 October 1906, having been built in a record year and a day, immediately running trials over the measured mile. The *Dreadnought* was revolutionary in every way, ushering in a completely new way for fleets to fight for control of the seas. Her appearance caused foreign navies to be taken completely by surprise. The shock of this revolutionary concept that upset all existing tactics threw their naval planners into utter confusion, to the extent that all battleship construction largely ceased, with Germany now recognising that, not only had all her existing battleships and armoured cruisers become obsolete, but that in order to compete against these new ships, the recently completed Kiel Canal – vital for the transfer of the German fleet between the North Sea and the Baltic – would have to be widened and deepened to accommodate the larger, new dreadnoughts then being designed.

This major reconstruction of the canal was to take eight years to complete, at a cost of £14,000,000. Once completed, as Lord Fisher had predicted with incisive prescience, Germany would consider herself powerful enough to challenge Great Britain at sea, heralding the start of hostilities.

Fisher was so sure that the two countries would inevitably clash at sea within a few years that in 1908 he proposed to King Edward VII that Britain should initiate a preventive war against Germany and destroy her fleet in the manner of Nelson at Copenhagen, while the Royal Navy still had an overwhelming advantage in ships and gun power. The king was horrified by the suggestion and told Fisher that he must be mad.

In Germany, all building of capital ships was suspended for eighteen months as plans were prepared for their own dreadnoughts, while in Britain construction raced ahead, so that by the end of 1909 the Royal Navy had four dreadnoughts in commission and three building, while the German Navy had only two ships in service and two building.

Against this tide of rising panic, a second and even more intensive naval arms race burst onto the international scene. The main protagonists were, of course, Great Britain and Germany, but the ramifications of these developments in the North Sea effected all the major naval powers. In shipyards from Brest to Constantinople, Taranto to Koenigsberg, the crash of the riveting hammers was heard with increasing frequency, as France, Russia, Italy, Austria, Japan and the United States poured ever more of their national wealth into the race to maintain parity with other nations by whom they felt threatened.

In Great Britain, such an expansion of naval armaments was anathema to the Liberal Government, but the introduction of supernumerary German naval law in 1908, which proposed the laying down of four dreadnought battleships in that year and a further four in 1909, caused great alarm in Parliament, the Admiralty and among the general public, who at that time followed military and naval matters with great interest through the popular press.

Powerful forces both within Parliament and outside, such as the influential Navy League, demanded immediate action. They saw Germany as the potential future enemy, having identified the rapid expansion of the German fleet as a threat to British commerce on the oceans of the world.

Prior to this, in January 1909, the British Foreign Secretary Sir Edward Grey tried to placate German opinion by suggesting to the German Ambassador in London, Count Metternich, that a 'naval holiday' should be instituted, with Britain offering to reduce the number of new ships laid down if Germany would promise proportionally to do the same. His proposals were rejected.

To counter the German move, Reginald McKenna, then the First Sea Lord, moved to introduce immediate expanded estimates in March 1909 where, after much debate, the Government offered four ships in one year and four the following year. After fierce debates within and outside Parliament, a compromise was reached where all eight ships were laid down in the same year.

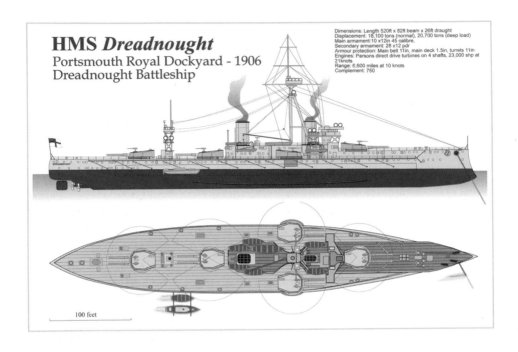

HMS *Dreadnought*
Portsmouth Royal Dockyard - 1906
Dreadnought Battleship

Dimensions: Length 520ft x 82ft beam x 26ft draught
Displacement: 18,100 tons (normal), 20,700 tons (deep load)
Main armament:10 x12in 45 calibre,
Secondary armament: 28 x12 pdr
Armour protection: Main belt 11in, main deck 1.5in, turrets 11in
Engines: Parsons direct drive turbines on 4 shafts, 23,000 shp at 21knots
Range: 6,600 miles at 10 knots
Complement: 750

100 feet

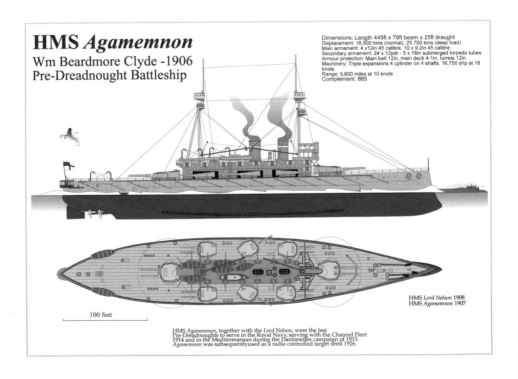

HMS *Agamemnon*
Wm Beardmore Clyde -1906
Pre-Dreadnought Battleship

Dimensions: Length 445ft x 79ft beam x 25ft draught
Displacement: 16,500 tons (normal), 20,700 tons (deep load)
Main armament: 4 x12in 45 calibre - 5 x 9.2in 45 calibre
Secondary armament: 24 x 12pdr - 5 x 18in submerged torpedo tubes
Armour protection: Main belt 12in, main deck 4-1in, turrets 12in
Machinery: Triple expansions 4 cylinder on 4 shafts, 16,750 shp at 18 knots
Range: 5,600 miles at 10 knots
Complement: 865

HMS *Lord Nelson* 1908
HMS *Agamemnon* 1907

100 feet

HMS *Agamemnon*, together with the *Lord Nelson*, were the last
Pre-Dreadnoughts to serve in the Royal Navy, serving with the Channel Fleet
1914 and in the Mediterreanean during the Dardanelles campaign of 1915.
Agamemnon was subsequentlyused as a radio controlled target until 1926.

Parallel with the development of *Dreadnought*, Fisher planned yet another new type of warship, the laying down of three of the *Invincible* class battle-cruisers in 1906. These ships, HMS *Invincible*, HMS *Indefatigable* and HMS *Indomitable*, were not originally intended to form part of the line of battle with the battleships. Their purpose would be to hunt down and destroy with their superior armament the enemy armoured cruisers and armed merchant cruisers that would in time of war be expected to harry our ocean trade routes.

From the start, however, they were seen as adjuncts to the battle-fleet, where their task was to operate as fast battle squadrons, preceding the main units to seek out and make first contact with the enemy fleet. In this role their inadequate armour was to prove their Achilles heel, as shown by the loss of three British battle-cruisers at Jutland.

These ships were generally similar in size to the *Dreadnought* but with much lighter armour protection, the main belt reduced to 6in and the turret armour to 7in, and mounting only eight 12in guns in four turrets to the other ships' ten 12in guns in five turrets, to allow for the installation of more powerful engines of 41,000hp, giving a speed of 25 knots.

Once again Germany was taken aback by the introduction of yet another revolutionary class of ship that they could see would completely outclass their standard armoured cruisers, and were further discomfited when misleading information was purposely allowed to leak out, indicating that the *Invincibles* would be armed with 9.2in guns.

HMS *Invincible*
Armstrong Whitworth, Elswick - 1907
Battle-Cruiser

Dimensions: Length 560ft x beam 78ft x 25ft draught
Displacement: 17,450 tons (normal), 20,130 tons (deep load)
Main armament: 8 x 12in 45 calibre
Secondary armament: 16 x 4in 45 calibre
Armour protection: Main belt 6in, main deck 1in, turrets 7in
Engines: Parsons direct drive turbines on 4 shafts, 41,000shp at 25 knots
Range and coal stowage: 6,300 miles at 10 knots / 1,000 tons
Complement: 1020

100 feet

Invincible Class Battle-Cruisers

HMS *Invincible*	1907
HMS *Inflexible*	1907
HMS *Indomitable*	1907

HMS *Invincible* served with the 3rd Battle-cruiser Squadron at Jutland in May 1916, where she was lost when her magazines exploded under heavy shell fire from the German Battle-cruisers *Lutzow* and *Derfflinger*.

Germany's response was to launch, in 1909, the heavy armoured cruiser *Blucher*, which was 15,000 tons and powered by the older reciprocating machinery capable of 26 knots and mounting twelve of the lighter 8.2in guns. Although she took her place in the line of the later German battle-cruisers, she was completely outgunned and sunk at the Dogger Bank action in 1915.

The Germans quickly realised their error, rapidly producing their first turbine-powered battle-cruiser SMS *Von der Tann*, capable of 27–28 knots and powerfully armed with eight 11in guns, followed in 1911–12 by the larger, more powerful 22,600-ton SMS *Moltke* and SMS *Goeben*, each carrying ten 11in guns, making them more than a match for the British ships.

The later German battle-cruisers were possibly also ship-for-ship superior to the British vessels. Having the advantage of being designed to operate largely in the North Sea or the Baltic, as opposed to the British requirement to protect the Empire, a greater proportion of tonnage on the German ships could be devoted to armour protection and more efficient watertight subdivision of the hull, where the inconveniences placed on restricted crew accommodation and comfort could be considered acceptable on short sea voyages.

With their greater beam, the German ships had better protection to their magazines and the advantage of cased cordite charges or cartridges which, unlike the silk bags of the British, were more likely to burn in the case of a hit on a turret.

It was not just in the design of capital ships that Fisher's reforms were felt. A whole new generation of fast, modern cruisers and destroyers were being laid down in this period. These ships would play a major part in the war that was all too soon to come.

4

FROM NAVAL REVIEWS
TO WAR

On 24 June 1914, in blazing summer weather without a cloud in the sky, the ships of the German High Seas Fleet were assembled in the roadstead at Kiel, as the Kaiser, aboard the Royal yacht *Hohenzollern*, cruised along the lines of stately grey-painted warships, each dressed with colourful flags, their sides manned by cheering sailors, as each succeeding ship fired their guns in salute.

From the deck of the yacht the Kaiser in turn reviewed thirteen of the latest dreadnought battleships, three sleek battle-cruisers, eight pre-dreadnought battleships, cruisers, torpedo boats and other vessels that represented the result of eight years of frantic and dedicated work costing millions of marks in order to challenge Great Britain's control of the seas.

That day represented the culmination of his own, and that of Grand Admiral Tirpitz's, vision to give Germany a powerful navy to complement her incomparable army, which at that time was the largest in the world.

As they viewed this vast array of powerful vessels they must have felt the thrill of accomplishment of their long-laid plans and were convinced that little could now stand in the way for the greater expansion of the German Empire to give Germany her rightful place in the sun.

Among the foreign ships present were four British dreadnoughts and three light cruisers – painted a darker grey and of a leaner profile than the German ships, but still projecting an impressive purposeful presence – which embodied the long tradition of Great Britain's command of the seas.

As guests during Kiel week, the officers and men of the British ships enjoyed a round of parties, balls and sporting events such as regattas and football matches that created a friendly rivalry between the competing nations.

Suddenly, however, this summer idyll came to an abrupt end, with the news of the assassination of the Archduke Franz Ferdinand on 28 June 1914 at Sarajevo in faraway Bosnia by a Serbian nationalist. This threw the complicated pattern of alliances and treaties that had evolved in Europe since the Treaty of Vienna in 1814 into chaos.

These same treaties dictated the responses of the European powers that moved with ponderous inevitability towards war.

Immediately, the festivities of Kiel week were abandoned, with the Kaiser ordering official court mourning and leaving on a train to Vienna to join the ageing Emperor Franz Joseph for the state funeral. Meanwhile, the British squadron, under orders from the Admiralty, weighed on 30 June, with the commander Sir George Warrender capturing the feelings of disquiet and uncertainty as to what the future held by signalling the German ships as the British squadron got underway with the message, 'Friends in the past, friends for ever'.

The tragic events in Sarajevo set in motion over the following month first the mobilisation of Austria-Hungary against Serbia and then the counter-mobilisation by Czarist Russia in support of Serbia, which in response caused Germany to mobilise her own army.

This threatening move led France to follow suit, concentrating her armies on her borders, seeing an opportunity to liberate her former provinces of Alsace and Lorraine, which had been under Prussian occupation since 1870.

In Great Britain the initial response that these events were merely a squabble between foreigners far away gave way to graver concern as the crisis deepened.

Over the next few weeks, as the world held its breath, intense diplomatic efforts were being pursued in the chancelleries of Europe in an effort to avoid war, but the unravelling pattern of events had an immutable logic that forbade any such accommodations being made to arrive at a peaceful solution to the crisis.

In the event, diplomacy failed and the generals took matters into their own hands, first with Austro-Hungarian troops invading Serbia and then, with an unstoppable inevitability, one nation after another taking up arms. Within days half of Europe was in flames.

The German response was to implement the execution of the long-laid 'Schlieffen Plan', where Germany demanded free passage for her troops through Belgium in order to outflank the French defences and sweep down on Paris from the north. The Belgian Government rightly refused this outrageous demand and stood to arms to defend their territorial integrity. When the grey-clad cavalry squadrons under General von Kluck's First Army rode across the Belgian border in the early morning mists of 4 August 1914, the die was irrevocably cast and (as a result of her obligations to Belgium that had guaranteed her neutrality) Great Britain was drawn with an almost somnambulant inevitability into the gathering storm.

Just prior to these dramatic events unfolding on the Continent, on the sun-drenched waters of Spithead, an even larger gathering of warships was taking place. On 1 July 1914 the great naval review was being attended by King George V. In this huge collection of warships three fleets were present. The First Fleet, under the command of Sir George Callaghan, was made up of all the first-line warships of the

Royal Navy, the dreadnoughts, battle-cruisers, and the most modern cruisers and destroyers that totalled over one hundred vessels in all.

The Second Fleet was composed of the older ships that were in commission, led by the more modern ships of the pre-dreadnought fleet; ships now outmoded by the introduction of the *Dreadnought*, but still powerful in their own right. These ships were normally only partly crewed with reduced complements, but with their armament and machinery were kept in first-class condition and able to put to sea for battle practice at regular intervals. In an emergency, the ships could be quickly manned with reservists to fully active commission status, if required.

Finally, the Third Fleet or reserve fleet was present. These much older ships were normally anchored in their home ports, tied up on a care and maintenance basis, again to be crewed by reservists when necessary.

The original plan when the review ended was for the various fleets to sail out for battle practice and on completion of these exercises for them to return to their home ports, or in the case of the First Fleet resume their deployment with the Channel and Atlantic fleets.

However, the First Lord of the Admiralty, Winston Churchill, and the First Sea Lord, Prince Louis of Battenberg, mindful of the deteriorating political situation in Europe, used the occasion to order a full-scale test mobilisation of the combined fleets on 27 July 1914.

Accordingly, at the end of the review, and as the Second and Third fleets were now fully manned, orders were issued to Sir George Callaghan to keep the First Fleet concentrated at Portland, while the Second and Third Fleets put to sea for battle practice. On completion of these manoeuvres they were to proceed to their home ports but to remain crewed in state of readiness.

Two days later, on 29 July, the First Fleet received Admiralty orders to sail to its secret war station, the location of which was known only to a select few in naval circles.

The ships of the First Fleet weighed anchor and, squadron by squadron, the great ships headed north from Portland to the lonely anchorage of Scapa Flow in the Orkney Islands in the far north of Scotland. These remote windswept islands, with their broad and seldom-visited vast, enclosed anchorage, previously the home of wandering seabirds and the occasional fishing boat, had been selected many years before by naval planners as the ideal base both for the concentration of the huge number of warships of the fleet. It was also seen as the perfect location from which to control the northern exits of the North Sea, in pursuance of the previously agreed government policy for a distant economic blockade of the German coastline in the event of war with Germany.

In the early light of dawn on 30 July the great battleships and attendant vessels slid like wraiths into the grey waters of the anchorage at Scapa Flow, with the roar of their anchor chains rumbling through the hawse pipes echoing across the broad waters as they took up their allotted positions in the anchorage.

The few local crofters and fishermen who witnessed the arrival of this great armada of ships must have been amazed by this demonstration of naval might that had appeared in their previously peaceful islands overnight. They were the representatives of another way of life, putting them at the centre of world-shattering events. Immediately after their arrival, an Admiralty order decreed that the First Fleet would, henceforth, be known by the altogether more splendid title of the Grand Fleet.

Matters now moved with increasing speed and on the afternoon of 29 July Admiral Sir John Jellicoe was travelling north by train, carrying Admiralty orders relieving Sir George Callaghan of command and appointing him as Commander-in-Chief of the Grand Fleet and to fly his flag in the fleet flagship HMS *Iron Duke*. The fleet Jellicoe took over was comprised of the 1st and 2nd Battle Squadrons, totalling sixteen of the latest dreadnought battleships, each armed with ten 12in or 13.5in guns.

Also at anchor was the 3rd Battle Squadron of eight pre-dreadnoughts, each mounting four 12in guns, while the 1st Battle-Cruiser Squadron of four battle-cruisers was armed with eight 12in guns. The attendant armoured and scouting cruiser squadrons and destroyer flotillas made up the rest of the fleet.

This awesome display of naval might now filled the Flow, their grey forms merging with the grey waters and sea mists, silent and deadly fortresses of steel, patiently awaiting the order to put to sea to seek out the enemy.

Scapa Flow, while being the ideal strategic location to control the northern routes into and out of the North Sea, was located so far in the north of the British Isles that any fleet composed of heavy units stationed there would, due to distance, be incapable of dealing with any raids the Imperial German Navy might launch against the east coast of the United Kingdom and southern waters.

Again, the possibility existed that, unless the fleet had prior knowledge through the interception of German wireless traffic or other intelligence, such raids could be carried out with impunity and the German ships could be on their way back to their bases before the Grand Fleet could interfere.

Initial steps to cancel out this disadvantage included the institution of the 'Harwich Force', comprising a powerful force of cruisers and destroyers, under the command of Commodore Tyrwhitt, based at Harwich. From here they could conduct sweeps into the southern North Sea, hopefully intercepting incursions by the German fleet and maintaining the all-important economic blockade by stopping and searching neutral ships for contraband from southern Norway to the Belgian coast, from where the Channel Fleet took over these duties.

Throughout the course of the war the Harwich Force was involved in many of the actions that took place in the southern North Sea and the German Bight, although, apart from an initial sortie on the day far to the south, they were absent from the Battle of Jutland.

Later in December 1914, following two raids by Admiral Hipper's battle-cruisers against east coast ports, Admiral Beatty's 1st Battle-Cruiser Squadron – comprising the battle-cruisers HMS *Lion*, HMS *Princess Royal*, HMS *Queen Mary* and HMS *New Zealand* and accompanying cruiser squadrons – were moved south to Rosyth on the Firth of Forth to afford greater protection to the east coast and, more importantly, to be better placed to cut off and engage an isolated portion of the German fleet from one of these raids.

Additionally, seven *King Edward* class pre-dreadnoughts, together with the *Dreadnought* herself, were also moved to the Thames, where it was hoped their 12in guns would provide powerful support to the cruisers of Harwich Force. Meanwhile, the Second or Channel Fleet was now concentrated at Portland and comprised the 5th and 6th Battle Squadrons, totalling thirteen pre-dreadnought battleships all armed with four 12in guns, together with several squadrons of older cruisers.

Within a few days, these ships of the Channel Fleet were to escort the first units of the British Expeditionary Force from the Channel ports to France, an operation that was conducted in perfect safety without any interference from the enemy and without any loss; such was Great Britain's complete control of the sea.

The Third Fleet, consisting of the 7th and 8th Battle Squadrons containing the oldest ships, had now returned to their home ports but remained crewed by the reservists, along with five of the older cruiser squadrons.

Due to the foresight of Churchill, Prince Louis of Battenberg and the Admiralty, the fleet, from the most powerful battleship to the smallest patrol boat, was fully prepared for action.

The sands of time had finally run out. In the words of the Foreign Secretary Sir Edward Grey on the evening of 3 August 1914, 'The lamps are going out all over Europe'. This was followed by an Admiralty signal issued by wireless on the afternoon of 4 August 1914 to all Royal Naval ships around the globe, 'Commence hostilities against the Empire of Germany'.

One of the first moves in the naval war occurred far from the cold, grey waters of the North Sea, in the warm, blue waters of the Mediterranean, where the British Mediterranean Fleet in the opening days of the war attempted, and failed, to intercept a German squadron whose subsequent escape to the safety of Constantinople was to encourage the Ottoman Empire to join with the Central Powers against the Allies.

In 1912 the battle-cruiser *Goeben* and the light cruiser *Breslau* were stationed at the Austrian port of Pola in the Adriatic as a squadron whose purpose in time of war was to interrupt the passage of troops from North Africa to France in conjunction with the Austria–Hungarian Navy.

HMS *Bellerophon*
Portsmouth Royal Dockyard -1907
Dreadnought Battleship

Dimensions: Length 522ft x 82ft beam x 27ft draught
Displacement: 18,590 tons (normal) 22,540 tons (deep load)
Main armament: 10x 12in 45 calibre
Secondary armament: 16 x 4in 50 calibre
Armour protection: Main belt 10in, main deck 3in, turrets 11in-12in
Engines: Parsons direct drive turbines on 4 shafts, 23,000 shp at 20.75 knots
Range /Coal stowage: 5,700 miles at 10 knots, 2,000 tons
Complement: 820

100 feet

Bellerophon Class

HMS *Bellerophon*	1907
HMS *Temeraire*	1907
HMS *Superb*	1907

However, at the outbreak of war between Austria-Hungary and Serbia on 28 July 1914, Admiral Souchon, commanding the *Goeben*, left Pola unsupported by his allies, with the intention of carrying out a bombardment of Bone and Philippeville and attacking any troop transports loading there.

On 1 August he put into the neutral Italian port of Brindisi, where the Italian authorities refused Souchon coal. He then sailed on to Taranto, where he was joined by the *Breslau*. The squadron continued westward on to Messina, where sufficient coal was obtained from four German merchant ships, and then set course towards the Algerian coast on 3 August.

At the Admiralty on 30 July, the First Lord, Winston Churchill, ordered the Mediterranean Fleet under Admiral Berkeley Milne to aid the French transportation of troops and, if possible, intercept and destroy the two German ships once war was declared.

Sailing from Malta on 1 August, the British fleet consisted of three battle-cruisers and four armoured cruisers, together with attendant light cruisers and destroyers. The battle-cruisers *Indefatigable* and *Indomitable*, accompanied by five cruisers and destroyers commanded by Rear Admiral Troubridge, Commander-in-Chief of the Mediterranean Fleet, were detached to the north-east to cover the Adriatic and watch for the Austrian fleet.

The German ships were reported at Taranto by the British Consul to the Admiralty in London, who ordered the *Indomitable* and *Indefatigable* to Gibraltar in order to prevent the German ships escaping into the Atlantic.

As Souchon closed the ports of Bone and Philippeville on 3 August and the ships prepared for bombardment of the ports, a wireless message from Berlin informed Souchon that war had been declared on France and the German ships should now turn eastwards to seek sanctuary at Istanbul. The two German ships shelled both ports briefly before retiring to the east, running into the two British battle-cruisers on a reciprocal course in the early morning of 4 August 1914.

The British ships, under Admiral Milne, turned to shadow the German ships, but at that time the two countries were not at war and, due to boiler problems, the British battle-cruisers fell behind the German ships, losing contact in fading light off the north coast of Sicily, which allowed the *Goeben* and *Breslau* to coal again at Messina.

Souchon was offered no help from the Austrian Navy and rather than being trapped in Pola he chose to continue to Istanbul.

At the Admiralty it was still believed that the German ships would go to the west and attempt to break out into the Atlantic and, therefore, the heavy British units were proceeding to the west.

On 6 August the *Goeben* and the *Breslau* entered the eastern Mediterranean, where they were spotted by the cruiser *Gloucester*, which began to shadow the German ships. The *Gloucester* was part of Admiral Troubridge's cruiser squadron, which comprised the armoured cruisers HMS *Defence*, *Black Prince*, *Warrior* and HMS *Duke of Edinburgh*, together with eight destroyers, then deployed off the Ionian Islands in the eastern Mediterranean. The armoured cruisers mounted 9.2in guns against the 11in guns of the *Goeben*. Troubridge considered his squadron of twelve ships, armed with a total of twenty-two 9.2in guns and torpedo armament in the destroyers, to be outgunned and outranged by the two German ships, and invoked Churchill's order 'to avoid engagement with superior forces' to break off the pursuit.

However, on her own initiative HMS *Gloucester*, with her superior speed to the rest of the cruiser squadron, engaged the fleeing German ships, scoring a hit on the *Breslau* on the water line, until Admiral Milne ordered her to break off the action off Cape Matapan.

From a tactical point of view Troubridge's ships could, had he closed with them again, have been used successfully against the fleeing German squadron by dividing into two columns and attacking on either quarter. In this way they could have divided their fire with every possibility of severely damaging the two German ships, or at least delaying their escape until the three British battle-cruisers could be brought up from their position off the Greek island of Zante.

After a string of inaccurate and conflicting signals from the Admiralty on 9 August, Milne was finally ordered to pursue the German squadron, but these instructions had arrived too late and, after refuelling once more, the German ships passed into the Dardanelles and into safety.

The failure of Admiral Milne to intercept the two German ships had serious consequences for the course of the war, and was a factor in Turkey joining the Central Powers. The Germans offered to sell the *Goeben* and *Breslau* to the Turks in compensation for two battleships that had been seized by the British Admiralty while building in Britain. The Turkish Government accepted the offer on 16 August 1914, renaming the ships *Yavuz Sultan Selim* and the *Midilli* respectively, retaining their German crews. Furthermore, Admiral Souchon became the Commander-in-Chief of the Turkish Navy when Turkey finally joined the war on Germany's side in October 1914.

Admiral Milne was severely criticised for his actions and court-martialled. Although he was acquitted, he was not to hold a senior post in the Navy again, dying in 1938 with his reputation damaged and still considered to be responsible for the debacle.

The first naval casualties of the Great War occurred when ships of the 2nd Destroyer Flotilla, led by the 3,440-ton light cruiser HMS *Amphion*, put to sea from Harwich in the early morning of 5 August to sweep the Heligoland Bight, where, while en route, the flotilla received reports from fishing boats that they had observed a large, two-funnelled ship laying mines to the north of the Outer Gabbard light vessel.

This ship was the SMS *Konigin Luise*, an auxiliary minelayer that had been dispatched from Wilhelmshaven on 1 August to lay mines at the mouth of the Thames Estuary.

The flotilla sighted the German ship in the forenoon in squally weather and gave chase as she turned eastward, working up to her maximum speed of 20 knots. She attempted to escape into neutral Dutch waters, hiding in a rain squall, while laying more mines in the path of her pursuers.

The destroyer HMS *Lance* opened fire at the minelayer with her 4in Mk IV gun, this being the first shell fired in anger at sea by either side, just 12 hours after the declaration of war, with the cruiser and the other destroyers joining in. After a brief engagement, Captain Biermann, realising escape was impossible, ordered the *Konigin Luise* to be scuttled, sinking at 12.22 p.m. in the position 5I2° 52'N/2° 30°E, with the loss of forty-six of her crew.

After picking up survivors from the minelayer, the flotilla continued their patrol and in the late afternoon intercepted a second German ship flying a large German flag, which the destroyers immediately opened fire on. The *Amphion* recognised her as being the *St Petersburg* and, knowing it was carrying the German Ambassador returning to Germany, ordered them to cease fire. When her signal was ignored, she placed herself between the opposing ships to allow the German vessel to proceed in safety.

On turning to return to Harwich at 3.30 a.m. on the morning of 6 August, the light cruiser *Amphion* ran into the minefield laid by the *Konigin Luise* the day before, striking a mine that caused the bow portion of the ship to be enveloped in flames. The majority of the bridge crew, including the captain, were killed.

The ship drifted back into the minefield, where she ran on to a second mine that broke the ship's back and caused the forward magazine to explode. The ship sank rapidly with the loss of 150 British sailors, together with fifteen German sailors who had previously been picked up from the sinking of the minelayer.

So, the first day of the war at sea had ended with equal honours – with both sides losing one ship each, *Konigin Luise* and *Amphion* – and the first of many more deaths to follow.

The destroyer *Lance* had only been launched in February 1914 and continued to serve with the 3rd Destroyer Flotilla for the remainder of the war, being present at the successful action off Texel in October 1914 when a German torpedo boat half flotilla was completely destroyed by a British force.

Lance was sold for breaking, along with her thirteen surviving sister ships, after only seven years' service, on the grounds of economy.

Equally as important as the need to seek out and destroy enemy warships was the need to institute an economic blockade on the German coastline and ports to deny them raw materials, food, oil and other supplies, so as to hamper their war effort.

Naively, the Germans initially assumed that the Royal Navy would impose a close blockade after the pattern employed against the French ports in the Napoleonic wars, where British ships patrolled in sight of the French coastline. Had such a close blockade been implemented, the Germans would have hoped to have waged a war of attrition on the Royal Navy by picking off the blockading ships by mine and torpedo, without having to risk their main units in a face-to-face confrontation. With the advent of the mine and the submarine, such tactics were, of course, suicidal and the Royal Navy elected to control the German coasts from a distance.

The anchorage at Scapa Flow, although long planned to be the main base of the fleet in time of war by the Admiralty, had not prior to the arrival of the fleet been prepared in any way to receive them. There were no defensive works or batteries installed on the islands and no administrative or onshore accommodation, while the various sea entrances into the Flow were devoid of any form of boom defences and were not considered by the Admiralty to be sufficiently secure from attack by U-boat.

During the first month of their tenure there were a series of false alarms within the anchorage, with imagined sightings of U-boat periscopes or torpedo tracks that, on occasion, resulted in the ships being ordered to raise steam and put to sea for safety; a complicated and onerous task that interfered with the normal duties and training schedules as the fifty or so ships steamed out of the anchorage, where they were probably in greater danger from the U-boats that were known to patrol the Pentland Firth and surrounding waters.

While immediate efforts were made to secure the anchorage with the installation of booms and protective artillery emplacements, the majority of the fleet, including all the dreadnoughts, were temporarily moved to Lough Swilly in Donegal on the north-west coast of Ireland. From here they continued their battle training in relative safety, or so it was thought.

On 27 October HMS *Audacious*, a modern *King George V* class battleship only commissioned in 1913, left Lough Swilly with other units of the 2nd Battle Squadron for battle practice to the north of Tory Island, when, at 8.45 a.m., she ran onto a mine laid by the German auxiliary minelayer *Berlin*.

The mine exploded on the port side and flooded the port engine room, the shell handling room and the magazine below 'X' turret where, after some hours, despite counter-flooding to correct the heavy list to port and the efforts of the cruiser *Liverpool* and the destroyer *Fury* to take her in tow, she capsized and sank with her forward magazine exploding, which caused the only fatality when a sailor on *Liverpool* was struck by debris.

A witness to the sinking was the White Star liner RMS *Olympic*, which offered assistance, and although the Admiralty made strenuous efforts to keep the sinking a secret, only announcing the loss at the end of the war, many of the passengers aboard the liner were American, who took photographs and even a cine film of the incident, so that the loss was known to the Germans.

By 14 November the anchorage at Scapa Flow was now considered to be safe and the battle fleet returned to what would be its home for the next four years.

HMS *Audacious*
Cammell Laird Shipbuilders, Birkenhead - 1912
Super Dreadnought Battleship

Dimensions: Length 600ft x 89ft beam x 27ft draught
Displacement: 23,000 tons (normal), 25,500 tons (deep load)
Main armament: 10 x 13.5in 45 calibre
Secondary armament: 12 x 4in 50 calibre
Armour protection: Main belt 12in, main deck 1.5in, turrets 11in
Engines: Parsons reduction turbines on 4 screws, 27,000 shp at 21 knots
Coal stowage / Range: 1,000 tons, 5,900 miles at 10 knots
Complement: 1,114

King George V Class

HMS *King George V*	1911
HMS *Ajax*	1912
HMS *Centurion*	1911
HMS *Audacious*	1912

100 feet

HMS *Audacious* served with the 2nd Battle Squadron in 1914, but was mined and sunk off Lough Swilly, Northern Ireland on 27 October 1914.

While further imagined scares still took place (in one unfortunate incident in July 1917 the battleship HMS *Vanguard* was destroyed by a magazine explosion, probably due to unstable cordite, with the loss of almost all her crew), it is unlikely that any U-boat did indeed penetrate the defences during the Great War. That honour fell to the brave and daring Kapitanleutnant Gunther Prien and his crew of the *U47*, when at the start of the Second World War in October 1939 he entered the anchorage through Kirk Sound to sink the battleship *Royal Oak* and make his escape.

5

ARMED MERCHANT CRUISERS AND SURFACE RAIDERS

Since the 1890s the British Admiralty through the Government had subsidised the building of express liners on the condition that the owners would allow them to be requisitioned in time of war to be used as armed merchant cruisers.

To this end, reinforced gun mountings were built into the liners' decks to allow for the fitting of guns, usually of 4.5in or 6in calibre, which were often stored aboard as a part of the ships' equipment to allow for the rapid fitting out as an AMC.

The *Mauretania*, *Aquitania*, *Olympic* and other smaller liners were immediately fitted out in this manner on the commencement of hostilities, but it was soon found that the larger super liners were unsuitable for these duties and they were relegated to more useful trooping work or as hospital ships. Under the 1912 Naval Act, Germany also directed that new liners and certain existing ships should be equipped to carry guns for employment as armed merchant cruisers.

With the opening of hostilities in August 1914, the British blockade came into immediate effect, with patrol lines established to control the northern exits of the North Sea and the English Channel, where cruiser patrols ordered ships to be stopped and searched for contraband materials.

The German Admiralty, in turn, wirelessed orders to all German merchant ships at sea on the world's oceans that those ships that were in a position to do so should seek the safety of the nearest German port, while other ships whose chances of returning to Germany or in avoiding British patrols were unlikely to be successful were advised to lay their ships up in neutral ports to avoid them falling into British hands.

Within weeks, the German red, white and black merchant flag had all but disappeared from the trade routes, as they either sought the safety of their home ports or chose to be interned, rather than taking their chance against the ubiquitous cruisers of the Royal Navy.

The brand new 54,000-ton Hamburg-Amerika Line *Vaterland*, completed in 1913 and then the largest liner in the world, having just completed her fourth Atlantic crossing, was advised by Grand Admiral Tirpitz to lay up in New York rather than attempt to run the British blockade. Her capture would hand a huge propaganda coup to the British.

The *Varterland*, *Kronprinz Wilhelm II*, *Kronprinzessin Cecilie*, *America* and the *George Washington* were all eventually interned in American harbours, where they remained for the next two years until the effects of the German policy of unrestricted U-boat warfare brought the USA into the war, after which the ships were pressed into US Naval service to provide troop transports to take the thousands of American troops to France.

The declaration of war found the Hamburg-Amerika liner *Kronprinzessin Cecilie* four days out from New York in the mid-Atlantic bound for Bremen, with 1,200 passengers and $12 million in gold and silver locked in her strong room.

On receipt of the news that his country was at war with Great Britain, Kapitan Karl Polack wirelessed the German Admiralty his intention to return to New York, taking the precaution of painting the tops of the ship's four yellow funnels black in the hope of passing for the White Star liner *Olympic*.

His decision to turn back was contested by a deputation of rich American businessmen who wanted to continue on to Europe, even proposing to buy the ship and put it under the American flag.

Invoking the age-old law of the sea that the captain is the sole arbiter of a ship's fate at sea, Kapitan Polack rejected their offer and, proceeding at high speed, evaded patrolling British cruisers to arrive safely off the coast of Maine to disembark her frustrated passengers at Bar Harbour, from where she was escorted to New York and internment.

Already converted for raiding, with an armament of six 4in guns, the liner *Kaiser Wilhelm der Grosse*, built in 1897 and the former holder of the Blue Riband but still capable of 22 knots, left Bremerhaven on 4 August 1914 with orders to attack British merchant shipping on the Atlantic sea lanes.

The fact that this ship was equipped so quickly as a surface raider following the deteriorating international situation after the assassination of the Archduke Ferdinand in June was one of the reasons that the deployment of this type of vessel was originally seen as such an attractive proposition to naval planners. The raiders were capable of pursuing a *course de guerre* form of warfare at the outset of hostilities.

Kapitan Reymann steamed his ship up the North Sea, passing undetected through the British Northern patrol line between Scotland and the Norwegian coast. Rounding the north of Scotland, he proceeded around the north of Iceland to enter into the broad waters of the Atlantic via the Denmark Strait.

His first capture was a large 250-ton trawler, which, after taking the crew off, was sunk by gunfire.

Heading southwards to the vicinity of the Canaries he next fell in with the Union Castle liner *Galician* of 6,700 tons, where, after sending a boarding party on to the liner and discovering that there were a large number of women and children on board, he gallantly allowed the liner to proceed to her destination, although by doing so he had revealed his position to the British Admiralty.

Later in the war the *Galician*, by then renamed HMHS *Glenart Castle*, was not so lucky when, while serving as a hospital ship in February 1918, she was torpedoed and sunk with heavy loss of life. Meanwhile, the *Kaiser Wilhelm der Grosse*, continuing her cruise, sank three other British merchant vessels in two days, but now being short of coal she put in to the Spanish colony of Rio de Oro on the coast of Africa. Despite the protests of the Spanish authorities concerning the legality of belligerent ships staying for nine days, she took on coal. (Under international law a belligerent vessel could only stay in a neutral harbour for 24 hours, either coaling or making repair, before being subject to internment.)

This delay allowed the British protected cruiser HMS *Highflyer* to arrive off the port on 26 August 1914 to demand the surrender of the German ship.

Kapitan Reymann refused and, after disembarking 400 of his crew in boats, he put to sea with a skeleton crew to accept action with the cruiser, bravely opening fire on the British cruiser with his six 4.1in guns, although it must have been obvious to Reymann what the outcome would be.

The *Highflyer*, with her superior armament of eleven 6in guns, fought a one-sided action, resulting in the German ship being sunk after an engagement of less than 1 hour, going to the bottom with her ensigns still proudly flying.

A further single-ship action was fought on 14 September 1914 off the Brazilian island of Trinidad between the Hamburg-Amerika liner SMS *Cap Trafalgar* of 18,500 tons and the 19,500-ton armed merchant cruiser RMS *Carmania* of the Cunard Line, built in 1903 and equipped with a heavier armament of eight 4.7in guns.

The German ship had earlier been armed off the River Plate, with two 4in guns and six machine guns from the gunboat *Eber*, while her commander Kapitanleutnant Wirth as a senior regular naval officer took command of the *Cap Trafalgar*, which originally had three funnels. The aft one, which was a dummy, was removed during conversion to an AMC and, oddly, the ship was disguised to resemble her nemesis the *Carmania*.

While exploring the several anchorages of the island, the *Carmania* surprised the *Cap Trafalgar* in a remote bay coaling from supply ships. With steam up, the German ship, having seen the *Carmania* approaching, slipped her cable and headed for the open sea to the north, working up to full speed. The *Carmania* opened fire at 8,000yd, immediately scoring several hits, and soon further hits were registered on the German vessel.

Wirth realised that his only chance against his heavier armed opponent was to close the range from where he could rake the British ship with combined 4in and machine-gun fire. The German ship was 2 knots faster than the *Carmania* and Wirth used this factor to his advantage.

Closing the range to 3,000yd in the face of heavy fire, Wirth caused extensive damage to the British ship, wrecking the bridge and starting serious fires from the seventy-nine shell hits and the continuous stream of heavy machine-gun fire that made it difficult for the British ship to serve the guns.

Captain Grant of the *Carmania* continued to shell the German ship, aiming at the water line. Despite its brave retaliation, after an hour the *Cap Trafalgar* was a smoking ruin, having been hit more than 300 times, and eventually rolled over on her beam ends and sank, taking Kapitan Wirth and most of his crew to the bottom.

A more successful commerce raider was the *Kronprinz Wilhelm* of the Nord Deutscher Lloyd, another former Blue Riband holder of 15,000 tons and commanded by Kapitan Thiefelder, which left New York at the outbreak of war and, evading British cruisers, headed south to the West Indies, where she rendezvoused with the light cruiser *Karlsruhe*, which, while being fitted out with two 88mm guns and ammunition, was surprised by the cruiser HMS *Suffolk* and other cruisers.

Having seen their smoke in good time, the two German ships sped off in opposite directions, and although the *Suffolk*, a *Monmouth* class cruiser built in 1904, pursued the more modern German cruiser, she was no match in terms of speed, where the extra 5 knots of the *Karlsruhe* allowed her to escape.

The *Karlsruhe* continued to operate in the West Indies and off the coast of Brazil, where time and again her speed allowed her to elude pursuit and during which time she sank sixteen merchant ships totalling 72,000 tons, until on the night of 4 November 1914 she was destroyed by an internal explosion 200 miles north of Trinidad, with the loss of the majority of her crew.

The *Kronprinz Wilhelm* also escaped the British cruisers, and in a cruise lasting eight months and covering 20,000 miles, the liner destroyed twenty-six merchant vessels, replenishing her coal bunkers from captured ships. Eventually, when running low on food and medical supplies together with signs of scurvy amongst the crew, Kapitan Thiefelder dropped anchor in Chesapeake Bay on 10 April 1915, ending his successful cruise and accepting the inevitable internment.

Of the forty-two German liners at sea on 4 August 1914 most ended up blockaded in neutral ports for the duration of the war, except for five of the ships, which were converted to surface raiders or auxiliary cruisers in German ports and dispatched to harry British and Allied shipping on the world's oceans. These ships were the equivalent of the British 'Q' ships that were employed to decoy unsuspecting U-boats into attacking them.

Similarly, the German ships were disguised as harmless merchantmen, but carrying concealed guns, torpedo armament and mine laying equipment. They would trick Allied ships to approach them under some pretext while flying a neutral flag before revealing their true purpose. After running up the Kaiserlicher Marine battle ensign to legitimise the action they would open fire on the unsuspecting vessel.

The first of these ships was the *Moewe*, an ex-refrigerated banana boat of 9,800 tons with a good turn of speed, which was converted in Hamburg as an auxiliary cruiser mounting four × 4.1in guns, four × 19.7in torpedo tubes and a complement of 300 mines. Her commander was Nikolaus zu Dohna-Schlodien and, disguised as a Swedish freighter, she left Wilhelmshaven on 29 December 1915. Eluding British patrols, she laid a minefield in the Pentland Firth and a few days later the pre-dreadnought battleship HMS *King Edward VII*, en route to Belfast, struck one of the mines off Cape Wrath. Notwithstanding efforts to take her in tow, she sank, although, despite heavy weather, all her crew were saved due to the skill of her destroyer escorts *Musketeer*, *Marne*, *Fortune* and *Nessus*.

Moewe next laid mines in the Gironde Estuary, sinking two merchant ships, before moving on to operate between the Canary Islands and the Brazilian coast, where she engaged an armed British merchant ship, which, after a short fight, was scuttled.

Between 16 January 1916 and April 1916, when she successfully ran the blockade again to return to harbour, she sank or captured fifteen ships. Following this successful sortie the ship was refitted for a second raiding voyage that began on 29 November 1916, again eluding the blockade to enter the North Atlantic.

Her first success came on 6 December when she captured the SS *Mount Temple*, carrying war supplies and 700 horses destined for the Western Front. It must have been a heart-wrenching decision to have to lay charges in the vessel and send the animals to the bottom.

Six days later, with the capture of the SS *Georgic*, a liner of 15,500 tons with a further 1,200 horses on board, they had to repeat the unpleasant duty once again. Continuing her cruise, she captured or sank a further twenty-five ships, including two that were in turn fitted out as raiders.

Finally, in March 1917, the *Moewe* was badly damaged in a fight with an armed New Zealand merchant ship, returning to Wilhelmshaven on 22 March 1917, having sunk 225,000 tons of Allied shipping in the two voyages.

All this had been accomplished despite the best efforts of the British and French cruisers searching for her, although never once sighting their elusive adversary.

The raider *Greif* had an altogether more unfortunate cruise. She sailed from Cuxhaven on 27 February 1916 disguised as a Norwegian ship of similar outline, but was unfortunately intercepted by the armed merchant cruiser SS *Alcantara* of 12,000 tons the very next day in the North Sea. The *Alcantara* ordered her to heave to and lowered a boat to inspect the suspect vessel.

The Germans ran up their colours and opened fire at 3,000yd. Closing the range, *Alcantara* responded with her 5.9in guns, smashing into the German ship and setting her on fire. The *Greif* in turn fired a torpedo that struck *Alcantara* amidships. As she started to settle, a further round from the British ship hit the *Greif*'s magazine, which exploded. With both ships sinking, the survivors were rescued by the accompanying AMC *Andes*.

Undoubtedly the most successful of all German raiders in the Great War was the renowned *Wolf*, a Hansa Line freighter of 11,200 tons. She was converted at Kiel, mounting six 5.9in guns concealed behind removable bulwarks, four 19.7in torpedo tubes and a complement of 450 mines. Uniquely, the *Wolf* also carried a Friedrichshafen FF33 seaplane known as the *Wolfchen* (Wolf Cub) for spotting potential targets. This revolutionary idea considerably increased the scouting range of the ship.

Under her resolute commander Fregattenkapitan Karl Nerger, the *Wolf* left Kiel escorted by a U-boat on 30 December 1916, passing to the north of Scotland into the Atlantic. She then headed undetected to the Cape of Good Hope in January, where she laid mines off Durban and Port Elizabeth before moving on to laying mines outside the harbours of Colombo and Bombay. Nerger planned to stay at sea for a year without recourse to using harbours or other facilities, thanks to the *Wolf*'s exceptional coal capacity of 8,000 tons, giving a range of 32,000 miles, with supplies and additional coal being obtained from captured ships.

From Bombay the *Wolf* cruised the Indian Ocean, using her seaplane to seek out shipping, then headed eastward to the waters off New Zealand, where her presence caused considerable alarm as she sank further ships and prompted fruitless searches by cruisers of the Royal Australian Navy.

Heading north through the islands of the East Indies, she continued her depredations, sinking ships and transferring supplies and prisoners, who were well treated as far as conditions allowed. Eventually, after capturing and sinking fourteen ships by gunfire or setting charge, and thirteen known ships to her mines, totalling in all 75,000 tons, the *Wolf* returned to a hero's welcome at her home port of Kiel on 24 February 1918 with 467 prisoners after a non-stop cruise of 451 days – a truly remarkable feat of endurance and seamanship.

The fourth of this group was a 1,570-ton sailing ship, SMS *Seeadler*, a renamed captured American vessel previously called the *Pass of Balmaha*. The rationale of using a sailing vessel was that it would obviate the need to replenish coal supplies and theoretically give it unlimited range, although it did have an auxiliary diesel engine of 900hp that would require fuel.

The *Seeadler* departed Cuxhaven on 21 December 1916 under the command of Kapitan Leutnant Felix von Luckner, disguised as the Norwegian ship *Irma*, with a crew selected for their ability to speak fluent Norwegian. Under this guise, she successfully passed through the British blockade inspection line to begin her cruise of 225 days, operating in the Indian Ocean and the Pacific, where she sank or captured fifteen ships, all of which were sailing vessels, totalling a surprising 30,000 tons. She was wrecked in a storm on Mopelia in the Society Islands in

French Polynesia, from where Luckner and some of the crew sailed in the ship's cutter to Fiji, where they were captured. The remainder of the crew seized a French schooner, sailing to Easter Island, where they were interned by Chilean authorities.

The final ship of the quintet of special converted auxiliary cruisers was the *Leopard*, formerly the SS *Yarowdale*, a British freighter of 7,000 tons that had been captured by the *Moewe* during her cruise in 1916. Armed with five powerful 5.9in and four 4.1in guns and torpedoes, she would have been a considerable threat to British shipping and represented the last effort by Germany to send a surface commerce raider to sea.

Fortunately for the British, she was intercepted by the armed boarding vessel *Dundee* and the armoured cruiser HMNZS *Achilles* midway between Scotland and Norway. The *Leopard* opened fire and launched a torpedo at the British ships. After a fierce fight, *Leopard* was sunk with all hands.

The German attempt to respond to the British blockade and to exact retribution by interfering with British trade on the high seas was a successful undertaking, and had more raiders been assigned to this task it would have seriously affected the importation of war material and food supplies.

As it was, the limited number of ships so employed by the Germans caused considerable disruption to British trade before they were eliminated and diverted a large number of warships from other duties. The converted commerce raider could be considered a very effective weapon that had an important negative effect on British strategy at the beginning of the war.

The main harbours used by Germany's extensive merchant fleets were Hamburg on the River Elbe and Bremerhaven on the River Wesser, serving the North Sea, while in the Baltic Rostock and Danzig in East Prussia were the main ports.

A small canal some 27 miles in length had been constructed in Schleswig-Holstein during the eighteenth century, linking the River Eider to Kiel Fjord and connecting the North Sea at the mouth of the Eider at Tonning to the Baltic, with a width of 95ft and a dredged depth of 10ft, which is still in use and capable of taking smaller ships of up to 200 tons.

The Kaiser Wilhelm Canal was begun in 1887 to allow for larger ocean-going ships to pass between the North Sea and the Baltic, saving around 200 miles as opposed to taking the route around the north of Denmark and avoiding the frequent rough weather often found in the Skagerrak.

The need for the expanding German Navy to transit quickly between the two seas was also key to building the new canal that employed 9,000 workers and was finished in June 1895. Running for 61 miles from Kiel to Brunsbuttel on the Elbe, it was 26ft in depth and between 90 and 120ft wide.

The German Navy used the canal to transfer ships between the naval bases of Kiel and Wilhelmshaven in the Jade Estuary for a number of years, until the launching of the *Dreadnought* in Great Britain, which revolutionised battleship construction and caused the Germans to follow suit by building dreadnoughts of their own. These vessels, being much larger than the existing pre-dreadnoughts and of greater draught, were incapable of passing through the existing canal, rendering it largely useless for the needs of the navy. In response, a programme to widen and deepen the canal was instituted to allow for the passage of dreadnoughts. The plan was approved in 1908 at a cost of 11 million marks, with the work finally being completed in June 1914.

Admiral Fisher had earlier predicted with great prescience that the long-expected naval war between Great Britain and Germany would start once the canal had been finished, and so it proved.

6

CORONEL AND THE FALKLANDS

In common with other major European powers during the latter years of the nineteenth century, the emergent German Empire joined in the scramble for overseas possessions in Africa, the Pacific and the Far East.

In Africa, Germany acquired Togo, the Kamerun, Tanganyika and the vast, seemingly barren area of German West Africa on the Atlantic coast, which as it transpired contained large mineral resources including diamonds, in 1884, followed with great rapidity by the equally large and tropical territory of German East Africa in 1885. Between 1885 and 1900, the Pacific island territories of the Marianas, the Caroline Islands, Samoa, the Bismarck Archipelago and the north-east portion of New Guinea were added to these acquisitions.

The conquest of these far-flung territories coincided with the expansion of the German Navy, from what was basically a coast defence force to a deep-water fleet. As such, it required the provision of modern long-range cruisers to protect these interests, which began to come down the ways of the shipyards at Hamburg, Stettin, Danzig, Bremen and Wilhelmshaven in ever increasing numbers.

Germany also attempted to extend her influence into China in search for new markets for her manufactured goods and to exploit the supply of raw materials. Even before the creation of the German Empire with the confederation of the majority of the German states under Bismarck in 1872, the Kingdom of Prussia had concluded a treaty with the Chinese Government, allowing German warships to operate in Chinese waters, although no base existed that they could use.

Later, in 1881, a Far East Squadron was created, with four cruisers deployed, but the African colonies were deemed to be of greater political and economic importance and an African Cruiser Squadron was formed in 1885, operating from their newly acquired bases. As a result, the Far East Squadron was disbanded in 1893. However, with the advent of the First Sino-Japanese War of 1894, the East Asiatic Squadron was recreated with the armoured frigate SMS *Kaiser* as flagship, together with the light cruisers SMS *Prinzess Wilhelm* and the SMS *Cormoron* under the command of Rear Admiral Hoffmann.

A major drawback to the operation of the squadron was that they were without a base and had to rely on the goodwill of the British at Hong Kong, as well as the Japanese and Chinese ports at Nagasaki and Shanghai in order to refit and supply their vessels.

In order to effectively protect German interests a permanent base on the Chinese coast was essential.

To this end the German Government ordered Admiral Hoffmann's replacement, Rear Admiral von Tirpitz (who was later in the Great War), to lead the High Seas Fleet at Jutland to look for an anchorage suitable to house the East Asiatic Squadron. The chosen site was the small fishing village of Tsingtao that lay on the Lioedong Peninsula.

Initial offers to buy the proposed anchorage from the Chinese were rejected, but fortuitously for the plan the murder of two German missionaries in November 1897 was used as a pretext to force the Chinese to cede the port on a ninety-nine-year lease in 1898 to the German Government. The Germans rapidly laid out a town and large harbour facilities suitable to support all the needs of the squadron to operate effectively and protect German interests in China and the Pacific.

Much of the original German infrastructure still survives, with the buildings of the town hall, railway station, post office and Lutheran church built in the German colonial style oddly juxtaposed with more traditional Chinese and modern architecture.

One of the enduring legacies of the German occupation of the town that was a veritable home from home for the German colonists is the Tsingtao brewery, which still produces its world-famous lager.

The protected cruiser SMS *Kaiserin Augusta* arrived in January 1898 with a contingent of marines to protect the base. The German commercial community began to grow and prosper with great rapidity, allowing them to extend their markets more effectively in south-east Asia.

During the Boxer Rebellion of 1900 the German ships and marines helped to subdue the Taku forts on the Peiho River, deploying the protected cruisers SMS *Hansa* and SMS *Hertha*, together with the light cruisers SMS *Gefion* and SMS *Irene*, whose guns made good practice, despite the danger posed by Chinese 'electric mines' laid in the river.

At the outbreak of war in 1914, the East Asiatic Squadron, under the command of Admiral Count von Spee flying his flag in the armoured cruiser SMS *Scharnhorst*, was already at sea, anchored in the lagoon of the atoll of Panope in the Caroline Islands, accompanied by her sister ship SMS *Gneisanau*.

Both these ships were powerful vessels of 11,600 tons, mounting eight 8.2in guns, with six 5.9in guns as secondary armament. Their triple expansion engines of 26,000hp gave a top speed of 22.5 knots and were protected by a 6in armoured belt and 2in deck armour, together with a wide radius of action, rendering them formidable warships in their own right.

Von Spee came from an aristocratic Danish family, with connections in Rhineland Westphalia. He chose to enter the Kaiserliche Marine in 1878 where he was recognised by his superiors as a talented officer, serving in the Kamerun where he was later promoted to commanding the port facilities, but was later repatriated to Germany due to contracting Malaria.

In 1897 von Spee was given command of the cruiser SMS *Deutschland* and dispatched to the Far East to safeguard German interests during the Spanish American War of 1898. In 1910, after various staff appointments, von Spee was promoted to Rear Admiral, serving with the North Sea scouting forces. In 1912 he took command of the East Asiatic Squadron and base at Tsingtao, where he flew his flag in the modern armoured cruiser *Scharnhorst*.

Back at Panope, on receipt of the news of the commencement of hostilities, as off-duty crew members swam in the crystal clear waters of the lagoon, von Spee had to rapidly reconsider his options. His situation was a desperate one. He was in the mid-Pacific, 2,500 miles from his base at Tsingtao, which he reasoned would soon be under siege from the Japanese, so to return there would be out of the question. He concluded that his southern base at Rabul would also be under threat from the Australian fleet and possibly already in their hands. To the north he was threatened by the ships of the powerful Japanese Navy, which even now were searching for his squadron, while to the south-east the Royal Australian Navy was also mobilised, equipped with modern light cruisers and the battle-cruiser HMAS *Australia*, whose 12in guns and high speed were rated by Von Spee as more than a match for his two armoured cruisers.

Fortunately for von Spee, in a wave of patriotism, the first action of the Australian fleet was to escort a military expedition to seize German possessions in the Bismarck archipelago and German New Guinea, an undertaking in which the Australian forces hardly covered themselves in glory, as the large force was only opposed by reservists and native police, who put up such a heroic and determined defence that it delayed the seizure of the island territories. This delayed the availability of the Australian ships to join the search for von Spee by several vital weeks.

The German forces in the island territories finally surrendered on 21 September 1914, by which time it was obvious that the battle-cruiser *Australia* and the modern light cruisers could have been better employed seeking out the ships of the East Asiatic Squadron.

Von Spee was joined at Ponape by the light cruiser SMS *Nurnberg*, which had just returned from Honolulu, where she had received news of the commencement of hostilities. Weighing anchor, the squadron steamed north to Pagan in the northern Marianas, where the cruiser SMS *Emden* and four supply ships joined them.

Here, von Spee decided that, despite all the obvious dangers, he would wreak what havoc he could against Allied shipping across the Pacific and lead the squadron around Cape Horn in an attempt to return up the Atlantic to Germany. While at Pagan taking on coal, Kapitan Karl von Muller of the *Emden* asked permission to take his ship on a raiding cruise into the Indian Ocean as a diversion and, if possible, also to make it home.

The Admiral agreed to the suggestion and, with the *Emden* detached on her cruise, the squadron turned north to the Marshall Islands, where Japan's entry into the war was confirmed.

Von Spee sent the *Nurnberg* back to Honolulu to get news and to advise the Admiralty in Berlin of his intentions. He then left the Marianas and set course for the Christmas Islands to rendezvous with the *Nurnberg*, from whom he learned of the capture of German Samoa. On receipt of this news he decided to head south to attack the invasion force, but arrived too late to affect the outcome, so turned east towards Tahiti.

Arriving on 22 September off the Papeete, the two armoured cruisers shelled the town and harbour facilities, causing considerable damage, and sank the French gunboat *Zelee* at anchor in the harbour, but were unable to secure the port's coal stocks.

Moving on to the French Marquesas Islands, von Spee captured more supplies and cut telegraph cables, before sailing south-east to the remote Easter Island, where after coaling from colliers that had been stationed in the Pacific since before hostilities began, he was joined by the light cruisers SMS *Dresden* and SMS *Leipzig*, which he had summoned earlier by wireless.

These same wireless transmissions alerted the Royal Navy of the presence of the squadron off the South American coast and the Admiralty instructed Sir Christopher Cradock's West Indies Squadron – comprising the armoured cruisers HMS *Good Hope* and HMS *Monmouth*, together with the light cruiser HMS *Glasgow*, which were stationed at the Falklands – to sail around Cape Horn to intercept the German ships on the Pacific coast of Chile.

Admiral Cradock entered the Royal Navy in 1875 and served in Egypt during the Arabi Pasha's revolt in 1881. He was present at the bombardment of Alexandria in July 1882 and the subsequent Battle of Tel-el-Kebir. He accompanied General Wolseley's column in an abortive attempt supported by gun boats on the River Nile to relieve General Gordon at Khartoum in the Sudan. Later he took part in the suppression of the Boxer Rebellion in China and by 1913 was given command of the prestigious North America and West Indies Station. He was a popular officer with crews and was recognised for his efficiency and personal bravery, a trait that was to influence his decision to engage von Spee's squadron, despite the knowledge that his own ships were vastly inferior in firepower to the German ships.

In this decision he was also conscious of the recent court-martial of Admiral Troubridge, whose failure to engage the *Goeben* and *Breslau* in the Mediterranean at the outbreak of war allowed them to escape to a Turkish port. He was resolved that the odium for failing to engage the king's enemy at sea would not fall on his shoulders.

The flagship *Good Hope* was 14,100 tons and armed with two 9.2in and sixteen 6in guns, the *Monmouth* mounted fourteen 6in guns and the *Glasgow* carried only two 6in and ten 4in guns.

On reflection, these ships were ill-suited to the task. The *Good Hope* was a *Drake* class battleship that had been launched in 1902 and her two older pattern 9.2in guns were no match for the rapid-firing 8.2in guns of the German armoured cruisers. The *Drake* class cruisers were regarded by 1914 as outdated, compared to the modern dreadnought generation of turbine-powered cruisers, and were due for scrapping. They had earlier served with the 2nd Cruiser Squadron until it went into the reserve fleet in 1913.

At the outbreak of war *Good Hope* was recommissioned and assigned to the Grand Fleet at Scapa with other units as a replacement for the 4th Cruiser Squadron, which had been dispatched to join the North American and West Indies Squadron sent to protect British interests during the Mexican Revolution. Subsequently, the *Good Hope* was first ordered to Halifax, Nova Scotia, and then to the Falklands, where she became Admiral Sir Christopher Cradock's flagship.

The *Monmouth* had earlier served on the China Station, before similarly going into reserve in January 1914. She was also recommissioned in August 1914 and was hurriedly equipped with a crew of reservists, as was the *Good Hope*. Both crews had little time to work up to a high state of battle practice efficiency.

The *Monmouth*'s older 6in guns were out-ranged by the faster firing modern 4.1in guns of the German light cruisers, while the lower battery of 6in weapons mounted in casements near the waterline were rendered unworkable in a heavy seaway, as was the case later when the cruiser went into action at Coronel.

As a result of the fate that was to befall the *Monmouth*, the eight survivors of this class had these lower guns moved to the upper deck and consequently gave good service throughout the war on convoy duty and on the China Station.

The *Monmouth* class of nine ships was commissioned as a response to the German 1898 fleet expansion programme. They were at best a quick, cheap and ineffectual solution to the problem, being equipped with a weak armament and wholly inadequate armour protection.

Before Cradock's squadron left Port Stanley it was joined by the armed merchant cruiser HMS *Otranto* of 12,100 tons, mounting four 4.6in guns and of doubtful use. At Port Stanley, Admiral Cradock also had the pre-dreadnought battleship HMS *Canopus*, which had sailed from Halifax to reinforce his squadron with her four 12in guns, but on arrival she was experiencing boiler trouble that reduced her speed from her best of 18 knots to around 12 knots, making her incapable of keeping up with the cruisers. Cradock therefore determined to search for the German ships with the four faster ships at his disposal.

The Japanese Navy was at the same time also searching the wide waters of the Pacific, with several powerful squadrons, trying to locate von Spee's ships. To the north, the new battleship *Kongo*, built in 1912 in Britain, together with the cruiser *Izumo*, searched the waters towards Midway Island, while Admiral Mabumura, with the battleship *Satsuma* and the cruisers *Yahagi* and *Hirado*, searched the shipping lanes along the Pacific coast of South America for the elusive foe.

On 15 October, the 1,600-ton German cruiser *Geier* appeared off the island of Honolulu, where the Japanese battleships *Hizan* and *Asama*, alerted to her presence, stood in towards Pearl Harbor. After some negotiation the German ship entered port, where she was interned by the US authorities, avoiding what could have been an unpleasant international incident.

Meanwhile, since 18 September the garrison at Tsingtao had been under siege by a mixed force of largely Japanese and British troops numbering 25,000, supported by overwhelming naval forces. After a spirited resistance, the German commander Mayer-Waldeck surrendered with his 3,400 troops on 7 November, bringing to an end German control of their Chinese enclave.

Winston Churchill had earlier telegraphed Cradock, instructing him to rely on the support of the 12in guns of the *Canopus* and to preferably wait for the assistance of the powerful Japanese ships before he attempted to intercept the German ships. Cradock's other ship, the light cruiser *Glasgow*, commanded by Captain Luce, was already scouting off Valparaiso where she had intercepted wireless transmissions from *Leipzig*. Having received the information that the German cruiser was on the Chilean coast, Admiral Cradock weighed from Port Stanley on 22 October 1914 with *Good Hope*, *Monmouth* and the AMC *Otranto*, leaving orders for the *Canopus* together with the armoured cruiser *Defence* that was hurrying down from the West Indies to follow on at best possible speed.

At the same time von Spee was aware that the *Glasgow* was on the west coast. *Glasgow* had put in to Valparaiso harbour on 31 October to collect Admiralty instructions, where she encountered the German collier *Gottingen*, which had wirelessed the information to von Spee, who sailed south intending to locate and destroy the lone British cruiser.

Quickly putting out to sea again, the *Glasgow* joined up with Admiral Cradock's ships off the Chilean coast, with the *Canopus* still 300 miles to the south, slowly coming up in support, while the *Defence* had been retained by Admiralty orders off the River Plate.

Heading northward, the British squadron now expected to locate the *Leipzig*, so that both squadrons of warships were acting under the misapprehension that they would encounter only a single enemy ship. Instead, at 4.20 p.m. on the afternoon of 1 November 1914, the *Glasgow* signalled Admiral Cradock leading his line that they had sighted the whole German squadron coming south close inshore some 20 miles off the Chilean port of Coronel.

Despite realising that he was at a severe disadvantage and faced overwhelming odds due to the superior armament and speed of the two German armoured cruisers and the three light cruisers, Admiral Cradock, instead of turning away to the south, formed his ships into line of battle and turned towards the enemy to run parallel to the oncoming German ships and to accept action.

On sighting the British ships von Spee worked his armoured cruisers up to full speed of 20 knots – with their superior speed the German ships could dictate the course of engagement – opening the range to 18,000yd, keeping his own ships well beyond the range of the British guns.

Admiral Cradock attempted to close the range but von Spee skilfully maintained his chosen range as the ships continued to run southward in heavy weather that boded ill for working the lower batteries of the British ships. At 6.50 p.m., with the setting sun outlining the British in stark silhouette, presenting perfect targets for the German gun crews, von Spee closed to 12,000yd and opened fire.

Immediately the German ships had the range, with the first salvoes straddling the British ships. In the rapidly failing light, the German ships were hard to see in the gathering gloom to the landward and within 5 minutes of opening fire an 8.2in shell from *Scharnhorst* scored a direct hit on *Good Hope's* forward 9.2in gun, wrecking the turret and causing a massive fire to rage on the forecastle, ensuring that the British ship was unable to make any effective reply.

Cradock closed the range to 6,000yd in order that his 6in guns could be brought to bear on the enemy, but this only allowed the German shells to find their mark with greater ease and, consequently, shell after shell smashed into the grievously wounded ship.

The *Monmouth* was also under severe fire, with the third salvo from the *Gneisenau* similarly destroying her forward 6in gun, and a furious fire raged on her bow and boat deck.

The burning ship was now a beacon for the German shells and as the fusillade of high explosive smashed into her she was able only to make a token response, where, due to damage and the high sea, her lower 6in casements, comprising half her armament, were unworkable.

HMS *Glasgow*
Fairfield Shipbuilders, Clydeside - 1909
Town Class Light Cruiser

Dimensions: Length 453ft x47ft beam x 15ft draught
Displacement: 4,800 tons (normal)
Main armament: 2 x 6in Mk10 40 calibre
Secondary armament: 10 x 4in-2 x 18in torpedo tubes
Armour protection: Main belt 6in-3in, main deck 1in-2in, turrets 10in
Machinery: Parsons direct drive on 4 shafts, 22,500 shp at 25 knots
Range: 3,600 miles at 10 knots
Complement: 450

100 feet

HMS *Glasgow* took part in the Battle of Coronel, where the Armoured Cruisers *Good Hope* and *Monmouth* were sunk by von Spee's East Asiatic Squadron in November 1914. She later served in the Battle of the Falkland Islands in December 1914, also serving in the 8th Light Cruiser Squadron in the Mediterranean during 1918.

Bristol Class

HMS *Bristol*	1909
HMS *Glasgow*	1909
HMS *Gloucester*	1909
HMS *Liverpool*	1910
HMS *Newcastle*	1910

By now both armoured cruisers were receiving terrible punishment as fierce fires raged in the darkness; both ships were obviously doomed.

The Armed Merchant Cruiser *Otranto* was also being shelled by the *Nurnberg* at long range, receiving several hits, and Cradock ordered her away to the south to save herself and seek the protection of the still distant *Canopus*.

Captain Luce of the *Glasgow* was being heavily engaged by *Gneisenau*, *Leipzig* and *Dresden* and was fortunate to only be hit five times. Against these odds and seeing no value in losing his ship for no useful purpose, Luce ceased offering return fire as the German gunners were using his own gun flashes as aiming points.

Turning away from the hail of shellfire the *Glasgow* fell in with the blazing *Monmouth* where she offered assistance to Captain Brandt, who ordered Luce to save his own ship.

Then, as the *Glasgow* passed down the disengaged side of the doomed and blazing ship, the survivors of her crew gave three cheers to the light cruiser as she slipped into the night and safety.

The *Good Hope* bravely continued to put up what resistance it could but by 7.50 p.m., an hour after commencement of the one-sided action, she ceased fire and with the ship a mass of flames, her forward magazine exploded and she sank unseen by friend or enemy alike in the dark cold waters, taking Admiral Cradock and all hands with her.

The *Nurnberg* came upon the blazing *Monmouth*, listing heavily to port, and, after offering the chance for the cruiser to surrender by shining a searchlight on her ensign, which was refused, she opened a rapid fire with her 4.1in guns at point-blank range, until at 8.20 p.m. the *Monmouth* rolled over and sank in the darkness, again with the loss of all her crew – a total of 720 officers and men. Speeding southward, the *Glasgow* counted seventy-five gun flashes in the dark from the position where they had last seen the *Monmouth*.

In the action only two 6in British shells had struck the *Scharnhorst*, doing only minor damage, while the *Good Hope* was hit more than thirty-five times. But the German ship had expended 70 per cent of her 8.2in ammunition, while *Gneisenau*, after receiving minor damage had only used 40 per cent of her supply of shells.

The *Leipzig* and the *Dresden* were ordered to pursue the *Glasgow* while the other ships of the squadron were ordered to Valparaiso. On 2 November 1914 the victorious East Asiatic Squadron entered Valparaiso harbour on the Chilean coast to take on coal and supplies.

Here they received a hero's welcome from the German residents and brought the British authorities the first news of the battle. After a stay of one day, the *Graf Spee* set sail intending to raid the Falkland Islands, where the ships would plunder Port Stanley's coal stocks and attempt to fight their way up the Atlantic and make for home.

Meanwhile the *Glasgow* had outrun the German cruisers and after a passage through the Strait of Magellan she met the *Canopus*, which reversed course back to Port Stanley, where after further boiler and machinery problems she was beached in the outer harbour to provide a defensive battery.

Back in London, news of defeat reached the Admiralty by cable from British embassy staff in Valparaiso, where it was received with shock and incredulity by their Lordships and public alike. This was the first defeat at sea of a British squadron since the naval war with the United States in 1812. It seemed inconceivable to the public that the Royal Navy, which for so long had been a sure shield against 'infection and the hand of war', could be so comprehensively defeated by a nascent naval power with no tradition of command of the seas. The news of this humiliating defeat arrived when news of the land fighting in France and Belgium was anything but encouraging.

From the outset, in August British troops had been defeated in the early battles at Mons and Le Cateau, followed by a retreat in the face of overwhelming odds to the very environs of Paris itself, where by a supreme effort the French and British armies threw the German juggernaut back at the Miracle of the Marne in early September, driving von Kluck's forces back to beyond the River Aisne. This success was short-lived as the Germans, going into prepared positions, settled into the near-static trench warfare in October that was to characterise the four-year struggle.

At sea, the Royal Navy, despite the success of their battle-cruisers in early August against their opposite numbers in the High Seas Fleet scouting squadron in the Heligoland Bight, had already suffered the loss of several major units to mines and torpedoes in the North Sea, where three cruisers were lost to a single submarine, and in the English Channel where the increasing sinking of merchant ships was causing great alarm.

Moreover, a modern dreadnought had been mined and sunk off the Irish coast and two days after von Spee's victory, units of the High Seas Fleet had bombarded Yarmouth and Lowestoft. These seemed to the British public to be the portents of more dreadful things to come and perhaps even the spectre of invasion.

Added to this litany of gloom, all was not well at the Admiralty, where the First Sea Lord Prince Louis of Battenberg had been receiving criticism due to his German antecedence, encouraged by the rise of anti-German feeling then running high in the country.

German businesses that had been established for years were targeted. Any shop displaying a vaguely German-sounding name would have its windows smashed and ransacked (as my own mother, living in Poplar at the time, witnessed).

Prince Louis, the eldest son of Prince Alexander of Hesse, had joined the Royal Navy in 1868, becoming a British subject. As an efficient officer he saw service in varied commands, rising to the rank of commander in the battleship *Dreadnought* (the earlier turret ship of 1871 and not the later 1905 ship of the same name).

Due to his organisational ability, he was further appointed to the prestigious position in 1902 of Director of Naval Intelligence, which was followed by promotion to Rear Admiral in 1904. This was followed in 1908 by promotion to commander of the Atlantic Fleet. In this role he supported the reforms to modernise the fleet, at that time being enacted under the control of the ageing First Sea Lord Admiral Sir John Fisher, who in turn recommended Battenberg to replace him as First Sea Lord, recognising him as an able administrator and the ideal candidate for the job. In 1911 Louis took the post of Second Sea Lord, where he worked with the new civil First Lord of the Admiralty, Winston Churchill, and finally became First Sea Lord in December 1912.

On the eve of war when, as fortune would have it, the combined fleets were assembled at Spithead in review, prior to sailing on battle manoeuvres, it was decided that instead of dispersing the fleets afterwards, the ships should be fully prepared for war and sent to their war stations.

Meanwhile, anti-German sentiment had reached such a pitch, with the press calling for Battenberg's resignation as a 'Dangerous alien' who had access to Britain's naval secrets, that Churchill was obliged to ask him to step down, which he did in October 1914.

Sir John Fisher, Churchill's choice, was recalled to the post of First Sea Lord on 30 October, the day before the battle off Coronel. It could be concluded that the preoccupation with arguments as to the suitability of Battenberg's position as

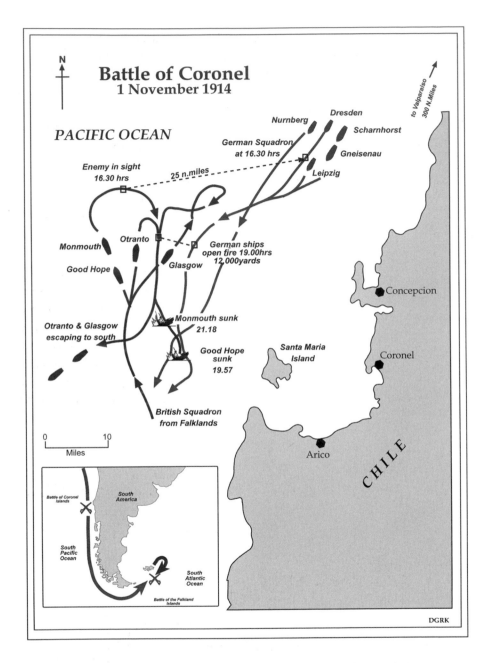

head of the navy and his replacement diverted attention of senior officers at the Admiralty away from earlier tactical problems in the South Pacific that had led to the recent disaster.

Now the problem of succession to the post of First Sea Lord was resolved, Fisher, together with Winston Churchill, prepared a response to the debacle that had occurred off the Chilean coast.

Speed was of the essence and, since von Spee's squadron had left the neutral port of Valparaiso on 3 November, the Admiralty were again in the dark as to his movements. However, they assumed that with the loss of his bases in the Pacific and the threat of the powerful Japanese fleet patrolling those waters, von Spee would soon attempt to round Cape Horn and either head directly for Germany or prey on Allied merchants in the sea lanes off the River Plate or the African coast until such time as his ships were either sunk by the Royal Navy or chose to accept internment in neutral ports in South America.

In fact, von Spee's squadron, after stopping the 24 hours as required by international law in Valparaiso harbour, had departed on 3 November, heading north to Mas Afuera, an island group including Juan Fernandez some 340 nautical miles off the Chilean coast. It remained there for several days, taking on coal at remote island anchorages from the remaining German colliers that were still at sea.

At the same time, there was nothing von Spee could do to replace the ammunition that had been expended in the battle, apart from a redistribution of 8.2in shells between the armoured cruisers, and similarly with the 4.1in shells of the light cruisers. While at Mas Afuera Island, von Spee received news from the colliers of the loss of the detached cruiser *Emden* at the Cocos Keeling Islands in the Indian Ocean on 9 November, when she was sunk by the Australian cruisers HMAS *Melbourne* and HMAS *Sydney*.

On 5 November the squadron sailed to Bahia San Quintin, a remote bay on the Chilean coast, where 300 Iron Crosses were presented to the crews in recognition of their recent action.

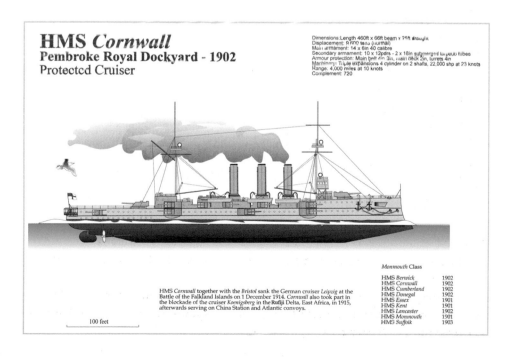

HMS *Cornwall*
Pembroke Royal Dockyard - 1902
Protected Cruiser

Dimensions: Length 460ft x 66ft beam x 25ft draught
Displacement: 9,800 tons (normal)
Main armament: 14 x 6in 40 calibre
Secondary armament: 10 x 12pdrs - 2 x 18in submerged torpedo tubes
Armour protection: Main belt 4in 2in, main deck 2in, turrets 4in
Machinery: Triple expansions 4 cylinder on 2 shafts, 22,000 shp at 23 knots
Range: 4,000 miles at 10 knots
Complement: 720

Monmouth Class

HMS *Berwick*	1902
HMS *Cornwall*	1902
HMS *Cumberland*	1902
HMS *Donegal*	1902
HMS *Essex*	1901
HMS *Kent*	1901
HMS *Lancaster*	1902
HMS *Monmouth*	1901
HMS *Suffolk*	1903

HMS *Cornwall* together with the *Bristol* sank the German cruiser *Leipzig* at the Battle of the Falkland Islands on 1 December 1914. *Cornwall* also took part in the blockade of the cruiser *Koenigsberg* in the Rufiji Delta, East Africa, in 1915, afterwards serving on China Station and Atlantic convoys.

100 feet

Finally, on 15 November the squadron raised anchor and steamed south, stopping at Picton Island in the Beagle Channel to take on water, redistribute the coal stocks and allow the men ashore to hunt, while time was taken to make minor repairs to the boilers. The squadron then rounded Cape Horn on the night of 12 December, with the intention of making a raid on the British outpost of Port Stanley in the Falkland Islands, where further stocks of coal could be obtained.

Von Spee's intelligence led him to believe that he would find the harbour defended by the pre-dreadnought HMS *Canopus* – old, but still a dangerous opponent due to her 12in guns, and a single armoured cruiser, perhaps supported by the light cruiser *Glasgow*, which had escaped at Coronel. However, unbeknown to von Spee, Churchill and Fisher were putting together a powerful squadron consisting of the armoured cruisers HMS *Carnarvon*, HMS *Cornwall* and HMS *Kent* to assemble at the Abrolhos Rocks, an archipelago off the north-east coast of Brazil, where they would be joined by two battle-cruisers.

On the same day Churchill requisitioned the battle-cruisers *Invincible* and *Inflexible* from the Grand Fleet, much against the Commander-in-Chief Admiral Jellicoe's wishes, and more particularly the objections of the Commander of the battle-cruiser fleet based at Rosyth, Vice-Admiral Sir David Beatty. He was anxious that the absence of the two battle-cruisers would seriously weaken the ability of the battle-cruiser squadrons to deal with any further coastal raids by the High Seas Fleet.

Churchill and Fisher eventually won the day and the two battle-cruisers left Rosyth for Devonport, from where, on 11 November, the two ships sailed at night on 'detached service' with only the commander, Vice-Admiral Doveton Sturdee, and his captains aware of their destination. Under conditions of the greatest secrecy, shipwrights and dockyard workers aboard the *Invincible* who had been carrying out work on board sailed with her, after being refused permission to go ashore on the grounds of security.

The two battle-cruisers headed south at an economical 10 knots, arriving at Abrolhos Rocks off the coast of Brazil on 26 November, where they met up with the other ships of the new squadron.

The augmented squadron left the Abrolhos Rocks on 27 November, arriving at the Falkland Islands on the morning of 7 December where repairs were carried out: *Invincible* had a wire cable that had wrapped around a propeller removed, *Bristol* overhauled one of her reciprocating engines, and *Cornwall* pulled her fires for boiler repairs.

While the ships coaled, the armed merchant cruiser *Macedonia* patrolled outside the harbour, watchful for the possible arrival of von Spee. Only the *Kent* had full steam up and was ready to sail immediately should it be necessary. At 8.00 a.m. on the morning of 8 December, only 24 hours since the arrival of the British ships, naval coast watchers above Stanley sighted smoke to the south-east closing on the island. The vessels were quickly identified as a four-funnelled armoured cruiser and a light cruiser, which could only be von Spee's squadron. On receipt of the electrifying news, Admiral Sturdee ordered all ships to raise steam with all dispatch, at the same time ordering hands to breakfast, knowing it would be some time before they could take up the pursuit.

By now the watchers could see the remainder of the German ships, which were shaping a course towards the island. The British ships were at this time in great danger if von Spee could catch them in harbour, where they would make perfect targets. However, as von Spee closed on the port, he was horrified to see the tripod masts that betokened the presence of battle-cruisers, and at the same time the old *Canopus* opened fire from her mud berth, hitting SMS *Gneisenau* with a 12in shell with her first salvo, while the *Kent* was already clearing the harbour and in pursuit of the enemy.

Realising that he had fallen into a trap, the outcome of which he knew would end in the destruction of his squadron, von Spee hauled sharply around to the south-east and worked his ships up to full speed, safety now lying only in escape. The British ships followed *Kent* out of Stanley harbour and by 9.45 a.m. the German ships were now some 13 nautical miles ahead, with the *Invincible* and *Inflexible* quickly working up to their top speed of 26 knots. They were accompanied by the armoured cruisers *Carnarvon* and *Cornwall* and the light cruisers *Bristol* and *Glasgow*, supported by the *Macedonia*.

Coast watchers had also sighted three colliers following the main German fleet, some 30 miles distance to the south, and accordingly *Glasgow* and *Macedonia* were detailed to hunt them down. After a long chase, two of the ships were sunk by gunfire around 9.00 p.m. that evening, while the third escaped but eventually handed herself over to internment in Chile. By 11.00 a.m., with the weather set fair, a light north-westerly wind, excellent visibility and long hours of daylight ahead of them that prevailed at that time of year in the South Atlantic, the British ships settled in to the pursuit of the German squadron, now some 20 miles ahead.

Admiral Sturdee was so confident he would overhaul the enemy ships by early afternoon that he slowed the battle-cruisers' speed to allow the armoured cruisers to catch up and sent the crews to the mess decks for breakfast. By 12.30 p.m. the battle-cruisers were closing rapidly on the German ships, with the *Inflexible* opening fire at 16,000yd at 12.47 p.m. while running parallel to their course.

The British ships on the windward side took a long time to find the range of the last ship of the German line, *Leipzig*, as the copious amount of smoke they were producing, which was drifting to leeward, obscured their view and made it difficult to observe the fall of shot effectively.

Admiral Sturdee tried to manoeuvre his ships into a more favourable position, while at the same time endeavouring to stay out of range of the German guns; in this he was unsuccessful thanks to von Spee's skilful evasive action.

Von Spee realised that in the contest between the battle-cruisers and his own armoured cruisers there could only be one outcome, so, after ordering the light cruisers away to the south to attempt to escape, he bravely turned the *Scharnhorts* and *Gneisenau* 90° to port and accept action.

Sturdee ordered the *Kent*, *Cornwall* and *Glasgow* to pursue the fleeing light cruisers, while *Carnarvon* followed the battle-cruisers as they turned to the east, gradually closing the range.

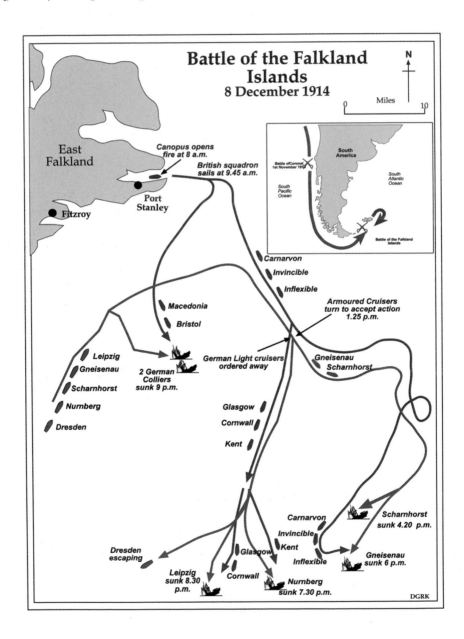

Soon the British ships found the range and the 12in shells began to take effect, as they smashed into the German ships with increasing regularity, but at 1.50 p.m. salvoes from the *Scharnhorst* straddled the British ships, causing Sturdee to increase the range once more, with a corresponding fall-off in the rate of British hits.

At 2.10 p.m., with both German ships now receiving severe damage, von Spee turned sharply to the south-west and, with Sturdee closing the range to 15,000yd, suddenly a full-rigged sailing ship crossed the *Invincible*'s track, heading south-east. One can only imagine with what consternation and incomprehension the barque's crew viewed a full-scale sea battle taking place in this lonely, unfrequented part of the world, as the great ships' guns thundered out, sending towering columns of water high into the air as the shells splashed into the sea, or sent sheets of flame and black smoke writhing into the clear air from wrecked and torn decks as they struck home.

At 2.45 p.m. the two German ships turned through 90° to port, closing the range to 15,000yd. Both ships were now receiving fearful punishment and the *Scharnhorst* was on fire with her third funnel shot away, while aboard *Gneisenau* fires raged uncontrollably.

Despite this punishment, the German gun crews continued to return fire, hitting the British ships over forty times between them, while the battle-cruisers expended a disproportionate amount of ammunition during the action, bringing into question the standard of British gunnery.

At 3.30 p.m. the *Scharnhorst* put about to the west, followed by the crippled *Gneisenau*. By 4.00 p.m., with most of her guns silent and a heavy list to port, *Scharnhorst* fell out of line and, following further salvoes, blazing from end to end, rolled over and sank into the cold waters of the South Atlantic, taking Admiral von Spee, two of his sons and the entire crew with her.

SMS *Scharnhorst*
Blohm & Voss Hamburg - 1907
Grosser Kreuser

Dimensions: Length 474ft x 71ft beam x 26ft draught
Displacement: 13,598 tons (deep load)
Main armament: 8 x 2in Mk10 10 turret
Secondary armament: 6 x 5.9in-4 x 18in submerged torpedo tubes
Armour protection: Main belt 6in-2in, main deck 2in, turrets 5in
Machinery: Triple expansions 4 cylinder on 3 shafts, 26,000shp at 22.5 knots
Range: 6,600 miles at 10 knots
Complement: 760

Wandering Albatross

100 feet

The *Gneisenau* maintained fire from all guns – even though she was a mass of flame, with her foremost funnel shot away and her decks a shell-torn charnel house – as the three British ships continued to pound her, until at 6.02 p.m. she rolled over on her beam ends and slipped beneath the waves. The British ships hove too and picked up 180 survivors aided by a fairly calm sea and good light – the sole survivors of more than 1,500 officers and men on the two ships.

Meanwhile, the three German light cruisers were running south at high speed, but were gradually being overhauled by the British ships. The *Leipzig* was being pursued by the *Cornwall*, while *Glasgow* was unable to catch the *Dresden*, whose boilers were in better condition than the British ship, enabling her to pull away and escape. By 7.40 p.m. the *Leipzig* was receiving heavy punishment from the 6in guns of the *Cornwall*, sinking at 9.20 p.m., with only eighteen of her crew surviving; British casualties being one man killed and four wounded.

The other German ship, *Nurnberg*, was being chased down by the old armoured cruiser *Kent*, the sister ship of the ill-fated *Monmouth*. Built in 1902, her design speed of 23 knots had seldom been attained in recent years, but the old ship excelled herself and by tying down the safety valves and feeding the wardroom furniture into the furnaces, she worked up to 25 knots, despite receiving a shell to a turret that started a magazine fire, which was dealt with by flooding the magazine. The German ship was sent to the bottom, with only eighteen survivors picked up.

The *Dresden* escaped to the south-west, rounding Cape Horn and making for the remote inlets along the Chilean coast, from where she attempted to carry on raiding merchant shipping, but succeeded in only sinking one ship between December and March 1915 due to lack of coal. Finally, she was located in Cumberland Bay on Juan Fernandez Island by the *Glasgow* and *Kent* where, after a short exchange of fire, the German ship was scuttled.

The *Invincible* and *Inflexible* were quickly returned to the battle-cruiser fleet, having received minimal damage, while the victory they had achieved was to be the most comprehensive to be gained by the Royal Navy throughout the whole course of the war. The news of the victory was welcome at home and did much to restore the prestige of the Royal Navy in the eyes of allies and neutrals alike.

7

EAST COAST RAIDS

Britain's long preoccupation with viewing France as a potential enemy over the preceding century had allowed military planners to largely disregard the building of extensive defensive works along the east coast; a region that was now seen to be dangerously unprotected and at risk of invasion from the sea.

It was along the flat coasts of Norfolk, Suffolk and Essex that the fear of invasion was most strongly felt in the years leading up to the Great War, as tension between Great Britain and Germany increased.

The British public, increasingly literate since the Elementary Education Act of 1870 that called for the compulsory education of children up to the age of thirteen, had for many years, thanks to the availability of cheap newspapers and magazines, taken an altogether more informed interest in politics and world affairs. The novel had become a popular diversion for this literate public and, following the Franco-Prussian war of 1870, in which an increasingly militaristic state, Prussia, had invaded and overwhelmed Europe's largest army in a matter of weeks (thanks to modern weapons and modern methods of warfare), the public felt a sense of unease that a new threat faced our islands.

This popular anxiety was immediately taken up by the author George Tomkyns Chesney, who, in 1871, produced the book *The Battle of Dorking*, the first of the genre of several hundred 'invasion scare' stories produced over the next forty years, up to the outbreak of the Great War. In *The Battle of Dorking*, an unnamed foreign army, that happen to speak German, invade the British Isles and, despite heroic resistance, they subject the country to their will.

Other works also led the British public to increasingly regard Germany as the potential enemy. These included Erskine Childers' *The Riddle of the Sands* of 1903, describing a seaborne invasion of the east coast, and H.G. Wells' *The War in the Air* of 1907, which describes a world war precipitated by the expansionist ambitions of an Imperial Germany. And then there was the self-styled secret agent and author, William le Queux, whose novel *The Invasion of 1910* again casts Germany in the aggressor role. Fuelled by these anti-German stories regarding possible invasion, a spy mania swept the country in the early years of the twentieth century, which in turn created calls for action on the part of the Government. In response they founded the 'Secret Service Bureau' that was to be the forerunner to MI5 and MI6, with the home section of the agency occupying itself by tracking down spies and saboteurs, although in fact no extensive network of spies existed in the country.

The main result in the years before the Great War of this anti-German invasion genre was to promote in the minds of the average Englishman the inevitability of war between the two countries. Voices were raised against this scare-mongering, such as when the Prime Minister Henry Campbell-Bannerman denounced Le Queux's book *The Invasion of 1910* as 'Calculated to inflame public opinion abroad, and alarm the more ignorant at home', but by then the seeds of conflict had been irrevocably sown.

As previously mentioned, while no actual invasion took place, the German High Command at the outbreak of war had expected, and indeed hoped, that the Royal Navy would impose a close blockade of their coast in the manner of that conducted during the Napoleonic wars against Brest, Toulon and other ports that had proved so successful in containing the French fleet.

It was hoped that under these favourable circumstances, with British warships patrolling close inshore to German naval bases, opportunities to sink them by use of submarine and mines would be greatly increased, or possibly to intercept smaller, isolated squadrons and lure them into a trap against superior enemy surface units in conditions that favoured the defending force. In the event the British had already come to the conclusion that with the advent of modern weapons the principle of close blockade was no longer a viable option.

Accordingly, plans were put in hand as early as 1908 that, in the event of war with Germany, Admiralty policy would be to close off the entrances to the North Sea from the Channel in the south and between Norway and Scotland in the north. The intention was to achieve the double goal of restricting the flow of foodstuffs and raw materials to Germany with an economic blockade and, conversely, to reduce the possibility of German surface raiders leaving the North Sea to prey on Britain's merchant shipping on the world's trade routes.

After some preliminary skirmishing between individual light units and the capture and sinking of AMCs and minelayers, it became more obvious that the British had no intention of offering themselves up as targets for torpedos and mines in a close blockade. The Commander-in-Chief of the High Seas Fleet, Admiral Friedrich von Ingenohl, resolved to use the High Seas Fleet in an aggressive manner, seeking out the enemy as occasion and opportunity warranted. But in this he was frustrated by the Kaiser who was intensely protective of the fleet he had created and was loath to risk his ships, and insisted that the fleet was not to put to sea without the express orders of the Kaiser himself. In his caution he was reinforced by an incursion into the Heligoland Bight by a strong force of

Royal Navy ships in August, including battle-cruisers, when the war was only three weeks old, that fell upon patrolling German light forces sinking three light cruisers.

On the other side of the coin the dangers to the Royal Navy of operating in the waters close to the German coastline was dramatically illustrated in September 1914 when three armoured cruisers patrolling at 10 knots in the Broad Fourteens off the Dutch coast were sunk in turn by a single submarine in an afternoon.

The armoured cruisers HMS *Aboukir*, HMS *Hogue* and HMS *Cressy* of the 7th Cruiser Squadron based at Dover, under the command of Captain Drummond of the *Aboukir*, were sister ships launched in 1902, each of 12,000 tons' displacement, mounting two 9.2in and twelve 6in guns apiece. They were cruising slowly at 10 knots in line ahead parallel to the Dutch coastline in the early morning of 22 September 1914, after their accompanying destroyers had been detached to refuel.

Unwisely, the ships were not steaming on the recommended zigzag course –the correct procedure in hostile waters – which made it easier for Kapitanleutnant Otto von Weddigen who, while running submerged, had sighted the trio from his U-boat *U9* of 500 tons' surface displacement and one of the earliest German submarines built.

Manoeuvring into an optimum position across their track, he fired a single torpedo from under 1,000yd range that struck the *Aboukir* amidships on the port side around 6.30 a.m.

HMS *Aboukir*
Fairfield, Clyde - 1900
Protected Cruiser

Dimensions: Length 472ft x 70ft beam x 26ft draught
Displacement: 12,000 tons (normal)
Main armament: 2 x 9.2in Mk10 40 calibre
Secondary armament: 12 x 6in, 8 x 18in submerged torpedo tubes
Armour protection: Main belt 6in-2in, main deck 3in, turrets 5in
Machinery: Triple expansions 4 cylinder on 2 shafts, 21,500 shp at 21 knots
Range: 4,600 miles at 10 knots
Complement: 760

HMS *Aboukir*, together with the *Hogue* and *Cressy*, were units of the Seventh Cruiser Squadron in September 1914 patrolling off the Dutch coast in the Broad Fourteens, when the *Aboukir* was torpedoed by the U9.

On going to her assistance, the *Hogue* was also torpedoed, whilst the *Cressy*, on attempting to render help, was also sunk.

Cressy Class

HMS *Aboukir*	1900
HMS *Bacchante*	1901
HMS *Cressy*	1899
HMS *Euryalus*	1901
HMS *Hogue*	1900
HMS *Sutlej*	1899

100 feet

Believing that she had struck a mine and having seen no torpedo tracks, Captain Drummond ordered the *Hogue* to his assistance as his ship began to settle, to aid in the rescue of survivors.

Captain Nicholson of the *Hogue* came alongside and lowered boats to help with the rescue, when at 6.45 a.m. the *U9* fired two torpedoes at the *Hogue* from a range of only 300yd, hitting her amidships on the starboard side.

The *Hogue's* boiler room flooded rapidly and within 10 minutes she slipped beneath the waves, followed at 7.00 a.m. by the *Aboukir*, rolling over on her beam ends and going down in a welter of steam with her screws still turning.

The third cruiser *Cressy* hastened to the aid of the two stricken ships and was in turn herself torpedoed, quickly followed by a second torpedo from *U9* 10 minutes later, exploding on her armoured belt at 7.20 a.m. where, after listing heavily to starboard, the *Cressy* sank at 7.35 a.m. carrying all but fifteen of her crew to the bottom. Within the course of an hour three large warships and 1,880 officers and men, many of them reservist or cadets, had been lost to one of the oldest U-boats in the German Navy.

On their return to Wilhelmshaven von Weddigen and his crew received a hero's welcome and were decorated and feted.

The following month, von Weddigen repeated his success with *U9* when on 15 October he sank HMS *Hawke*, a protected cruiser of 7,700 tons built in 1891 in the North Sea, with a single torpedo that hit her magazine, causing the ship to explode with the loss of all hands.

Otto von Weddigen was later to meet his nemesis when in March 1915 his next command, the *U29*, was rammed and sunk by *Dreadnought* in the Moray Firth, with the loss of von Weddigen and his crew. It is interesting to consider that the revolutionary dreadnought – the ship that ushered in new concepts of the war at sea – should employ the most archaic of naval weapons, the ram, to gain her victory.

In Britain the news of the loss of three armoured cruisers to a U-boat was received with disbelief and profound shock, while the Admiralty were forced to realise that the submarine which had been seen as a peripheral weapon of doubtful use, apart from perhaps harbour defence or patrolling inshore coastal waters, was in fact a dangerous new weapon of great potential that could fundamentally affect the balance of power at sea.

A hastily convened court of inquiry was held, at which Captain Drummond was criticised for his failure to follow a zigzag course as contained in his orders, while the senior officer of the squadron, Admiral Christian, was similarly criticised for his lack of leadership and failing to follow correct procedures, instituting these high-risk patrols using old ships in distant waters that were of limited value, against repeated advice from experienced senior officers.

Although these older ships, of which the Royal Navy possessed around thirty-four armoured cruisers and twenty-odd protected cruisers that had been built since

1900, were still of considerable use in their scouting function to the fleet, they were patently inferior to the modern types of turbine-driven cruisers and in almost any engagement would be at a severe disadvantage.

Although most of the later armoured cruisers were still attached to the Grand Fleet, from now on they were employed with greater circumspection now that their inherent weakness had been exposed and were increasingly detailed to the less dangerous work of trade protection. As a result of the disaster, these patrols were suspended and the practice of major units stopping to go to the aid of their fellows in enemy waters was banned, with any rescue being affected by destroyers or smaller craft if practical.

Frustrated by the British policy, the German Admiralty devised a series of raids on the English coast that would not only deliver a propaganda coup to the German nation, but could possibly lead to the isolation of a section of the Grand Fleet, by drawing it into a trap consisting of a squadron of superior heavy ships placed across the British line of advance and preferably located in or near to German waters.

Admiral Friedrich von Ingenohl proposed a daring scheme to take a squadron of battle-cruisers and light cruisers on a lightning raid on the British east coast, the first target chosen for this raid being the port of Great Yarmouth. Accordingly, at 4.30 p.m. on 2 November, the battle-cruiser squadron under the command of Admiral Reinhard Scheer left Wilhelmshaven in the Jade Basin heading westward. It was to be followed by two squadrons of battleships sailing some hours later that would be positioned several miles behind the battle-cruisers, ready to fall upon any British ships that might be enticed into pursuing Scheer's ships into a trap.

In the early morning light of 3 November 1914, the old gunboat HMS *Halcyon*, patrolling off the Cross Sands light vessel, sighted and challenged a group of unknown vessels emerging from the mist to seaward. *Halcyon*'s challenge was met with a withering blast of fire from the German battle-cruisers *Seydlitz*, *Von der Tann* and *Moltke*, the armoured cruiser *Blucher* and three accompanying light cruisers, commanded by Admiral Franz von Hipper.

Against these overwhelming odds, the *Halcyon* pluckily returned fire with her two 4.7in guns before seeking shelter in a smoke screen laid by the destroyer HMS *Lively*, which allowed the gunboat to turn away with only minor damage and escape to the south-west, raising the alarm with a wireless message of the presence of enemy ships close inshore.

The German squadron standing off Great Yarmouth then proceeded to bombard the town for 30 minutes with their 11in-high explosive shells – which fortunately did little damage, with most of the shells landing on the beach – while the light cruiser SMS *Stralsund* laid mines along the coast. In the harbour four destroyers were raising steam, while three submarines prepared for sea. One of these ran onto a mine near the harbour entrance and was lost.

At 10.00 a.m. Admiral Beatty, alerted to the raid, led the 1st Battle-Cruiser Squadron south from Rosyth on the Firth of Forth in hope of intercepting the raiders, but by that time Hipper's ships were already 50 miles east of Great Yarmouth. The returning German ships were delayed by fog from entering harbour and anchored overnight in the Schillig Roads. In the fog, the armoured cruiser SMS *Yorck*, which had not been involved in the raid, while crossing the Jade estuary went off course and ran into a German defensive minefield, sinking with a heavy loss of life.

The raid could be seen as a propaganda victory for Germany, particularly among the neutral nations and, although little material damage had been done, it did demonstrate the ability of the German Navy to raid the British coast with impunity. On the British side, with a submarine lost and twenty-three killed, the lack of an effective response to this form of incursion exercised the minds of the Lords of the Admiralty as to the best way to respond.

The widely publicised news of the raid coincided with the receipt at the Admiralty in London on the same day of the report of the loss of the *Good Hope* and *Monmouth* of Admiral Cradock's squadron at the Battle of Coronel off the coast of Chile. This added to a feeling of outrage and disbelief from the general public, who had long trusted in the invincibility of the Royal Navy and had expected them to be successful in any confrontation with an enemy.

In government circles the ease with which the German ships had been allowed to approach Britain's coast (to be met with only minimal resistance) was a worrying development that exposed a lack of an integrated and effective scheme to protect Britain's east coast harbours and shipping lanes from this form of incursion.

Additionally, the raid seemed to be a portent of worse to come and in response the Government hurriedly stationed two additional regiments of infantry in East Anglia, should these raids be the precursors to an actual invasion. At the same time, the naval bases at Dover, Harwich, Great Yarmouth and Sheerness were reinforced with additional destroyer and cruiser flotillas, while the battle-cruiser squadrons remained at their northerly harbours.

The Germans had hoped that by this and later raids it would persuade the Admiralty to bring a portion of the battle-cruiser fleet south and encourage the dispersal of other units to protect the east coast, thereby increasing the chance of the Germans catching an isolated group of British ships in a trap during a subsequent sortie, while at the same time weakening the main fleet at Scapa Flow.

The Commander-in-Chief of the High Seas Fleet, Admiral Friedrich von Ingenohl, was satisfied with the outcome of the raid, as, more importantly, was the Kaiser (although still ever fretful about hazarding his ships). Its success, together with the news of von Spee's victory, did much to boost the confidence of the fleet and encourage a more aggressive and daring use of its ships in future.

Buoyed up by the success of the Yarmouth raid, von Ingenohl now proposed an even more ambitious raid, with the chosen target being the Yorkshire coastline between the River Humber and Hartlepool.

From early August, German minelayers had laid mines along the coastwise sea lanes and at the approaches to the ports of Hartlepool, Scarborough, Whitby and Hull, resulting in a number of merchant ships being sunk. The British, in turn, attempted to keep the approaches to these harbours open by sweeping the channels, initially employing drifters and other fishing craft for the task until specialist mine sweepers could be developed.

The German mines were laid by fast converted merchant ships, or *Hilfekreusers*, which could carry up to 300 mines, laying them during the hours of darkness before fleeing back to their bases, eluding the Royal Navy patrols.

In choosing to attack ports on the Yorkshire coast, von Ingenohl was taking a greater risk with his ships, as these targets were much closer to Scapa Flow and Rosyth where Beatty's battle-cruisers were based, which would allow them to be in a more favourable position to intercept the raiders than had been the case during the Yarmouth raid.

The advent of the introduction of wireless telegraphy to the Navy in the early 1900s opened up the possibility of instant communication between ships and their home ports, where instructions and reports of enemy ship movements that previously could only be transmitted by visual signal could now be instantly available to an admiral leading a squadron into battle, enabling him to make instant tactical decisions that could affect the outcome in his favour.

An area where the British excelled was that of intelligence and the dissemination of the data they had gained. At the outbreak of war, Sir Alfred Ewing, a former scientist, was appointed Controller of Intelligence at the Admiralty, with Commander Alasdair Denniston acting as his ADC. The centre of this intelligence-gathering network was located in Room 40, Old Building, at the Admiralty in Whitehall. The whole undertaking was overseen by the redoubtable Admiral Sir Reginald 'Blinker' Hall in his role as Director of Naval Intelligence (DNI), who had formerly served as captain of the battle-cruiser RMS *Queen Mary*, but was forced to give up seagoing duties due to ill health.

As an officer of outstanding intellect and organising ability, Hall was offered the post of DNI, taking over from Captain Oliver, and quickly set up a highly efficient code-breaking and intercept service, establishing links with other British intelligence services such as MI5, MI6 and Scotland Yard.

Throughout the war a team of specialised cryptographers, drawn from a wide variety of civilian and service backgrounds, worked tirelessly on wireless code intercepts of German military and naval traffic, together with telephone and commercial cable traffic and other information garnered from neutral sources, commercial and business sources, and information supplied by spies.

By itself this information, randomly gathered, meant very little, but in the hands of the Admiralty cipher experts each piece was made to fit the complicated jigsaw that helped to understand the military and naval intentions of the Central Powers.

In this they were aided by an approach in the autumn of 1914 to the First Lord Winston Churchill by two English wireless amateurs: Barrister Russell Clarke and Colonel Richard Hippisley.

They informed him that, using their own private civilian equipment, they had for some time been picking up German military and naval wireless traffic and that these intercepts included wireless bearings issued to Zeppelin airships in the air and warships at sea. Recognising the significance of this information, Churchill immediately installed the two men at a remote coastguard station near Hunstanton on the Wash to listen in on the German frequencies.

A further refinement was added in February 1915 when, following successful wireless direction-finding experiments on the Western Front by the Marconi Company, Admiral Hall ordered the establishment of a further fourteen listening stations sited from Dover to the Humber and staffed by hand-picked GPO personnel. These stations were equipped with the latest equipment capable of taking cross-bearings on Zeppelin airships or surface warships as they approached the British coast and accurately pinpointed their locations.

In contrast, the Germans and their allies paid scant heed to the requirements of an effective military or naval intelligence service to aid their fighting services throughout the war. Their own efforts in this field were fragmentary and lacking a single, unified central department for sifting the large amount of varied information they received. The German High Command failed to appreciate the value of the information available to the British military and naval command and little realised to what extent their own efforts were being compromised by the highly efficient British secret service and the untiring work of the skilful analysts of Room 40.

The Admiralty cryptographers had a further advantage over their German counterparts, when in August 1914 the German light cruiser SMS *Magdeburg* was sunk by Russian cruisers in an engagement in the Gulf of Finland. Russian divers were subsequently able to dive on the wreck and recovered a haul of secret German naval codebooks and maps, which included the SKM code that was the main cipher then in use.

In an uncharacteristic spirit of co-operation on the part of the Russians, these codebooks were immediately dispatched to the Admiralty in London, arriving on the desk of Admiral Sir Reginald Hall, chief of naval intelligence in Room 40. These codebooks and others, such as the GN and VB codes, similarly retrieved from the German destroyer *T119* that had been sunk at the Dogger Bank action, gave valuable insights into not only the current codes but also the system employed in the construction of new codes. This piece of good fortune allowed the Admiralty to read almost all German wireless traffic throughout the whole course of the war.

Another code that fell into British hands early in the war was the *Handelsschiffsverkehrsbuch*, or HVB code, which was the standard German merchant service code book, long compromised by British intelligence, the first copy of which was seized from an interned German merchant ship in Australia. This particular code was also used by the German Naval Airship Service where, due to an oversight of German security, Zeppelins departing their bases would transmit the message 'Only HVB on board', which meant that the more secret code books had been left behind, which in turn indicated to the code breakers of Room 40 that the destination of the airships was to be a raid on the British Isles, giving time for appropriate defensive countermeasures to be taken.

In December 1914 naval intelligence became aware through coded wireless intercepts of a planned sortie by units of the German High Seas Fleet. Accordingly, at noon on 15 December the 1st Battle-Cruiser Squadron under Admiral Beatty in his flagship *Lion* rendezvoused off the Scottish coast, with the 2nd Battle Squadron comprising the battleships HMS *King George V*, HMS *Ajax*, HMS *Centurion*, HMS *Orion*, HMS *Monarch* and HMS *Conqueror*, together with the 3rd Cruiser Squadron from Rosyth and attendant destroyers. The whole fleet was under the overall command of Admiral Warrender. At 3.00 p.m. the combined fleet moved southward to take up a position to the south of the Dogger Bank where they expected to meet and engage the German ships.

To the south, the Harwich Force, under Commodore Tyrwhitt, with the light cruisers HMS *Aurora* and HMS *Undaunted* leading forty destroyers, was ordered to sea, while Commodore Keyes departed Dover with eight submarines and two destroyers to patrol off Terschelling and intercept any attempt by the German ships to enter the English Channel. As a further precaution, Admiral Jellicoe dispatched four armoured cruisers of the 3rd Cruiser Squadron stationed at Rosyth to bolster the defending force in the event that more powerful German units accompanied the raid.

The German forces were led by Admiral Hipper, leading his 1st Scouting Group, including the battle-cruisers *Seydlitz*, *Moltke*, *Von der Tann* and *Derfflinger* and the armoured cruiser *Blucher*, together with light cruisers of the 2nd Scouting Squadron. Hipper headed west across the North Sea at high speed towards the British coast.

Following some miles behind, Admiral von Ingenohl directed his course towards the south of the Dogger Bank, where he intended to lay in wait with his battleships, as well as being able to protect the returning battle-cruisers and hopefully overwhelm any pursuing British vessels.

At 5.20 a.m., just west of the Dogger Bank, the German light forces accompanying Hipper's battle-cruisers came into contact with British destroyers and exchanged fire in thick weather. News of this contact was wirelessed to von Ingenohl, who

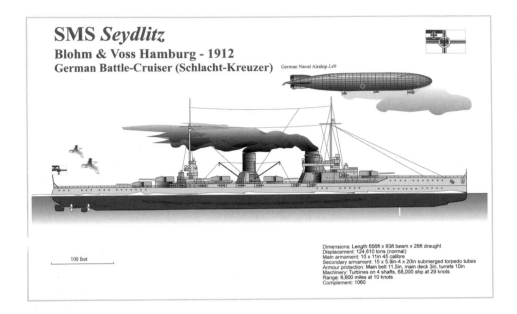

SMS *Seydlitz*
Blohm & Voss Hamburg - 1912
German Battle-Cruiser (Schlacht-Kreuzer) German Naval Airship *L49*

100 feet

Dimensions: Length 656ft x 93ft beam x 26ft draught
Displacement: 24,610 tons (normal)
Main armament: 10 x 11in 45 calibre
Secondary armament: 15 x 5.9in-4 x 20in submerged torpedo tubes
Armour protection: Main belt 11.5in, main deck 3in, turrets 10in
Machinery: Turbines on 4 shafts, 68,000 shp at 29 knots
Range: 6,600 miles at 10 knots
Complement: 1060

reasoned that the destroyers could represent the screening forces of the British battle fleet and, having no idea what strength they might be and in accordance with the Kaiser's orders not to risk the High Seas Fleet, he ordered his ships back to Wilhelmshaven at 5.45 p.m.

The chance of the two fleets meeting was now dashed, although some of Warrender's ships pursued the German cruiser *Roon* for several hours, which enabled her to make her escape and led them away from the main German fleet retiring eastwards.

Meanwhile, Hipper's battle-cruisers were unaware that the main fleet had put back and that they now did not have the support of the heavy ships as they raced on towards the English coast.

At 8.00 a.m. on the morning of 16 December, in heavy weather that reduced visibility, the German battle-cruisers were standing off Hartlepool and Scarborough and began to shell the two towns, causing considerable damage. Over 1,100 heavy shells were fired by the attacking ships, with 300 houses being hit along with damage to the steel works, gasworks and railway, resulting in eighty-six people killed and up to 424 wounded. The scale of the destruction was unprecedented, and the sense of total shock to the survivors, many of whom had fled the attack to the surrounding countryside, fearing it was an actual invasion, caused panic along the coast.

In Hartlepool harbour, the light cruiser HMS *Patrol* put to sea only to be hit by two 8in shells, and on taking water was run aground by her captain to save her from sinking.

Hartlepool was defended by three 6in guns, which opened up on the raiders, causing some slight damage to the *Seydlitz* and *Derfflinger* and disabling two 6in guns on the *Blucher* while the attackers were briefly engaged ineffectively by a small force of destroyers.

After shelling Scarborough, the attacking force of three ships ran south to pour a rain of shells into the fishing port of Whitby before both groups reversed course to head home again at high speed.

Coming down from the north, Beatty's cruisers came upon the German light cruisers scouting ahead of the main fleet and an indecisive, confused action followed until they were lost in the mist. At around 1.45 p.m. Beatty turned north, where, unbeknown to him, Hipper's ships were on a converging course. But, on receiving an erroneous signal that the German ships had turned south, he turned his ships away to the south, allowing Hipper to escape.

Admiral Warrender finally called off the search at 4.00 p.m. on 16 December, turning his ship on course for harbour, disappointed that he had failed to bring under his guns the German fleet. Meanwhile, at Scapa Flow reports received at 1.50 p.m. indicated that the German High Seas Fleet was now at sea some 70 nautical miles north-west of Heligoland.

Fearing that they were planning to fall upon Beatty's battle cruiser squadron, Admiral Jellicoe ordered the entire Grand Fleet to sea. Pounding southwards in misty weather, the Grand Fleet rendezvoused with Beatty's ships, but by that time the German ships were long gone.

British opinion was outraged by the flagrant disregard of the laws of civilised warfare shown by the German ships in bombarding the undefended towns of Scarborough and Whitby, which under the Hague Convention of 1899 were deemed immune from attack, while Hartlepool, with its three 6in guns, was considered a 'defended place' and as such a legitimate target. To the British public, however, with fresh accounts of recent atrocities and the shooting of civilians in Belgium, this was yet another example of 'Hun frightfulness'.

Once again, the seeming ease with which the German ships had carried out their attack and returned safely to port almost unmolested by the Royal Navy, called into question the whole policy of the defence of Britain's islands, a failure made all the more unpalatable by the fact that the Admiralty had prior warning of the raid and yet failed to respond effectively. Churchill demanded answers.

Following the seemingly successful and almost uncontested raids on the British coast in 1914, the Admiralty strengthened and increased the cruiser and destroyer patrols in the southern North Sea and the English Channel, with additional ships deployed to Admiral Tyrwhitt's Harwich Force.

On the German side, von Ingenohl was anxious to repeat this form of attack in order, as before, to entice British ships into a well-laid trap; an eventuality he was planning for.

However, despite the loss of the cruiser *Blucher* and the severe damage sustained to Sheer's flagship *Seydlitz* at the Dogger Bank battle in January 1915, where, due to poor communications and misunderstood orders between Beatty's ships, the German ships were allowed to escape from a position where they should have been destroyed, the German Admiralty were dertermined to pursue the policy of coastal raiding.

The Kaiser was furious at the loss of the *Blucher* and the hazarding of his precious ships, and as a result von Ingenohl was replaced in February 1915 by Admiral Hugo von Pohl. Von Pohl more closely followed the Kaiser's views of not hazarding the fleet on such risky ventures and saw the need to preserve the fleet in being by transferring a portion of the fleet through the Kiel Canal to the somewhat safer waters of the Baltic, and to a large extent ceding the control of the North Sea to the Royal Navy. He was, however, a sick man and dying of cancer, being forced to step down in favour of Admiral Scheer, who now became Commander-in-Chief of the High Seas Fleet. Scheer had for some time militated for a more offensive position to be taken on the employment of the fleet. Great Yarmouth and Lowestoft were again the targets selected for attack.

Lowestoft was the main British base for mine-laying activities, while Great Yarmouth was the centre of submarine activity in the southern North Sea and the English Channel, where they both contributed considerably to damaging and reducing German coastwise trade, so if severe damage could be done to either warships in harbour or harbour installations and workshops it would materially assist the enemy war effort and disrupt the British.

The date of the raid, 25 April 1916, was chosen to coincide with the Easter Uprising of Irish nationalists that had broken out the day before. Earlier German help had been sought by the rebel groups, the Irish Republican Brotherhood and the volunteers, and shipments of rifles and ammunition were secretly landed around the Irish coast in the preceding months from coasters and yachts to arm the dissident groups. A notable rebel leader was Sir Roger Casement, who had landed from a U-boat in Tralee Bay to co-ordinate the rebellion, but was captured almost immediately and subsequently executed by firing squad for treason.

On 23 April, German intelligence had reports of two separate light units of the Royal Navy operating independently off the Norwegian coast and in the Hoofden off the Dutch coast. Taking advantage of this disposition of British ships, Scheer planned to strike at the two harbours, which would attract these forces to their line of retreat, where the battle-cruisers would engage whichever of the two hopefully inferior forces first crossed their path.

Fortunately for the Germans, and unbeknown to them, three ships of the northern force – the battle-cruisers *Australia*, HMS *New Zealand* and the battleship *Neptune* – had been involved in collisions due to fog off the Danish coast and had abandoned their operation and returned to port.

A feature of the raid was the inclusion of eight Zeppelin airships, under the command of Fregattenkapitan Peter Strasser, leader of Naval Airships, which, while operating independently of the fleet intending to raid the Midlands, provided a limited reconnaissance function that augmented the light cruiser screen, with their reports being available to Admiral Scheer by wireless as they flew westward.

The German battle-cruisers sailed from the Jade Basin mid-morning of the 24 April, followed by the battleship squadrons some 2 hours later, and escorted into the German Bight by the Zeppelin *L7* cruising ahead of the fleet. At 2.30 p.m. the *Seydlitz* struck a mine off the home island of Norderney. She was seriously damaged with a 50ft hole on her starboard side, took on over 1,000 tons of water and suffered eleven crewmen killed. Initially it was thought she had been torpedoed, but the *L7* flying overhead saw no torpedo tracks and escorted the badly damaged battle-cruiser back to Wilhelmshaven.

The new commander of the battle-cruiser fleet, Admiral Bodicker, transferred his flag from the *Seydlitz* to the *Lutzow* and, in order to avoid more minefields, sailed close to the West Frisian Islands, even though there was now a greater chance of his ships being sighted from the Dutch islands and reported to the British.

At 7.30 p.m. the Grand Fleet was ordered to weigh anchor and sail south, while at midnight Tyrwhitt's Harwich Force put to sea with three light cruisers and eighteen destroyers heading north. Admiral Beatty's battle-cruiser fleet had already put to sea from Rosyth and was battling heavy seas southward, 100 miles ahead of Jellicoe's battleships. At 3.50 a.m. the cruiser SMS *Rostock* of the scouting group sighted Tyrwhitt's Harwich Force, which in turn reported four battle-cruisers and six light cruisers to the Grand Fleet racing southward at high speed.

The German ships reached the British coast and opened fire on Lowestoft at 4.10 a.m. While only lasting 10 minutes, the barrage sent a storm of high explosive shells into the town, destroying almost 200 houses, two gun batteries and fortunately only killing three civilians and wounding fifteen. The German ships then moved up the coast to Great Yarmouth, where a dense fog made the target difficult to observe and made only a limited practice before they retired to join the light cruisers that had been in action with Tyrwhitt's ships to the south, causing serious damage to the cruiser *Conquest* and the accompanying destroyer HMS *Laertes*. Bodicker did not pursue the retreating British ships, as he feared they might be leading them into a trap, so he turned away to the north-east to rendezvous with the battle fleet off Terschelling.

Tyrwhitt's squadron followed the German ships in heavy seas until ordered to turn back at 8.30 a.m. Similarly, the units of the Grand Fleet, fighting heavy seas that had caused their escorting destroyers to fall behind, was also instructed to abandon the chase at 11.00 a.m., when they were still 150 miles behind the battle-cruiser force. The rival battle-cruiser squadrons had in fact come within 50 miles of each other but, due to the poor weather and confused reporting of the disposition of various units, had failed to meet.

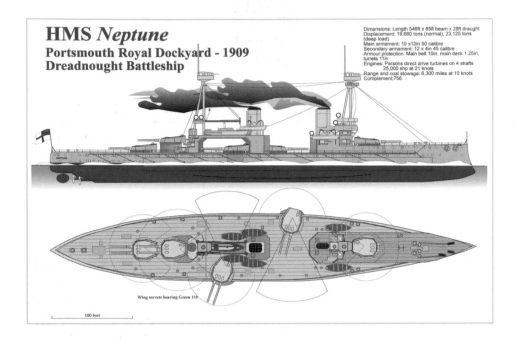

HMS *Neptune*

Portsmouth Royal Dockyard - 1909
Dreadnought Battleship

Dimensions: Length 546ft x 85ft beam x 28ft draught
Displacement: 19,680 tons (normal), 23,125 tons
(deep load)
Main armament: 10 x12in 50 calibre
Secondary armament: 12 x 4in 45 calibre
Armour protection: Main belt 10in, main deck 1.25in,
turrets 11in
Engines: Parsons direct drive turbines on 4 shafts
25,000 shp at 21 knots
Range and coal stowage: 6,300 miles at 10 knots
Complement:756

Wing turrets bearing Green 110

100 feet

The German ships regained their harbours without further incident and the Germans could reflect that the raid had been a failure and achieved very little, with the *Seydlitz* mined, one U-boat sunk and another captured when it ran aground. None of the objectives of causing heavy damage to the harbour installations that would disrupt the mine-laying operations or curbing submarine activity in the two ports had been achieved.

Once again public outrage was expressed on this further attack on civilian targets and the Germans were regarded in neutral world opinion to have behaved in a barbaric fashion. In the United States in particular opinion hardened against them and their war aims.

Following these events, the 3rd Battle Squadron that previously had been part of the Grand Fleet at Scapa Flow was moved down to the Thames and stationed at Sheerness to reinforce the Harwich Force.

8

HELIGOLAND BIGHT AND THE CHRISTMAS DAY RAID

At the outbreak of war the British Expeditionary Force, consisting of four army corps comprising six divisions of infantry, five brigades of cavalry and artillery, totalling some 150,000 men and everything necessary to support the army in the field, under the command of Sir John French and his general staff, was safely transported across the southern North Sea to France by the Royal Navy between 11 and 21 August without any loss to or interference from the German Navy.

The speed and efficiency with which the British movement of troops to the continent had been accomplished took the German high command by surprise, as they had assumed Britain would take much longer in mobilising her land forces. The British Army was in fact following a long-established War Office plan, formulated by Lord Haldane in concert with their French counterparts some years prior to the war, for the rapid deployment of British troops in the event of conflict with Germany.

The troopships were strongly protected by destroyer and cruiser flotillas and included aerial surveillance by two naval airships over the route, which deterred any interference from German torpedo boats or submarines.

Following the initial reverses suffered by the British and Allied armies through August 1914, with the retreat from Mons and the Battle of Le Cateau where the British at brigade strength faced whole German divisions, the Allies fell back toward Paris and faced defeat. The tide turned, however, at the 'Miracle of the Marne', when the British and French threw von Kluck's army back at the beginning of September and then rapidly advanced northward to the River Aisne.

Here the war of movement came to a halt as the struggle inexorably settled into the trench warfare that was to characterise the four-year war. Under these circumstances the Government turned to the Royal Navy to strike an inspirational blow against the enemy that would boost public confidence and demonstrate Britain's command of the seas, in keeping with its historic record of over 500 years of unchallenged naval ascendancy.

In early October 1914 the Fleet Commander Admiral Jellicoe communicated a memorandum to the Admiralty in which he expressed his contention that, in the event of meeting the High Seas Fleet in battle, the enemy would contrive that such an action would take place near to their home ports in the eastern portion of the North Sea, and that they would in all probability refuse to accept direct action, instead turning away with the intention of drawing the British ships into prepared minefields and ambuscades of torpedo boats and submarines.

Under these circumstances, Jellicoe stated that he would not pursue the enemy ships into their home waters, which he perceived would hazard his ships disproportionately due to the new threats posed by the mine and torpedo. This was a complete reversal of policy from the accepted battle instructions, which were based on the close pursuit and destruction of an enemy as the primary purpose of the fleet. Plans to carry the war against the enemy at this early stage were formulated and submitted to the Admiralty by Commodore Tyrwhitt, commanding the destroyer force at Harwich, who on their forays into the German Bight had observed a repetitive pattern of patrol by the German ships, where each evening destroyer flotillas would be escorted out by cruisers to patrol deeper into the North Sea and escorted back again in the morning.

Such a formation, comprising relatively lightly armed enemy warships, posed a tempting target. Despite the chosen scene of action being in dangerous proximity to the island of Heligoland, it promised the opportunity to wreak havoc among the lightly protected German ships. An emphatic British victory would do much to restore the morale of the British public following the setbacks in the land war in France referred to earlier.

The attack would have to be made as a lightning strike, quickly destroying as many German torpedo boats, and hopefully also light cruisers, as possible before the enemy could send heavier units from the Jade Basin in support. Tyrwhitt proposed the dispatch of a strong force of cruisers and destroyers in conjunction with Commodore Keyes' submarine force, based at Dover, which would intercept the returning ships at first light and overwhelm them.

The plan was enthusiastically endorsed by First Lord Winston Churchill, who was delighted by the audacity of the plan in keeping with the offensive Nelsonian spirit of the Royal Navy. While he recognised the dangers of implementing such an attack by pushing so deep into enemy waters, he considered that a successful raid into Germany's backyard would reap benefits in terms of an increase of prestige in the eyes of neutral opinion and a much needed boost to public morale at home.

In order to strengthen the raiding squadron, Churchill initially requested the additional support of the 2nd Battle-Cruiser Squadron, comprising *New Zealand* and *Invincible* under Admiral Moore, to be stationed some 40 miles to the west of the proposed scene of action, together with Cruiser force 'C' of five armoured cruisers *Cressy, Bacchante, Hogue, Aboukir,* and *Euryalus* a further 100 miles westward.

The submarine force consisted of the E class submarines *E4*, *E5* and *E9* accompanying the attacking force, while *E6*, *E7* and *E8* took station on the surface 3 nautical miles to the west of the planned battle area to entice the German ships out to sea and under the guns of the cruisers. Two further older submarines, *D2* and *D8*, were ordered to close the Ems estuary and watch for any sign of reinforcements being sent to the German destroyers' aid.

Before the sortie, planned to take place on 26 August, was sanctioned by the Admiralty, Admiral Jellicoe was concerned that in being so close to the German bases the hunters could become the hunted and therefore requested additional powerful support for the venture in the shape of three more battle-cruisers, *Lion*, *Princess Royal* and the *Queen Mary*, led by Vice-Admiral Sir David Beatty.

Also included were the ships of the 1st Light Cruiser Squadron from Rosyth, with Admiral Goodenough leading in the 5,400-ton 6in cruiser HMS *Southampton*, accompanied by HMS *Liverpool*, HMS *Birmingham*, HMS *Falmouth*, HMS *Lowestoft* and HMS *Nottingham*, where, once agreed to by the Admiralty, the ships steamed southward through the night to the rendezvous.

Jellicoe wirelessed a signal to both Tyrwhitt and Keyes informing them of the reinforcements but, due to delay in forwarding the message, neither were aware of the extra support available until they saw Goodenough's ships emerging from the mist later in the action, causing some concern before they could be identified as friendly. At 7.00 a.m. on the morning of 26 August, in misty conditions, the *Arethusa*, leading a force of sixteen destroyers of the 3rd Flotilla, steaming at high speed in a position 12 miles north-west of Heligoland, sighted the German torpedo boat *G194*.

The British ships were followed at a distance of 2 nautical miles by the 1st Destroyer Flotilla, also composed of sixteen destroyers, with Goodenough's six light cruisers a further 8 miles behind them. The deteriorating weather favoured the enemy – due to fog and misty conditions, visibility was only of the order of 2½ miles.

On sighting the British ships, the *G194* reversed course towards Heligoland, working up to 34 knots, at the same time reporting the British presence to the commander of the torpedo boat flotilla, who passed the information on to Rear Admiral Franz Hipper, who was commanding the battle-cruisers in the Jade Basin. Here, due to the shallow waters of the anchorage, the battleships would have to wait until high water before they could negotiate the narrow channels and the bar at the mouth of the estuary leading to the open sea.

Admiral Hipper, assuming that the attacking ships only included two destroyer flotillas, ordered the light cruisers SMS *Stettin* and SMS *Frauenlob* – each armed with ten 4.1in guns – as well as six other light cruisers, the *Stralsund*, *Strassburg*, *Koln*, *Ariadne* and *Kolberg*, moored in the River Jade, and *Mainz* at anchor on the River Ems to raise steam and put to sea as soon as possible.

Off Heligoland, four of Tyrwhitt's destroyers went in pursuit of the *G194*, opening fire on her and the rest of her flotilla when they were occasionally revealed to the British rangefinders through the encroaching mist.

Arethusa and her attendant destroyers began to overhaul the retreating Germans, opening fire at 8,000yd. Hits were registered on the torpedo boat *V1* and two other torpedo boats, which requested the coastal batteries on Heligoland to lay fire on the British ships. However, the German gunlayers were unable to identify friend from foe in the fog and held their fire.

At 07.27 a.m. the British destroyers sighted and gave chase to a further force of ten German torpedo boats of the reconnaissance group, steaming at high speed towards the island of Heligoland. After chasing them for 30 minutes and coming within 2 miles of the island, where they found themselves being engaged by the cruisers *Stettin* and *Frauenlob* coming rapidly up from the east, they were forced in turn to fall back on the support of the *Fearless* and *Arethusa*.

With the German torpedo boats now safe in the island's harbour, the German cruisers turned south-west to engage Tyrwhitt's destroyer flotillas, with the *Frauenlob* coming into action against the *Arethusa* and the two ships trading shots through the increasing mist, as they ran on parallel courses to the south.

Although more heavily armed than the German ship, the *Arethusa*, having only recently been commissioned, was mainly crewed by reservists and was experiencing machinery problems, with two of her smaller 4in guns inoperative. Trouble was also experienced with the training mechanisms of the 6in batteries. Under these circumstances the *Frauenlob* was able to lay down an accurate fire in the British ship, causing severe damage to the cruiser.

Despite these drawbacks, the *Arethusa* returned fire at close range, causing terrible damage to the German ship, until finally a 6in shell struck the bridge of the *Frauenlob*, killing the captain and the entire bridge crew. The ship had to turn away towards the security of her base in a badly damaged condition and make her way slowly towards Wilheimshaven. She was the first serious casualty of the engagement in the first major fleet action of the war.

By 8.00 a.m. Goodenough's cruisers *Nottingham* and *Lowestoft* had arrived at the scene of action south-west of Heligoland, crossing the path of the fleeing German torpedo boat *V187*, which reversed course with the intention of slipping through the pursuing destroyers and escaping eastwards. In this she failed to break through and was quickly sunk. As the British destroyers attempted to rescue survivors by lowering boats, the *Stettin* appeared from the north-east opening fire, which caused the British to abandon the German survivors and the British sailors in the lifeboats.

Running on the surface was the British submarine *E4*, which fired a single torpedo at the *Stettin*. Unfortunately it missed its target and caused the alerted cruiser to attempt to ram the *E4*, which in turn submerged to escape. Upon resurfacing when safe to do so, with the battle having moved away, the submarine retrieved the British crewmen and put the German survivors into the lifeboats, equipping them with a compass to row to the nearby German coast, as the submarine was too small to take them all aboard.

Commodore Keyes coming into action with the *Fearless* and his destroyer flotilla, who was still unaware of the approach of the additional force of cruisers and battle-cruisers sent by Jellicoe, sighted two four-funnelled cruisers on his port bow that he took to be enemy ships and informed *Invincible* he was in contact with German cruisers. Fortunately, Keyes identified them as British ships and rejoined Tyrwhitt's squadron, continuing their sweep.

The British submarines, likewise, had not been informed of the cruiser reinforcements and at 9.30 a.m. one of them fired two torpedoes at the *Southampton*, which fortunately missed, and the submarine was lucky to avoid being run down by the cruiser.

Admiral Tyrwhitt joined with Keyes and, sighting *Stettin*, briefly opened fire on her before she disappeared into the mists.

By 8.15 a.m., the British 12th Flotilla led by *Fearless* had turned to the south-west, attempting to draw the German light cruisers towards the battle-cruisers *Invincible* and *New Zealand*, while still being unaware of the additional three battle-cruisers added to the squadron by Jellicoe.

The destroyers engaged German torpedo boats, sinking the *V167* and two others, while damaging several more with accurate fire.

Fearless and her destroyer flotilla at 10.15 a.m. had fallen in with the *Arethusa*, which had been badly mauled and needed assistance with temporary repairs to her boiler room before she could proceed.

By this time, as reports of the action were received in Wilhelmshaven, Admiral Maas aboard his flagship the cruiser *Koln*, although still unaware of the scale of the attack and accurate whereabouts of the British ships, ordered to sea the cruisers *Koln* and *Strassburg*, modern ships both of 4,500 tons mounting twelve 4.1in guns, together with the smaller *Ariadne* armed with ten 4.1in guns, while the *Mainz*, also armed with twelve 4.1in guns, was coming up from the south-east.

The *Strassburg* came upon the damaged *Arethusa* heading south-west and attacked her with shellfire and torpedoes, but was herself forced to turn away thanks to heavy shellfire and determined torpedo attacks from the accompanying British destroyers.

By 11.00 a.m. Tyrwhitt's flotilla led by the *Arethusa* was running to the south-west pursued by the German cruisers *Stettin* and *Ariadne*, who were firing on the retreating ships and gradually gaining on the British squadron.

At the same time the *Koln* was coming up independently from the south-east to join the action, but was similarly repulsed by torpedo attacks and badly damaged by shellfire, causing her also to turn away to the south.

Admiral Tyrwhitt, leading the German ships towards the rendezvous, had wirelessed for immediate assistance from Beatty's battle-cruisers, which at that time were 40 nautical miles to the north-east, with Admiral Goodenough's armoured cruisers some miles ahead. Beatty ordered his ships to maximum speed as they plunged southward towards the sound of gunfire.

At 11.30 a.m. Tyrwhitt's ships engaged the lone cruiser *Mainz* as it crossed their track, into which they poured a storm of shellfire and torpedo hits, in which they were joined by the arrival of Goodenough's cruisers, who also opened fire on the unfortunate German ship – by now a mass of flame and in a sinking condition. British destroyers lowered boats and brought a destroyer alongside to take off survivors, after which her captain ordered her scuttled and she finally sank at 12.45 p.m.

To the west, at 12.30 p.m., Beatty's five battle-cruisers came rushing into action, throwing up high, curling bow waves as their 13.5in and 12in guns sought out their targets in the misty conditions that still persisted.

At 12.45 p.m. *Lion* and *Princess Royal* opened fire at 7,800yd on the *Koln*, *Stettin* and *Ariadne*, scoring hits with the first salvoes and causing the German cruisers to abruptly reverse course to the east.

Closing the range to 7,000yd, Beatty's battle-cruisers wreaked terrible havoc to the German ships and, to add to their discomfort, from the south the *Fearless* also engaged the *Stettin* and *Köln* simultaneously.

The German ships attempted to escape to the north but Beatty brought the battle-cruisers and Goodenough's squadron around to the north-east and continued to punish the enemy ships.

Although grievously damaged, the *Stettin* managed to disengage from the action and escape to the north-east and finally gain the Jade Basin and safety. The *Köln*, bearing Admiral Mass, staggered away to the north-east, as she was continuously being hit by the heavy shells from Beatty's battle-cruisers, reducing the vessel to a fire-ravaged wreck.

Yet, despite the terrible damage being inflicted, the German ship still attempted to return fire and the superior quality of her construction and watertight integrity of her hull to a comparable British cruiser enabled her to remain afloat longer.

Eventually, however, as the battle-cruiser's squadron swept round in an arc to the west, heading homeward after a final barrage of heavy shellfire, the *Köln* rolled over, slipping beneath the waves at 1.35 p.m.

Now the cruisers *Danzig* and *Stralsund* cautiously approached the area as the British ships departed westward and attempted to pick up survivors, but had to withdraw when British submarines were sighted manoeuvring to attack.

Admiral Mass went down with his ship, and of the estimated 250 survivors in the water only one was eventually rescued two days later by a passing fishing boat.

The final loss of the day was the *Ariadne*, which had been furiously engaged not only by the battle-cruisers but by the armoured cruisers of Goodenough's squadron, finally sinking at 3.00 p.m. and effectively bringing the battle to a close, as far as the British were concerned.

Meanwhile, in an effort to support the beleaguered German ships, as wireless reports came in of the nature of the attacking force, Admiral Pohl ordered the battle-cruisers to sea.

In the Jade Basin the tide had now risen sufficiently to allow heavier units to put to sea and the *Moltke* and *Von der Tann* steamed out at 2.10 p.m., followed at 3.10 p.m. by Rear Admiral Hipper with the *Seydlitz*. But by the time they reached the area south-west of Heligoland the British ships were long gone and the battle was over.

From the British point of view the battle was a comprehensive victory and on the surface seemed to represent an example of an action that had been carried out with meticulous planning and attention to detail, executed with traditional verve and the bulldog spirit the public expected from the senior service.

Yet the whole episode had been characterised by muddled planning, poor communications and signalling to an extent that hazarded the success of the operation, as in the case of the cruisers *Nottingham* and *Lowestoft*. Although present during the initial stages of the operation, they somehow managed (due to poor communications) to lose contact with the ensuing action and took no further part in a battle in which their 6in guns could have been employed to good effect.

Nonetheless, the Admiralty must bear a large proportion of the blame, as they failed to communicate to the commanders of the various elements involved an overall united plan of action, or even to inform, for instance, Commodore Tyrwhitt and Keyes that additional powerful units had been dispatched to assist and support him in the operation.

Commodore Keyes was disappointed that the opportunity for a greater success had been lost, as the additional cruisers had not been included from the outset in the plan that was proposed by Jellicoe but rejected by the Admiralty.

The Germans had fought bravely, but by bringing their ships into the action as individual units rather than in the squadron formation adopted by the British they put themselves at a disadvantage, as the British could bring a heavier weight of fire to bear on individual ships. That being said, German ships were class for class superior to their British counterparts and due to their strong construction and watertight integrity they were, despite severe punishment, hard to sink. On this occasion, however, their faster firing 4.1in guns were no match for the slower firing but heavier 6in guns of the British cruisers. They had lost three light cruisers, *Mainz*, *Ariadne*, *Köln*, and the cruiser *Frauenlob* was severely damaged, as were to a lesser extent the *Strassburg* and *Stettin*. The destroyer *V187*

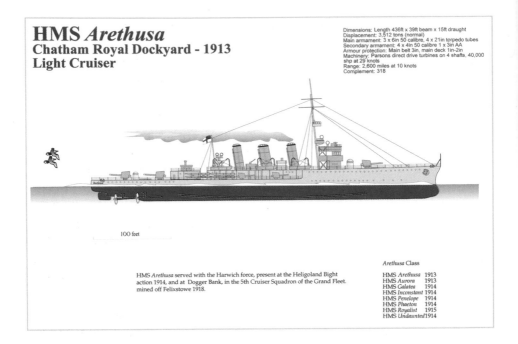

HMS *Arethusa*
Chatham Royal Dockyard - 1913
Light Cruiser

Dimensions: Length 436ft x 39ft beam x 15ft draught
Displacement: 3,512 tons (normal)
Main armament: 3 x 6in 50 calibre, 4 x 21in torpedo tubes
Secondary armament: 4 x 4in 50 calibre 1 x 3in AA
Armour protection: Main belt 3in, main deck 1in-2in
Machinery: Parsons direct drive turbines on 4 shafts, 40,000
shp at 29 knots
Range: 2,600 miles at 10 knots
Complement: 318

100 feet

Arethusa Class

HMS *Arethusa* served with the Harwich force, present at the Heligoland Bight action 1914, and at Dogger Bank, in the 5th Cruiser Squadron of the Grand Fleet. mined off Felixstowe 1918.

HMS *Arethusa* 1913
HMS *Aurora* 1913
HMS *Galatea* 1914
HMS *Inconstant* 1914
HMS *Penelope* 1914
HMS *Phaeton* 1914
HMS *Royalist* 1915
HMS *Undaunted* 1914

and two other torpedo boats were also sunk and other torpedo boats and mine sweepers damaged.

The German casualities included 714 killed, including Rear Admiral Mass, and 336 captured as prisoners of war, while, although several Royal Navy ships were damaged, none had been lost and casualties were limited to thrity-five killed and forty wounded.

The effect on the Germans of this encounter was one of profound shock and it was a damaging blow to the morale of the High Seas Fleet. The immediate result was that the Kaiser ordered all future naval operations to be personally approved by him before being implemented.

Bad communications on the German side also had a bearing on the outcome of the battle, as the presence of the British cruisers had not been communicated to Admiral Hipper until as late as 2.35 p.m., by which time the British ships were retiring. Had Hipper been made aware earlier, his battle-cruisers could have created a very different outcome to the battle.

The daring nature of the raid, with the British risking their most powerful vessels so deep in enemy waters, deeply impressed the Germans. As Winston Churchill wrote in *The World Crisis*: 'The British did not hesitate to hazard their greatest vessels and light craft in a most daring offensive action, and had escaped apparently unscathed.' The Germans felt as the British would have done had German destroyers broken into the Solent and their battle-cruisers had penetrated as far as the Nab Tower.

To the logical German mind such an attack so close into their home waters, an area protected by minefields and submarines, with a battle squadron prepared to sail only an hour away, was utter madness and it was beyond their comprehension that it could have been countenanced by the Lords of the Admiralty. However, it only served to increase the respect in which they held the Royal Navy, as well as increasing the feeling of inferiority felt within their own fleet.

The immediate effect of the raid over the next months severely curtailed the patrolling of the German Bight by the torpedo-boat flotillas, with only the most essential mine-laying sorties to maintain the defensive mine barrages being carried out, together with limited scouting by the torpedo boats. During the years preceding the Great War, the German Navy had concentrated on building dreadnought battleships in an effort to maintain a sufficient number of these vessels to challenge the Royal Navy's position. To achieve this end, vast amounts of the nation's wealth was required to support the building programme, so that cruisers and other types of warship for the fleet were produced in lesser numbers than were required to create a balanced fleet.

The numbers of cruisers built from 1900 onwards were also below the figure that Admiral Tirpitz would have considered necessary to perform the varied scouting duties, fleet protection and distant patrol work for which they were designed. A unique alternative to perform the vital role of scouting ahead of the fleet and to provide the essential early warning to the fleet commander of the presence

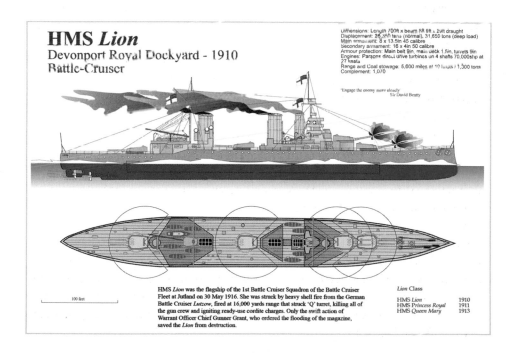

HMS *Lion*
Devonport Royal Dockyard - 1910
Battle-Cruiser

Dimensions: Length 700ft x beam 88 ft x 2½ft draught
Displacement: 26,350 tons (normal), 31,650 tons (deep load)
Main armament: 8 x 13.5in 45 calibre
Secondary armament: 16 x 4in 50 calibre
Armour protection: Main belt 9in, main deck 1.5in, turrets 9in
Engines: Parsons direct drive turbines on 4 shafts 70,000shp at 27 knots
Range and Coal stowage: 5,600 miles at 10 knots / 3,300 tons
Complement: 1,070

'Engage the enemy more closely'
Sir David Beatty

100 feet

HMS *Lion* was the flagship of the 1st Battle Cruiser Squadron of the Battle Cruiser Fleet at Jutland on 30 May 1916. She was struck by heavy shell fire from the German Battle Cruiser *Lutzow*, fired at 16,000 yards range that struck 'Q' turret, killing all of the gun crew and igniting ready-use cordite charges. Only the swift action of Warrant Officer Chief Gunner Grant, who ordered the flooding of the magazine, saved the *Lion* from destruction.

Lion Class	
HMS *Lion*	1910
HMS *Princess Royal*	1911
HMS *Queen Mary*	1913

of an approaching enemy squadron could, it was asserted, be provided by the scouting airship.

An airship from its elevated vantage point flying at 3,000ft could scout a far greater area of ocean more rapidly than was possible from the deck of a cruiser, and could be built at the fraction of the cost of a surface ship.

Count Zeppelin's first airship had flown over Lake Constance in July 1900 and in the intervening fourteen years had developed into a viable flying machine, first as a commercial carrier, then to be employed for war purposes, initially by the Army and later the Navy.

At the outbreak of war the German Army possessed ten airships, which they used to support their advancing troops by bombing frontier fortresses and strong points, but in doing so quickly lost three Zeppelins to ground fire.

Before the Great War there was a widely held belief amongst the British public that, in the event of war with Germany, fleets of giant Zeppelin airships would launch bombing attacks on major cities within hours of a declaration of war. Such attitudes had been encouraged during the years of mounting international tension by sensationalist writers of the day such as William le Queux, a novelist and self-styled secret agent. They were also influenced by the works of H.G. Wells. In his prophetic novel, *The War in the Air* of 1908, he describes how a German attack on the United States by a fleet of giant airships destroys the American Atlantic fleet and then obliterates New York, before they are, in turn, overwhelmed by a superior Asiatic air fleet, with the ensuing worldwide war leading to the breakdown of organised government and the total disintegration of civilised society.

In the event, at the outbreak of war the German Navy had only one Zeppelin in service, the *L3* based at Fulhsbuttle near Hamburg, but by December 1914 it had been joined by five new airships numbered from *L4* to *L8* whose primary duty was to scout ahead of the High Seas Fleet.

The Committee for Imperial Defence prior to the war, when considering the protection of naval dockyards, forts and magazines, had decided that the Army would be responsible for all home defence matters. However, once the war had started, with all the existing army's Royal Flying Corps squadrons quickly accounted for supporting the BEF in France, it was apparent that the task of supplying aircraft for home defence was beyond the capability of the War Office.

Accordingly, the responsibility for the aerial defence of the British mainland passed by default to the Royal Navy, with the army still maintaining the fixed-gun defences. At this stage of aeronautical progress the airship was considered to be almost invulnerable to attack and could easily out-climb the primitive aircraft available by dropping water ballast and ascending at a rate that left the aircraft standing.

Once again the First Lord Winston Churchill convened a conference to discuss how to deal with the Zeppelin menace.

In response to the news that the Germans had established airship bases in occupied Belgium, bringing the threat of an attack closer to the capital, the Admiralty proposed a bold plan to strike at the Zeppelin bases in Belgium and on the North Sea coasts, with the intention of destroying the airships before they could be used.

The first of these raids by aircraft of the Royal Naval Air Service based at Dunkirk was launched on 9 October 1914, when Commander Spencer Grey and Flight Lieutenant Marix, flying Sopwith Tabloid biplanes, set out to bomb the Zeppelin sheds at Cologne and Dusseldorf.

After a flight of 100 miles, Marix located the Dusseldorf shed and in the face of heavy machine-gun fire dropped his two 25lb bombs, scoring a direct hit and destroying the army Zeppelin *Z9* inside. This was the first success of its kind by the Royal Naval Air Service. Meanwhile, Spencer Grey, frustrated by thick fog over Cologne and being unable to locate the sheds, dropped his bombs on the main railway station instead.

A further attack of an even more daring nature was carried out by the Royal Naval Air Service on 21 November 1914 from Belfort near the Alsace-French border. It was aimed at the very heart of the Zeppelin empire at Friedrichshafen. Early in the morning three Avro 504s, each carrying four 25lb bombs, flew 125 miles through the mountains on a route carefully designed to avoid Swiss territory to emerge on the south side of Lake Constance before climbing to attack the Zeppelin works.

British airmen claimed a direct hit on one of the main sheds; however, German sources to this day continue to claim that the raid caused no damage, although the testimonies of Swiss workers in the factory maintain that a partly built airship was destroyed.

A particularly audacious air raid was planned for Christmas Day 1914 to attack the airship shed at Cuxhaven and, simultaneously, attack warships at anchor at Wilhelmshaven. Commodore Tyrwhitt again led the Harwich Force of three light cruisers and a destroyer flotilla of eight ships and supporting submarines under the command of Commodore Keyes, these submarines leaving port on the evening of the 24th to be in position off the German coast next morning. Further support was supplied by the 1st Battle Squadron under Sir David Beatty, led by *Marlborough* and seven other dreadnoughts, together with the 6th Cruiser Squadron being ordered south to Rosyth from Scapa Flow on 21 December.

Accompanying the Harwich Force were three fast cross-channel steamers, *Empress*, *Engadine*, and *Riviera*, that had been converted as seaplane carriers, each carrying three Short type 74 or type 81 seaplanes with folding wings that allowed them to be stored in the hangers aft. The three seaplane carriers departed Harwich at 5.00 a.m., followed at intervals by the Harwich Force, reaching the launching point for the seaplanes 40 nautical miles north-west of Cuxhaven at 6.00 a.m. on the morning of 25 December.

Amazingly, the seaplane carriers had reached the rendezvous point undetected and, coming to a halt, lowered the nine planes, each armed with three 25lb bombs, onto the calm water.

The engines of two of the machines failed to start and they were hoisted back aboard, with the remaining seven machines taking off from the smooth water at 7.00 a.m., climbing slowly as they headed eastwards towards Cuxhaven and Wilhelmshaven – the main targets of the raid.

Although the weather was clear over the sea, on reaching the coast the British aircraft encountered a thick fog bank reaching far inland, which made it impossible to locate the main target, the Zeppelin shed. Instead, the aircraft attacked what targets they could find, with flight commander Hewlett attacking a destroyer at 8.20 a.m. and flight commander Oliver attacking the seaplane base on Langeoog Island, while Flight Lieutenant Edmonds attacked the cruisers *Stralsund* and *Graudenz* in the Jade Estuary.

Lieutenant Erskine Childers, author of the novel *The Riddle of the Sands*, which was set in these very waters, was an observer in one of the machines that reconnoitred the Schillig Roads, identifying several dreadnoughts and heavy cruisers.

At the Zeppelin base of Nordholz near Cuxhaven, two airships, the *L6* with Kapitanleutnant Horst von Buttler Brandefels in command and the *L5* under Kapitanleutnant Hirsch, had taken off at 6.00 a.m. on a reconnaissance of the waters beyond Heligoland.

As a clear dawn was breaking on a north-westerly course, *L6* steered over Heligoland, where, after an hour, three ships were spotted cruising slowly to the north-east. Von Buttler Brandenfels identified these as minelayers and was preparing to wireless the discovery to base when the wireless set went dead. Fortunately for them, a German seaplane came up on their port side and they were able to relay the warning by signal lamp for it to be sent on to Wilhelmshaven.

The *L6* had arrived after the seaplanes had departed so had no idea of the true purpose of the operation, but on seeing more British ships, cruisers among them, von Buttler Brandefels took his airship lower and dropped three bombs on one of the carriers, all of which missed.

Soon the *L5*, alerted by radio, appeared on the scene accompanied by German seaplanes, just as the British seaplanes were returning after almost 3 hours and were short of petrol. As they landed alongside the carriers to be recovered, they were subjected to bombing attacks, which were largely ineffectual and turned into a general melee of ships against aeroplanes and airships with no conclusive result, and tellingly no interference from German surface forces.

Only two aircraft were recovered and hoisted on board, the remainder landing short of the rendezvous, where the crews were picked up by British submarines and destroyers, while the aircraft were sunk to avoid them falling into enemy hands.

One pilot originally posted as missing was picked up by a Dutch fishing boat and eventually returned to England. Once all the naval flyers had been recovered, Commodore Tyrwhitt ordered the Harwich Force to withdraw, which it did at 11.45 a.m. without loss.

Although the raid failed to achieve its main objective, the destruction of the airship sheds demonstrated that the combined British surface and air arms had successfully carried out an operation that both demonstrated that the Royal Navy could operate with impunity deep into the enemy's heartland and give a much needed boost to morale at home once news of the raid was made public.

9

CRUISER WARFARE

Nelson once famously observed that if he were to die, the lack of frigates would be found engraved on his heart.

During the long French revolutionary wars, the stormbound ships of the line of the Royal Navy kept their unceasing watch on the ports of Brest, Toulon, Cadiz and other continental harbours. They would constantly tack back and forth, often in the most appalling weather conditions, standing sufficiently far offshore to have the weather gauge, but close enough in to observe any sign of the enemy making ready for sea, as the frigates continued their unrelenting work.

Under these conditions the frigate was in constant demand as the maid-of-all work, performing a variety of duties for which the larger three-deck wooden walls were too valuable to hazard: scouting ahead of the fleet, intercepting enemy ships trying to run the blockade, or delivering urgent dispatches between the blockading fleet and the Admiralty at home. Other duties could also include being ordered to undertake some military operation on a hostile shore, where the frigate would deliver the troops ashore and act as a floating battery to support the landing.

A typical frigate of the period was *Lively*, launched in 1804 at Woolwich, of 1,076 tons burden, with a main gun deck of 154ft in length and armed with twenty-eight 18pdr cannon and six 32pdr carronades. With a complement of 300 officers and men, she was able to maintain herself as a completely self-contained unit at sea for up to six months. Ships like her were fast, formidable opponents, ideally suited for independent command to be dispatched to the most distant parts of the globe, operating as cruisers carrying out the manifold duties demanded by the Admiralty and Parliament to protect British trade and to project British power.

The advent of steam power was slow in arriving in the ships of the Royal Navy, where, in 1845, although there were over one hundred steam ships on the navy list, none were in the main battle fleet, which were still wooden three-decker sailing ships. The reason for this seeming discrepancy, when steam power on land in factories and railways was pointing the way to the future, was that the existing method of steam-paddle propulsion, while adequate for merchant ships, was unsuitable for warships where the paddle machinery would be vulnerable to fire in combat and interfered with the ship's sailing qualities when under sail alone. Furthermore, the cumbersome installation of the paddle boxes, engines and so on reduced the number of guns available in the broadside battery. The application of the screw propeller to ship propulsion solved these problems, and a range of fast wooden hulled steam sloops and frigates of various sizes were built between 1845 and 1860.

During this period, construction methods were increasingly changing from wood to iron. With the building of the iron frigate *Warrior* in 1860, in response to the French ironclad *Gloire*, a new designation appeared in the navy list, that of the ironclad steam frigate. Ships like the *Warrior* at 9,000 tons, and mounting a formidable broadside battery of twenty-six 64pdr muzzle-loading, smooth-bore cannon, rendered at a stroke the fleets of wooden ships of the line obsolete, although they continued to be employed in the Royal and other navies, with some of the ships converted to steam propulsion.

With their single gun deck, the new iron ships had the appearance of frigates, albeit on a much larger scale, and now represented the new ships of the line, or, as they became known, ironclad battleships.

By the 1870s, long broadside batteries were beginning to be replaced by armoured turrets, as the gradual transition to the design of the modern battleship of the 1880s began. The term frigate during this period gradually fell out of usage and was replaced by the term cruising ship or cruiser, referring to a new class of vessels of between 3,000 and 7,000 tons built in the 1870s that were equipped with steam propulsion, with screws that could be raised to allow the ship to operate under sail alone and armed with smooth-bore cannon and early examples of breech-loading rifled guns.

These smaller vessels were variously constructed from wood, iron and composite construction; that is to say with iron frames and wooden hulls. These ships took on the role and duties of the old frigates, working with the battle fleet and, importantly, protecting British merchant trade around the world or being dispatched on distant commissions, securing overseas interests and possessions.

The cruiser as an identifiable and distinctive type evolved in the mid-1880s; two categories of vessel were created. First was the protected cruiser, by now built in iron, steam propelled and mounting a mixed armament of muzzle and breech-loading guns. They did not have side armour but had their vitals below the waterline, the engines, boilers and magazines protected by an armoured steel deck ranging in thickness from 1 to 6in, with additional protection being afforded by arranging the coal bunkers along the sides of the ship and by careful sub-division of the hull.

Secondly came another variation of the armour theme, the armoured cruisers, which were generally of larger displacement than the protected cruisers. While having armoured decks, they relied on thick side armour for protection.

Two early armoured cruisers typical of this period were HMS *Warspite* and HMS *Imperieuse*, both of 8,500 tons and launched in 1883–84. These ships were the first cruisers to do away with a sailing rig entirely, relying solely on the 8,000hp compound engines that gave them a speed of 16 knots.

Equipped with a 1in armoured deck and a 10in armoured belt, their armament consisted of four 9.2in breech-loading rifled guns mounted in single barbettes, with gun shields and armoured shell hoists down to the level of the armoured deck. Both these ships gave good service and, despite drawing 2ft more than their designed draught, were powerful vessels for the day, pointing the way ahead for the development of the cruiser.

Some 130 cruisers of various designs were launched between 1885 and 1900, most of which had been sent to the breakers by the outbreak of war in 1914 under Lord Fisher's reforms. Of those older ships that remained in service, a dozen or so of the more modern ships were converted to minelayers, while others performed duties as accommodation ships, submarine depot ships or escorting troopships and convoys.

Between 1899 and 1907, thirty-three armoured cruisers of between 9,000 to 14,000 tons were built that were intended amongst other duties to take their place alongside the battleships as part of the battle fleet. Two particularly large examples of the armoured cruiser, *Powerful* and *Terrible*, were launched in 1895, each of 14,200 tons, armed with two 9.2in and twelve 6in guns, with a 6in armoured belt and 2–6in armoured deck.

Their triple expansion engines of 25,000hp gave them a speed of 22 knots and, impressive though these ships were in service, they were found to be uneconomic to run, due to their high coal consumption. They did their best work during the Boxer Rebellion in 1902 and in the second Boer War (1899–1902) where, during the relief of Ladysmith, four 12pdr and smaller guns from *Powerful* were mounted on gun carriages and accompanied the quickly formed Naval Brigade to raise the siege, with the help of another similarly equipped brigade from *Terrible*.

The Naval Brigade, together with the ship's guns, fought in several actions against the Boers, and the stirring exploits of the Bluejackets raised them to new levels in the esteem of the British public. By the 1890s the protected cruisers had evolved into a distinctive class and were efficient ships, well suited for their role, with good sea-keeping qualities and adequate coal storage for undertaking extended cruises.

The function of the protected cruiser was to guard the worldwide trade routes, as Great Britain at the outbreak of the Great War operated over half of all the merchant shipping tonnage afloat.

The *Vindictive* class of four ships of 1896–97 were typical of the period. They were three-funnelled cruisers of 5,700 tons, 320ft long, armed with four 6in and six 4.7in guns plus smaller guns and three 18in submerged torpedo tubes. The armoured deck protecting magazines and machinery was 4in thick, with 1.5in of additional armour on the upper deck. Their triple expansion engines of 10,000hp gave the class a speed of 19 knots. The succeeding *Highflyer* class of 1898, consisting of five ships, was a similar layout but mounting eleven 6in guns, making it a more formidable opponent by recognising the need to lay down a heavier and faster rate of fire, particularly against the threat posed by the quick-firing guns of the newly emerging fast torpedo boats.

Of the fifty protected cruisers launched between 1885 and 1901, a high proportion were still considered to be of use and were in service at the start of the war. *Vindictive* won immortality in the Zeebrugge raid of 1918, along with three other protected cruisers, sunk as block ships in an attempt to seal the harbour entrance against the passage of U-boats.

The *Vindictive* also played an unusual and important part in the destruction of Graf von Spee's East Asiatic Squadron at the Battle of the Falkland Islands in 1914 when, while being used for testing experimental long-range wireless equipment, she was able to transmit wireless messages over far greater distances than the standard sets used in other ships. When Churchill ordered the battle-cruisers to the South Atlantic under Admiral Sturdee, the *Vindictive* was stationed at a point just below the Equator in a position from which her powerful wireless equipment could serve as a link between the Admiralty in London and the battle-cruiser squadron.

A step towards the modern light cruiser of the Great War was taken in 1904 with the launch of the protected cruiser HMS *Amethyst* of 3,000 tons, armed with ten 4in quick-firing guns. It was the first of Britain's cruisers to be fitted with steam turbine propulsion of 12,000hp, which gave a speed of 23.5 knots, while the remaining three ships of the class, equipped with triple expansion engines, could reach 22 knots. This was 3 knots faster than the preceding *Pelorus* class, commissioned three years earlier.

The next four classes of small cruisers, the *Sentinel*, *Forward*, *Pathfinder* and *Adventure*, comprised eight ships in total and were all built during 1905. All were under 3,000 tons and carried a similar armament of ten 4in guns and triple expansion engines, all capable of 25 to 26 knots.

These were followed by the seven ships of the *Boadicea* and *Active* classes, built between 1910 and 1913 and of similar displacement. These were designed as new light and fast cruisers, collectively designated Scouts and designed specifically to work with and protect the new larger destroyers that in turn were by 1905 accompanying the fleet to sea.

In the event, these cruisers turned out to be slower than their destroyer charges by 5 knots or more, as the destroyers themselves were fitted with turbines. By 1915, as the faster light cruisers came into service, these older ships were transferred for service in the Mediterranean and the Atlantic.

Eventually, as the destroyers themselves increased in tonnage, they were led by flotilla leaders that were somewhat larger, with accommodation being made for the Commodore of the flotilla and his staff.

The four ships of the *Boadicea* class were each attached to the Grand Fleet Battle Squadrons at Scapa Flow, leading the attached destroyers, with HMS *Fearless* leading the 1st Flotilla, HMS *Active* the 2nd and *Amphion* the 3rd Flotilla of the Grand Fleet. HMS *Adventure*, HMS *Attentive* and HMS *Foresight* served with the 6th Dover Patrol, while *Active* and *Foresight* served at Jutland.

Of those lost during the war, *Amphion* was mined in the Thames Estuary in August 1914, while HMS *Pathfinder* was torpedoed off St Abb's Head in September 1914.

The circumstances of her sinking are of interest. In the early afternoon the U-boat *U21*, commanded by Kapitan Otto Hersing, had penetrated the Firth of Forth as far as the battery under the Forth bridge, when she observed the *Pathfinder* leading destroyers of the 8th Destroyer Flotilla from the south-south-west towards their anchorage in the pens above the bridge. The *Pathfinder* was very low on coal – a recurring problem with this class due to insufficient bunkerage being built into the design – and, therefore, was proceeding slowly at only 5 knots without zigzagging, making it an easy target for the U-boat.

At 3.45 p.m. the *U21* fired a single 50cm torpedo from 2,000yd, which, despite the destroyer attempting to take evasive action, struck it under the bridge. It exploded with great violence, rapidly sinking and taking 260 of the crew to the bottom, with only eighteen survivors being rescued. The remaining fourteen ships of the *Scout* class survived the war before being scrapped in 1920–21.

The following class, the *Towns*, were much larger vessels, being up to 5,000 tons with better sea-keeping qualities and more suited than the preceding classes for long-range cruising missions, as well as general duties with the fleet. This class had been introduced in response to similar ships that were being brought into service with the High Seas Fleet that were more powerfully armed and faster than their British contemporaries.

The five classes of *Towns* were all instantly recognisable with their four-funnel layout and a displacement of around 5,200 tons, mounting eight to ten 6in weapons on the upper deck and two 21in torpedo tubes. All ships had turbines of 25,000hp on four shafts, giving a speed of around 26 knots and a complement of between 450 and 500 officers and men.

The *Towns* led an active life during the war. As mentioned earlier, *Glasgow* was involved in the Battle of Coronel, where her speed allowed her to escape the fate of the *Monmouth* and *Good Hope*.

The five *Town* class cruisers of the *Bristol* class of 1910 were initially rated as second-class protected cruisers, but in effect were light armoured cruisers due to their relatively heavy armament compared to the Scouts.

The *Bristol* was on the West Indies station at the outbreak of war where, on 6 August 1914, she engaged the German cruiser *Karlsruhe*. Thanks to its superior speed *Karlsruhe* was able to escape, only to be destroyed by an internal explosion, possibly due to unstable cordite, on 4 November 1914 with the loss of the majority of her crew.

The *Nottingham* of the later *Birmingham* class was more heavily armed, with nine 6in guns and two 21in torpedo tubes. The ship was in action at the Battle of the German Bight in 1914 and served at Jutland with the 2nd Cruiser Squadron. A few months later, on 19 August 1916, while on a sweep in the North Sea, she was struck by two torpedoes from the *U52*, sinking after a third hit was registered. Fortunately most of her crew was saved.

The final examples of the *Towns* were HMS *Birkenhead* and HMS *Chester*, two ships that were originally ordered for Greece but were taken over by the Admiralty prior to the outbreak of war, with both ships serving with the battle-cruiser force. Both ships were larger than the preceding *Towns*, being 5,750 tons and armed with ten 5.5in guns on individual mountings, which fired a shell of 85lb weight, compared to the 6in shell of 100lb, which gave a faster rate of fire for a small loss in hitting power. Armour protection was provided by 2in armoured belt, and 1.5in over the deck. Another feature of these two ships was that they oil fuelled and their Parsons compound reaction turbines gave a top speed of 26.5 knots.

At Jutland, the *Chester* was fiercely engaged by four German cruisers at a range of 6,000yd. As Captain Lawson turned his ship away, he received a storm of shells with over seventeen 150mm shells bursting on the deck, causing terrible damage among the gun crews, where many lost legs to shell splinters, as the open-backed gun shields did not reach to deck level as was standard British practice. The British cruiser was smothered in so many shell splashes that two of the enemy cruisers were ordered to cease fire so that the other two ships could more clearly see the target. Eventually the *Chester* succeeded in escaping to the north-west with only a single gun still working.

Among the crew of the forward 5.5in gun on the forecastle was Boy First Class Jack Cornwall, a 16-year-old sight setter who was at his post behind the protective gun shield.

As previously mentioned, the gun shields were open at the back, with a gap between the base of the shield and the deck exposing the gun crews to shrapnel injuries from behind and at lower leg level.

At least four heavy shells fell close to the gun, causing blast damage and throwing shrapnel into the unprotected rear of the gun shield, killing or wounding all of the crew and mortally wounding Jack Cornwall, who, despite his injuries, stood to his post awaiting orders in the highest tradition of loyalty and duty inculcated into British servicemen in time of war. Repair and first-aid parties discovered him still at his post some 15 minutes later during a lull in the battle, as the ship steamed out of danger and he was taken to the sick bay.

Badly damaged, the *Chester* retired from the battle and steered for Immingham for repair. Here Jack Cornwall was taken to Grimsby General Hospital, where he died on the morning of 2 June 1916, before his mother was able to arrive from London. He was awarded a posthumous Victoria Cross. The citation includes the sentiment that Boy First Class John Travers Cornwall remained standing alone at a most exposed post, quietly awaiting orders until the end of the action, with the guns crew dead and wounded all around him. He was less than 16½-years of age.

The *Chester* was subsequently repaired and served with the 3rd Light Cruiser Squadron until the end of the war, where she was offered for sale to the Greek Government together with the *Birkenhead*. The offer was refused and both ships were sold for scrap in 1921.

The next class of ship represented a more modern type, the light cruiser, which was more suited for North Sea operations, where the emphasis was on speed rather than protection, essential for working with and supporting the newer high speed destroyers.

The first of these ships was the *Arethusa*, launched in 1914 from Chatham dockyard. She was 436ft in length, displacing 3,512 tons and armed with a rather odd armament of three 6in and four 4in guns. She was much more heavily armed with torpedoes than the preceding classes, mounting eight 21in torpedo tubes that gave notice that while working with the flotilla the new cruisers would press home their own attacks along with the destroyers.

Engine power was greatly increased in this class, with turbines of 40,000hp on four shafts installed, giving a speed of over 36 knots. Their appearance differed from that of previous classes of cruiser, as they had only three funnels instead of four – the standard arrangement in most classes of larger cruiser over the past fifteen years. Hull protection was provided by 3in armoured belt and 1in deck armour, which was similar to the earlier class but was less extensive in area to save weight.

The *Arethusa* was commissioned in August 1914 as the flotilla leader of the Harwich Force, almost immediately seeing action at the Battle of the Heligoland Bight where, due to the ship and her new crew not being fully worked up, she experienced difficulties with her gunnery and mechanical problems. During the battle, while flying the flag of Commodore Tyrwhitt, she was badly damaged by the German cruisers *Frauenlob* and *Stettin* and had to be towed home.

By December of the same year, *Arethusa* was repaired and took part in the Cuxhaven Raid on Christmas Day 1914 where she engaged a Zeppelin airship, this also being the first occasion when aircraft and Zeppelins had attempted to attack warships at sea, albeit without success on either side.

HMS *Chester*
Cammell-Laird, Birkenhead - 1915
Belted Light Cruiser

Dimensions: Length 458ft x 47ft beam x 15ft draught
Displacement: 5,200 tons (normal)
Main armament: 10 x 5.5in Mk10 50 calibre 2 x 21in
torpedo tubes
Secondary armament: 1 x 3in AA
Armour protection: Main belt 2in, main deck 1.6in,
Machinery: Parsons compound turbines on 4 shafts, 31,00 shp at
25 knots
Range: 3,600 miles at 10 knots

Boy First Class Jack Cornwall VC
Jutland 1916

100 feet

Birkenhead Class

HMS *Chester* and *Birkenhead* were laid down for the Greek navy, but taken over
by the Admiralty at the outbreak of war, entering the Royal Navy with the 3rd
light Cruiser Squadron. Served at Jutland, where *Chester* was badly damaged,
and where Boy 1 Cornwall won a posthumous VC.

HMS *Birkenhead* 1915
HMS *Chester*   1915

In January 1915 she was again in action when she fought at the Dogger Bank, together with other ships of the same class. After this she was transferred to the 5th Light Cruiser Squadron at Harwich, leading an active life of continuous patrol duty in the Southern North Sea.

On 11 February 1916, after a comparatively short life, the *Arethusa* struck a mine off Felixstowe and, although grounding in shallow water, where strenuous efforts were being made to salvage her, she became a total loss.

The succeeding C class comprised twenty-eight ships in seven separate groups of ships, all of which, apart from the first group of six including *Caroline*, were distinguishable by carrying only two funnels. The *Caroline* class of six ships was slightly larger at 3,800 tons and were less cramped, with better accommodation than the *Arethusa*. The first of the group laid down in 1913 were described as a light armoured cruiser with two single 6in guns in super-firing mountings aft and eight 4in guns as main armament.

After war service, HMS *Caroline* became a drill ship for the Royal Naval Volunteer Reserve in Belfast in 1924, where she still performs this service as the only surviving example of a First World War light cruiser.

The six associated classes of cruiser were generally similar in layout, being of approximately 4,200 tons' displacement, with a length of 450ft and an armament of either two × 6in and eight × 4in guns or in later ships five × 6in guns. The armour protection consisted of 3in to machinery spaces, with 2in armour to magazines and 1in deck.

Propulsion was provided by 40,000hp Parsons steam turbines, giving a speed of 29–30 knots, with a range of 5,900 nautical miles.

During the Great War, cruisers of the C class were involved in most of the actions in the North Sea, being present at Jutland with the 4th Light Cruiser Squadron under Commodore C. Le Mesurier, where in the twilight of the evening action while seeking to locate the retreating High Seas Fleet they came under heavy close-range fire from several German battleships, with HMS *Calliope* being badly hit.

Also present were the 1st and 2nd Light Cruiser Squadrons, which were scouting ahead and on the beam of the Grand Fleet before it deployed in line ahead to engage the High Seas Fleet. Both cruiser squadrons were involved in some of the heaviest fighting during the battle where, in spite of heavy damage, all the ships of the class survived.

In March 1916 HMS *Cleopatra* rammed and sank the German destroyer *G194* during the air raid on the airship sheds at Tondern. During this action, while both ships were locked together, hand-to-hand fighting briefly broke out on the German ship's decks before she went down.

In 1917 HMS *Centaur* ran into a minefield, striking two mines that blew off the bow and the stern of the ship. Although she suffered extensive damage, she managed to reach port and was subsequently repaired and returned to service. Despite their hard usage throughout the war, no C class cruiser was lost during hostilities, until HMS *Cassandra* struck a mine after the armistice. The high point of the C class war service came in November when HMS *Cardiff* steamed out to a point 40 miles east of the Bell Rock to lead the surrendered High Seas Fleet through two parallel lines of British, French and American ships, their crews at battle stations as they escorted the German ships into internment.

The last of the light cruisers built during the war period were the D class of very similar layout to the Cs – 4,600 tons, carrying the heavier armament of six 6in guns and a heavy torpedo armament of twelve 21in torpedoes. Thanks to their Trawler bow these ships also had better sea-keeping qualities than the earlier class that were very wet in a heavy seaway. Engine power was again provided by turbines of 40,000hp, giving a top speed of 29 knots.

By the outbreak of the Second World War the C and D classes were considered to be out of date but, at a time when every ship was required, some were converted into flak ships while the others gave good service, particularly in the Mediterranean and on convoy duty in the Atlantic, where one of the class, *Curacoa*, had the misfortune to be run down by the RMS *Queen Mary* while escorting a convoy, sinking the cruiser and damaging the great liner.

The armoured cruiser was conceived as a fast armoured warship that could operate either independently to protect trade or in a squadron as part of the battle fleet, capable of defeating most classes of enemy warships apart from a battleship, which with its superior speed it could outrun.

With the development of more powerful engines and longer-range weapons at the end of the nineteenth century, the need for thicker side or belt armour, which had been dropped in earlier versions of the protected cruisers because of the disproportionate weight of early armour, could now be reintroduced. The advent of the lighter Harvey and Krupp compound armour led to the building of several classes of new larger armoured cruisers.

The first of the new ships were the six ships of the Cressys of 1899. These ships were of 11,000 tons, powered by triple expansion engines of 21,000hp, capable of 20 knots and with an armament of two 9.2in and twelve 6in guns. The armoured belt was 11in deep, with a thickness of 6in, tapering to 2in at the bow and stern, with 3in armour to the deck. On paper these ships appeared to be well protected by the standards of the day, but the loss of three of this class on the same day in September 1914 to a U-boat demonstrated that their and the later armoured cruisers' protection was inadequate.

The *Drake* class of four ships were larger at 14,000 tons with an increase in power to 30,000hp, increasing the speed to 25 knots, while carrying the same armament and protection as the Cressys. The *Good Hope* of this class together with the smaller, three-funnelled *Monmouth* of the following class were both overwhelmed and sunk at Coronel in November 1914, while the name ship *Drake* was torpedoed off Church Bay, Rathlin Island, in October 1917.

Sir Philip Watts succeeded Sir William White as Admiralty Chief Constructor to the Royal Navy in 1902, where he continued in that post until 1912, during which time all but four of the battleships that fought at Jutland were built to his designs. Watts' first armoured cruisers were the *Duke of Edinburgh* and the *Black Prince*, both of 13,550 tons and 505ft in length. Her triple expansion steam engines produced 23,000hp and oil could be sprayed into her coal-fired furnaces to increase the burning rate, giving a speed of over 23 knots and a range of 8,200 nautical miles. The hull was protected by a 6in belt with 1in to the decks and 7in to the turrets. This represented a major increase in gun power, with six 9.2 Mk10 guns in single turrets, four set on the corners of the upper deck and one each mounted on the forecastle and the quarter-deck.

At main-deck level ten 6in guns were mounted in casements, but this arrangement was unsatisfactory and the guns were sited too low and were unworkable in seaway, to the extent that in the succeeding and almost identical *Warrior* class (that were to have been copies of the *Duke of Edinburgh* class) the ten 6in guns were dropped in favour of four heavier 7.5in guns, all mounted on the upper deck and the 6in casements plated over.

The *Black Prince* built at the Thames Ironworks and Shipbuilding Co at Blackwall was launched in 1904 and was stationed in the Mediterranean at the outbreak of war where she took part in the unsuccessful pursuit of *Goeben* and *Breslau*. The *Duke of Edinburgh* and the *Black Prince* were part of Admiral Arbuthnot's 1st Cruiser Squadron at the Battle of Jutland, where during the night battle the *Black Prince*, scouting ahead of the battle fleet, lost contact with the

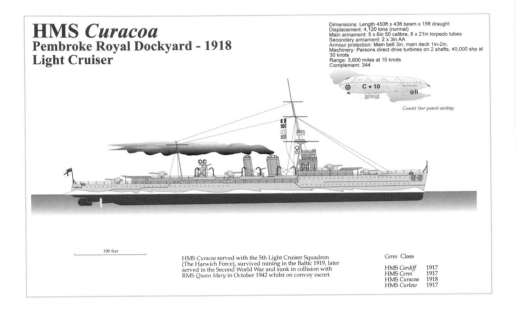

HMS *Curacoa*
Pembroke Royal Dockyard - 1918
Light Cruiser

Dimensions: Length 450ft x 43ft beam x 15ft draught
Displacement: 4,120 tons (normal)
Main armament: 5 x 6in 50 calibre, 8 x 21in torpedo tubes
Secondary armament: 2 x 3in AA
Armour protection: Main belt 3in, main deck 1in-2in
Machinery: Parsons direct drive turbines on 2 shafts, 40,000 shp at 30 knots
Range: 3,600 miles at 10 knots
Complement: 344

Coastal Star patrol airship

C ✶ 10

100 feet

HMS *Curacoa* served with the 5th Light Cruiser Squadron
(The Harwich Force), survived mining in the Baltic 1919, later
served in the Second World War and sunk in collision with
RMS *Queen Mary* in October 1942 whilst on convoy escort.

Ceres Class

HMS *Cardiff*	1917
HMS *Ceres*	1917
HMS *Curacoa*	1918
HMS *Curlew*	1917

remainder of the squadron and ran into the German main force. After engaging the *Rheinland* at around 11.30 p.m., scoring two hits with 6in shells, the *Black Prince* turned away to the north at midnight but came under sustained fire from the German battle line, which included the battleships *Thuringen*, *Ostfriesland* and *Friedrich der Grosse*. With the range reduced to 1,000yd, and illuminated by searchlights, she was struck by over twenty heavy shells and was soon reduced to a blazing wreck, sinking unseen in the dark by friend and foe, taking her entire crew of 860 to the bottom.

Earlier in the same action at 6.05 p.m., Rear Admiral Arbuthnot's flagship of the First Cruiser Squadron, the *Defence*, together with the *Warrior* and the *Black Prince*, were surprised in an area between the two fleets by Admiral Hipper's battle-cruisers coming out of the mist from the south, accompanied by the German 3rd Battle Squadron at a distance of only 8,000yd.

Immediately, the German ships opened fire on the van of Arbuthnot's cruisers, smothering the *Defence* with shells, causing a huge fire to break out. With a tremendous explosion she blew up at 6.20 p.m., leaving only a tower of black smoke to mark her passing.

The *Warrior* was also heavily engaged, being hit by fifteen or more heavy shells, and was only saved from the same fate as the *Defence* when the German ships switched their fire against the battleship *Warspite*, whose helm had jammed, causing her to circle out of the British battle line and make two turns close towards the German ships.

The *Warrior* withdrew to the westward, heavily damaged and badly flooded, where, despite being taken in tow by the seaplane carrier HMS *Engadine*, she was

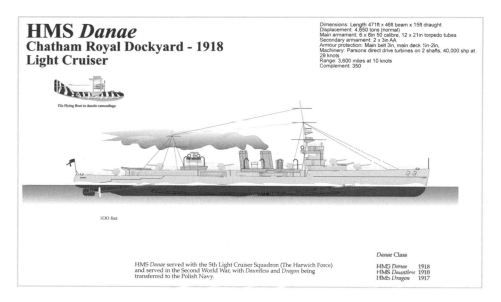

HMS *Danae*
Chatham Royal Dockyard - 1918
Light Cruiser

Dimensions: Length 471ft x 46ft beam x 15ft draught
Displacement: 4,650 tons (normal)
Main armament: 6 x 6in 50 calibre, 12 x 21in torpedo tubes
Secondary armament: 2 x 3in AA
Armour protection: Main belt 3in, main deck 1in-2in,
Machinery: Parsons direct drive turbines on 2 shafts, 40,000 shp at 29 knots
Range: 3,600 miles at 10 knots
Complement: 350

F2a Flying Boat in dazzle camouflage

100 feet

HMS *Danae* served with the 5th Light Cruiser Squadron (The Harwich Force) and served in the Second World War, with *Dauntless* and *Dragon* being transferred to the Polish Navy.

Danae Class

HMS *Danae*	1918
HMS *Dauntless*	1918
HMS *Dragon*	1917

HMS *Carnarvon* armoured cruiser in dry dock, Gibraltar, 1910. (Author's collection)

abandoned after taking off the surviving crew of 743, sinking 80 miles east of the Humber on the morning of 1 June.

An unusual loss was that of the armoured cruiser *Natal* while lying at anchor in the Cromarty Firth. Captain E. Black was hosting a film show on board, having invited fellow officers, their wives and children together with nurses from the nearby hospital.

Suddenly, at 3.25 p.m. a series of violent explosions shook the ship and she rolled over and sank, with the loss of 390 lives. Originally it was thought that a mine was responsible, but subsequent examination by divers revealed the ship had been destroyed by internal explosions possibly caused by faulty cordite.

By the outbreak of the Great War and the introduction of the dreadnought battleship and the battle-cruiser in 1907, the armoured cruiser was rendered obsolete. The offensive power of their 9.2in, 7.5in and 6in guns that fired 300lb, 200lb and 100lb shells respectively were hopelessly inferior to the 900lb 12in shells of the battle-cruisers, while their inadequate armour was demonstrated forcibly by the loss of four of their number at Jutland.

10

DOGGER BANK

By January 1915, after five months of war, the long expected clash between the fleets had failed to materialise, while the hit-and-run tactics of the German Navy with their attacks on the east coast had caused outrage among the civilian population.

The victory over von Spee's squadron at the Battle of the Falkland Islands in December was a much advertised and much needed boost to civilian morale, as was the sortie into the Heligoland Bight, where three German light cruisers and three destroyers were sunk. Against these achievements, in the same period, the Royal Navy had already lost the dreadnought HMS *Audacious* to a mine in October 1914 and the pre-dreadnought HMS *Bulwark* in November to an internal explosion at Sheerness while taking on ammunition, together with the loss of the three large *Cressy* class armoured cruisers to a single U-boat. This was a worrying trend that if continued threatened to reduce the superiority in numbers enjoyed by the Royal Navy.

In the early hours of 1 January 1915 the pre-dreadnought battleship HMS *Formidable*, together with HMS *Implacable*, HMS *Irresistible* and the light cruisers *Diamond* and *Topaz*, part of the 5th Battle Squadron stationed at Portland, had completed gunnery exercises in the Channel and were returning to base at 10 knots on an easterly course in good visibility, 20 miles west of Start Point, when at 2.00 a.m. the *Formidable* at the rear of the line was struck by a torpedo below the foremost funnel on the starboard side, cutting off all steam. She heaved to with a heavy list and the deteriorating weather made rescue hazardous in the dark. Forty-five minutes later, a second torpedo struck on the port side, the flooding from which brought the ship back onto an even keel.

Boats from the light cruisers worked in worsening conditions to rescue some of the crew but at 2.45 a.m. she suddenly rolled over and sank, taking 562 of her crew with her.

A further setback had occurred a few days before on 27 December as ships of the 2nd Battle Squadron Grand Fleet were entering Scapa Flow at night in a half gale. The battleship *Monarch*, leading the line, altered course and slowed her engines to avoid a patrol vessel that loomed across her bow.

In the dark, the following ship, the 23,000-ton *Conqueror*, collided with the *Monarch*'s stern, causing severe damage to both ships, which were put out of action for several months.

Admiral Jellicoe, with the responsibility of Britain's only battle fleet weighing on his shoulders, was worried that these accumulated losses, plus the storm damage to his cruisers and destroyers in the recent gales and the detachment of the battle-cruiser squadron, together with the attendant cruiser and destroyer flotillas under Beatty to Rosyth in response to the east coast raids, were reducing the strength of the battle fleet. Additionally, the battle-cruiser *Queen Mary* was in dry dock at Portsmouth, while HMS *Invincible* and HMS *Inflexible* were on duty in the Mediterranean.

Jellicoe was aware that, through their extensive network of spies in Britain and on the Continent, the Germans would be aware of these losses and dispositions of ships and would take every opportunity to exploit the temporary weakness of the fleet.

On 15 January British coastal wireless listening stations picked up traffic indicating that Admiral Hipper's flagship *Derfflinger* and the *Seydlitz* had put out to sea from the Jade Basin.

Along the east coast, from Dover to Rosyth, squadrons of cruisers, destroyers and battle-cruisers made ready for sea, but in the event the flurry of activity on the German side of the North Sea came to nothing. As an assurance, Commodore Tyrwhitt led a reconnaissance into the Heligoland Bight in force on 19 January, supported by the battle-cruisers further to seaward, but found no sign of the German fleet, so returned to harbour. Jellicoe was, however, still convinced that something was in the wind and ordered a further reconnaissance for 23 January. Almost immediately, the listening stations again detected increased wireless traffic indicative of the preparation for the German fleet putting to sea.

This time, instead of an all-out raid on British coastal seaports, Admiral von Ingenohl planned a low-key attack on the unprotected British fishing fleets on the Dogger Bank, as German Naval Intelligence claimed that the fishermen were spying on naval movements and passing the information on to Room 40.

On the evening of the 23rd, Admiral Hipper's squadron, consisting of his flagship the battle-cruiser *Seydlitz*, *Moltke*, *Derfflinger* and the armoured cruiser *Blucher*, together with the light cruisers *Stralsund*, *Rostock*, *Kolberg* and *Graudenz* and a flotilla of torpedo boats, moved seawards from the Schillig Roads.

The *Blucher* had been built to match the first of the British battle-cruisers *Invincible*. The British deliberately leaked disinformation, claiming that the new ship would be armed with 9.2in guns, instead of the 12in guns actually fitted. Acting on this misinformation, the German ship was built mounting twelve 8.2in guns and equipped with reciprocating engines instead of turbine propulsion. As a consequence, she was slower and under-gunned compared to her British counterparts and should not have been included in the battle-cruiser line; she suffered accordingly.

This time Jellicoe had definite information that the Germans would be launching a sortie and orders were given on 23 January to prepare for sea. By 9.00 p.m. the last of the battle squadrons of the Grand Fleet were at sea, steaming south-east from Scapa Flow to rendezvous in daylight with the cruisers midway between Scotland and the Danish coast.

From Rosyth, Admiral Beatty aboard *Lion* led the battle-cruisers *Princess Royal*, HMS *Tiger*, *New Zealand* and *Indomitable* – the 3rd Battle Squadron of pre-dreadnoughts and Commodore Goodenough's 1st Light Cruiser Squadron.

The assembly of warships was due to meet Commodore Tyrwhitt's hard-working light cruiser force at dawn from Harwich on 24 January on the north-east side of the Dogger Bank, from where, assuming the German purpose was a further coastal raid, the British ships would be perfectly positioned to contest the passage of the German ships as they attempted to retire from our coasts.

In the black darkness of the winter's night, ship after ship, showing no lights, slid out of the Firth of Forth and Scapa Flow, only the wash from their passing bursting on the rocky shore to show that the king's ships were at sea in pursuit of his enemies.

Admiral Tyrwhitt's force had more difficulty getting to sea because of fog, but eventually the squadron cleared the coastwise sandbanks that still make navigation a danger and by 6.00 a.m., in the still, dark early morning, Tyrwhitt's flagship *Arethusa* and seven destroyers approached the rendezvous point, with the remainder of the force, consisting of the light cruisers *Aurora* and *Undaunted*, together with a further twenty-eight destroyers some miles behind, putting on speed to join up.

From the bridge of the *Lion* a cruiser was sighted in the dim early dawn light to the south-east and a signal lamp sent out a rapid challenge. The *Arethusa* flashed back the recognition, the rendezvous having been accomplished at the correct spot on time.

The battle-cruisers continued their course to the south in line ahead, while the light cruisers took up a scouting line at right angles. On either side, lookouts peered through their glasses for any sign of the German ships.

Suddenly, at 7.05 a.m. gun flashes were sighted away to the south-east in the half light, followed by the electrifying signal from *Aurora*, 'I am engaging enemy cruisers'. *Arethusa* had earlier crossed the bows of the enemy ships in the dark 30 minutes before *Aurora* came upon them. The *Aurora's* Captain W.S. Nicholson saw a cruiser emerge from the mist some 4 miles ahead and, assuming it was *Arethusa*, flashed a challenge, which was answered by a salvo of shellfire from the light cruiser *Kolberg*.

Shell splashes leaped around the British ship and, in spite of the poor pre-dawn light, three of the German shells found their mark, although no serious damage was done. Now the *Aurora's* guns found the range and the red glow of striking shells was visible as the *Kolberg* hauled away to the eastward.

Meanwhile, the *Aurora*, *Undaunted* and the destroyer flotilla pressed on to the north and as the light grew stronger, more enemy ships were sighted on their starboard quarter to the south-east and the flotilla, after reporting the contact by wireless, turned to keep contact with them.

Further north at 7.30 a.m., with the sun coming up, Goodenough's flagship *Southampton*, scouting ahead of the battle-cruisers, was anxious for news of the German dispositions and on towards the spot where the *Kolberg* was engaged.

When news of the brush between *Kolberg* and *Aurora* reached Hipper, he immediately suspected and feared that he was running into a prepared trap and at once recalled his scouting group. Turning his heavy units on a south-easterly course and working up to full speed, the whole fleet set course for home.

As he turned away at 7.50 a.m. the *Undaunted* and *Aurora* sighted Hipper's ships in the morning light, this being the first time in the war that Goodenough and his men actually saw the German battle-cruisers as they were outlined against the clear sharp line of the horizon 14 miles distant, pouring out thick oily black smoke in their efforts to escape what must seem inevitable destruction. With the trap prematurely sprung, the chase was now on, with the German ships straining for every knot, escape now their sole purpose as they drove eastwards, throwing up huge white, churning bow waves.

With Goodenough's cruisers a mile ahead on the starboard bow, Beatty's battle-cruisers raced in line ahead in pursuit at 25 knots, which was the maximum speed his rearmost and oldest ship *Indomitable* was supposed to be capable of. But as the Admiral asked for 26 knots, she managed through the superhuman efforts of her stokers to keep her place in the line, eliciting a 'well steamed *Indomitable*' from Admiral Beatty.

Beatty was anxious to overhaul the German ships quickly before he was brought too close to waters where there was the possibility of running into heavy units, which he reasoned must by now be at sea coming to the aid of the German battle-cruisers, and ordered 29 knots.

At this speed his two older battle-cruisers and the accompanying destroyers dropped slowly behind, while *Lion*, *Tiger* and *Princess Royal* speeded ahead, gradually overhauling the German squadron. In the lead ship, *Lion*, the eyes of the range finders in the control top strained through their instruments as they estimated the range of the rearmost enemy ship. Then finally at 8.53 a.m. the range was called out – 10 nautical miles – and at 8.32 a.m. a single round from the *Lion's* forward turret crashed out. The first round fell short and subsequent salvoes gradually found the range until at 9.09 a.m. a 13.5in armour-piercing shell found its target on the quarter deck of the rearmost ship in the German line, the armoured cruiser *Blucher*.

Now a deliberate fire was laid on the comparatively lightly armoured *Blucher*, repeatedly finding the mark, and to which she was unable to answer with her smaller 8.2in guns. She was also slower than the other German ships, being capable of only 26 knots, and started to fall behind. As the *Tiger* came within range, she, too, started to fire on the unfortunate vessel, allowing *Lion* to shift her aim to the next German ship in the line, *Moltke*.

Now the German ships were able to respond and at 9.28 a.m. an 11in shell from *Moltke* hit *Lion* on the waterline, where by good fortune much of the force of the explosion was absorbed by the coal bunkers. Soon, however, *Lion*, at the head of the column of British ships with the range closing, became the target for all three German battle-cruisers and started to receive ever more damaging hits from plunging shellfire.

Beatty ordered his five battle-cruisers to deploy into echelon to port to divide the enemy fire and directed that each should engage her opposite number in the German line in order that all the German ships should be under fire. At this stage, with five British ships firing on four German, some degree of misunderstanding of these orders crept in, with captains being uncertain as to which ship was in fact their opposite number. This would later allow two of the German ships to be unmarked for a short period of time.

The second from last ship in Beatty's line, *New Zealand*, was now in range and engaged the damaged *Blucher*, which was already falling behind the other fleeing German ships. This allowed the *Princess Royal* to shift her aim to the *Moltke*, while *Tiger* moved her aim onto *Seydlitz*, the lead ship, in accordance with the established principle where the leading ship should be engaged in order to destroy the cohesiveness of the squadron.

The situation at 9.30 a.m. was that two British ships, *Lion* and *Tiger*, were both firing on *Seydlitz*, with the *Princess Royal* and *Indomitable* firing on the already badly damaged *Blucher*.

Captain Pelly of the *Tiger* continued to direct fire against the *Seydlitz*, unaware that he was mistaking the *Lion's* shell splashes, which were falling with increasing accuracy on the German ship, for his own, which were falling some 2,000yd beyond his intended target. This mix-up of targets went unnoticed for some time, allowing the two unengaged battle-cruisers *Derfflinger* and *Moltke* to make accurate and undisturbed practice on *Lion*. Despite the punishment *Lion* was now receiving from three German ships, she was still racing along at 29 knots and scoring telling hits on Hipper's flagship.

At 9.42 a.m. a 13.5in armour-piercing shell penetrated the rear turret of the *Seydlitz*, bursting with near catastrophic effect that was later to have far reaching repercussions in the lessons learned that would determine the differing fates of British and German battle-cruisers during the Battle of Jutland fifteen months later. The shell penetrated the right-hand corner of the aft turret barbette, totally wrecking the turret and all parts of the stern, including officers' quarters, messes and so on and causing an ammunition fire in the reloading chamber, rapidly spreading

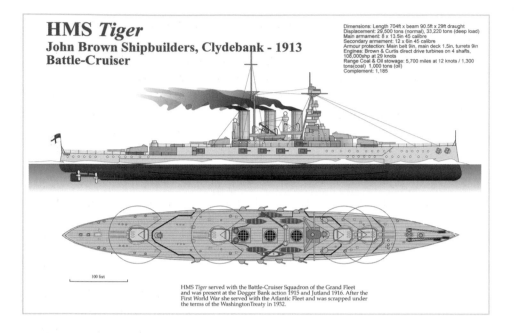

HMS *Tiger*
John Brown Shipbuilders, Clydebank - 1913
Battle-Cruiser

Dimensions: Length 704ft x beam 90.5ft x 29ft draught
Displacement: 29,500 tons (normal), 33,220 tons (deep load)
Main armament: 8 x 13.5in 45 calibre
Secondary armament: 12 x 6in 45 calibre
Armour protection: Main belt 9in, main deck 1.5in, turrets 9in
Engines: Brown & Curtis direct drive turbines on 4 shafts,
108,000shp at 29 knots
Range Coal & Oil stowage: 5,700 miles at 12 knots / 1,300
tons(coal) 1,000 tons (oil)
Complement: 1,185

100 feet

HMS *Tiger* served with the Battle-Cruiser Squadron of the Grand Fleet
and was present at the Dogger Bank action 1915 and Jutland 1916. After the
First World War she served with the Atlantic Fleet and was scrapped under
the terms of the Washington Treaty in 1932.

from one compartment to the next. The fire ignited ready-use propellant charges, with the flames racing down to the magazine and spreading to the upper turret as the crew attempted to escape through a connecting door that was normally closed. The flames rose as high as the mainmast and the ship was only saved from destruction by the prompt action of the turret crew and the brave action of one sailor, Wilhelm Heidkamp, who flooded the magazine, dousing the flames. Although the ship was saved, both turrets were burnt out and wrecked, with both crews of 165 men perishing.

In this near catastrophe a valuable lesson was learned by the Germans for the future, which was aided by the superior system of protection employed in the design of their turrets and methods of handling shells in their magazines to that practised in British warships.

In the British system, if an armour-piercing shell penetrated a turret, the flash from an explosion could set off the cordite propellant charges stored in open-topped bins in the turret itself and the working chamber below the turret, as were the ready-use shells themselves.

Additionally, the cordite propellant in the British case was packed in silk bags as opposed to the German practice of having their charges encased in brass cases. Again, in German ships all shells in the magazine and charges in the handling room above were protected by double interlocking doors and in closed bins, unlike the British single door and open bin system.

This German system of protection extended from the magazine in the lower part of the ship, up the ammunition hoist and into the working chamber, a system that more effectively prevented flash and flame travelling down to the magazine than was the case in the British ships.

It was not until after the loss of three battle-cruisers at the Battle of Jutland that the British took more stringent precautions to protect their magazines, with the introduction of double doors and closed shell bins. A further failing was that the British were still using the older formula of a Vaseline-based solvent in the manufacture of cordite that made it extremely unstable. In fact, tests indicated that the so-called stabiliser actually reduced stability and made it more likely to explode rather than burn if set off. The Germans, on the other hand, benefiting from their highly developed chemical industry, were using the much more stable, non-solvent based cordite. Apart from the loss of the *Karlsruhe* in 1914, which was using the older Vaseline-based solvent, no German ships were lost due to accidental magazine explosion, unlike the British, Italian and Japanese navies, who lost two battleships each to this cause.

As the chase continued, the British ships gradually gained on Hipper's cruisers, but the early accurate shooting of Beatty's ships deteriorated, while that of the Germans became more accurate, with *Lion* bearing the brunt of the fire.

Finally, at 10.18 a.m. the flagship *Lion*, after having been hit several times, was struck by a salvo of twelve shells from *Derfflinger* on the waterline, causing extensive flooding and taking on hundreds of tons of water up to the level of the main deck, causing her to slow slightly. Then at 10.41 a.m. a heavy shell hit and penetrated A turret, causing a fierce fire in the ready-use cordite bins, but fortunately this was quickly brought under control by the fire parties before the flames could spread down into the magazine *Lion* continued to be the main target for the German ships, having been hit over fifteen times by heavy shells, and was taking heavy punishment.

Hipper's ships were now running low on ammunition and were in no position to support the damaged *Blucher*, which they would need to abandon if they were to save themselves. At 11.00 a.m., as they continued the chase, a suspected U-boat was reported on the starboard beam. In response, Admiral Beatty ordered a 90° turn away to port for the squadron, but almost immediately countermanded the order, as the ships beginning to turn were being too drastic, opening the range unnecessarily and causing the British ships to lose ground on the enemy. In order to reduce the angle of turn to 45°, the flag signal course north-east was hoisted.

As the ships returned to the chase at 10.46 a.m., the *Lion* again received a 12in-shell hit on the waterline that smashed through the armour belt, causing more flooding and wrecking a boiler room, cutting off steam to the port turbines and reducing her speed to 15 knots.

Because of the damage suffered to the *Lion*, Beatty realised that he was now in danger of losing control of the battle, so he hoisted a succession of flag signals (wireless communications being largely non-existent due to the aerials being shot away) that were instrumental in creating confusion in the minds of the captains of the British battle-cruisers at this critical point in the action.

The signal 'Engage the enemy's rear' raced to the masthead, while the previous course north-east signal was still flying, much to the puzzlement of Rear Admiral Sir Archibald Moore, Beatty's second in command aboard the *New Zealand*, who was unaware of the reason for the 90° turn to port and assumed the two signals indicated that he should attack the damaged *Blucher*, which was to his north-east and led his ships towards her, inadvertently breaking off the pursuit of the German main force.

As the *Lion* fell out of line, Beatty summoned the destroyer *Attack* alongside and, transferring his flag, raced off in pursuit of his squadron. Confident that he was on the verge of a great victory that would see Hipper's battle-cruisers sent to the bottom, he ran up another signal in the tradition of Nelson, 'Engage the enemy more closely', which only added to the confusion.

By now Beatty had become aware that his intentions had been misinterpreted by his second in command, as he realised that the four battle-cruisers were concentrating their fire on the luckless and already doomed *Blucher* instead of chasing Hipper's three ships that were slipping away to the east and safety. In desperation, Beatty hoisted yet another signal, 'Keep closer to the enemy', but by now Rear Admiral Moore's ships were too far away to read the signal and the chance to destroy the German ships had been lost through poor communications.

Meanwhile, the *Blucher*, fighting valiantly and despite having been hit by over fifty British shells, had managed to seriously damage the destroyer *Meteor* and hit two of the battle-cruisers, even as she was being smashed into a burning wreck. Finally, after the cruiser *Arethusa* fired two torpedoes into her, she capsized and sank at 12.13 p.m., taking 792 men down with her.

British ships attempted to rescue survivors from the water, but these operations were interrupted by the appearance of a German Zeppelin *L5* and seaplanes that dropped bombs causing the ships to withdraw. Later, after the airship had departed, the British destroyers, on returning to the spot where the *Blucher* had sunk, managed to pull 234 survivors from the water.

Admiral Beatty aboard the *Attack* came up with the *Princess Royal* at 12.20 p.m., to which he transferred his flag once more and was furious to learn that his instructions had been misinterpreted by Rear Admiral Moore, who had abandoned the pursuit to turn all three of his ships onto the *Blucher*, thereby missing the chance of what could have been an overwhelming victory. Admiral Moore's decision to abandon the chase is a difficult one to understand.

The damaged *Lion* was taken in tow by the *Indomitable* to Rosyth, crawling along dangerously exposed to possible attack by U-boats at 10 knots, with both ships escorted by a huge fleet of destroyers and Commodore Goodenough's cruiser squadron, where on arrival the damage to *Lion* was found to be so severe that she was in dockyard hands for four months under repair.

Commodore Tyrwhitt's Harwich Force had accompanied Beatty's battle-cruisers but, when the chase was finally abandoned at 12.45 p.m., they turned for home with only minor damage to *Aurora* and *Undaunted*. Similarly, the battle squadrons of the Grand Fleet, which had hoped to bring their guns to bear on the German ships, put about to Scapa, this being the first of many similar occasions when the great ships would embark on a North Sea sweep in the expectation of engaging the enemy, only to return empty handed.

The battle was hailed as a great victory and Beatty became the hero of the hour to the British public, and the dramatic picture carried on the front page of the *Daily Mail* of the *Blucher* rolling over on her beam ends in a welter of water, with crewmen sliding down her sides, was seen as an example of what the Hun could expect if they attempted to cross swords with the Royal Navy.

At the Admiralty the errors inherent in the handling of the action were glaringly obvious, with Beatty failing to communicate his intentions clearly and Captain Pelly of the *Tiger* failing to engage his opposite number *Derfflinger*, leaving her free to fire unmarked by a British ship. The greatest odium, however, fell upon Rear Admiral Moore, who had abandoned the pursuit at a vital juncture in the battle; he was quietly removed from command.

More worrying when the course of the battle came to be analysed was, first, the chaotic and primitive methods of signalling that led to a failure to effectively communicate and pass on the Commander-in-Chief's orders to his subordinates, and, secondly, the poor standard of shooting by the British ships.

On the German side, the three battle-cruisers reached the protection of the Jade Basin safely in the early afternoon, with the *Seydlitz* having received the most damage. Despite Beatty's later exaggerated claims on reporting the battle to have repeatedly hit and severely damaged all three German battle-cruisers, the truth was very different.

Out of the expenditure of over 1,100 shells that had been fired by the British battle-cruisers, the *Seydlitz* and *Derfflinger* had only been hit three times each. Admittedly these were telling blows that severely damaged both vessels, while the *Moltke* was not hit by any shell throughout the entire action. Conversely, the *Lion* was struck by seventeen German shells and the *Tiger* seven, indicating a higher standard of German gunnery.

The Germans took to heart the lesson learnt from the 13.5in shell that had penetrated the turret of the *Seydlitz* and caused the near-fatal fire that came within an ace of destroying the ship. They took additional precautions to protect the ammunition hoists and shell rooms from the danger of the flash from a hit on a turret reaching down to the magazine, by the installation of further interlocking fireproof doors in the hoists, ensuring that a cordite fire could not be transmitted

SMS *Blücher*
Kaiserliche Werft, Kiel - 1909
Grosser Kreuser

German Naval Airship *L3*

100 feet

Dimensions: Length 530ft x 780ft beam x 26ft draught
Displacement: 15,000 tons (normal)
Main armament: 12 x 8.2in 40 calibre
Secondary armament: 8 x 5.9in-3 x 18in submerged torpedo tubes
Armour protection: Main belt 6in-2in, main deck 2in, turrets 6in
Machinery: Triple expansions 4 cylinder on 3 shafts, 34,000 shp at 26 knots
Range: 8,600 miles at 10 knots
Complement: 860

from the turret to the magazine; a lesson the British, who had experienced a similar near disaster, failed to recognise, with disastrous results fifteen months later at Jutland.

The battle was celebrated as a great victory, and, thanks to Churchill and Fisher, who admired his dash, Beatty, despite the errors of judgement he had displayed, continued in their and the public's imagination to be the hero of the hour. So much so that within a few months Beatty became the commander of the newly instituted battle-cruiser fleet, an independent entity from the Grand Fleet.

The Kaiser was furious when he learnt of the loss of the *Blücher*, which, as an inferior class of vessel, had no place in the line of battle-cruisers. Von Ingenohl took the blame for the loss and, criticised for what was seen to be a dangerously risky series of operations, was replaced by the more cautious Admiral Hugo von Pohl, who more closely followed the Kaiser's views on the necessity to preserve the fleet by not hazarding it unnecessarily.

11

THE GRAND FLEET AT SCAPA FLOW

In his book *The Riddle of the Sands*, published in 1903, Erskine Childers – one-time Royal Naval officer and fervent Irish nationalist, who was to die at the hands of a Free State firing squad and to whom the whole genre of the modern spy novel can be ascribed – presented the contention that Imperial Germany was making preparations to invade England's east coast with a seaborne invasion issuing from the small harbours laying in the shallow waters behind the East Frisian Islands.

In the book, the German efforts are frustrated by two young British yachtsmen who, while sailing the waters around and behind the low-lying islands of Borkum, Norderney, Baltrum, Langeoog and the twisting torturous channels and sandbanks between the River Ems and the Weser, expose the German invasion plan and alert their government to the danger.

At a time of increasing international tension, the publication of the book caused great excitement and disquiet both in the general public and in Parliament, where rapid German naval expansion was being viewed with increasing concern. Although there was in reality no such invasion plan in the German archives emanating from the Frisian Islands, there had earlier in 1894 been a plan for a seaborne invasion that had briefly been considered by the High Command, but was already abandoned by 1900.

However, the hypothesis expressed most forcibly in the novel was that the east coast and its ports that faced Germany across the North Sea were at that time almost totally unprotected, lacking any form of effective defence and open to invasion. The reason why the coast from Norfolk to the north of Scotland was so thinly defended by defensive works or coastal batteries has a long historical origin.

For the preceding five centuries or longer any seaborne threat to these islands had come from our traditional enemy, France, together with Spain, and for a period the Dutch in the 1600s. The geography of these threats necessitated positioning British major naval bases and defences mainly along the south coast at harbours where they could concentrate their naval strength, such as Dover, Portsmouth, Plymouth and Torbay, and from where the 'wooden walls', taking advantage of the prevailing westerly winds, would be in an advantageous position to sail out before the wind to keep watch and blockade the French ports of Brest, L'Orient, La Rochelle and other harbours.

Historically, British control of the narrow seas was so complete that any landing on Britain's eastern shores seemed a remote possibility, although with changing alliances such threats did occur.

During the Dutch Wars in the 1650s–70s, for instance, English control was sorely contested, with defeats at sea. In 1667 the Dutch fleet, sweeping aside the paltry defences, sailed up the Medway, burnt the shipyard at Chatham and captured or destroyed sixteen ships.

By 1900, although there were existing fortifications and batteries controlling the entrances to the major seaports, advances in naval gunnery meant that modern warships far outperformed the obsolete artillery installed in most of these shore batteries that could no longer offer the protection to Britain's shores, as had been the case in the past. The 3-mile limit – the distance of a cannon shot – that for centuries had been the arbiter of our safety was now no longer a shield against infection and the hand of war.

The paradox was that, following the rapid expansion of the German fleet after the ratification of the First Navy Law in 1898 under Tirpitz's direction, and the British response, the Royal Navy found itself with an ever-growing fleet of huge modern battleships that, under the strategy for their use, dictated that they largely operated as a single unit to maximise their massive destructive power and ability to completely overwhelm any opposition.

The need to concentrate such a huge assembly of ships required the need to find a suitably large anchorage to accommodate them, and at the same time to be in a geographically advantageous location that answered to the strategic requirements of our naval policy.

By 1900 the requirement for a new naval base to control the east coast became ever more urgent and coincided with the recognition that in a future war the close blockade of enemy, or more particularly German ports, by our ships would be impractical and undesirable due to the developments of modern weapons such as long-range artillery, the mine and the development of fast torpedo boats and, latterly, submarines that could threaten capital ships. The new policy of distant blockade also required that the German fleet should be effectively contained within the North Sea or preferably within its harbours so as not to offer a danger to our merchant fleets on the world's trade routes.

In March 1904 the Prime Minister Arthur Balfour announced to the House of Commons that a new naval base was to be established at Rosyth on the Firth of Forth where the main battle fleet, then referred to as the Home Fleet, would in future be based.

From here it was suggested the Royal Navy could exert control over the German fleet and their bases in the German Bight some 350 miles across the North Sea.

The choice of Rosyth as a base had many advantages: being near to the cities of Dunfermline and Edinburgh across the Firth, there was an availability of labour to construct and service the port. Moreover, it was connected by the main rail line to all other parts of the country for the supply of materials, munitions, coal and so on.

A disadvantage to the location was voiced early in the scheme by the First Lord Admiral Fisher and others, who objected on the grounds that it lay on the upstream side of the great iron Forth railway bridge, which, should it be damaged or destroyed in an attack or through some act of sabotage, would effectively trap the entire fleet, rendering it impotent.

Fisher also suggested that the long and relatively narrow sea entrance to the proposed harbour rendered it vulnerable to the laying of mines and attacks from torpedo craft in a similar manner to that experienced by the Russians at Port Arthur at the hands of the Japanese.

Progress on building the base over the next few years proceeded slowly, as there were conflicting views both in Parliament and at the War Office, as well as the Admiralty, as to the value or the necessity of building it at all.

The influential Admiral Fisher, in the throes of developing his revolutionary fleet of dreadnought battleships and completely reorganising the Royal Navy from the top down to make it fit for purpose under the changed conditions, considered Rosyth to be unsuitable, being too far inland. Instead, it favoured the more northern Cromarty Firth, or the River Humber, and expressed his opinion that Rosyth was an unsafe and poor choice for a fleet anchorage.

The defence of harbours and ports devolved on the War Office, as did the protection of naval storehouses, building facilities and magazines – a situation that was far from satisfactory, as the amount of money the War Office was prepared to expend fell far below that necessary to adequately ensure their security.

By 1912 the strategy of the distant blockade had become the accepted plan to be employed. In the event of war with Germany, and while the narrow waters of the English Channel were seen to be adequately taken care of by the naval forces at Harwich, Dover and Portsmouth, the gap between Scotland and Norway required further northern bases to be developed.

Belatedly, work on Rosyth and the Cromarty Firth were accelerated with a minimum of shore-based artillery being installed, sufficient only to fend off light enemy forces, but at the time inadequate to repel any determined attack. The rate of progress and lack of political will to complete these bases left them largely unfortified at the outbreak of war in 1914.

The other anchorage being considered was Scapa Flow, a vast body of enclosed water in the Orkney Islands at the northern point of the Scottish mainland, covering 120 square miles of protected water, and considered to be one of the great natural harbours in the world.

Separated from the Scottish mainland by the Pentland Firth, Scapa Flow consists of 10 miles of stormy water where daily tides flow between the North Sea and the Atlantic at a rate of between 8 to 10 knots. The tides also flow strongly in and out of the various entrances, making navigation difficult when, as frequently occurs, sea fogs, mists and storms beset the anchorage, particularly in winter, when due to its northerly position the short days mean the Flow can be in darkness for up to 18 hours a day.

It has a fairly shallow (around 50 to 100ft in depth), sandy bottom and three main entrances: Hoy Sound to the west and Hoxa Sound to the south, a mile wide and used during the Great War as the main entrance and exit for the fleet. Apart from other very much smaller entrances used by fishermen, the Switha entrance leading in to Longhope Sound was used as the base for trawlers and other boats such as boom vessels that were required for the management of the anchorage.

Scapa Flow had been used as a harbour since historical times, being known to the Romans and the Vikings, and King Haakon IV of Norway anchoring his fleet there in 1263 before the Battle of Largs, in an attempt to reassert Norwegian rule over northern Scotland. This came to nothing when the Scottish forces of King Alexander III beat them off, ending Norwegian control.

During the flight of the Spanish ships around the wild rocky coastline of Scotland following the defeat of the Spanish Armada in 1588, several unfortunate vessels were cast ashore on its inhospitable coastline.

Scapa Flow had previously been used since the 1890s by ships of the Royal Navy for summer fleet exercises, and from 1909 under Fisher's directions more frequent use was made of it, with the Home Fleet using it as the base for exercises from April to October.

In 1909 no less than eighty-two warships were anchored in its environs, consisting of thirty-seven pre-dreadnought battleships and cruisers including the new *Dreadnought*, supported by forty-four destroyers, colliers and repair and store ships.

The following year, ninety warships under the command of Prince Louis of Battenberg, including battleships, cruisers and destroyers, conducted summer manoeuvres and night-firing exercises during August and September from Scapa Flow. In 1911, with the international situation worsening again, the anchorage was used for naval exercises, with destroyer and cruiser flotillas conducting practice torpedo attacks and countermeasures exercises, while the battleships practised deploying from cruising formation to line of battle, and firing exercises in the Atlantic.

Even though up to the outbreak of war Scapa Flow was extensively used by the Royal Navy, the thought of using it as a permanent war station was not seriously considered until 1912 when the policy of the distant blockade had been reluctantly accepted by a Liberal government who were unenthusiastically supporting the massive naval rearmament programme, and who were anxious to cut expenditure in other areas to save money.

At the time Scapa Flow was being considered as a base, it was completely lacking in any form of defence and there was no will within Parliament to expend vast sums on making it safe.

At the same time, the discussions on the various merits of Scapa, Rosyth and Cromarty were seemingly endless and served only to put off any decision on a final choice of a preferred base.

At Scapa, apart from the light guns landed with the Royal Marine Artillery during exercises and a few field guns used by the local Territorial Army artillerymen, the islands were without any other form of defence. Furthermore, apart from the town of Kirkwall and the even smaller community of Stromness, there were no social amenities on the islands to cater for the off-duty crews or any dockyard facilities to service and repair the ships.

In 1912 a proposal was made to mount twenty-four guns and searchlights to secure the harbour, but nothing came of this. It was only in 1913, with a further change of plan after Winston Churchill had belatedly announced in Parliament that Cromarty had been chosen as the preferred major North Sea base, that work at last started, much to the relief of all concerned.

The parsimonious attitude towards expenditure on the construction of new harbour facilities and coastal defences was in contrast to the German approach to the problem, where, following the introduction of the larger dreadnought battleships into their fleet, they had constructed new docks of larger dimensions which allowed for ships of greater beam than their British counterparts to be built and, therefore, possessed of greater protection. Over a seven-year period they had also spent millions of marks in enlarging and deepening the Kiel Canal to allow the rapid passage of their ships between the North Sea and the Baltic, while at the same time installing modern protective batteries and forts.

In Britain the naval defence estimates year by year, while providing the necessary money to build new dreadnoughts, were lacking in the provision for new harbour construction or their defence. British naval estimates for 1913–14 were a massive £46,500,000, of which as little as £5,000 was set aside for improvement work to Scapa Flow.

The Admiralty requested £380,000 for the installation of what they considered minimum defences to secure the anchorage, but even this cost, the price of a destroyer, was turned down by the Liberal chancellor Lloyd George as being too expensive. So, when war broke out, the fleet found themselves entering what was the ideal anchorage, but wholly unprotected from the enemy.

As the British fleet departed Portland on 29 July for their war station, colliers had already been sent ahead, together with fleet oilers and supply and repair ships, anchoring in protected inlets to form the basis of a real base.

The first to drop anchor were the destroyers of the 4th Flotilla, returning from duty in the Irish Sea, where tensions were high with the continuing Home Rule problem that had seen opposing groups arming for a possible confrontation.

The battle fleet arrived on 31 July, with the great ships entering through Hoxa Sound to anchor in lines off Scapa pier on the north side of the Flow off Flotta Island, their arrival largely concealed by a fog, and the last ships arriving in the short hours of the summer night.

By 1 August, Scapa Flow was the home to ninety-six ships, with three battle squadrons consisting of twenty-one dreadnoughts, eight pre-dreadnoughts and four battle-cruisers.

The Commander-in-Chief Admiral Sir John Jellicoe flew his flag in the *Iron Duke* with the 1st Battle Squadron under Vice-Admiral Sir Lewis Bayly, composed of *Marlborough* flag, with ten 13.5in guns and seven dreadnoughts with ten 12in guns.

The 2nd Battle Squadron contained eight of the later 13.5in super-dreadnoughts, with Vice-Admiral Sir George Warrender flying his flag aboard the *King George V*. The 3rd Battle Squadron was made up of eight pre-dreadnoughts, each mounting four 12in guns, with Vice-Admiral E. Bradford commanding aboard the *King Edward VII*.

The 1st Battle-Cruiser Squadron was under the command of Vice Admiral Sir David Beatty and comprised the *Lion*, *Princess Royal*, *Queen Mary* and *New Zealand*. Also present were eight armoured cruisers, thirteen cruisers and forty-two destroyers. Overnight the population of these remote islands had swollen by 40,000 souls. Also under the command of the Commander-in-Chief was the Channel Fleet based at southern harbours and on the south coast, commanded by Vice-Admiral Sir Cecil Burney and composed of the 5th, 6th, 7th and 8th Battle Squadrons, containing twenty-eight pre-dreadnought battleships armed with four 12in guns apiece.

It is customary for modern writers to regard these older ships as useless, but, while inferior to the dreadnoughts in gun power, they performed much valuable work during the war.

The first task at Scapa Flow was to strip the ships for action, with any unnecessary woodwork and fittings, wardroom furniture or any other fire hazards, together with spare boats that were surplus to requirements, taken ashore and dumped. Although now installed at his northern base, Jellicoe (as had been his predecessor Admiral Callaghan), was deeply concerned by the lack of defences and was afraid of the possibility of an attack by either German destroyers or submarines.

He immediately stationed destroyers at the entrances to the Flow and instituted cruiser patrols off the islands. His confidence was hardly improved when the cruiser *Birmingham* rammed and sank the U-boat *U15* in the first few days of the war off Fair Isle.

Alarmed by the dangers of an unprotected anchorage, Jellicoe took the fleet to sea in the first few weeks, as he felt his ships would be safer and in October he took the entire fleet to Lough Swilly on the north-west coast of Ireland while boom defences and gun emplacements were hurriedly installed, until by November Jellicoe was at last satisfied that the anchorage was secure.

The old battleship HMS *Hannibal* was permanently anchored to cover the entrance into Hoy Sound, while her sister ship HMS *Magnificent* was similarly positioned to protect Hoxa Sound. In addition, several old ships were sunk as block ships in the smaller entrances on the eastern side of the islands to discourage U-boats. Other anti-submarine measures included commandeering dozens of fishing trawlers equipped with light guns and towed explosive sweeps that could be detonated from the ship. The trawlers laid the steel anti-submarine nets of the boom defences and electrically controlled mines were also laid, which between them registered two successful sinkings.

On the morning of 24 November 1914, the *U18* commanded by Kapitan von Hennig attempted to enter the Flow through Hoxa Sound, but her periscope was sighted by a patrolling trawler and rammed her, though not fatally. The damaged U-boat tried to run for home but had to be scuttled near the Pentland Skerries, where her crew were rescued by British destroyers.

Later, near the end of the war, great advances had been made in the protection of the entrances, with arrays of hydrophones installed to detect incoming submarines, and on 25 October 1918 a mine-laying submarine, the *UB116*, also attempted to enter Hoxa Sound. She was detected by hydrophones and was quickly destroyed when an electric mine was triggered from the shore. There were no survivors and it was the last German U-boat to attempt an entrance until Gunther Prien's successful sinking of the *Royal Oak* in October 1939.

The island of Flotta was taken over and began to be developed as the on-shore headquarters establishment, with piers and an oil storage and ammunition dump being established. An athletics ground and a football field were constructed for the recreational use of the men, where games and boxing tournaments were entered into with great enthusiasm and in an intense spirit of competition between ships' crews, while a nine-hole golf course was dug for the officers on the exposed treeless island that was frequently used by the Commander-in-Chief when he went ashore.

Other amenities added as the years went by included a much appreciated cinema and a YMCA hut that gave a welcome taste of the civilian world and a break from the strict naval discipline that prevailed on board ship. When the weather permitted, sailing and rowing regattas were a pleasurable diversion from the monotony of the regular and everyday duties.

Within the Flow, the battle fleet lay off Flotta Island, often in appalling weather conditions, when frequent gales struck the islands where the ships rode out the storm with both anchors down. Fog and rain were a regular part of the scene, with each ship isolated from its fellows when the sea state was too rough for boats to be lowered to visit neighbours.

Much praise must be given to the work of the attached steam drifters, manned by Scottish fishermen, who in all but the very worst weather continued their important work of delivering mail, provisions and supplies from the depot ships at Long Hope, while each day the attached minesweepers put to sea to clear the swept channels.

Once a month, one of the battle squadrons would leave the Flow in rotation to sail down to Invergordon on the Cromarty Firth, which now belatedly was fully protected with guns and anti-submarine nets. Here conditions were more bearable for the crews, and the off-duty liberty men were able to enjoy some of the more normal everyday pleasures of life in a large town, such as pubs and cinemas, and the company of females available in the average seaport that were so lacking at Scapa Flow.

From here the same routine of training prevailed, with the Squadron putting to sea on North Sea sweeps, on the receipt of intelligence reports, searching for the elusive enemy, which all too often involved steaming at high speed at action stations, only to find the intelligence in error or that the alerted enemy had long slipped away.

The Grand Fleet through constant exercise were working the crews up to a high degree of efficiency, and at sea during battle practice the guns were fired at targets and signal-flag and wireless communications and the complicated manoeuvres necessary to deploy the fleet were practiced over and over again.

At any time the battleships and cruisers of the fleet needed to put to sea for battle practice, while the destroyers, between their duties in screening the larger warships from submarine attack, also had to take part in weapons training and tactical exercises in co-ordinated flotilla attacks and night-fighting training.

The process of organising the Grand Fleet to put to sea, whether for practice or North Sea sweep, was a complicated operation that required careful planning and timing, with instructions being sent to the various units to raise steam many hours before the indicated departure time.

The destroyer flotillas would be dispatched first to form a protective screen for the big ships, while the patrol vessels already at sea would be searching for any U-boats that might be laying off the approaches to the harbour.

Next, the cruiser squadrons and the armoured cruisers that were to scout ahead of the battle squadrons would depart to their rendezvous points and, finally, the battleships were ordered to sea by divisions.

Sometimes these operations would take place at night, often in atrocious weather conditions, with perhaps sixty ships showing no lights, steaming at speed into the darkness, with the danger of collision an ever present threat, requiring the highest standards of seamanship to accomplish successfully.

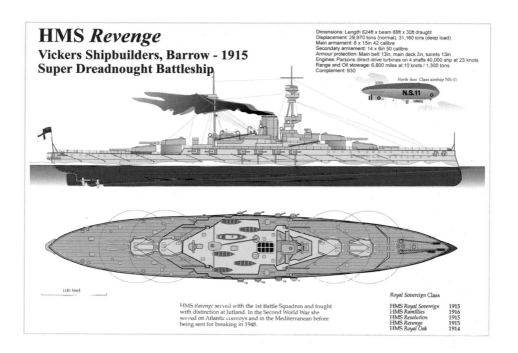

HMS *Revenge*
Vickers Shipbuilders, Barrow - 1915
Super Dreadnought Battleship

Dimensions: Length 624ft x beam 88ft x 30ft draught
Displacement: 29,970 tons (normal), 31,160 tons (deep load)
Main armament: 8 x 15in 42 calibre
Secondary armament: 14 x 6in 50 calibre
Armour protection: Main belt 13in, main deck 2in, turrets 13in
Engines: Parsons direct drive turbines on 4 shafts 40,000 shp at 23 knots
Range and Oil stowage: 6,800 miles at 10 knots / 1,300 tons
Complement: 930

North Seas Class airship NS-11

100 feet

HMS *Revenge* served with the 1st Battle Squadron and fought
with distinction at Jutland. In the Second World War she
served on Atlantic convoys and in the Mediterranean before
being sent for breaking in 1948.

Royal Sovereign Class

HMS *Royal Sovereign*	1915
HMS *Ramillies*	1916
HMS *Resolution*	1915
HMS *Revenge*	1915
HMS *Royal Oak*	1914

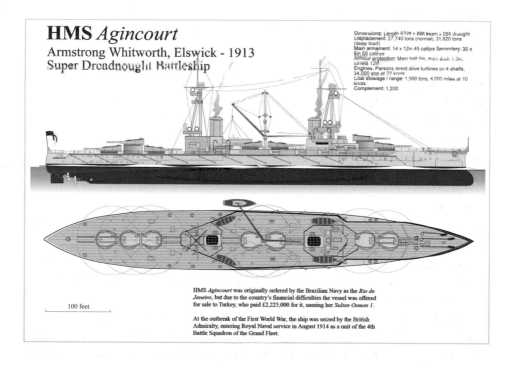

HMS *Agincourt*
Armstrong Whitworth, Elswick - 1913
Super Dreadnought Battleship

Dimensions: Length 632ft x 89ft beam x 20ft draught
Displacement: 27,740 tons (normal), 31,620 tons
(deep load)
Main armament: 14 x 12in 45 calibre Secondary: 20 x
6in 50 calibre
Armour protection: Main belt 9in, main deck 1.5in,
turrets 12in
Engines: Parsons direct drive turbines on 4 shafts,
34,000 shp at 22 knots
Coal stowage / range: 1,500 tons, 4,000 miles at 10
knots
Complement: 1,200

100 feet

HMS *Agincourt* was originally ordered by the Brazilian Navy as the *Rio de
Janeiro*, but due to the country's financial difficulties the vessel was offered
for sale to Turkey, who paid £2,225,000 for it, naming her *Sultan Osman 1*.

At the outbreak of the First World War, the ship was seized by the British
Admiralty, entering Royal Naval service in August 1914 as a unit of the 4th
Battle Squadron of the Grand Fleet.

A line of twenty-four battleships at sea in the closest order would be 6 miles in length and, although this line of battle would be the preferred formation that an admiral would want to present to an enemy as he crossed his line of advance, putting him in the advantageous position of crossing the enemy's T, it had severe disadvantages. For instance, to pass a flag signal from one end to the other could take 10 minutes and such a line would be the ideal target for a submarine attack.

Prior to disposing into line of battle, the fleet would adopt the cruising formation, where, for instance, twenty-four ships would form six columns of four ships in line ahead disposed abeam of each other, forming a compact box where signals could be more rapidly communicated.

The problem was to effect a smooth transition from this compact formation into the battle line, which was dependent on the direction the enemy approached. Only constant practice to cater for all possible variations could bring the ships and crews to the highest standard of efficiency.

The German High Seas Fleet in 1914 was composed of thirteen dreadnought battleships, comprising four *Westfalen* class ships – these being the first German dreadnoughts built and launched in 1909, mounting twelve 11in guns, together with four similarly armed *Helgoland* class of 1911, armed with twelve of the heavier 12in guns, and five *Kaiser* class of 1913 which, with a superimposed turret arrangement aft in the manner of the British *Colossus* class, carried ten 12in guns. There were also ten pre-dreadnought battleships, each with four 11in guns, and four modern battle-cruisers carrying ten 11in guns.

The German battleships had greater displacement than their British counterparts, class for class, as well as thicker armour protection and, while the calibre of the main armament was less in each case, thanks to the superior subdivision of their hulls and watertight integrity their ability to absorb punishment was greater. The provision in their construction of additional armoured longitudinal and transverse bulkheads to protect their vitals was superior to that found in the British ships, and rendered them almost unsinkable.

During 1915 the fleet were joined by three ships of the new and powerful *Queen Elizabeth* class, carrying eight of the new MkI 45 calibre 15in gun that fired a shell of 1,920lb at a muzzle velocity of 2,575ft per second to a range of 30,000yd. The three ships were HMS *Queen Elizabeth*, HMS *Warspite* and HMS *Barham*, each of 32,000 tons' displacement and with a length of 640ft.

With geared turbines of 75,000hp they could achieve 25 knots and were not only remarkably fast, but were also more heavily armoured than earlier classes, with 13in belt and 6in armour to the upper deck, 2in anti-torpedo protection and later retrospectively fitted with anti-torpedo bulges. They were joined in 1916 by HMS *Valiant* and HMS *Malaya*, which was a gift from the Government of Malaya.

These ships formed the 5th Battle Squadron of the Grand Fleet and were considered to be the most effective and successful British battleships ever built and gave sterling service in both World Wars. They were oil fired, and the extra 4 knots allowed them to be used as a fast battle squadron that supported Sir David Beatty's battle-cruisers most effectively at Jutland.

The name ship *Queen Elizabeth* was sent shortly after completion to the Dardanelles in 1915 to assist in reducing the Turkish forts during efforts to force the narrows, but was soon withdrawn after receiving hits from Turkish batteries, as it was considered to be too hazardous and an ineffectual way to employ such a modern vessel that had cost £2,400,000 to build.

The following class were the *Royal Sovereigns*, which entered service in 1916–17. They were originally designed as 21-knot coal-burning versions of the *Queen Elizabeth* class, as there was concern over the possible interruption of oil supplies during a conflict, whereas Britain had all the secure reserves of coal required to serve the needs of the fleet.

The *Revenge*, *Royal Oak* and *Royal Sovereign* joined the fleet in May 1916, allowing the first two ships to be in action at Jutland on 1 May 1916, while *Resolution* and *Ramillies* joined the 1st Battle Squadron at Scapa in late 1916. These ships had only eighteen boilers, compared to the Queen Elizabeths' twenty-four, reducing the horse power from 75,000 to 40,000, which, with the change to oil-fired boilers, gave the very respectable speed of 23 knots.

The length of this class of ship was reduced to 620ft, while the tonnage remained approximately the same, with the reduction of the number of boilers allowing for the installation of a single funnel, giving these ships a distinctive outline. They were regarded as having too low a freeboard and proved to be very wet forward in heavy weather, with a tendency to roll heavily, but, like their predecessors, they were to serve with great distinction in both world wars.

As the war progressed into 1915, with newer battleships and cruisers being added to the fleet, our strength increased with further units of the *Iron Duke* and *King George V* class being added, together with the purchase of HMS *Canada* in October 1915 that was being built for Chile as the *Almirante Latorre* of 32,000 tons armed with ten 14in guns, unique at that time in the British fleet. The *Canada* was present at Jutland with the 4th Battle Squadron, where she made good practice on the German line.

This ship was subsequently sold back to Chile in 1920, together with three modern *Tribal* class destroyers, for £1,400,000. Two other acquisitions made in 1914 were the *Agincourt* and the *Erin*. Both these ships had been under construction for Turkey.

The *Agincourt* had originally laid down as the *Rio de Janeiro* for Brazil, but due to financial difficulties in that country it was offered for sale to Turkey for £2,225,000. She was renamed *Sultan Osman I*. This was a powerful vessel of 27,750 tons, 632ft in length, and her Parsons direct drive turbines of 34,000hp gave her a speed of 22 knots.

HMS *Erin*
Vickers Shipbuilders, Barrow - 1913
Super Dreadnought Battleship

Dimensions: Length 559ft x beam 91ft x 28ft draught
Displacement: 23,000 tons (normal), 25,470 tons (deep load)
Main armament: 10 x 13.5in 45 calibre
Secondary armament: 16 x 6in 50 calibre
Armour protection: Main belt 12in, main deck 1.5in, turrets 10in
Engines: Parsons direct drive turbines on 4 shafts, 26,600shp at 21 knots
Range and coal stowage: 5,300 miles at 10 knots / 1,300 tons
Complement: 1,130

100 feet

HMS *Erin* was originally laid down as the *Reshadieh* for the Turkish Navy, but was seized by the British Admiralty at the outbreak of the First World War whilst undergoing trials, and enterted service with the Royal Navy as a unit of the 4th Battle Squadron of the Grand Fleet.

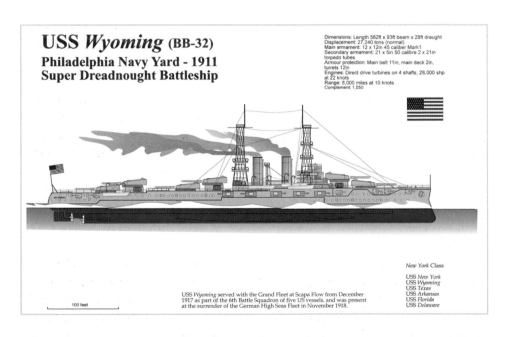

USS *Wyoming* (BB-32)
Philadelphia Navy Yard - 1911
Super Dreadnought Battleship

Dimensions: Length 562ft x 93ft beam x 28ft draught
Displacement: 27,240 tons (normal)
Main armament: 12 x 12in 45 caliber Mark1
Secondary armament: 21 x 5in 50 calibre 2 x 21in torpedo tubes
Armour protection: Main belt 11in, main deck 2in, turrets 12in
Engines: Direct drive turbines on 4 shafts, 28,000 shp at 22 knots
Range: 8,000 miles at 10 knots
Complement: 1,050

New York Class

USS *New York*
USS *Wyoming*
USS *Texas*
USS *Arkansas*
USS *Florida*
USS *Delaware*

USS *Wyoming* served with the Grand Fleet at Scapa Flow from December 1917 as part of the 6th Battle Squadron of five US vessels, and was present at the surrender of the German High Seas Fleet in November 1918.

100 feet

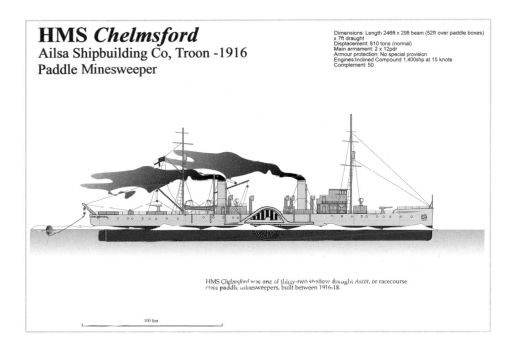

HMS *Chelmsford*
Ailsa Shipbuilding Co, Troon -1916
Paddle Minesweeper

Dimensions: Length 246ft x 29ft beam (52ft over paddle boxes)
x 7ft draught
Displacement: 810 tons (normal)
Main armament: 2 x 12pdr
Armour protection: No special provision
Engines:Inclined Compound 1,400shp at 15 knots
Complement: 50

HMS *Chelmsford* was one of thirty-two shallow draught *Ascot*, or racecourse class paddle minesweepers, built between 1916-18.

100 feet

At the time of her launch she was considered the largest and most heavily armed warship in the world, mounting fourteen 12in guns in seven turrets, each named for the days of the week, although her armour protection was poor, with only a 9in main belt and as thin as 1.25in deck armour.

At the outbreak of war Turkey had paid £2,000,000 for the vessel, almost crippling the country financially in the effort, but the British Government was alarmed at the prospect of so powerful a battleship coming into the hands of a potential enemy and seized her from the Armstrong Whitworth yard at Elswick, sending her to Devonport Royal Dockyard for completion.

HMS *Agincourt* joined the 4th Battle Squadron at Scapa Flow in August 1914, later serving at Jutland in the 1st Battle Squadron, firing 144 12in shells at the enemy while receiving superficial damage herself. After a life of ten years, the *Agincourt* was scrapped in 1924.

The second ship, HMS *Erin*, had also been commissioned by the Turks for Vickers Shipbuilders Barrow as the *Rashadiea* and was complete and running sea trails, with a Turkish crew waiting ready to sail for home, when it was also seized by the Royal Navy in August 1914, entering service with the Grand Fleet. The *Erin* was very similar in layout to the *King George V* class and with her ten 13.5in guns was a welcome addition to the fleet.

With these additions, the 3rd Battle Squadron of pre-dreadnoughts under Vice-Admiral Bradford, which was comprised of ships of the *King Edward VII* class, was withdrawn from Scapa in April 1915 to be based at Sheerness, as a support to the Harwich Force should there be further German raids on the east coast.

Of the six ships in this class the *King Edward VII* was sunk by a mine off Cape Wrath in 1916 and the *Britannia* had the misfortune to be the last British battleship sunk in the war in November 1918 off Cape Trafalgar.

With the advent of the entry of the United States into the war on 6 April 1917 as a result of the German policy of resuming unrestricted submarine warfare, the US Navy sent a squadron of dreadnought battleships to be attached to the Grand Fleet at Scapa Flow in December of that year.

The squadron consisted of the flagship USS *New York*, USS *Wyoming*, USS *Texas*, USS *Arkansas*, USS *Florida* and USS *Delaware*, together with escorting cruisers and destroyers, which soon had their own anchorages in the Flow. The ships were under the command of Rear Admiral Hugh Rodman, where they formed the 6th Battle Squadron of the Grand Fleet.

The American ships worked up to full efficiency in a remarkably short period of time to achieve the same high standards as the Grand Fleet. Their arrival was greeted as a welcome addition by the war weary crews, who had for the past four years kept the watch on the German fleet in their harbours across the North Sea. The American ships were employed on convoy duty and joined the other ships of the Grand Fleet on their regular North Sea sweeps. The flagship *New York* rammed and sank an enemy U-boat in the Pentland Firth on one of these patrols.

The *New York* class ships were of 27,240 tons' displacement, with a length of 562ft and a beam of 93ft. Their armament was rather mixed, with *New York* and *Texas* carrying ten 14in guns, while *Wyoming* and *Arkansas* were fitted with twelve 12in guns and *Florida* mounting only ten 12in guns, but with all ships carrying a 5in-gun secondary armament.

Direct drive turbines of 28,000–30,000hp gave the ships a speed of 22 knots. Their oil fuel gave them a radius of action of 8,000 miles and they carried a crew of 1,050. Their characteristic wire-cage masts were a distinguishing recognition feature of these American ships. The six ships of the squadron were also present as representatives of the US Government at the surrender of the German High Seas Fleet in November 1918. Equally important as the battleships were the support vessels that allowed them to operate efficiently far from their well-equipped home dockyards. The fleet repair ships were mobile workshops that could provide spare parts and repair facilities, being fully equipped with forges and machine tools that could cope with all but the most serious mechanical problems that would need to be carried out in a dry dock at a main naval base. A floating dock was, however, towed up to Scapa Flow, where it was able to take the largest of the fleet's battleships and proved a great asset throughout the war.

Five fleet repair ships were commissioned from converted merchantmen, not all of which worked at Scapa Flow. They were HMS *Aquarius* 2,800 tons, HMS *Assistance*

9,600 tons, HMS *Bacchus* 3,500 tons, HMS *Cyclops* 11,500 tons and HMS *Reliance* 3,250 tons. Of these most were sold at the end of the war, while *Cyclops* was converted to a submarine depot ship and continued in use, serving throughout the Second World War, being finally scrapped in 1947.

Destroyer depot ships were often old cruisers, but ex-merchant ships were deemed more convenient for use due to the larger compartment spaces available. Five converted merchant ships were in use from 1913 onwards. They were HMS *Diligence* 7,400 tons, HMS *Greenwich* 8,584 tons, HMS *Hecla* 5,600 tons, HMS *Sandhurst* 11,500 tons, HMS *Tyne* 3,590 tons and HMS *Woolwich* 3,400 tons, with *Greenwich* and *Sandhurst* surviving to serve in the Second World War.

The submarine depot ships were also originally eight or so old cruisers, but were substituted for the same reasons when suitable merchant ships became available as follows: HMS *Ambrose* 6,400 tons, HMS *Lucia* 5,800 tons, HMS *Pandora* 4,500 tons, HMS *Titania* 5,250 tons, HMS *Adamant* 935 tons, HMS *Alecto* 1,600 tons and HMS *Maidstone* 3,600 tons.

Mine laying was initially conducted by old converted warships, but it soon became apparent that high speeds were required to reach the locations in enemy waters in the hours of darkness and to get clear before daylight. Accordingly, destroyers, fast cruisers and submarines were increasingly used for this duty, together with fast cross-channel ships including two Canadian Pacific Railway steamers, HMS *Princess Irene* and HMS *Princess Margaret*, each carrying over 400 mines. The dangers inherent in performing these duties were demonstrated when the *Princess Irene* blew up at Sheerness in 1915 while loading mines.

Minesweeping was carried out by a variety of craft, with trawlers and steam drifters being employed in large numbers, that were augmented by over one hundred *Hunt* class and a further thirty-six paddle minesweepers designed to work in the shallow waters of estuaries.

Over 200 sloops were also built during the war that gave invaluable service, being used for convoy escort work and for a variety of other duties, including minesweeping, anti-submarine duties and as Q ships to counter the U-boat menace. The *Flower* class sloop *Azalea* was typical of the type, being of 1,200 tons' displacement, 262ft in length, with a beam of 33ft and powered by a four-cylinder triple expansion engine of 2,400ihp on a single shaft, giving a speed of 16 knots. Offensive armament consisted of two 4in or 12pdr guns and depth charges, with a complement of eighty officers and men.

Other smaller craft included the small steam-driven patrol or PC boats, eighty or so being built of around 600 tons, specially designed to hunt down U-boats and equipped with a hardened steel ram in the bows and carrying a 4in gun and two torpedo tubes. Turbines of 4,000ihp gave a speed of 23 knots.

Numerous Motor launches served on varied duties with the fleet, many of these being built in the USA being of 35 to 40 tons' displacement.

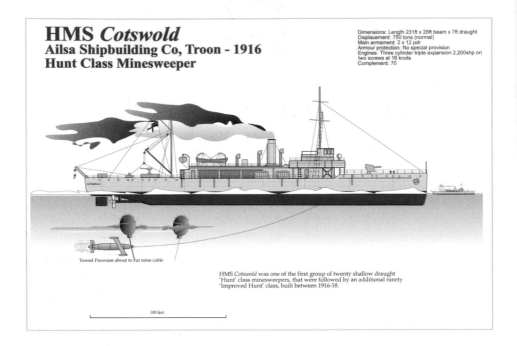

HMS *Cotswold*
Ailsa Shipbuilding Co, Troon - 1916
Hunt Class Minesweeper

Dimensions: Length 231ft x 28ft beam x 7ft draught
Displacement: 750 tons (normal)
Main armament: 2 x 12 pdr
Armour protection: No special provision
Engines: Three cylinder triple expansion 2,200shp on two screws at 16 knots
Complement: 70

Towed Peravane about to cut mine cable

HMS *Cotswold* was one of the first group of twenty shallow draught 'Hunt' class minesweepers, that were followed by an additional ninety 'Improved Hunt' class, built between 1916-18.

100 feet

CMBs were developed from pre-war racing motor boats to become the basis of a new type of fast torpedo boat, built largely at small yards on the Thames such as Thornycroft. The 70ft-long CMB of 24 tons, powered by 1,500ihp petrol engine, could reach 30 knots, carrying five torpedoes and six Lewis guns with a crew of six.

12

DESTROYERS AND TORPEDO BOATS

Probably the most charismatic class of ship, and the one that excited the imagination of the public on both sides of the conflict, was the destroyer or torpedo boat. They were produced in their hundreds, essential for the work of defending the larger and more valuable ships of the fleet such as the battleships.

A destroyer was small and fast, dashing into the attack under a storm of shells that left towering columns of water erupting around her, with thick black smoke pouring from her funnels and a great white bow wave curling away from her prow, as she heeled into a turn to deliver a torpedo attack on the enemy line, or to beat off an attack of enemy torpedo boats. Their dashing exploits were the stuff of legend on both sides in the Great War that spawned countless stories of heroism and called for a special type of officer and seamen to man them.

The early destroyers were cramped and uncomfortable, with the engines, boilers and machinery crammed into their narrow hulls, taking up most of the space below deck, and where the roaring furnaces, escaping steam from the boilers and thundering machinery, as the little ship pitched and rolled as it sped forward, made conditions in such a small space almost unbearable for the crews.

With the introduction of the Whitehead torpedo into the world's navies in the 1870s, various experiments were conducted in its use, being initially installed in battleships as a defensive weapon to be used against other battleships. Later, small steam picket boats were equipped to launch torpedoes against an enemy fleet at anchor, which was seen as their main tactical use, but the range of the early torpedoes was limited and the boats themselves too small and slow.

In the 1880s many foreign navies started to build larger, fast and highly manoeuvrable torpedo boats, seeing this as a relatively cheap way to counter the advantages of an enemy that possessed more battleships by using a flotilla of torpedo boats to attack warships in their harbours.

The threat of the torpedo boat in the 1880s and the increasing range of the torpedo itself required battleships and cruisers to mount batteries of 4in quick-firing breech-loaders as secondary armament as a defence against torpedo attack. In the late 1880s a new type of boat was introduced specifically to deal with the torpedo boat, known initially as the torpedo boat catcher or torpedo gun boats, being larger and more heavily armed than their prey.

The *Sharpshooter* of 1888 was a typical torpedo gunboat of the period, being of 730 tons' displacement, 230ft in length and armed with two 4.7in quick-firers, four 3pdrs and carrying five 14in torpedo tubes. Although they appeared to be a solution to the problem due to their large size, they proved to be slower than the torpedo boats they were set to catch.

An improved type of craft was devised with the building in 1887 at the Yarrow yard in Poplar of what was to be the first true torpedo boat destroyer. The *Kotaka* (Falcon) was built for the Japanese Navy according to their specifications, being of 203 tons and armed with four 1pdr guns and six 14in torpedo tubes. *Kotaka* was shipped out to Japan in parts, where she was assembled at Yokosuka Naval Arsenal, being capable of 20 knots and able to operate with the fleet at sea, where she participated in the Sino-Japanese War of 1894–95 and the Russo-Japanese War of 1904–05. Her builders, Yarrow, later stated that they considered that Japan had invented the modern destroyer.

With the continuing development of high-pressure boilers and ever more powerful triple expansion reciprocating engines, the speed of the new torpedo boat destroyers now being introduced rose rapidly, but they were often susceptible to mechanical breakdowns and unable to keep up top speed for prolonged periods of time.

In 1885 the Spanish Admiralty placed an order with the George Thomson Shipyard on Clydebank for a torpedo boat, the *Destructor*, with a displacement of 380 tons and armed with one 6pdr and four 3pdrs and capable of 22.5 knots. Upon completion, the *Destructor* made the passage from Falmouth to El Ferrol across the Bay of Biscay, demonstrating her sea-keeping qualities in a record 24 hours, making her the fastest ship in the world at the time. The design of the ship was said to have influenced the naval constructor Sir William White in the design concept for later destroyers.

It was not until the launching of HMS *Viper* in 1889, powered by Charles Parsons steam turbine machinery, that the Royal Navy had a vessel that could maintain sustained high speeds for long periods and was almost vibration free and quieter, which was a welcome relief to the crews, who in the earlier boats had to endure the constant thundering gyrations of the reciprocating engines. *Viper* was capable of over 33 knots and even 37 knots under forced draught, an astonishing speed for 1889 when a battleship like the *Canopus* could only manage 17 knots.

The *Viper* was of 375 tons, being 223ft on the waterline by 20ft beam and carried one 12pdr quick-firer on the foredeck, two 6pdrs and two 18in torpedo tubes, with turbines of 11,500hp. She had a whaleback forecastle, with a diminutive open bridge platform and narrow walkways past the boiler uptake casings that served as decks, while the combination of low freeboard and high speed ensured that she was a very wet ship inside and out and, as with the earlier boats, her interior was still crammed full with steam pipes, boilers and engines that left little space for crew accommodation or any semblance of comfort.

Following the success of the *Viper*, the Admiralty ordered forty-two boats to a similar specification from fourteen different builders between 1889 and 1902 that varied in aspects of design and layout, although the specified armament was universal.

The early Whitehead torpedo of the period had a range of around 3,000yd at 26 knots, carrying a warhead of 200lb of explosive. However, with the introduction of the heater torpedo in the early 1900s, performance had greatly improved so that by the outbreak of the First World War the British Mk X 21 torpedo of 1914 had a range of 8,000yd at 38 knots, carrying a warhead of 500lb of Torpex, which greatly increased the destroyer's offensive capacity.

This increased threat to capital ships was appreciated by commanders on both sides, dictating that in the event of a torpedo attack by destroyers the approved response was to turn away to allow the ships to comb the tracks. This method of dealing with an attack could result in the ships being attacked, losing contact with the enemy fleet if they were on a parallel course until it was safe to return to the original course.

So it could be seen that, even though a torpedo attack was unsuccessful, it could aid the tactical position of the retiring fleet by increasing the distance between them and allowing them a better chance of escape. It should be noted that a turn towards a torpedo attack was also available to the commander, allowing him, conversely, to gain on his retiring enemy while avoiding torpedoes, but this was generally considered to be a more risky manoeuvre and rarely employed in action.

The main builders of the new destroyers and torpedo boats were some of the smaller boat builders, such as Thornycroft, Yarrow and Hawthorn, while larger yards like Denny and Palmers also produced their own designs. The first class of torpedo boat destroyers delivered during 1893–95 were the A class of 27-knot turtle-backs. These boats were between 180 and 206ft in length, with a beam of 20ft and a draught of 12ft.

As stated, coming from a variety of builders, they varied in detail, but their average displacement was between 200–300 tons. Their machinery consisted of two sets of triple expansion engines with water tube boilers, developing 4,000hp on two shafts to give a speed of a very respectable 27 knots. Their armament comprised one 12pdr gun on the turtle back forecastle, plus three to five 6pdrs and two 18in torpedo tubes and carried a complement of fifty-five.

All of these first-generation destroyers served in the First World War, largely on coastal patrol and harbour protection work. Only one, HMS *Lightning*, was lost to mines and two others sunk as result of collisions.

Several of these vessels were sent out to serve on the China station, a long voyage, which says much of these little ships for their sea-keeping qualities, if not for their crew comfort.

Between 1895 and 1902, seventy-six larger turtle-back destroyers were added to the Admiralty list of the B, C and D classes of 30 knot boats, of gradually increasing size, with the D class being of between 310 to 440 tons, with a length of 210ft and a beam of 21ft.

The *River* class of 1903 was an attempt to improve the sea-keeping qualities of destroyers by giving them higher forecastles, in imitation of the German torpedo boats, and although these boats were slightly slower at 26 knots, this speed could be maintained in a seaway, where in the turtle-backs speed would fall off after a short period steaming at high speed. Armament was similar to the earlier boats, with one 12pdr quick-firer and five 6pdr guns being mounted.

The first destroyers to be considered to be truly ocean going were the F class of 1907, these being the first of the famous *Tribal* class. In their design Admiral Fisher had insisted that they should be capable of 33 knots, and to achieve this speed required an unprecedented increase in power to 15,000hp, or twice that of the previous class. They were 270ft in length, with a displacement of 890 tons. Powered by turbine engines developing 13,000hp on three screws, these boats could reach 33 to 36 knots. They were more heavily armed than their predecessors, with five 12pdrs and two 18in torpedo tubes.

The Tribals were the first class to be oil-fired but had a limited fuel capacity of around 100 tons, and while they were excellent ships this defect limited their endurance due to their high fuel consumption. Of this group of ships, HMS *Tartar* reached 37.4 knots on her trials, making her the fastest ship of her day in 1907. All twelve ships of the *Tribal* class led active lives during the war, with HMS *Ghurka* being mined off Dungeness in 1917 and HMS *Maori* off Zeebrugge in 1915. Perhaps the most fascinating story involving these ships is the phoenix-like rebirth of two of them after being severely damaged in action.

On 21 October 1916 the destroyer HMS *Nubian* was coming to the end of her patrol off Folkestone when she was hit by a torpedo from a submerged U-boat, blowing off her bow. With her pumps working and the engine room still functioning, she remained afloat and able to proceed, being beached near Dover, where the wreck was examined by Admiralty inspectors.

Just over two weeks later, on 8 November, a second of the class, HMS *Zulu*, was mined off Gravelines, Dunkirk, blowing half her stern off. Again, the damaged ship remained afloat and was towed into Calais harbour. The *Zulu* had already led a busy life in the war, capturing the German barque *Perhns* on the first day of the

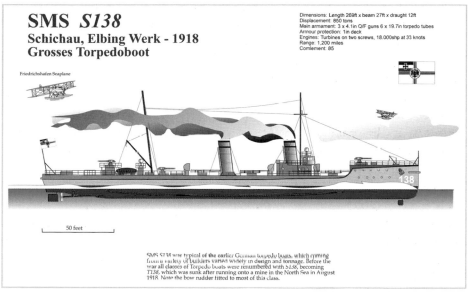

SMS *S138*
Schichau, Elbing Werk - 1918
Grosses Torpedoboot

Dimensions: Length 269ft x beam 27ft x draught 12ft
Displacement: 850 tons
Main armament: 3 x 4.1in Q/F guns 6 x 19.7in torpedo tubes
Armour protection: 1in deck
Engines: Turbines on two screws, 18,000shp at 33 knots
Range: 1,200 miles
Comlement: 85

Friedrichshafen Seaplane

50 feet

SMS S138 was typical of the earlier German torpedo boats, which coming from a variety of builders varied widely in design and tonnage. Before the war all classes of Torpedo boats were renumbered with S138, becoming T138, which was sunk after running onto a mine in the North Sea in August 1918. Note the bow rudder fitted to most of this class.

HMS *Zubian*
Hawthorne Leslie, Tyneside, Thornycroft, Woolston - 1909
F (Tribal) Class Torpedo-Boat Destroyer

Dimensions: Length 280ft x beam 26ft x 12ft draught
Displacement: 1,090 tons (normal)
Main armament: 2 x 4in Q/F, 2 x 18in torpedo tubes
Armour protection: 1in deck
Engines: Turbines on 3 shafts,15,500hp at 35 knots
Range: 3,500 n.miles at 15 knots
Complement: 72

100 feet

Area where hulls were joined

The after part of HMS *Zulu* was destroyed by a mine, whilst the bow section of HMS *Nubian* was wrecked by a German torpedo. The fore portion of the *Zulu* and the after portion of the *Nubian* were salvaged and joined together to form a new ship, the *Zubian*, thus HMS *Zubian* acquired three battle **honours before** being laid up in 1919.

war and later involved in almost continuous patrols in the Dover Straits and in supporting the coastal monitors bombarding German positions at the seaward end of the Western Front.

After inspection, *Zulu* and *Nubian* were both towed to Chatham dockyard, where fore section of *Zulu* and the after part of *Nubian* were joined together, despite there being a 4in difference in the beam of both vessels.

As *Nubian*, the newly created ship served throughout the remainder of the war with distinction, sinking the German mine-laying submarine *UC50* off the Essex coast in 1916 by ramming and depth charge. The *Nubian* thus acquired three battle honours before being sent for breaking in 1919.

The ship that followed the Tribals was a one-off experiment built by Cammell Laird of Birkenhead as a flotilla leader and completed in 1907.

HMS *Swift* was almost the size of a light cruiser, being 2,200 tons' displacement, with a length of 353ft and 34ft beam, with turbines of a massive 45,000hp. She could reach 40 knots, being originally armed with four 4in guns, with the two on the forecastle being replaced by a single 6in weapon in 1913, this being the heaviest gun mounted on a destroyer. Although she was referred to as the fastest ship in the Navy, she proved to be unsatisfactory, with recurring mechanical breakdowns and a high fuel consumption, at a speed of 27 miles per hour from a capacity of only 180 tons.

On 20 April 1917, together with HMS *Broke*, she engaged six German destroyers in the Dover Straits, during which *Swift* torpedoed the German destroyer *G85* but received gunfire damage herself. In the meantime, the *Broke* had rammed the *G42* where, with both ships locked together, hand to hand fighting broke out on the decks before the German crew of the sinking ship surrendered. The other four German destroyers retired from the action and the *Swift* went to the aid of *Broke*, rescuing the German crew of the sinking *G42*.

Originally planned by Admiral Fisher to be a new class of high-speed destroyer leader, and originally attached to the 4th Torpedo Boat Flotilla of the Grand Fleet, her performance was judged unsatisfactory, as were her sea-keeping qualities that made her unsuitable to operate with the fleet, despite her large size. No further boats of this class were built.

As war approached the Admiralty recognised the need for uniformity in the design of destroyers so that they could operate in flotillas of fifteen to twenty ships that would all have comparable performance.

The sixteen ships of the G or *Basilisk* class of 1910 conformed to this requirement and returned to coal-fired boilers, as it was considered that the supply of oil could be compromised in the event of war. These were the last British destroyers to burn coal.

These three-funnelled ships were projected under the 1908–09 estimates, and were 270ft in length with a beam of 28ft, making them roomier than the earlier ships. They displaced 900 tons, while turbines of 12,500hp on three shafts gave a speed of 28 knots. Armament consisted of a 4in Mk VIII breech-loading gun, three 12lb quick firers and two 21in torpedo tubes.

In order to improve their sea-keeping qualities, the bridge was placed higher and the bandstand which mounted the 4in gun was also positioned higher to fight in heavy seas.

The subsequent H class of twenty ships laid down in 1910, the I class of 1911 consisting of thirty ships, and the K class of a further twenty ships of 1913, were the last to be launched before the war and between them were the most modern destroyers available at its outbreak.

The L class were the first British class to exceed 1,000 tons' displacement, at 1,072 tons, with engines of 24,000hp giving a speed of 31 knots, and were more heavily armed with three 4in guns and four 21in torpedo tubes. The effectiveness of these powerful destroyers was amply demonstrated on 17 October 1914 at the Battle of Texel when four L class destroyers, accompanied by a light cruiser, completely destroyed four German torpedo boats.

Following the Battle of the Heligoland Bight in August 1914, the High Seas Fleet were under orders to avoid further large-scale engagements, naval activity being reduced to the occasional coastal raid and minelaying in British coastal waters, where, despite the absence of German capital ships, their light forces continued to operate.

Performing a routine patrol off the Island of Texel at 2.00 p.m., the light cruiser *Undaunted*, commanded by Captain Cecil Fox and accompanied by the destroyers HMS *Lennox*, *Lance*, HMS *Loyal* and HMS *Legion*, encountered the German 7th Half Flotilla of four torpedo boats under the command of Korvettenkapitan Georg Thiele en route to lay mines in the Thames Estuary. As the British ships closed, the German torpedo craft made no attempt to challenge the approaching ships, nor was any attempt to retire initially made.

The British squadron was more heavily armed than the German ships, with *Undaunted* carrying two 6in guns and the four destroyers mounting three 4in guns apiece. The German torpedo boats S115, 117, 118 and 119, on the other hand, were of 1898 vintage and carried three 4pdr guns apiece, but did possess three 18in torpedo tubes that constituted a significant danger to the British squadron.

The German ships had at first mistaken the British ships for German reinforcements but, realising their mistake, began to scatter. By then, however, the *Undaunted* was within range and opened fire on S118, while *Lance* and *Lennox* attacked S115 and S119. *Legion* and *Loyal* joined the flagship in the pursuit of S118 and S117. Although the S119 managed to hit the destroyer *Lance* with a torpedo, it failed to explode and by 3.45 p.m. all four German ships were battered sinking wrecks. Total German casualties were four torpedo boats sunk, 300 killed and thirty prisoners taken, while on the British side losses were three destroyers damaged and five wounded.

A fortunate windfall from the encounter came when on 30 November a British trawler fishing the area recovered a lead-bound box containing German codebooks, which was delivered to code breakers in Room 40 at the Admiralty. This find aided the deciphering of future German secret messages.

The larger M class that followed were produced in four groups. The first eighty-five ships, known as the Admiralty M class, were three-funnelled boats of 1,042 tons' displacement, with turbines on three shafts delivering 25,000hp. Armament was increased over the previous group of ships to three 4in guns and four 21in torpedo tubes. Two other Hawthorn M types with two funnels and six Thornycroft Ms, with two funnels of similar displacement were also built.

Two further and very similar groups of ships, the R and S classes consisting of two funnels with geared turbines and capable of 36 knots, followed, making a grand total of 163 ships for the M, R and S groups.

The following V and W classes represented a great step forward and were proportionally larger, being of 1,340 tons' displacement, with geared turbines of 27,000hp They were of 312ft in length and 30ft beam and were true ocean-going destroyers, again armed with four 4in guns and one 3in gun, plus a heavier torpedo armament of six 21in torpedo tubes.

Fifty-one of this class were built, with the majority surviving to serve in the Second World War. These boats were designed to deal with the new generation of large German destroyers being built at the end of 1917, namely the V115 class, built as destroyer leaders and of 2,300 tons' displacement, the size of a light cruiser. These large ships were armed with four 5.9in guns and four 23in torpedo tubes, plus the ability to carry forty mines at 37 knots. On paper, they were the most powerful destroyers in the world at that time and should have been formidable opponents, but in the event only two of the type was built, as they failed to come up to specification and were top-heavy, given to rolling badly in heavy weather.

German destroyer development generally followed similar lines to the British, but favoured a heavier torpedo armament than their British counterparts. A typical example of the German torpedo boat was the *S138* of 1906 that took an active part in the war, serving in the Battle of Jutland . The *S138* (later renumbered *T138*) was built at the Schichau-Werke, Elbing. Completed in 1907, she was 269ft in length with a beam of 27ft and displaced 850 tons. Turbine propulsion of 18,000hp on two shafts gave a speed of 33 knots and had a range of 1,200 miles and a crew of eighty-five. To aid manoeuvrability, many of these ships were fitted with an additional rudder under the bow.

This particular torpedo boat was lost to a mine off Ostend in August 1918, not an unusual fate for torpedo boats and destroyers; the Royal Navy losing sixty-seven destroyers from all causes during the war.

At Jutland sixty-four German torpedo boats took part in the action where, surprisingly, considering the fierceness of the encounter, only five were lost against the eight British destroyers. For their time, they were exceptionally heavily armed, with three 4.1 Q/F guns and six 19.7in torpedo tubes and a 1in armoured deck.

The German torpedo flotillas at Jutland were bravely led and their torpedo attacks on Jellicoe's battle squadrons on two occasions caused the British line to turn away, saving Admiral Scheer's battleships from certain destruction.

The United States, with its need to maintain a presence in both the Atlantic and Pacific Oceans, was greatly aided by the completion of the Panama Canal in 1914 that enabled it to rapidly transfer warships from the east to the west coast or vice versa.

The US Navy similarly built large numbers of destroyers during the war which, class for class, were larger and possessed of greater range than contemporary German craft.

Of the destroyers that accompanied the US 6th Battle Squadron when it joined the Grand Fleet in November 1917, the USS *Wickes* was one of a class of no less than 111 ships, while with its great productive capacity between 1917 and 1923 under the War Emergency Programme eleven shipyards produced a total of 273 ships of a generally similar design, being flush decked and carrying four funnels, and known colloquially as four stackers.

The *Wickes* was large for a destroyer, having a length of 314ft and a beam of 30ft on a displacement of 1,240 tons. An armament of four 4in Q/F guns was carried, together with six 21in torpedo tubes. She carried a complement of 105 crew and had an exceptional range for the period of 5,000 miles. Engine power varied from 18,000 to 27,000hp and speed from 30 to 35 knots when new.

After the war most of this class of ships, after performing convoy duty work in the Atlantic and working with the Grand Fleet, were laid up in reserve, from where at the beginning of the Second World War under the Lend Lease agreement between Britain and the United States fifty of these ships were leased to the

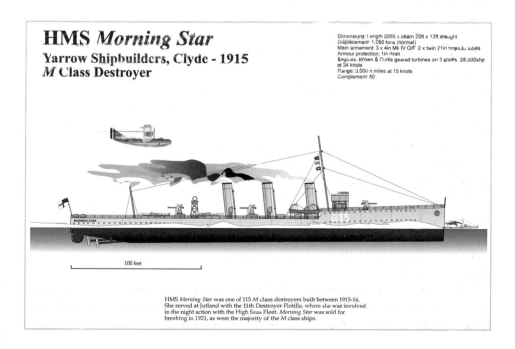

HMS *Morning Star*
Yarrow Shipbuilders, Clyde - 1915
M Class Destroyer

Dimensions: Length 288ft x beam 25ft x 12ft draught
Displacement: 1,050 tons (normal)
Main armament: 3 x 4in Mk IV Q/F 2 x twin 21in torpedo tubes
Armour protection: 1in deck
Engines: Brown & Curtis geared turbines on 3 shafts 25,000shp at 34 knots
Range: 3,000 n.miles at 15 knots
Complement: 80

100 feet

HMS *Morning Star* was one of 115 M class destroyers built between 1915-16. She served at Jutland with the 11th Destroyer Flotilla, where she was involved in the night action with the High Seas Fleet. *Morning Star* was sold for breaking in 1921, as were the majority of the M class ships.

Royal Navy in exchange for 99-year leases on British bases in the Caribbean and elsewhere.

In British service they were known as the *Town* class, with the *Wickes* being renamed *Monmouth* and spending her service with the Royal Canadian Navy on convoy and patrol work, being finally sent to the breakers in 1946.

In May 1916 intelligence reports being analysed in Room 40 at the Admiralty in Whitehall indicated the High Seas Fleet were preparing to put to sea in force, which subsequently was to reveal itself as the great fleet action of the First World War: Jutland.

During this epic encounter the destroyer flotillas played an important and active part in the battle, where the way they were employed tactically ensured that they would find themselves invariably in a position of great danger between the two fleets. During the night action, the German fleet heading south-east towards its base at Wilhelmshaven crossed the rear of the British fleet that had been cruising on a divergent course seeking them. In the darkness in a time before the advent of radar, although only separated by 12 miles or so, the German ships passed behind the searching battle squadrons of the Grand Fleet to escape to safety.

In the aftermath of the battle and the perceived failure to punish the High Seas Fleet more fully, or indeed defeat it decisively, much criticism was levelled at the commanders of the scouting cruiser and destroyer groups that had made contact with the main portion of the German fleet in the darkness. They had failed to fully report these contacts in a comprehensive way that would make the situation clear to Admiral Jellicoe as he led the fleet towards the Horns Reef, where at 3.00 a.m. on the morning of 1 June he finally abandoned the pursuit and led his battle-damaged ships back to port.

Jellicoe was to complain in later years that the Admiralty had failed to pass on intercepted signals from the German fleet indicating Scheer's position and speed, which they were reading in wireless traffic on an hourly basis and that would have been of incalculable value to the Commander-in-Chief. As the two fleets crossed their tracks a series of confused night actions occurred, with ships of opposing forces stumbling into each other in the darkness, where the brilliant glare of searchlights and the blast of gunfire close at hand were the first indications of the enemy presence.

Typical of these encounters was that of the 12th and 4th Destroyer Flotillas at 11.00 p.m. Captain Stirling aboard the flotilla leader HMS *Faulknor* commanding the Twelfth Flotilla was leading fourteen boats in the darkness, sailing on a gradually converging south-easterly course that was about to cross less than 4 miles behind the ships of the 1st and 5th Battle Squadrons and, unknown to Jellicoe, parallel to the leading ship of the retreating German line led by SMS *Westfalen*.

Six miles to the south-west, the Fourth Flotilla, commanded by Captain Wintour aboard HMS *Tipperary*, led the eleven boats of his flotilla in line ahead, comprising the destroyers HMS *Spitfire*, HMS *Sparrowhawk*, HMS *Contest*, HMS *Garland*, HMS *Broke*, HMS *Achates*, HMS *Ambuscade*, HMS *Ardent*, HMS *Fortune*, HMS *Porpoise* and HMS *Unity*.

At 11.00 p.m. Garland lookouts reported to Captain Wintour destroyers to starboard, but as they approached it became apparent that the ships were not destroyers but battleships. Unsure of the identity and nationality of the fast approaching ships, Wintour flashed the challenge. Almost immediately, *Tipperary*'s challenge was answered with dazzling searchlights illuminating his ship and a storm of shellfire. Within less than a minute, *Tipperary* was reduced to a blazing wreck, her bridge and all on it swept away in a blast of fire, as she fell out of the line.

In the darkness, the first five destroyers of the flotilla pressed home their torpedo attacks and opened fire with their deck guns, while the German battleships blasted away with their main armament at maximum depression because the range was so close. The *Spitfire*, next in line of the *Tipperary*, swung to starboard to avoid the wreckage of the blazing destroyer. Her captain, Lieutenant Commander Trelawney, then turned his ship to starboard to attempt to rescue the destroyer's crew. As he did so, he unknowingly passed between the tracks of the first three German ships, when on his starboard bow he suddenly saw close at hand the towering bow of the second German battleship in the line, SMS *Nassau*, which, together with the other ships of the German 1st Battle Squadron having turned away from the torpedo attacks, were now turning to port to regain their south-easterly course.

Too late, the *Spitfire* attempted to avoid being run down by the massive battleship, but with a rending crash of metal the two ships came together port bow to port bow. As the *Spitfire* ground past the *Nassau*, the battleship depressed her forward 11in guns and fired a salvo at point-blank range that flew overhead, but the effect of the blast was powerful enough to wipe away the *Spitfire*'s bridge, killing most of her bridge crew and splitting her hull open like a tin can.

Scraping past her mighty opponent, the heavily damaged *Spitfire* drew off into the protecting darkness with 20ft of side plating ripped from the *Nassau*'s hull firmly wedged to her bow; evidence of her close encounter. Despite her grievous injuries, the damaged *Spitfire* limped home, and was subsequently repaired to fight again.

Although none of the British torpedoes had found a mark in the attack, the cruisers of the German Second Scouting group which had been accompanying the German battleships to port were thrown into confusion. After midnight, in the melee, the light cruiser SMS *Elbing* was in turn rammed by the battleship *Posen*, which tore a hole in her hull, flooding the engine room and the ship, although it was not in danger of sinking. A torpedo boat took off most of the crew and efforts were made to save the ship, but when enemy destroyers were sighted at 2.00 a.m. the captain ordered the *Elbing* scuttled, fortunately with only four of her crew lost.

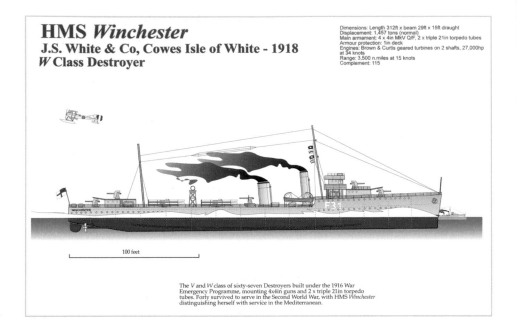

HMS *Winchester*
J.S. White & Co, Cowes Isle of White - 1918
W Class Destroyer

Dimensions: Length 312ft x beam 29ft x 15ft draught
Displacement: 1,457 tons (normal)
Main armament: 4 x 4in MkV Q/F, 2 x triple 21in torpedo tubes
Armour protection: 1in deck
Engines: Brown & Curtis geared turbines on 2 shafts, 27,000hp at 34 knots
Range: 3,500 n.miles at 15 knots
Complement: 115

100 feet

The *V* and *W* class of sixty-seven Destroyers built under the 1916 War Emergency Programme, mounting 4x4in guns and 2 x triple 21in torpedo tubes. Forty survived to serve in the Second World War, with HMS *Winchester* distinguishing herself with service in the Mediterranean.

The Fourth Flotilla now was under the command of Commander Allen in the *Broke*, which, followed by *Sparrowhawk*, *Garland*, *Contest*, *Ardent*, *Fortune* and *Porpoise*, now returned to the attack. Leading his force toward the German line, Allen sighted the cruiser *Rostock*. Once again the German line seized the initiative and the Fourth Flotilla was again swept by searchlight and a storm of shellfire, initially from *Rostock* and then from the 11in guns of *Westfalen* and SMS *Rheinland*.

The *Broke* was immediately reduced to a burning wreck, with her helm jammed hard to port and careering at high speed towards the unfortunate *Sparrowhawk*, which was turning to fire her torpedoes when the *Broke* crashed into her, locking both ships together.

The following ship, *Contest*, also managed to ram into the *Sparrowhawk*'s stern, where the blazing wreckage attracted still more unwanted attention of enemy ships, until the *Broke* drifted away. After a hazardous voyage of over two days, eventually made safety in the River Tyne.

The *Sparrowhawk* was taken in tow by the destroyer HMS *Marksman* but had to be abandoned the next day, while the *Conquest* also made it safely back to port and, after repair, re-joined the fleet to serve to the end of the war with honour.

The Fourth Flotilla still bravely pressed their attacks on the German line, but in so doing quickly lost the *Fortune* when again the *Westfalen* and five other battleships opened fire at close range. The *Fortune* was quickly reduced to a flaming wreck and sank, while the *Porpoise* was under heavy fire but managed to limp away to safety on the Humber.

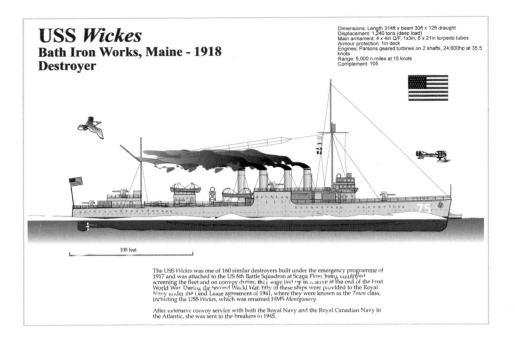

USS *Wickes*
Bath Iron Works, Maine - 1918
Destroyer

Dimensions: Length 314ft x beam 30ft x 12ft draught
Displacement: 1,240 tons (deep load)
Main armament: 4 x 4in Q/F, 1x3in, 6 x 21in torpedo tubes
Armour protection: 1in deck
Engines: Parsons geared turbines on 2 shafts, 24,600hp at 35.5 knots
Range: 5,000 n.miles at 15 knots
Complement: 105

100 feet

The USS *Wickes* was one of 160 similar destroyers built under the emergency programme of 1917 and was attached to the US 6th Battle Squadron at Scapa Flow, being employed screening the fleet and on convoy duties, they were laid up in reserve at the end of the First World War. During the Second World War, fifty of these ships were provided to the Royal Navy under the Lend Lease agreement of 1941, where they were known as the *Town* class, including the USS *Wickes*, which was renamed HMS *Montgomery*.

After extensive convoy service with both the Royal Navy and the Royal Canadian Navy in the Atlantic, she was sent to the breakers in 1945.

The remaining ships of the flotilla scattered to save themselves, but not before Lieutenant Commander Marsden of the *Ardent*, attempting to escape, was also sunk as he once again blundered into the German line.

Despite all their bravery, and being responsible for two German cruisers being sunk, the Fourth Flotilla had been destroyed or scattered. Twice the ships of the Fourth Flotilla had bravely thrown themselves against the might of the German 1st Battle Squadron and their gallantry was in the highest traditions of the service.

13

THE DARDANELLES OPERATION

From classical times at the eastern end of the Mediterranean, the Dardanelles, which lead through the Sea of Marmara to the Bosporus to what, at that time, was the Turkish capital Constantinople, have been the crossroads between Asia and Europe. Invading armies and ideas have crossed this narrow stretch of water, determining the fate of nations from ancient times. The area has always had great strategic importance, as it controls the only entrance into the Black Sea. From the time when the fabled city of Troy was built on its southern shore over three millennia ago, to Allied attempts to force the straits in the First World War, the Dardanelles have been constantly fought over.

In August 1914 the two German cruisers *Goeben* and *Breslau*, eluding the pursuit of Admiral Troubridge's squadron, found sanctuary in the Dardanelles, where the Turkish Government allowed them free, unchallenged passage through the Sea of Marmara to Constantinople.

At this stage of the war Turkey was uncommitted and neutral and, under the existing international agreements concerning the passage of war vessels between the Black Sea and the Mediterranean, they should have refused them entry. Instead, the Turkish Government, in the shape of two soldiers of fortune Enver Pasha and Talaat Bey, had decided to throw in their lot with the German Empire and arranged the purchase of the two cruisers.

Germany had for some years been establishing a relationship with the Ottoman Empire, supplying military advisors and weapons, as they saw the Turks as a possible future ally against Russian expansion. Turkey had for years been considered the sick man of Europe and was to all intents and purposes bankrupt, so the purchase was worth no more than the paper it was written on.

Following the capture by the Royal Navy of a Turkish torpedo boat in September in Turkish waters, the Turkish Government closed the Dardanelles to all foreign shipping on 1 October 1914, in contravention of international agreements. This was followed by a violent anti-British campaign in the press engendered by British actions and for the earlier seizure by the British Government of two battleships being built in Britain for the Ottoman Empire.

In response to these provocative actions, a part of the British Mediterranean fleet under the command of Admiral Sackville Carden was concentrated at the island of Tendos at the mouth of the Strait on 27 October.

From the Turkish point of view, the acquisition of the German ships was a timely addition to their navy – replacements for those seized in British yards, the *Rashadiea* of 23,000 tons and the *Sultan Osman I*, a huge 27,000-ton warship mounting fourteen 12in guns, at that time the most powerful battleship in the world.

As part of the sale agreement of the German ships, the German crews under their commander Rear Admiral Wilhelm Souchon were in effect transferred to the Turkish Navy, which suited German plans relative to compromising Russian naval strength in the Black Sea.

The German crews adopted the fez headgear but were otherwise in all but name a German squadron based in the Black Sea.

Britain and France immediately imposed a blockade on the Dardanelles to ensure that the two cruisers did not emerge again into the Mediterranean and were for the time being satisfied that two dangerous German warships were isolated in the Black Sea out of harm's way.

The possession of the two ships, renamed *Yavuz Sultan Selim* and *Midilli*, completely changed the situation in the Black Sea, where the Russian fleet based at Sevastopol had no ships that could match the two ex-German cruisers in gun power.

On 28 October the Ottoman fleet led by the *Yavuz Sultan Selim* raided the Russian harbours of Sevastopol and Odessa, where despite some small success sinking two small gunboats, the Russian Black Sea fleet was still left intact. Russia declared war on the Ottoman Empire on 2 November 1914, with Great Britain following suit on 6 November.

On 3 November the fleet at Tendos weighed anchor and sailed to the mouth of the Dardanelles where the battle-cruisers *Indefatigable* and *Indomitable*, together with the French battleships *Verité* and *Suffren*, laid down a 10-minute fire on the outer forts, with two objectives in view: first to demonstrate British naval power and secondly to determine the range and arcs of fire of the Turkish guns.

Lacking any form of air reconnaissance during the operation, the British fleet commander Admiral Carden was unaware of the severity of the damage that short bombardment had inflicted on the forts. Although one lucky shot hit a magazine in the Sedd el Bahr fortress, causing great damage, this was not to be repeated in later attacks, due to the flat trajectories of the naval gunfire, where the short range militated against plunging shellfire that would have better suited the purpose.

This premature attack only alerted the Turks to British intention and allowed them to strengthen what were already formidable coastal defences on the Gallipoli peninsula.

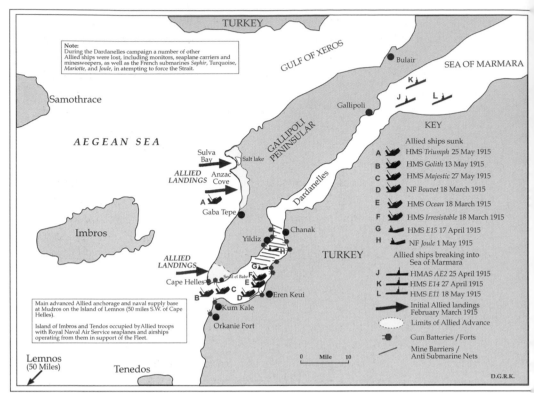

The Dardanelles and the Gallipoli Campaign, February 1915 - January 1916

As far back as 1906 the British General staff had discussed the possibility of forcing the Straits by a combined military and naval operation in the event of war with Turkey, but had come to the conclusion that such an adventure would be extremely costly both in ships and difficult for the Army to gain a foothold due to the extensive fortifications, and should be avoided as a policy, and so it was later to prove.

However, one Cabinet member, Winston Churchill, at that time still First Lord of the Admiralty as early as September 1914, proposed to Prime Minister Herbert Asquith the setting up of a second front to break the stalemate that had already begun to develop with the start of static trench warfare on the Western Front. He also saw such a demonstration as a way of diverting the Turks from attacking Egypt and seizing the all-important Suez Canal. The canal was the gateway to India and vitally important for trade and bringing Empire troops from India, Australia and New Zealand to the battlefields of France and the Middle East.

Initially, plans to open two new fronts were proposed for consideration, with Admiral Fisher devising a scheme for a naval attack to land troops on the German coastline in the Frisian Islands, and even had the special light draught battle-cruisers HMS *Courageous*, HMS *Glorious*, HMS *Furious* and other vessels laid down for the purpose.

This scheme was considered by the War Council to be too risky and wisely was taken no further. However, Winston Churchill's plan to launch a purely naval attack on the Dardanelles was accepted with the intention of forcing the Strait and entering the Black Sea, where it was naively expected that the appearance of a combined British and French fleet off Constantinople would persuade the Turks to surrender.

Churchill and Admiral Fisher disagreed about the form such an action should take, with Fisher putting forward his contention that a purely naval attack would fail and would have to be supported by a military action with the landing of troops on the Gallipoli peninsula and advancing on Constantinople.

In January 1915 Churchill requested the commander of the Royal Navy's Mediterranean Fleet, Vice-Admiral S. Carden, to produce a plan for forcing the Strait, employing battleships, submarines and minesweepers. On 13 January the Government War Council approved the plan. A fleet was put together comprising two modern pre-dreadnought battleships HMS *Lord Nelson* and HMS *Agamemnon*, armed with 12in and 9.2in guns, and ten pre dreadnought battleships, HMS *Ocean*, HMS *Albion*, HMS *Vengeance*, HMS *Majestic*, HMS *Prince George*, HMS *Canopus*, HMS *Irresistible* and HMS *Cornwallis*, all with four 12in guns, together with HMS *Swiftsure* and HMS *Triumph* with four 10in guns apiece.

Also included were the new super-dreadnought *Queen Elizabeth* with eight 15in guns, the battle-cruiser *Inflexible*, minesweepers and other small craft, together with a French squadron of four pre-dreadnoughts (*Suffren*, *Charlemagne*, *St Louis* and *Gaulois*, all armed with 12in guns) and a Russian cruiser.

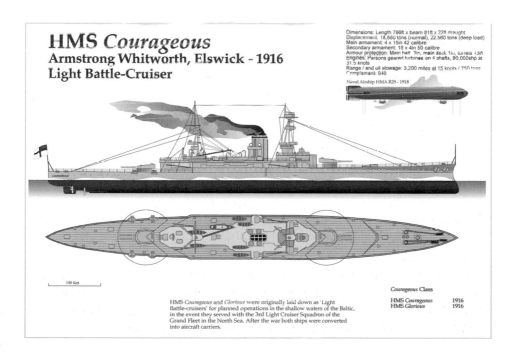

HMS *Courageous*
Armstrong Whitworth, Elswick - 1916
Light Battle-Cruiser

Dimensions: Length 786ft x beam 81ft x 22ft draught
Displacement: 18,560 tons (normal), 22,560 tons (deep load)
Main armament: 4 x 15in 42 calibre
Secondary armament: 18 x 4in 50 calibre
Armour protection: Main belt 3in, main deck 1in, turrets 13in
Engines: Parsons geared turbines on 4 shafts, 90,000shp at 31.5 knots
Range / and oil stowage: 3,200 miles at 15 knots / 750 tons
Complement: 848

Naval Airship HMA R29 - 1918

100 feet

HMS *Courageous* and *Glorious* were originally laid down as 'Light Battle-cruisers' for planned operations in the shallow waters of the Baltic, in the event they served with the 3rd Light Cruiser Squadron of the Grand Fleet in the North Sea. After the war both ships were converted into aircraft carriers.

Courageous Class

HMS *Courageous*	1916
HMS *Glorious*	1916

On 19 February Admiral Carden led ten battleships into action against the outer forts. The *Cornwallis* and *Vengeance* opened fire at 12,000yd on the Orkanie fort, with the remaining ships firing from 8,000yd. However, it soon became evident that the ships needed to be anchored as the gunners were experiencing great difficulty in spotting the fall of shot on the flat, featureless landscape, where only a direct hit on a gun position or a magazine could knock it out.

After 8 hours of bombardment in which only 140 shells had been fired and with little to show for their efforts and with the forts left largely undamaged the fleet withdrew.

The next day a further bombardment took place that had better results, as other ships had been stationed on the flanks of the battleships to accurately record fall of shot.

Among the ships was the new *Queen Elizabeth*, whose 15in guns with only eighteen rounds quickly destroyed two large guns at Cape Helles, while the older *Irresistible* firing thirty-five 12in rounds destroyed the fort at Orkanie.

In the afternoon, the battleships moved closer inshore, bringing their secondary armament into play, silencing all the outer forts. Landing-parties of marines were put ashore at Kum Kale and Orkanie, spending two days ashore placing demolition charges in the forts and destroying fifty guns. At the same time the minesweepers were able to clear several of the layers of minefields the Turks had laid in the entrance to the Strait.

The inner defences proved harder to deal with where the Straits widen out above Seddulbahir, the range being too great for accurate firing. For the first time the Allied warships became targets for the mobile batteries, which included 6in howitzers, positioned on either shoreline.

Between 2 and 8 March, three more bombardments took place that proved ineffective. The *Queen Elizabeth*, firing indirectly over the Gallipoli peninsula at 14,000yd range, was hit seventeen times by the mobile artillery and only managed to fire at a rate of one round per hour due to spotting problems, while throughout the conflict no guns were put out of action in the forts.

The *Queen Elizabeth* came under fire from an unexpected source when, while firing on Fort Chemenlik on the Asiatic shore, the Turks brought up the old pre-dreadnought *Hayreddin Barbarossa*, the ex-German *Kurfurst Friedrich Wilhelm* built in 1894. A great advantage of the old ship was that her 11in guns had an elevation of 25° and her first three rounds landed near the British ship, causing her to move out to sea an additional 1,000yd, as it was assumed due to the plunging trajectory that the shells had come from onshore howitzers.

The *Queen Elizabeth* identified and destroyed the spotting position, but soon found herself under plunging shell fire, with the *Hayreddin Barbarossa* hitting the battleship with three shells on her armoured belt below the waterline.

As the deck armour of ships of the period was not designed to withstand plunging fire, it was possible that the old Turkish battleship could seriously damage or even sink a modern dreadnought fresh from the shipyard. The Admiralty belatedly decided that the *Queen Elizabeth* was too valuable to be risked in such a dangerous situation and, additionally, they were reluctant to use too many of the 15in shells until the stocks had been built up. They insisted that she be recalled to serve with the Grand Fleet, but not before she was employed in a final attempt to break through to the Narrows.

On the night of 13 March the cruiser *Amethyst* led six minesweepers into the Strait in an attempt to clear the mines, when four of the trawlers were hit by shell fire and the *Amethyst* was also damaged.

Unbeknown to the Allies, earlier on the night of 8 March the Turkish minelayer *Nusret* had laid mines in Eren Koy Bay on the Asian shore. The Turks had observed that the Allied ships made a turn to starboard as they withdrew from the wide bay, and accordingly sowed a line of twenty-five mines parallel to the southern shore at intervals of 100yd and a depth of 15ft.

Admiral Carden planned a massive sweep using all eighteen battleships that was to silence the guns that protected the five lines of minefields stretched across the bay. The attack was to be accompanied by thirty mine sweepers that in reality were fishing trawlers manned by civilian crews tasked to clear the minefields once and for all.

Unfortunately, before the operation could begin Admiral Carden suffered a nervous breakdown – his place was taken by his second in command, Vice-Admiral de Robeck.

In brilliant sunshine on 18 March and perfect visibility the fleet stood in towards the Narrows, with the ships arranged in five lines as shown:

Line A	*Queen Elizabeth* – *Agamemnon* - *Lord Nelson* – *Inflexible*(**D**)
Line B (French)	*Gaulois*(**D**) – *Charlemagne* - *Bouvet*(**S**) – *Suffren*(**D**)
Line B (British)	*Vengeance* – *Irresistible*(**S**) – *Albion* – *Ocean*(**S**)
Line C	*Majestic* – *Prince George* – *Swiftsure* – *Triumph*
Reserve line	*Canopus* – *Cornwallis*
	Key : (**D**) Damaged (**S**) Sunk

The *Queen Elizabeth* was the first to open fire, followed by the others in the first line and the second French line from Eren Koy Bay at 11.00 a.m.

After 2 hours of heavy naval gunfire the Turkish batteries were still largely intact. Although their fire had been reduced, it was still accurate, with the *Gaulois*, *Suffren*, *Agamemnon* and *Inflexible* all taking damaging hits.

At 1:25 p.m., with most of the Ottoman batteries now silenced, Vice-Admiral de Robeck decided to withdraw the French line and bring up the British Line C, plus the *Swiftsure* and *Triumph*.

Around 1:50 p.m., as the French ships led by the *Suffren* began to swing round in a wide turn to starboard towards Kum Kale heading for the open sea, the second ship in the line, the *Bouvet*, struck one of the mines laid by the *Nusret* ten days before. Her companions watched horrified as an enormous explosion followed, and within a matter of 30 seconds, with the ship still going ahead, she capsized and sank, taking 600 of her crew to the bottom.

Despite this setback, the fleet continued the bombardment until 2 hours later when the *Inflexible* also struck a mine in the same area as she was withdrawing, but although she took on many tons of water, her captain nursed her back to Tendos where she was beached while temporary repairs were effected.

A further disaster occurred when the *Irresistible* was also mined and began to drift towards the shore under heavy fire from the coastal batteries.

Vice-Admiral de Robeck ordered *Ocean* to take her in tow, but her captain considered the water too shallow, and after standing off the derelict ship was herself mined, jamming her steering gear and both ships drifted off up the Straits under heavy fire as efforts were made to rescue the crews.

In the face of these losses, de Robeck ordered the fleet to withdraw, while after dark Commodore Keyes took a destroyer into the Strait to look for the two battleships, but after searching for several hours concluded that both the *Irresistible* and *Ocean* had sunk.

NF* *Bouvet*
Lorient Naval Arsenal - 1896
French Pre-Dreadnought Battleship

Dimensions: Length 386ft x 70ft beam x 27ft draught
Displacement: 12,050 tons (normal)
Main armament: 2 x12in, 2 x 10in
Secondary armament: 8 x 5.5in - 2 x 18in submerged torpedo tubes
Armour protection: Main belt 18in, turrets 15in
Machinery: Triple expansion 4 cylinder on 3 shafts, 15,500 shp at 18 knots
Range: 5,600 miles at 10 knots
Complement: 710

100 feet

At the outbreak of the First World War, the *Bouvet* served in the Dardanelles campaign in 1915, where on 18 March she struck a mine, sinking in less than one minute with the loss of almost all hands.

Bouvet Class

FN *Bouvet*	1896
FN *Charles Martel*	1897
FN *Jaueguiberry*	1898
FN *Carnot*	1898
FN *Massena*	1898

* 'Navire Française'

The battle of 18 March 1915 was a great victory for the Ottoman Empire and demonstrated the folly of attempting a naval action in enclosed waters against fixed defences without military support onshore. For the loss of 118 Turkish casualties they had sunk three battleships, severely damaged a battle-cruiser by mine and inflicted over 800 casualties on the combined fleet.

The catastrophic losses of three Allied capital ships in a single afternoon – while a shock to the commander Admiral de Robeck, as he saw himself responsible for the most serious loss suffered by the Royal Navy since Trafalgar – had been anticipated by Churchill, who regarded such losses as a necessary sacrifice to achieve the breakthrough. Indeed, he regarded the old battleships as expendable gun platforms that could easily be replaced and even described them as useless for any other purpose.

This, quite apart from Churchill's apparent lack of concern for the lives of the crews of these ships, could also be considered a harsh opinion of the fighting capabilities of these older pre-dreadnoughts, which were placed in a situation, under the guns of shore based batteries at close range, and sailing into areas of intensively sown minefields, which any warship would be lucky to survive. It says more about the poor strategic and tactical decision making of those planning such campaigns.

Although outdated by the introduction of the dreadnought and their increasingly demonstrated vulnerability to mine and torpedo, where eleven British pre-dreadnoughts were lost during the war as opposed to only two dreadnoughts, they were still powerful ships in their own right and, properly employed in conditions that suited their vulnerability, they gave useful service throughout the war on convoy duty, as guard ships, harbour protection and on coastal bombardment work.

With the launching of the *Majestic*, designed by Sir William White in 1895, battleship design achieved a uniformity of layout that was to persist until the launch of the *Dreadnought* in 1906, with two funnels arranged side by side and two 12in guns mounted in barbettes at either end of a central armoured citadel, displacing 14,000 tons and capable of 17.5 knots. These nine ships were the oldest pre-dreadnoughts employed in the war.

From 1900 to 1904 a further twenty battleships were laid down that were generally similar in layout and armament, but with their two funnels set behind each other fore and aft. The *Albion* was typical of this class of ship. Laid down in 1899 at the Thames Ironworks at Blackwall and commissioned in 1901, she was of 12,950 tons' displacement, 430ft in length with a beam of 75ft. Her triple expansion four cylinder engines produced 13,500hp on two shafts giving a speed of 18 knots and sufficient coal stowage for a range of 5,600 miles at 10 knots.

Her main armament was four 12in 35 calibre Mk IX guns, which at an elevation of 15°, had a range of 15,000yd, firing a 850lb armour-piercing shell at a muzzle velocity of 2,400fp. Secondary armament consisted of twelve 6in Mk VII 45 calibre guns, firing a 100lb shell with a range of 14,000yd and four 18in submerged torpedo tubes. With a complement of 810, these ships served in all theatres, with eight ships of the *King Edward VII* class forming the 3rd Battle Squadron of the Grand Fleet at the outbreak of war in 1914 until replaced by modern dreadnoughts.

Also under the command of the Commander-in-Chief was the Channel Fleet, or Second Fleet, comprising the 5th and 6th Battle Squadrons of fourteen pre-dreadnought battleships and the reserve fleet – the 7th and 8th Battle Squadrons containing twelve of the oldest ships.

Two other ships present at the Dardanelles were the *Agamemnon* and her sister ship *Lord Nelson*, which had been designed by Sir Philip Watts, who had succeeded Sir William White as Chief Constructor to the Royal Navy in 1902. While excellent ships, as they were completed after the launch of the *Dreadnought*, they had the misfortune to be obsolete before they were built. Watts believed that, with the development of the torpedo boat and the increased range of engagement, a more heavily armed type of battleship was required, and these two ships could be seen as proto-dreadnoughts. They were of 16,500 tons and represented the last expression of the pre-dreadnought design.

Like the preceding ships, the main armament comprised four 12in Mark IX 50 calibre guns, but in these ships the 6in secondary batteries were replaced with ten 9.2in Mark XI 50 calibre guns mounted in four two-gun turrets on the beam at each end of the citadel and two single-gun turrets amidships. They also carried five 18in submerged torpedo tubes and were the first to carry a single distinctive tripod mast on her mainmast.

Armour protection consisted of a 12in belt tapering to 4in at either end or 12in on the turret, and 1in deck armour. With a length of 443ft and a beam of 79ft, the four-cylinder triple expansion engines, the last to be used in British battleships, were of 17,000hp that imparted a speed of 18.5 knots. With a crew of 780, these two ships were fine sea boats and very manoeuvrable, having a small tactical diameter.

Agamemnon had the distinction of shooting down a Zeppelin in Salonika in 1915 and after the war was used as a radio-controlled target.

At this distance in time, it seems incredible that the combined military minds of Great Britain and France, with the example of what was already taking place on the battlefields of Flanders, should propose to attempt to force the straits solely by warships, without a supporting land assault by troops. It was naively expected that once the combined British and French fleet arrived off the Golden Horn that the Ottomans would tamely surrender.

Perhaps it is as well that they never succeeded at the first attempt, as the thought of the assembled might of two Allied nations trapped, as indeed they would have been within 24 hours in the Black Sea, would have handed a huge propaganda victory to the Central Powers.

As it was, the British Secretary of State for War appointed General Sir Ian Hamilton to command the combined Mediterranean Expeditionary Force to undertake the landings on the Gallipoli peninsula.

This force comprised, along with British troops of the 29th Division, Australian and New Zealand infantry stationed in Egypt where they were training prior to being sent to the Western Front. Also present were the Royal Naval Division and the French Oriental Expeditionary Force that included four battalions of Senegalese colonial troops. Unfortunately, due to the delay between the cessation of the naval attacks and the start of the land campaign, a period of over four weeks, this allowed the Ottoman forces sufficient time to defend the peninsula in depth and to replace the guns that had been destroyed in the forts during the naval bombardment.

The Turkish forces were under the joint command of Mustafa Kemal and the German military advisor to the Ottoman Empire Otto Liman von Sanders, both of whom were extremely experienced and capable soldiers.

The land invasion commenced on 25 April 1915, with the British 29th Division landing at Cape Helles at the tip of the Gallipoli peninsula. The Anzacs were put ashore at Gaba Tepe, or Anzac Cove as it became known, on the Aegean coastline, where they planned to advance across the peninsula. Meanwhile, the French made a diversionary landing at Kum Kale on the Asian shoreline before re-embarking to reinforce the British sector at Hellas.

These initial landings met little resistance and, had they been quickly followed up with a determined advance, much of the peninsula could have been secured, allowing British warships to enter the Strait in greater safety.

As it was, this was not to be the case as by the following day Turkish troop reinforcements swept down the peninsula to halt any further advances by the Allies. The force of Allied battleships based at Mudros on the island of Lemnos 50 miles to the south-west provided covering fire for the landing of troops, pouring an accurate fire into the Turkish trenches. Accuracy was achieved by the troops onshore correcting the fall of shot, and on occasion spotting was carried out from aeroplanes carrying wireless sets launched from the seaplane carrier HMS *Ark Royal*, a converted collier of 7,450 tons that carried ten seaplanes in her hold.

At Cape Hellas on V beach, the Royal Munster Fusiliers and the Hampshire Regiment were landed under heavy fire from the collier SS *River Clyde* with appalling losses.

From then on, for the next eight months, the battle for control of the Gallipoli peninsula raged, with a constant round of attack and counter attack which left the Allied forces confined to the narrow beach areas they had first seized. Despite enormous losses, they were unable to make a breakthrough.

On the night of 12–13 May, a Turkish torpedo boat *Muavenet-i Milliye* steamed unseen slowly down the Strait into Morto Bay off Cape Helles and fired two torpedoes at HMS *Goliath*, striking her amidships under the funnels.

Following a tremendous explosion, the *Goliath* began to settle when a third torpedo struck her under the aft gun turret and she rolled over on her beam ends, rapidly sinking and taking 570 of her crew of 700 to the bottom. The Turkish torpedo boat, although fired on, managed to escape in the confusion.

On land, a constant war of attrition was fought under appalling conditions, with the opposing entrenchments often within a few score yards of each other. The searing summer heat, combined with non-existent sanitation and the uncollected corpses putrefying in the sun, were the cause of dysentery and other diseases that were to flourish in the summer, while interminable rain and frostbite made the winter months miserable. By August, and following the failure of the Allied offensive, the land campaign had ground to a halt and the question of evacuation was raised in Paris and London on 11 October 1915, which was strongly rejected by Sir Ian Hamilton who, like many of those responsible, was fearful of the damage to British prestige that a withdrawal would evoke.

The War Council, however, voted in favour of evacuation and dismissed General Hamilton, replacing him with General Sir Charles Monro, who oversaw the withdrawal. The evacuation of the army can be considered the sole success of the campaign, with the last troops departing the beaches on 20 December 1915.

The evacuation in winter rain and snow was expected to incur heavy casualties, but thanks to a steady reduction of the ranks, with large numbers of troops being taken off in the preceding days and the use of self-firing rifles that gave the impression that the Allied trenches were still manned, fourteen divisions of infantry and artillery were successfully spirited off the bloody beaches for the cost of only two wounded.

During the ill-starred campaign, 44,000 British and French troops had been killed, together with 10,000 Anzacs, while the Ottoman forces lost 86,000 dead. Of those responsible for the planning of the operation Lord Kitchener's reputation only suffered to a small degree as he was such a popular figure, while Churchill was demoted from First Lord of the Admiralty to a minor post until he resigned at the end of the year to command an infantry regiment on the Western Front.

The losses in capital ships incurred during the first 2 months of the campaign were the British battleships *Ocean* and *Irresistible*, the French battleship *Bouvet* on 18 March, followed in May by the British ships *Goliath*, *Triumph* and *Majestic*. These seemingly unacceptable losses were considered on the contrary by Churchill and the War Cabinet to be perfectly acceptable, as Churchill's view was that they were old and useless and fit for nothing else.

None of this could conceal the truth that Great Britain had suffered the greatest loss of capital ships since Nelson's day.

In September, in response to the failure of the land campaign, Admiral de Robeck put forward another plan for a further naval assault on the narrows to clear the minefields with better equipped minesweepers. The plan was supported by Churchill, but strongly opposed by Fisher, as he feared that more of the ships of the Grand Fleet would be frittered away on what was patently a lost cause.

Admiral Sir Roger Keyes, still a great supporter of aggressive naval action as a way to secure the Straits and capture Constantinople, presented more detailed plans to the War Council in conjunction with Admiral de Robeck to sweep the mines and enter the Sea of Marmara, while Lord Kitchener proposed a landing on the isthmus of Buldair with 40,000 infantry, capturing the entire peninsula that would allow Allied ships into the Sea of Marmara unchallenged.

With the entry of Bulgaria into the war on the side of the Central Powers in October 1914, the Ottoman Empire now had a direct supply line to their German allies and the defences on the peninsular were rapidly strengthened still further, making the chances of success in the land campaign an even more remote possibility.

If the Allies were unable to force the Strait with surface ships, the submarine, in theory, offered a better chance of success. Even before the campaign had started, the old British submarine *B11* had worked her way past five consecutive minefields to torpedo the old Turkish battleship *Mesudiye* that dated from 1874 in Sari Sighlar Bay, where it was moored as a floating battery.

The sinking was rightly seen as a major success for the Royal Navy and her captain Lieutenant Commander N. Holbrook was awarded the first naval Victoria Cross of the war.

This early success by submarine combined with the initial seemingly successful bombardment of the outer forts on 3 November was key to encouraging the adoption of the original plan to force the Strait by naval forces alone.

The French submarine *Saphir* was the next Allied submarine to work her way through the ten mine barriers that stretched across the narrows, where she ran aground at Nagara Point after coming under fire from shore batteries and was scuttled by her crew, with fourteen dead and thirteen taken prisoners of war.

On the next British attempt on 17 April the *E15* was caught in unsuspected underwater currents and she ran aground in Sari Siglar Bay under the guns of the Dardanos battery, where she came under heavy fire that resulted in the death of her captain Lieutenant-Commander Theodore Brodie.

The Turks made strenuous efforts to capture the boat, but were frustrated in this when the remaining crew exploded a torpedo that wrecked the interior of the submarine before surrendering.

The Australian submarine *AE2* was the first to succeed in passing through the Strait on the night of 24–25 April 1915 under the command of Lieutenant Commander Henry Stoker.

The *AE2* attacked the Turkish light cruiser *Plykisrvket*, badly damaging her, but due to defective torpedoes failed to sink her other targets. The *AE2*'s luck finally ran out in Artaki Bay on 29 April when she was shelled by a Turkish torpedo boat and sank, with the crew abandoning her as she settled, where they, too, became prisoners of war.

Undeterred by the fate of the earlier attempts, on 27 April 1915, Lieutenant Commander Edward Boyle broke through into the Sea of Marmara in his boat *E14*, where, in a three-week campaign, he and his crew sank a gunboat and a minelayer and several thousand tons of assorted small steamers. Although the tonnage sunk was small, the effect on Turkish morale of having an enemy submarine at large in the Sea of Marmara was a powerful propaganda coup for the Allies.

On the return to Murdos of the *E14*, Lieutenant Commander Boyle was awarded the Victoria Cross. Under Boyle the *E14* made two further incursions into the Sea of Marmara where he sank further ships and, more importantly, disrupted coastwise traffic for weeks at a time.

Perhaps the most successful British submarine commander in the Great War was Lieutenant Commander Martin Nasmith. His boat, the *E11*, was the standard type employed during the First World War.

Some sixty E class boats were built. With a surface displacement of 660 tons and armed with five torpedo tubes and a 12pdr gun, and with a range of 3,000 nautical miles carrying a crew of thirty, they proved to be Britain's most handy and effective submarines.

The *E11* had already seen service in the Baltic at the beginning of the war and had taken part in the Cuxhaven raid on Christmas Day 1914. The *E11* passed through the Strait and entered the Sea of Marmara on the night of 18 May 1914. On surfacing, Nasmith captured a trading schooner, which he lashed to the submarine's conning tower as a decoy to allow the submarine to approach other Turkish ships unseen. However, after several days without attracting any targets, he set the boat adrift. On 23 May he sank a gunboat and a minelayer, while on the 24th near the port of Tekirdag *E11* attacked and sank an ammunition ship after the crew had taken to the boats.

Going closer inshore, Nasmith sank a troop transport and forced a second aground by gunfire. He was so close to shore that he was attacked by a Turkish cavalry squadron, to which he replied with his deck gun.

The day of 25 May brought the *E11* into the waters off Constantinople, with the intention of seeking out the two ex-German warships *Goeben* and *Breslau*. Brazenly surfacing off the Golden Horn 1 hour after midday, Nasmith found instead a troop transport, the *Stamboul*, which he attacked within sight of the Turkish capital, hitting her with a torpedo but failing to sink her, as the damaged ship was beached, after which the *E11* came under sustained fire from shore-based artillery, causing Nasmith to submerge and escape back into the Sea of Marmara.

However, the very appearance of a British submarine, the first enemy warship in over one hundred years to attack Constantinople, was a tremendous blow to Turkish morale, causing great panic within all sections of the city.

The *E11* returned into the Bosphorus again on 27 May, sinking in total eleven ships before heading back through the Dardanelles to re-arm and refit on 5 June, where on the way he torpedoed another troop transport, before joining the fleet at Murdos. On arrival, Nasmith learnt that for his actions he had been awarded the Victoria Cross, the third naval recipient of the honour in the campaign.

As a new British landing was under way at Suvla Bay, on 8 August as the *E11* again prepared to enter the Strait, she sighted the Turkish battleship *Hayreddin Barbarossa*, which she sank with a salvo of two torpedoes, then again appearing before Constantinople and repeating her earlier success by sinking still more ships.

The *E11* made three sallies into the Sea of Marmara and the Black Sea, where she sank a total of twenty-seven steam vessels and over fifty-eight smaller sailing ships, while in a cloak and dagger operation the *E11* first officer Lieutenant Guy D'Oyly-Hughes was put ashore to blow up a bridge and culvert on part of the Constantinople railway line, earning him the Distinguished Service Order.

In other operations on 1 May the French submarine *Joule* attempted to enter the Strait, but struck a mine with the loss of all on board. A second French effort on 27 July by the *Mariotte* also failed when she became entangled in anti-submarine nets and was forced to surface, where it was shelled by shore batteries, forcing her commander to scuttle his boat before accepting captivity to prevent it falling into Ottoman hands.

The French submarine *Turquoise* managed to enter the Sea of Marmara on 30 October, but unfortunately ran aground and was captured intact before her captain could scuttle her. Along with the crew, who were taken prisoner, documents were discovered with details of British plans and of a proposed rendezvous with a British submarine, the *E20*, on 6 November; a rendezvous which was instead kept by a German U-boat, the *U14*, which torpedoed and sank the unsuspecting British boat.

The Allied submarine offensive was the most successful aspect of the entire Gallipoli campaign, and indeed the only success. Over the period April 1914 to January 1915, nine British submarines sank two battleships, one destroyer, two minelayers, five gunboats, nine troop transports, thirty-five steam ships and 180 other craft, for the loss of eight Allied submarines.

14

EAST AFRICA AND THE
INDIAN OCEAN

Far from the grey misty waters of the North Sea, on the warm, clear sparkling waters of the Indian Ocean and among the tropical spice islands of the East Indies, the quiet, ordered course of maritime trade that for so many years had been largely imposed on the region by the presence of the Royal Navy was shaken during the latter months of 1914 by the appearance of a single German surface raider. It all but brought trade to a complete halt and disrupted shipping over the whole of the Indian Ocean.

The cause of this alarm was the three-funnelled German Light cruiser, *Emden*, a ship of 3,650 tons' displacement, 388ft in length with a beam of 43ft, powered by two 16,000hp three-cylinder triple expansion reciprocating engines that gave a top speed of 24 knots and, importantly, a range of 3,700 nautical miles.

Her armament consisted of ten of the very effective 4.1in quick-firing guns in single mountings, protected with gun shields and two 17.7in torpedo tubes, which was also protected by a 2in armour deck and a 2.25in armoured belt.

She had been launched in 1908 at the Kaiserliche Werft Danzig in East Prussia and, on being commissioned in 1909, was assigned to join von Spee's German East Asiatic Squadron at Tsingtao. She was a particularly graceful ship, painted in the German tropical colours of white hull with buff funnels and upper works, and acquired the name *The Swan of the East*.

Operating from Tsingtao, she experienced her first taste of action in 1911 when, together with the cruiser *Nurnberg*, she helped to put down a rebellion on the island of Ponape in the German Caroline Islands.

Again, during the Chinese Revolution of 1913 led by Sun Yat-Sen, the *Emden*, under her new commander Korvetten Kapitan Karl von Muller, co-operated with British and Japanese warships to subdue a rebel fort during a revolt on the Yangtze River.

Kapitan von Muller was born in Hanover in 1873, the son of a Prussian army officer, and entered the Imperial Navy in 1891. He was described as a true gentleman, admired by friend and foe alike. During the cruise of the *Emden* he became recognised as a daring and chivalrous opponent who treated his captives well and did everything in his power to minimise civilian casualties.

The *Emden* left Tsingtao on 31 July 1914 and received the news of the outbreak of war on 2 August while at sea.

On 4 August the *Emden* captured a Russian steamer which she took back to Tsingtao. At Tsingtao, after assessing the situation, Kapitan von Muller considered the base to be too vulnerable to attack by enemy troops that were advancing on the town and elected to depart to join the ships of von Spee's Squadron at Pagan Island in the Marianas.

Reaching Pagan on 8 August, von Muller persuaded Admiral von Spee – who planned to take the combined squadron of six warships plus colliers across the Pacific, around Cape Horn, into the Atlantic and hopefully to reach home – to allow him to be detached to conduct an individual commerce-raiding cruise against British and Allied merchant shipping in the Indian Ocean, and possibly in turn to attempt to reach a German home port via the Cape of Good Hope.

On 14 August 1914 the *Emden*, accompanied by the collier *Markkomannia*, left the Squadron at Pagan and headed west. Her course took her to the Palau Islands, a German colony, where she rendezvoused with the old gunboat SMS *Geier*, which herself was to pursue a course as a commerce raider before being interned in Hawaii in October 1915.

Several days later, while taking on coal off the island of Timor in the Dutch East Indies, she was sighted by the Dutch coastal defence ship *Tromp*, whose captain entertained the German commander on board his ship while ensuring the German ship observed the Dutch neutrality laws in their waters.

Upon departure von Muller rigged a dummy fourth funnel to resemble in silhouette the British cruiser HMS *Yarmouth* that was stationed at Hong Kong. With his disguise complete, on 28 August the *Emden* sailed through the straits between Lombok and Bali to enter the Indian Ocean. Her cruise had begun.

Allied fleet dispositions in the Far East and the Indian Ocean at the outbreak of war included the powerful Japanese fleet with the 1st fleet, or Sentai 1, based at Kure in the home islands and comprising eight battleships, four cruisers and sixteen destroyers and other craft, together with the Sentai 2, similarly composed and based at Yokosuka and Sasebo.

With the fall of the German colony of Tsingtao in November, the besieging Japanese fleet consisting of six battleships were free to search for Admiral von Spee's Squadron, which by that time was on the coast of Chile.

The British presence in the Pacific was much smaller, in line with the Anglo-Japanese naval agreement made in 1902, where Japan assumed many of the duties to protect British interests in the region, allowing Great Britain to concentrate her naval power in the North Sea.

Consequently, a small yet powerful presence was maintained at Hong Kong, where the battleship *Triumph* was based, supported by the armoured cruisers HMS *Minotaur* and HMS *Hampshire* and the *Town* class cruisers HMS *Newcastle* and HMS *Yarmouth*. Southern Pacific waters were protected by the Australian fleet, which included the modern battle-cruiser *Australia* and the light cruisers *Melbourne* and *Sydney*, together with several older cruisers and three ships of the Royal New Zealand Navy.

In the Indian Ocean itself, the Cape of Good Hope Squadron was composed of three older protected cruisers, which were hardly a major deterrent to a determined surface raider and, although a number of French ships were also on the African coast, the ships of the China station and the Australian squadron were needed to help hunt the *Emden* down.

Moving swiftly along the coasts of Java and Sumatra, *Emden* began to prey on Allied merchant shipping along the busy shipping lanes, all of which sailed independently without any form of escort. By the end of September, von Muller had captured and destroyed seventeen ships, either by gunfire or the setting of demolition charges, in every case once the crews had been removed to safety.

With his disguise as the four-funnelled *Yarmouth*, von Muller had little difficulty in closely approaching his victims, when, after hoisting the German ensign and signal flags instructing the ship to stop and not to use their wireless, he would fire a warning shot across their bow. Kapitan von Muller behaved in an exemplary and gentlemanly manner to captured crews and passengers, treating them well and transferring them to another captured ship when possible, and sending them to a neutral port.

The Admiralty in Whitehall were not aware of the *Emden's* presence in the Indian Ocean until 14 September which, once it became known, resulted in widespread panic in the shipping offices, with insurance rates going sky high and the cessation of all shipping movements over the whole of the Indian Ocean, as shipping companies were afraid to risk ships and valuable cargoes while the raider was at large.

Sailing northwards, the *Emden* eluded the searching cruisers of five nations as they vainly sought the Swan of the East.

The day of 10 September found the *Emden* in the Bay of Bengal, where over the next five days she took eight further prizes before turning towards the east on 18 September, where she was reported harrying shipping off Rangoon, adding more prizes to her tally.

Having taken on coal from her collier, the *Emden* next sped westward, arriving off the port of Madras on the night of 23 September, where creeping inshore in the darkness she opened fire from 3,000yd on the oil storage tanks of the Burmah Oil Company, setting them ablaze and damaging several merchant ships in the harbour, causing a large number of casualties in an action that lasted 35 minutes.

Towards the end of the action, shore-based artillery attempted to reply against the raider, but without success, and after the expenditure of 125 rounds of 4.1in shells the *Emden* slid away into the darkness.

As a result of the raid, 125,000,000 gallons of kerosene and oil were destroyed, while the blow to British prestige and morale was devastating and caused a panic evacuation of parts of the city by the populace who feared further attacks.

Heading southwards, von Muller took his ship along the east coast of Ceylon, keeping a sharp lookout for Allied cruisers, which he expected would be active in the area. He brought his ship close in towards Colombo harbour at night, with the intention of bombarding the harbour facilities, but was dissuaded by the numerous searchlights that were continually sweeping the harbour approaches and turned away to the north-west, heading towards the Laccadive Islands. Here, between 26 and 28 September, he took six more prizes, before heading south to the Chagos Archipelago. He reached the islands on 4 October, where due to their remote location and absence of a cable station the inhabitants were unaware that the war had even started.

Meanwhile, the British cruiser *Hampshire*, together with the Japanese cruiser *Chikuma*, were dispatched to hunt the *Emden* among the Laccadive islands, but failed to locate her as she had already slipped away by the time they arrived.

At the Chagos Archipelago (a British possession) von Muller dropped anchor in the lagoon of Diego Garcia on 4 October, where the unsuspecting residents regarded him as a visiting representative of a friendly power.

For the next week, von Muller overhauled the ship's machinery, serviced the guns, scraped the marine growth from the hull and re-provisioned with fresh fruit and water. The crew were given much appreciated shore leave, which allowed them to relax and swim in the warm waters of the lagoon and generally stretch their legs ashore, where they all behaved with courtesy to the British officials and native islanders.

On 10 October the rejuvenated *Emden* weighed anchor and, having learned from Allied wireless traffic that coastal shipping was again plying the waters off Ceylon and the Indian west coast, headed north again to the Laccadive Sea.

Here von Muller quickly sank seven more ships, including the Blue Funnel steamer *Troilus* which was carrying a cargo of rubber and copper – valuable commodities that would have been welcome in Germany, as already at this early stage the country was beginning to suffer from the effects of the British blockade. The effects of these latest sinkings resulted in a further suspension of coastal traffic, with ships tied up for weeks in harbour losing hundreds of thousands of pounds for their owners.

In order to deal with these latest depredations, a larger squadron, comprising the British cruisers *Hampshire*, *Yarmouth*, HMS *Gloucester* and HMS *Weymouth*, together with the Japanese cruisers *Chikuma* and *Yahaghi* and the Russian cruiser *Askold*,

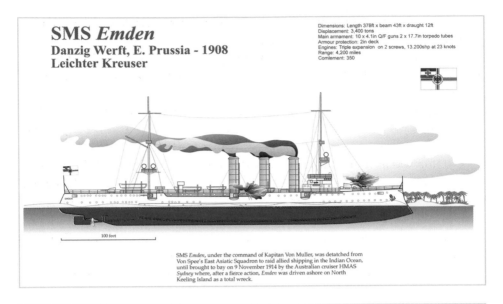

SMS *Emden*
Danzig Werft, E. Prussia - 1908
Leichter Kreuser

Dimensions: Length 378ft x beam 43ft x draught 12ft
Displacement: 3,400 tons
Main armament: 10 x 4.1in Q/F guns 2 x 17.7in torpedo tubes
Armour protection: 2in deck
Engines: Triple expansion on 2 screws, 13.200shp at 23 knots
Range: 4,200 miles
Comlement: 350

100 feet

SMS *Emden*, under the command of Kapitan Von Muller, was detatched from
Von Spee's East Asiatic Squadron to raid allied shipping in the Indian Ocean,
until brought to bay on 9 November 1914 by the Australian cruiser HMAS
Sydney where, after a fierce action, *Emden* was driven ashore on North
Keeling Island as a total wreck.

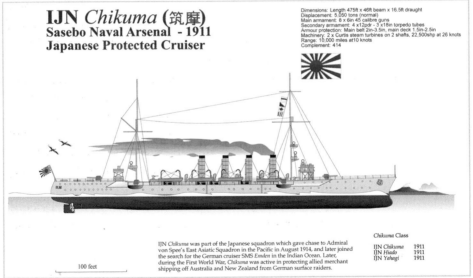

IJN *Chikuma* (筑摩)
Sasebo Naval Arsenal - 1911
Japanese Protected Cruiser

Dimensions: Length 475ft x 46ft beam x 16.5ft draught
Displacement: 5,050 tons (normal)
Main armament: 8 x 6in 45 calibre guns
Secondary armament: 4 x12pdr - 3 x18in torpedo tubes
Armour protection: Main belt 2in-3.5in, main deck 1.5in-2.5in
Machinery: 2 x Curtis steam turbines on 2 shafts, 22,500shp at 26 knots
Range: 10,000 miles at10 knots
Complement: 414

Chikuma Class

IJN *Chikuma*	1911
IJN *Hiado*	1911
IJN *Yahagi*	1911

IJN *Chikuma* was part of the Japanese squadron which gave chase to Admiral
von Spee's East Asiatic Squadron in the Pacific in August 1914, and later joined
the search for the German cruiser SMS *Emden* in the Indian Ocean. Later,
during the First World War, *Chikuma* was active in protecting allied merchant
shipping off Australia and New Zealand from German surface raiders.

100 feet

were assembled and dispatched in a more determined effort to hunt the *Emden*
down amongst the Laccadive islands, but once again without success.

The *Emden* now swung eastward, again towards the Nicobar Islands in the Bay
of Bengal, eluding the searching cruisers that crossed her track unseen in heavy
rain squalls.

The Japanese cruisers *Tokiwa* and *Yakumo* were also sent into the Bay of Bengal to
augment the *Chikuma* and the Russian cruiser *Zhemchug* that were already searching
the Andaman and Nicobar Islands.

Rendezvousing at sea, the *Emden* filled her bunkers from her collier, and set course for the port of Penang in Malaya.

In the early morning of 28 October, still sporting her false fourth funnel, she swept at high speed into the harbour, breaking out the German battle flag at the masthead.

Laying inside the harbour entrance was the 3,100-ton Russian cruiser *Zhemchug*, armed with eight 4.7in guns; a survivor from the Battle of Tsushima in 1904 that had just returned from patrolling the Nicobar Islands.

The ship was anchored in such a way that only one gun covered the harbour entrance and her commander, Captain Baron Cherkassov, feeling he had done his duty in his long and fruitless patrol, was ashore in a hotel entertaining his mistress. On board the ship, in an evident lack of discipline, the crew were in a similarly relaxed mood. Aboard the anchored vessel there were no officers or lookouts on duty or searchlights manned, while the ship itself was lit up *en fête* and a party of sixty Chinese prostitutes was on board, as part of the standard Russian R&R programme.

At 5.15 a.m. the *Emden*, speeding past the Russian ship, launched a torpedo at a range of 700m that struck her amidships, at the same time firing several salvoes of shells into the unfortunate ship, which surprisingly managed to fire back from a single gun manned by two unknown Russian heroes.

Turning sharply within the harbour, the *Emden* passed the Russian ship again, launching a second torpedo which, striking the hull by the forward magazine, caused a tremendous explosion, sinking the ship instantly in 30ft of water with the loss of half of her crew, while the fate of the unfortunate prostitutes is not recorded. As the *Emden* left the harbour, the old French cruiser *Diberville*, anchored without steam up, opened fire on the speeding German ship, but without scoring any hits.

Three French torpedo boats belatedly took up the chase, but when the *Mousquet* eventually came up with the *Emden* later in the morning a few well-aimed salvoes sent the French ship to the bottom.

Von Muller stopped to pick up survivors, who were later transferred to a British steamer, the *Newburn*, which took them to Sumatra in the neutral Dutch East Indies. Not so lucky were the commander and first officer of the *Zhemchug*, who were court-martialled and received prison sentences of 2½ years and 1 year respectively.

The raid on Penang caused a further panic all round the Indian Ocean. Shipping companies once again cancelled sailings and demanded from the Admiralty that something be done about this intrepid raider that was ruining their trade and could strike with impunity wherever she chose without any of the fifty or so Allied warships that were searching for her even catching a fleeting glimpse of her funnel smoke.

After sinking the *Mousquet* and shaking off two other French torpedo boats, von Muller sailed into the Sunda Strait, passing the island of Krakatoa to take on coal before heading south-west towards the Cocos Keeling Islands. Here he intended to destroy the important Eastern Telegraph Company cable and wireless station on Direction Island to disrupt Allied naval communications in the area.

Arriving at Direction Island before dawn on 8 November, von Muller sent a landing party comprising fifty fully armed marines ashore under the command of Leutnant zur See Hellmuth von Mucke, to whom the civilian employees of the wireless station surrendered without putting up any resistance. This allowed the German landing party to seize the station, where in the course of destroying the wireless equipment and cutting the undersea cable, they courteously agreed that in blowing up the wireless aerial they would ensure that it did not fall across the island's tennis court.

However, as the *Emden* approached the island, the wireless station superintendent Dover Ferrant, alerted by the sight of a unknown three-funnelled cruiser (von Muller having removed the fourth false funnel some days before) and knowing most British cruisers had four funnels, sent out a wireless call to all stations before the Germans came ashore. The message was picked up clearly by the Australian light cruiser *Sydney* which, together with the *Melbourne* and the Japanese cruiser *Ibuki*, were escorting a troop convoy bound for Colombo and a mere 55 miles to the south of the Cocos Keeling Islands.

At 6.30 a.m. the *Sydney* was detached from the convoy and at best speed came in sight of Direction island at 9.00 a.m.

The *Sydney* was a modern *Chatham* class light cruiser launched in 1913, of 5,400 tons' displacement equipped with Parsons turbines of 25,000hp, giving a speed of 25.5 knots and armed with eight 6in Mk XI guns and two 21in torpedo tubes – more than a match for the *Emden*.

The alarm was raised on the *Emden* as the Australian ship came over the horizon at full speed, leaving von Muller with a dilemma. He had no option but to weigh anchor and engage the enemy ship while leaving the landing party on shore.

The *Emden* opened fire at the extreme range of 20,000yd and, although during a fight of 1½ hours with the range continuously closing *Emden*, managed to hit *Sydney* fifteen times, destroying her range finder and disabling a 6in gun. In her turn the *Sydney* hit the German ship with one hundred armour-piercing shells, requiring only two of her early salvoes to destroy two of the *Emden*'s funnels, as well as the foremast and wireless, wrecking her steering gear and starting a fierce engine room fire.

With a large number of the crew killed and wounded and the ship battered into a burning wreck, von Muller ran his ship aground on the reef of North Keeling Island at 11.15 a.m. to avoid foundering.

Captain Glossop of the *Sydney* broke off the action at this time in order to pursue the accompanying collier SS *Buresk*. After a short chase the German ship scuttled herself. Captain Glossop then returned to North Keeling Island where he found the stranded wreck of the German ship still flying her battle ensign. A flag signal requesting the *Emden* to surrender bore no response, and Captain Glossop had no option but to recommence fire on the vessel.

After a few salvoes the German ensign was hauled down and von Muller and the remaining crew surrendered to be made prisoners of war, but as a mark of respect the officers were allowed to retain their swords.

The Australian ship suffered a loss of fifteen and forty wounded, while German casualties were 131 dead and sixty-five wounded.

The *Sydney* steamed back to Direction Island in order to aid repair of the wireless apparatus and the cable.

By the time the *Sydney* arrived off the island as darkness had fallen, Glossop elected to anchor offshore until the morning, with working parties making essential repairs through the night.

During the cruiser action, Leutnant Mucke had taken possession of the island in the name of the German Empire. Their reign was, however, short-lived, and having seen the *Emden* battered into a smoking wreck and knowing it was only a matter of time before the landing party were taken into captivity, von Mucke commandeered an old, leaky 96-ton, three-masted topsail schooner – the *Ayesha* – on to which, after some hasty repair, he loaded all the landing party complete with weapons, and sailed away before sunset.

After a 1,056-mile voyage, the leaking *Ayesha* arrived at the port of Padang in Dutch Sumatra. Here the party transferred to a steamship provided by the German agent sailing for the Yemen, where they travelled up the Arabian peninsula in a variety of transport, including dhows, horses and camels, to reach Syria, but not without brushes with Bedouin tribesmen on the way. They eventually arrived in Constantinople to a heroes' reception.

Von Muller and his surviving crew were sent to a POW camp in Malta, although von Muller, who suffered from malaria that was eventually to kill him, was later released as part of a prisoner exchange scheme. On return to Germany he was awarded the Pour le Mérite by Kaiser Wilhelm II.

In a unique mark of respect for what they had achieved, the Kaiser allowed all surviving officers and men to add the suffix *Emden* to their family names, as an inherited honour – evinced by German citizens still proudly bearing the name today.

Over a period of 4 months, a lone German cruiser had completely brought maritime trade to a halt over a vast area, disrupting the essential flow of raw materials and important troop movements, while a disproportionate number of Allied warships were tied down in ineffectual attempts to hunt her down.

The effect of her success on neutral powers was a severe blow to Allied morale and British prestige in the region, with a corresponding boost to German civilians at home.

In the days before the advent of radar, satellite technology and modern high-frequency radio communications, it was all too easy for a lone raider to hide in the vastness of the ocean where her interception relied on outdated reports of her presence and, most importantly, chance and good luck.

On the other side of the Indian Ocean another drama was being played out along the steaming tropical coastline of Africa. Here in the colony of German East Africa, German forces under General Paul von Lettow-Vorbeck were conducting what was to be a most successful land campaign. With a force of less than 14,000 troops, that included 3,000 European and 11,000 native soldiers, he held at bay an Imperial and Allied force of 300,000 by conducting a guerrilla war, over a 4-year period, even invading British territory. It became the only German colonial force never to be defeated during the war, finally surrendering two weeks after the armistice on the Western Front.

From its colonisation in the 1880s by Germany, commerce expanded rapidly in German East Africa with the building of an extensive railway network to serve the

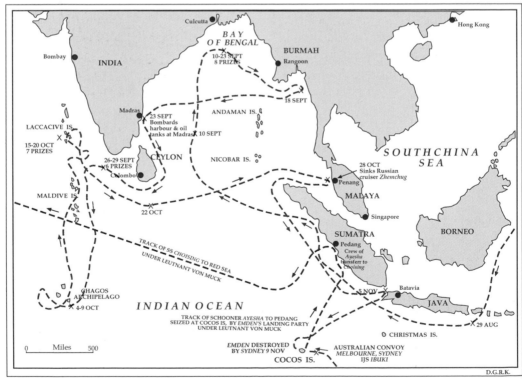

Cruise of the SMS *Emden*, August-November 1914

needs of the cotton and rubber businesses, along with sisal and coffee plantations that were established in the hinterland.

After suppressing dissident tribes, the German authorities began a programme of modernising the colony, introducing an education system of secondary and vocational schools for the native people that was far in advance of any other European African colony.

The port of Dar es Salaam was expanded and modernised to become by 1914 a busy trading port with a city of over 166,000 inhabitants. To protect this important trading centre, the German Government stationed warships on the coast based on Dar es Salaam. In accordance with this plan, the light cruiser SMS *Konigsberg* was in April 1914 detailed to undertake a two-year deployment on the East African station, under the command of Fregattenkapitan Max Looff, sailing via the Suez Canal to the protectorate.

The *Konigsberg* was a modern vessel built at the Kaiserliche Werft, Kiel, being completed in 1907. She was a three-funnelled cruiser of 3,400 tons, 378ft in length, with a beam of 43ft. Power was provided by three-cylinder triple expansion engines of 13,000hp, giving 23.5 knots on two shafts and range of 5,700 miles. Her armament consisted of ten of the excellent 4.1in quick-firing guns in single mountings and two 17.5in torpedo tubes and carried a crew of fourteen officers and 300 men. The guns had an elevation of 23°, allowing engagement of targets at a maximum range of 15,000yd or 8.5 miles.

Each gun was provided with 150 rounds and the ship was extremely well protected with a 2–2.5in armoured deck against plunging shellfire. In size, armament and appearance she was almost identical to the *Emden* and was to prove to be as much of a problem to the Allies in tying down ships urgently needed elsewhere.

As it became likely in the last days of July 1914 that war with Germany was an increasingly possible scenario, the Admiralty in London ordered the Cape Squadron under the command of Admiral King-Hall to proceed north to lay off Dar es Salaam in order to blockade the German cruiser and other ships in port. Although by the time they arrived the birds had flown, perhaps fortunately for the rather ineffective British ships.

The British ships comprised two very old protected cruisers, HMS *Astraea* of 4,300 tons, built in 1894 and armed with two 6in and eight 4.7in guns of limited range, together with the equally old HMS *Pegasus*, smaller at 2,300 tons, and sporting eight rather ineffective old-pattern 4in guns.

The third ship of the blockading squadron was the HMS *Hyacinth*, a more recent (1900) large protected cruiser of 5,600 tons more powerfully armed with ten 6in guns. However, none of the ships were capable of a speed in excess of 20 knots, against the *Konigsberg's* 24–25 knots.

On 31 July 1914, with war having been declared between Germany and Serbia, Kapitan Loofff sailed out of the port, quickly working up to full speed and easily outpacing the British cruisers, losing them in a heavy rain squall.

Five days later, Kapitan Looff, standing off the port of Aden, received orders from Berlin advising of the outbreak of war with Great Britain and to attack British maritime commerce at the southern entrance of the Red Sea.

The following day, 6 August, the German collier *Somalia* departed Dar es Salaam, taking advantage of the absence of the ships of the Cape squadron, with her holds crammed with coal for the *Konigsberg*.

By 8 August the British warships were again off Dar es Salaam, preventing a second collier from sailing, while British agents also bought up all the coal supplies in Portuguese East Africa to stop it falling into German hands.

The *Konigsberg* stopped two German ships en route for the Suez Canal to warn them that they would be interned, causing them to risk internment in neutral territory. Next, off the coast of Oman, Kapitan Looff intercepted his first British ship, HMS *City of Westminster*, which, after taking off the crew, he sank with demolition charges and gunfire; their first prize.

The same day the *Konigsberg* made a rendezvous with the collier *Somalia*, taking on 860 tons of coal to her bunkers then heading south to the Madagascar Channel, usually a busy shipping route, in search of British and French shipping, but drew a blank.

Returning north and to another assignation with the *Somalia* on 23 August, where, after taking on a further 800 tons of coal, Kapitan Looff had to consider some unwelcome news.

In his absence British warships of the Cape Squadron had shelled the harbour at Dar es Salaam, destroying the wireless station and damaging harbour facilities, rendering the port unusable, and leaving Kapitan Looff to seek a new safe base of operations on the African coast.

Fortunately, the Captain of the *Somalia* had a concise knowledge of the protectorate's coastline, having taken part in a survey some years earlier that had charted the Rufiji Delta area, which he now recommended to Looff as a suitable hiding place from where he could sally forth to attack commerce.

So, on 3 September the *Konigsberg*, riding the high tide, entered the steaming mangrove-lined Rufiji River, pushing further up-stream where there was a good depth of water below her keel.

Her place of refuge was a maze of intersecting channels covering 200 square miles, the shores of which were covered in a dense riotous growth of mangrove and palm trees forming a barrier of impenetrable vegetation, where in this confusion of waterways were five possible main outlets to the sea.

Once anchored far up a main watercourse, coast watchers were stationed at the mouth of the river and telephone lines were laid to the ship to ensure that the *Konigsberg* would not be taken by surprise should British ships approach the delta. With General von Lettow-Vorbeck commencing his campaign against the British and Imperial forces in the interior, Kapitan Looff did not have to wait long to be called to action, when on 19 September information was received that a two-funnelled cruiser was laying at anchor within the harbour of Zanzibar, which could only be British.

Having again taken on coal the *Konigsberg* slipped down river, passing the bar at high water, and set course 150 miles north for Zanzibar.

The *Pegasus,* which had been on patrol, had put into Zanzibar harbour, anchoring up with engine and boiler problems. While engineers were at work in the engine rooms, at dawn on 20 September 1914 the *Konigsberg* appeared off the port and opened fire on the British cruiser.

The engagement was a one-sided affair. *Pegasus* was a protected cruiser launched in 1896 of 2,135 tons, armed with four old pattern 4in guns, against the ten modern 4.1in quick-firing guns of the *Konigsberg.*

After a bombardment of 45 minutes, the *Pegasus* had been hit over one hundred times. The captain and his crew fought back as best they could, but they were outranged and out-gunned. Finally, with twenty-eight killed and fifty-five wounded, Commander Ingles struck his colours to avoid further casualties, with the ship eventually sinking at her moorings.

As he left the scene, Kapitan Looff also sank a captured German prize, the gunboat *Helmut.* Having taken on sufficient coal from her collier for two weeks, Kapitan Looff now decided his mission was accomplished in these waters and was preparing to attempt the long voyage back to Germany around the Cape of Good Hope, hoping to secure further supplies of coal from captured Allied ships en route. However, he had barely started on the long journey when a serious engine breakdown caused him to abandon the plan and return to the Rufiji Delta for repair.

Anchoring 5 miles up one of the main channels, the damaged and worn engine parts were dismantled and carried overland to Dar es Salaam 100 miles away, where new parts were made in the dockyard workshops.

While these repairs were going on, the ships of the Cape Squadron were urgently searching the African coastline for the elusive cruiser, with a reinforced squadron commanded by Captain Sidney Drury-Lowe.

On 19 October, the cruiser *Chatham* boarded the German steamer *President* at Lindi, where captured documents indicated that she had recently supplied *Konigsberg* with coal.

Finally, on 30 October, the British cruiser HMS *Dartmouth*, nosing into the Rifiji, located the German cruiser and her collier *Somalia* in the Delta, their presence being confirmed by a fierce artillery fire being directed against the cruiser from the shore.

This information being instantly wirelessed brought the other ships of the squadron, the cruisers *Weymouth*, *Dartmouth* and *Chatham*, hurrying to blockade the German ships in the Delta.

The pre-dreadnought *Goliath* was brought up in November, where it was hoped her four 12in guns could be used to good effect, but drawing too much water she was unable to pass over the bar.

Additionally, as a further safeguard, the steamer *Newbridge* was successfully sunk close to the main channel to prevent escape; an operation that drew shell fire from both banks of the river where the Germans had earlier landed light field artillery.

The *Konigsberg* was in a well-protected position hidden amongst the dense growth of trees in the mangrove swamps that helped to conceal the vessel and offered a degree of shelter from shellfire.

Knowing the game was up as far as further raiding was concerned, Kapitan Looff now moved his ship 12 miles further up the river, with the intention of assisting the war effort by tying up British ships that could be better employed elsewhere and which would be tied up watching his ship.

The Admiralty were now aware that the *Konigsberg* was anchored in the Delta but were unaware of her precise position and decided to engage a civilian exhibition pilot and his Curtis Model F flying boat to locate the enemy cruiser.

The aircraft was shipped aboard HMS *Kinfauns Castle* from Simonstown to Niororo Island, 18 miles south of the Rufiji Delta.

The pilot, Mr H.D. Cutler, was quickly commissioned into the Royal Naval Air Service, with the rank of Flight Sub-Lieutenant.

The Curtis was a single-engined wooden hulled and very leaky biplane flying boat whose engine power, not high to start with, was much reduced by the tropical climate and for the first reconnaissance was unable to carry the observer Midshipman A. Gallehawk.

This first flight was unsuccessful as Cutler could not locate the delta, and made an emergency landing for lack of petrol.

A second attempt was made two days later and Cutler had the good fortune to find the *Konigsberg* concealed and camouflaged amongst the mangroves. Cutler flew directly over the ship and observed she had steam up as though preparing for sea.

His report was initially not taken seriously, as Admiralty charts indicated an insufficient depth of water, and ordered a further reconnaissance. As the hull of the flying boat was now leaking so badly, a second Curtis was brought up from Simonstown and Cutler, together with the captain of the *Kinfauns Castle* on board, took the little flying boat staggering into the air, flying over the German ship and verifying her position.

The nearest ship capable of dealing with the *Konigsberg* was the cruiser HMS *Chatham*, which was hurrying up from Mombasa. In a further flight the

Curtis experienced engine failure and came down on the river, where Cutler was captured by German troops. He remained a prisoner of war until November 1917.

Once the entrances to the Delta were secured by warships, a mixed assortment of unsuitable aircraft continued the surveillance of the German ship, including an elderly Short seaplane, which, on 25 April, took photographs of the ship but, as it could only climb to 600ft, it was shot down before completing the mission.

Plans were made to attack the ship with motor boats armed with torpedoes, but before this could take place news came through that the two monitors, HMS *Mersey* and HMS *Severn*, armed with 6in guns, were arriving from England Monitors were special vessels that were of shallow draft, mounting heavy guns that were used for coastal bombardment. The *Mersey* was of 1,260 tons, being 266ft in length, with a beam of 49ft mounting two high-angle 6in guns and two 4.7in howitzers. These ships had previously been employed to good effect, bombarding German front-line positions in Belgium from the sea.

Vice-Admiral King-Hall, commanding the squadron, was anxious to undertake action before the onset of the monsoon season and ordered his ships into the delta.

On 6 July 1915, 8 months after the *Konigsberg* had secreted herself in the Delta, the *Mersey* and *Severn* made their way slowly up the main channel under rifle and artillery fire from the banks.

Finally, at 6.45 a.m., with a Henri Farman biplane to spot for them, the *Mersey* and *Severn* opened fire at 11,000yd. The *Konigsberg* returned a very accurate fire that hit and put out of action the *Mersey*'s forward 6in gun before she had even hit the German ship.

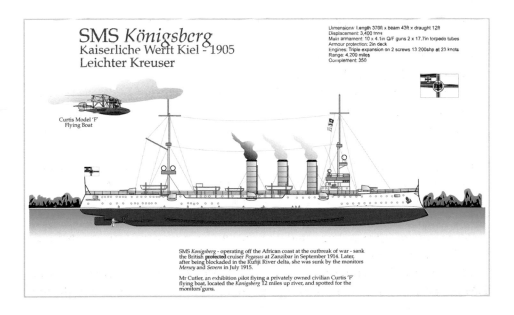

SMS *Königsberg*
Kaiserliche Werft Kiel - 1905
Leichter Kreuser

Dimensions: Length 370ft x beam 43ft x draught 12ft
Displacement: 3,400 tons
Main armament: 10 x 4.1in Q/F guns 2 x 17.7in torpedo tubes
Armour protection: 2in deck
Engines: Triple expansion on 2 screws 13,200shp at 23 knots
Range: 4,200 miles
Complement: 350

Curtis Model 'F'
Flying Boat

SMS *Konigsberg* - operating off the African coast at the outbreak of war - sank the British protected cruiser *Pegasus* at Zanzibar in September 1914. Later, after being blockaded in the Rufiji River delta, she was sunk by the monitors *Mersey* and *Severn* in July 1915.

Mr Cutler, an exhibition pilot flying a privately owned civilian Curtis 'F' flying boat, located the *Konigsberg* 12 miles up river, and spotted for the monitors' guns.

The reason for this accurate fire was a German observation post sighted in a tree within a few hundred yards of the British ships, and which was not discovered for an hour.

Once discovered, however, it was swiftly wiped out by a salvo of 6in shells and, thereafter, the German fire became less accurate while the British position improved. By 8.00 a.m., the *Severn* had scored six hits on the *Konigsberg*, with both ships continuing to rain shells on the German ship until evening before retiring to the open sea to replenish their magazines and repair damage.

The two monitors re-entered the Delta again on 11 July and, with a Caudron biplane as spotter, the two ships opened an accurate fire, hitting the German ship after the seventh salvo. During a 5-hour bombardment the Caudron was hit, but as the aircraft glided down it was able to report that the *Konigsberg*'s middle funnel had been shot away and the ship's stern was enveloped in flames. After a further twenty-five salvoes, resulting in heavy explosions, the ship was on fire from stem to stern and was a total loss.

With fire raging throughout the ship, Kapitan Looff, himself wounded, ordered demolition charges laid which blew out the ship's bottom, causing the battered wreck to settle on the riverbed, extinguishing most of the fires.

Earlier in December General von Lettow-Vorbeck, commanding German land forces, had requested Loofff to supply as many sailors as possible from the ship to augment his troops ashore and 150 of the crew were transferred to the Schutztruppe, where they served in the guerrilla campaign until the war's end. Additionally, the undamaged 4.1in and smaller guns were removed from the wreck and mounted on carriages and gave good service throughout the 4-year campaign. The wreck lay in the Rufiji River for many years as a reminder of a great naval action until finally being broken up for scrap between 1963 and 1965.

15

JUTLAND – EQUAL SPEED CHARLIE LONDON

By early 1916 a deep sense of frustration was being felt by the Lords of the Admiralty, politicians, the officers and men of the Grand Fleet and the general public alike at the seeming inability to bring the German fleet under the guns of the Royal Navy in a major sea battle that in everyone's expectation, or at least that of the man in the street, would end in the destruction of the High Seas Fleet, creating a victory of Nelsonian proportions.

Time and again over the past twenty-one months, the Grand Fleet had put to sea on the receipt of some intelligence to seek out their opposite numbers across the North Sea, but when the German ships had briefly emerged from their harbours to raid Britain's east coast or carry out some other operation off the Norwegian coast – due to bad communication or just bad luck - the British ships would arrive in the area of action too late to force a decision, allowing the High Seas Fleet frustratingly to slip away to safety.

The commander of the High Seas Fleet at the outbreak of war had been Admiral von Ingenohl, who was replaced following the Battle of the Dogger Bank in January 1915, where he was held responsible for the debacle, and for other losses that had occurred in the early months of the war.

His replacement, the former Chief of Naval Staff Admiral von Pohl, was under strict orders from the Kaiser that he should not risk the fleet unnecessarily, and that all future major operations should be personally approved by the Kaiser before being implemented.

Under these restrictions, the naturally cautious von Pohl conducted an even more timid policy throughout 1915, seldom ordering the fleet to venture more than 150 miles from base.

However, von Pohl's tenure as Fleet Commander was short-lived as he was terminally ill, dying of cancer, and he was replaced in January 1916 by Admiral Reinhard Scheer.

Reinhard Scheer had been born in 1863 in Obernkirchen, Lower Saxony, joining the Kaiserliche Marine at the age of 15 in 1879, serving in the Far East and on the East African Squadron from 1884 to 1890. After various commands, including the battleship SMS *Elsass*, Scheer was promoted in 1909 as Chief of Staff to the Commanding Officer of the High Seas Fleet.

In December 1913 Scheer was again promoted, this time to Vice-Admiral with the 2nd Battle Squadron, remaining in that position until January 1915.

After his eventual appointment to Fleet Commander, Scheer advocated for more aggressive tactics to be implemented, with a series of raids on the British coast to be undertaken, with the intention of drawing out isolated units of the Grand Fleet and luring them into a trap where they could be overwhelmed by a major portion of the High Seas Fleet lying in wait near the German coast.

By this method, together with the use of U-boats and raids by Zeppelins on the British mainland, Scheer intended to persuade Admiral Sir John Jellicoe to risk his precious ships in pursuing the German raiding squadrons deep into the German Bight.

A new offensive spirit now imbued the High Seas Fleet under its new commander and plans were made to employ Admiral Hipper's fast battle-cruisers to draw part of the Grand Fleet into a trap at the first opportunity.

In Room 40 at the Admiralty in London, towards the end of January 1916 the increase in monitored wireless traffic indicated that some form of sortie was being planned by the German fleet.

On 9 February, the listening stations detected a peak in wireless communications at Wilhelmshaven and the Grand Fleet and the Harwich Flotilla were alerted for action. When it was revealed that a force of German light cruisers and torpedo boats had left the Jade Basin, the Grand Fleet, including the battle-cruiser force, put to sea at midnight on 10 February, heading south to join up with Tyrwhitt's Harwich Force.

However, once again they were too late, as the German ships had fallen on a flotilla of minesweeping sloops off the Dogger Bank. After sinking one and inflicting damage on the others in an action lasting 35 minutes, they immediately ran for home, once again frustrating their would-be adversaries.

Although there appeared to be little to gain from Scheer's minor sortie, it was all part of his plan to divide the British fleet, but Jellicoe was not to be moved, either by the German actions or demands from politicians at home, to base some of his battleships further south in the Humber and the Forth, thus splitting his force, a course of action which he firmly rejected.

Apart from the dreadful and seemingly unending carnage on the Western Front that was soon to climax in the Battle of the Somme that commenced in July, other troubles were at hand, with the outbreak in Ireland of the Easter rebellion in April led by Sinn Fein, providing a suitable diversion that Admiral Scheer felt he could take advantage of.

The British for their part were now convinced that such an action at sea might well take place, and accordingly the Harwich Force were recalled to harbour to prepare for action. Similarly, the battle squadrons at Scapa and the battle-cruiser force at Rosyth were coaled, stored and took on ammunition, and raised steam in readiness for action.

Again, the first indication of a suggested sortie came via the listening stations and on 24 April, while a fierce southerly gale beset Scapa, the Admiralty informed Jellicoe that conditions in the southern North Sea were more favourable and ordered the fleet to sea. This included the new powerful ships of the fast Queen Elizabeth 5th Battle Squadron.

At the same time Beatty's battle-cruiser squadron departed Rosyth for the rendezvous point off the Dogger Bank.

The German fleet led by Admiral Bodicker, temporarily in command of the first Scouting Group, had sailed that evening, but had a mishap when SMS *Seydlitz* ran onto a mine off the Danish coast and was forced to return to Wilhelmshaven. The other ships of the scouting group pressed on westward, creating a very threatening situation, as the Grand Fleet were still too far to the north, and only Commodore Tyrwhitt's Harwich Force stood between them and the vulnerable towns and harbours of the east coast.

In the first light of dawn, as Tyrwhitt's cruisers sped north, they saw to eastward the unmistakable outline of three German battle-cruisers and accompanying warships on course for Lowestoft.

HMS *Canada*
Armstrongs Whitworth, Elswick - 1913
Super Dreadnought Battleship

Dimensions: Length 654ft x 92ft beam x 28ft draught
Displacement: 28,000 tons (normal), 32,200 tons (deep load)
Main armament: 10 x 14in 45 calibre Mark1
Secondary armament: 16 x 6in 50 calibre
Armour protection: Main belt 9in. main deck 1.25in. turrets 10in
Engines: Brown & Curtis direct drive turbines on four shafts 37,000shp at 22 knots
Coal stowage / range: 1,500 tons, 4,000 miles at 10 knots
Complement: 1,150

HMS *Canada* was originally laid down for the Chilean Navy as the *Almirante Latorre*, but was taken over by the Royal Navy at the outbreak of the Great War. At the end of hostilities the vessel was returned to Chile in April 1920, where she served as fleet flagship under her original name until she was scrapped in1959.

100 feet

Completely outnumbered and outgunned, Tyrwhitt nevertheless closed on the enemy and, when sure that he had been seen, reversed course to the south to give time for Beatty's battle-cruisers to come within range. Admiral Bodicker was not, however, deceived and held his course for Lowestoft, where he bombarded the town for 30 minutes with 12in shells before heading up the coast to Great Yarmouth, where he planned to mete out similar treatment.

Seeing this, the Harwich Force again reversed course to engage the German light cruisers at extreme range – an action which caused the battle-cruisers to abandon their attack on Great Yarmouth and pour heavy shell fire on the now retreating British ships, damaging the cruiser HMS *Conquest* and the destroyer *Laertes*, after which the enemy ships set off at high speed eastward for their home ports.

Tyrwhitt again turned his damaged ships to shadow the enemy and by 8.30 a.m. had their smoke in sight, but the British heavy ships were still too far away to bring the Germans to action and at 10.00 a.m. the chase was called off.

Dejectedly, as so often in the past, the British squadrons set course for their bases. Once again the Germans had escaped punishment while achieving a propaganda victory.

In Germany, the effect of the seeming ease with which ships of the High Seas Fleet could raid Britain's coasts at will and escape pursuit and damage demonstrated the power of their fleet that could defy the Royal Navy with impunity. With this and other minor successes over the Royal Navy, the Chancellor Bethmann-Hollweg called for the suspension of the policy of unrestricted submarine warfare that had caused a dangerous situation to develop between Germany and the United States.

Eventually, on 4 May, the policy was suspended and relations with the United States improved temporarily. Throughout May 1916 the commanders on both sides of the North Sea prepared their plans for what they now saw as an inevitable and imminent clash of arms.

Scheer was now aware that a new powerful force of fast capital ships, the 5th Battle Squadron, was now based in the Forth and he resolved to draw them out on their own by a bombardment of Sunderland, and to engage and overwhelm them quickly before the slower main units of the Grand Fleet could interfere.

Additionally, and important to his plan, was the disposition of U-boats now released from commerce raiding to form a barrier along the lines of advance of the British fleet to attack them as they left harbour. He also planned to use Zeppelin airships to patrol ahead of the fleet to give an early warning of the approach of British ships.

As a result of the Lowestoft raid, and in response to public opinion but against the advice of Admiral Jellicoe, the First Lord of the Admiralty, Arthur Balfour, announced a redistribution of naval forces, with the 5th Battle Squadron being permanently based at Rosyth under the direct command of Admiral Beatty.

Admiral Scheer deployed fourteen U-boats to take up station off the British bases but they arrived too late, as Jellicoe's ships had already passed through their patrol lines hours before.

Similarly, five Zeppelin airships were detailed on the morning of 31 May to patrol the North Sea to scout ahead of the High Seas Fleet as it made its way up the Jutland coast, followed by five other airships later in the evening, but in the event their reports were fragmentary and confusing and did little to help Admiral Scheer in understanding the movements of the British fleet during the Battle of Jutland. Although Admiral Beatty was later incorrectly convinced that the Zeppelin airships were the key that enabled Scheer's ships to escape.

As both sides prepared their plans throughout May, increased wireless traffic alerted the Admiralty, and when, at 3.30 p.m. on 30 May, a signal originating from the German fleet flagship SMS *Friedrich der Grosse* had been decoded by Room 40 as 'Carry out secret instruction 2940 on 31 May', it was deduced that a major fleet operation was about to take place. In response Jellicoe ordered the entire Grand Fleet to sea.

Aboard the 148 ships at Scapa Flow, Rosyth and Invergordon, a scene of intense activity prevailed as the ships prepared for sea. All liberty men ashore were hastily recalled to their ships and with thick clouds of black smoke pouring from their funnels as they raised steam with all facility, each ship soon hoisting the signal to their yard arms, ready to proceed. By early evening the boom-defence trawlers had drawn back the anti-submarine nets and floating booms to allow the great ships through marked channels to the open sea.

At 11.30 p.m. the flag signal 'weigh anchor and point ship' was run to the masthead of the fleet flagship *Iron Duke* and from Scapa, squadron by squadron, the ships of the Grand Fleet gathered way and slid out through Hoxa Sound, showing no lights, in ordered succession to their rendezvous eastward of the Long Forties. The King's ships were at sea.

Jellicoe's force consisted of twenty-four dreadnought battleships of the 4th and 1st Battle Squadrons (leaving from Scapa), the 2nd Battle Squadron (leaving from the Cromarty Firth), three battle-cruisers of the 3rd Battle-Cruiser Squadron, eight older armoured cruisers of the 1st and 2nd Cruiser Squadrons, together with eleven light cruisers and fifty-one destroyers.

Similarly, at Rosyth Beatty's flagship *Lion* at 11.00 p.m., the ships of the 1st Battle-Cruiser Squadron and four of the brand new 15in gunned *Queen Elizabeth* class super-dreadnoughts of the 5th Battle Squadron were lead out, a total force of four super-dreadnoughts, six battle-cruisers, one seaplane carrier, twelve light cruisers and twenty-nine destroyers. They set course direct for the Skagerrak at high speed, although the position of the German fleet was at that time still unknown to the British commanders. After joining forces with the 2nd Battle Squadron at 11.00 a.m. on 31 May, 200 miles east of the Cromarty Firth, Jellicoe continued

German Dreadnought SMS *Ostfriesland* with zeppelin *L33* flying overhead. (Airship Heritage Trust)

east-south-east at a more leisurely pace towards the Jutland Bank until the German dispositions could be confirmed.

The German forces were led by Admiral Hipper's 1st Scouting Group of five battle-cruisers and four light cruisers of the 2nd Scouting Group, which left the Jade Basin at 1.00 a.m. on 31 May, 2 hours ahead of Admiral Scheer's fleet of sixteen dreadnought battleships, a squadron of six pre-dreadnoughts, five light cruisers and four flotillas of torpedo boats that now followed them to spring the trap on Beatty's ships, once Hipper's battle-cruisers had drawn them in.

Typical of the German battleships facing Jellicoe was the SMS *Konig*, one of nine battleships comprising the 3rd Squadron of the High Seas Fleet.

The Germans had the advantage that their ships were designed to operate almost exclusively in the North Sea, whereas the British ships had to serve all over the world – a feature the Germans took full advantage of in their construction. Their systems of subdivision and damage control by flooding were superior to the British, as was their armour protection, which allowed their ships to take terrific punishment.

As mentioned earlier, cordite charges in the German ships were handled in brass canisters, and their system of magazine protection was clearly vastly superior to the British system, as demonstrated by the loss of three British battle-cruisers at Jutland. German gunnery was also superior to the British. The accuracy of German opening salvoes was remarkable and the quality of the German shells was excellent,

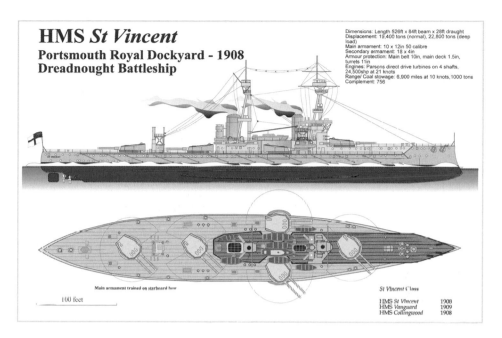

HMS *St Vincent*

Portsmouth Royal Dockyard - 1908
Dreadnought Battleship

Dimensions: Length 526ft x 84ft beam x 28ft draught
Displacement: 19,400 tons (normal), 22,800 tons (deep load)
Main armament: 10 x 12in 50 calibre
Secondary armament: 18 x 4in
Armour protection: Main belt 10in, main deck 1.5in, turrets 11in
Engines: Parsons direct drive turbines on 4 shafts, 24,500shp at 21 knots
Range/ Coal stowage: 6,900 miles at 10 knots,1000 tons
Complement: 756

Main armament trained on starboard bow

100 feet

St Vincent Class

HMS *St Vincent*	1908
HMS *Vanguard*	1909
HMS *Collingwood*	1908

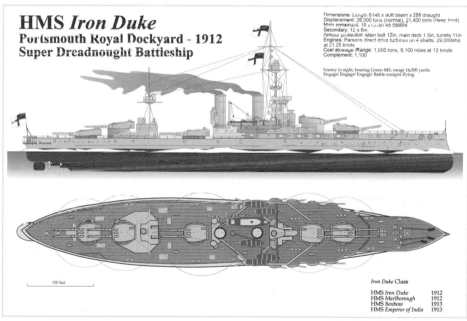

HMS *Iron Duke*

Portsmouth Royal Dockyard - 1912
Super Dreadnought Battleship

Dimensions: Length 614ft x 90ft beam x 28ft draught
Displacement: 26,000 tons (normal), 31,400 tons (deep load)
Main armament: 10 x 13.5in 45 calibre
Secondary: 12 x 6in
Armour protection: Main belt 12in, main deck 1.5in, turrets 11in
Engines: Parsons direct drive turbines on 4 shafts, 29,000shp at 21.25 knots
Coal stowage /Range: 1,500 tons, 8,100 miles at 12 knots
Complement: 1,100

Enemy in sight, bearing Green 045, range 16,500 yards.
Engage! Engage! Engage! Battle ensigns flying.

100 feet

Iron Duke Class

HMS *Iron Duke*	1912
HMS *Marlborough*	1912
HMS *Benbow*	1913
HMS *Emperor of India*	1913

in contrast to the British, where often the faulty armour-piercing shells broke up on impact without penetrating the German armour. Without a doubt the German ships, class for class, were superior to the British.

The *Konig* had 25,390 tons' displacement and was 580ft in length with a beam of 97ft. Her main armament consisted of ten 12in 45 calibre guns, with a secondary armament of fourteen 5.9in guns mounted in embrasures at upper-deck level turbines on three shafts of 34,000hp, which gave her a speed of 21 knots and a range of 4,600 miles at 10 knots. It carried a crew of 1,160.

The day broke clear and calm with only a gentle swell as Jellicoe's battleships proceeded on a south-easterly course towards the rendezvous point in cruising formation of six columns of four ships in line abreast, steaming at 15 knots.

Visibility at that time of day was excellent, though it was to deteriorate later, while the cruiser screen, spread in a line 2 miles ahead of the fleet, anxiously scanned the clear horizon for the first signs of smoke that would indicate enemy ships.

After 7 hours of searching an empty sea, at 2.00 p.m., with Beatty's battle-cruisers in the lead on a south-easterly course and with the 5th Battle Squadron following 5 miles astern of them, the two squadrons were approaching their turning point, from where they would reverse course to the north-east at what was seemingly the end of yet another fruitless search.

Unknown to Beatty, just beyond the horizon Hipper's ships were steaming north-east, on a course that if nothing interfered would place them directly in the path of the British battle squadrons.

At 2.15 p.m., the signal to turn was given and Beatty's ships began to swing round on to a north-easterly course.

As the turn commenced, the ships on the eastern side of the cruiser screen initially sighted the smoke and then the masts and upper works of a steamer to the east-south-east.

Commodore Alexander-Sinclair of the 1st Light Cruiser Squadron, flying his flag in HMS *Galatea*, turned towards the east to investigate the strange vessel, being followed in this change of course by the cruisers HMS *Phaeton*, HMS *Inconstant* and HMS *Cordelia*.

Simultaneously, 15 miles to the east on the west wing of the German scouting line, the cruiser *Elbing* had also sighted the steamer and, accompanied by two torpedo boats, turned to the west to investigate. The mystery vessel was the Danish steamer *N.J. Fjord* and, as the German and British ships closed on her, they each recognised the masts and funnels of enemy ships and flashed the flag and wireless signal 'enemy in sight' to their respective commanders. At 2.28 p.m. the *Galatea* opened up with her 6in guns at the *Elbing*, the first shots in the great sea battle.

The initial Morse wireless reports from both sides indicated the presence of only light units and, unknown to either Beatty or Hipper, the opposing battle-cruiser forces were at this time some 40 miles apart, heading towards each other at a combined closing speed of 45 knots.

In the initial exchange of gunfire the *Galatea* had been hit by a shell that had failed to explode, while Beatty, on receipt of a report 'smoke to the south-east', increased speed and turned onto that course, at the same time ordering the seaplane carrier HMS *Engadine* to launch a seaplane to scout ahead.

Due to the time it took to become airborne and the misty conditions now developing, the reconnaissance contributed no useful information to assist Beatty's deliberations. A confused gun duel commenced, with either side struggling to discern what was the strength and class of ship ranged against them so that they could communicate the information to their respective commanders.

Beatty's six battle-cruisers had now worked up to 25 knots, altered course and raced off to support the scouting cruisers, but Beatty's flag signal instructing his squadron to go round to a south-easterly course could not be read by the *Barham*, the flagship of the trailing 5th Battle Squadron under Rear Admiral Evan-Thomas, it continued on its previous track for over 10 minutes before it altered course to follow the 1st Battle-Cruiser Squadron to the south-east. By then, however, due to its slower cruising speed, a gap of 10 miles now separated the two sections of Beatty's command, which was to have repercussions later.

Pressing on regardless, Beatty led his six battle-cruisers towards the smoke on the horizon that presaged the advancing column of the German battle-cruisers, and at 3.30 p.m. the *Lion*, leading the line, had them in sight. Unknown to him, Admiral Hipper, in the recently commissioned SMS *Lutzow*, had spotted the British line 10 minutes earlier as he raced north at 24 knots. He immediately reversed course to the south in accordance with the plan to draw the British ships on to the main body of the High Seas Fleet hurrying north some 50 miles to the south.

Jellicoe and the Grand Fleet were in turn at this time around 60 miles to the north of Beatty's ships and, having received partially incomplete reports as to the position of the German ships, were increasing speed as they pounded south to what they hoped would at last be a chance to bring the enemy under their guns. So began the first part of the battle, known to historians as The Run to the South.

Meanwhile, Beatty held his fire, being unable due to deteriorating visibility to accurately estimate the range. Hipper had no such problem, with the British ships starkly outlined against a westering sun, while they themselves were partially concealed by the mists to the east, and at 3.48 p.m. the German ships opened fire at 16,500yd.

Simultaneously, great tongues of flame leapt from the *Lion's* fore turrets as her first salvo crashed out, but the range had been overestimated and the shells flew harmlessly over the German line to land almost a mile beyond them. The Germans on the other hand quickly found the range and after only a few salvoes the *Lion*, *Tiger* and *Princess Royal* had already been hit two or three times each.

The *Princess Royal* had her A turret put out of action and *Tiger* temporarily found her fore turrets jammed and unable to traverse, while her gun-laying director was badly damaged.

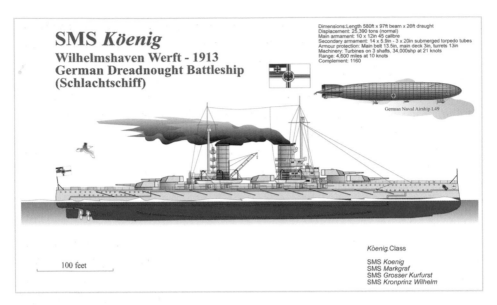

SMS Köenig
Wilhelmshaven Werft - 1913
German Dreadnought Battleship
(Schlachtschiff)

Dimensions:Length 580ft x 97ft beam x 26ft draught
Displacement: 25,390 tons (normal)
Main armament: 10 x 12in 45 calibre
Secondary armament: 14 x 5.9in - 3 x 20in submerged torpedo tubes
Armour protection: Main belt 13.5in, main deck 3in, turrets 13in
Machinery: Turbines on 3 shafts, 34,000shp at 21 knots
Range: 4,600 miles at 10 knots
Complement: 1160

German Naval Airship L49

100 feet

Köenig Class

SMS Koenig
SMS Markgraf
SMS Grosser Kurfurst
SMS Kronprinz Wilhelm

Jacky Fisher's maxim of hit first, hit hard and keep hitting was patently not working for the British ships, and it was not until 3.55 p.m., with the range down to 12,800yd, that the first German ship to be hit was the *Seydlitz*. Two 13.5in shells from *Princess Royal* pierced a forward barbette and started a fierce cordite fire in the handling room below the turret, killing all the gun crew, which only by prompt flooding of the magazine saved the ship from a major disaster.

Once again, confusion with signalling resulted in two British ships firing on a single target leaving the *Derfflinger* to practise unhindered on the British line.

At 3.58 p.m. the *Queen Mary*, realising she was unengaged, shifted her fire to the *Derfflinger*, immediately scoring hits.

As both protagonists sped to the south-east with the range closing, both flagships were hit at the same time, and while the *Lutzow*'s damage was relatively minor, the *Lion* was almost lost when a 12in armour-piercing shell penetrated the midships Q turret, causing terrible carnage and sending a flash of flame through the open flash doors to the handling room, starting an intense cordite fire. The swift action of Major Harvey of the Royal Marines, who with his dying breath ordered the turret flooded, saved the ship. The order was carried out by Chief Gunner Warrant Officer Alfred Grant, who seized the red-hot flood-valve wheels, burning his hands terribly, to flood the chamber. Major Harvey was awarded a posthumous Victoria Cross.

The German fire in contrast to the British efforts was extremely accurate, with *Lion* receiving six hits in rapid succession, while the *Princess Royal* had had Y turret aft disabled by a shell hit.

At 4.04 p.m. the rearmost ship *Indefatigable*, which had just started trading shots with the *Von der Tann* for 4 minutes, firing some forty shells without scoring a hit on the German ship, was hit herself with two 11in shells that struck together by the aft turret, penetrating the 3in armoured barbette. This caused a massive cordite fire that spread rapidly to the after magazine, exploding with great violence and blowing the bottom out of the ship. The ship began to sink rapidly by the stern, only to receive two further 12in shells on the A turret, which penetrated the forward magazine and caused a catastrophic explosion. The *Indefatigable* disappeared beneath the waves, and from her crew of 1,019 there were only two survivors.

The effect on the crews that witnessed the violent end of one of their much vaunted battle-cruisers must have been a profound shock, which together with the poor shooting of the British ships must have caused Beatty to question the wisdom of including these ships in the line of battle, for which they were not originally designed.

About this time, *Lion*, with damage-control crews struggling to control the fires raging on her, turned away from the German line, increasing the range to 21,000yd as Evan-Thomas's 5th Battle Squadron eventually arrived on the scene, where, after sweeping the German light cruisers aside, at 4.08 p.m. at a range of 19,000yd brought a concentrated and accurate fire of fifteen salvoes to fall on the rear of the German line, with the *Barham* hitting the *Von der Tann* below the waterline and *Moltke* also receiving serious hits. With her fires partly under control, Beatty now turned back to close the range first to 16,000yd then to 14,000yd, with the *Lion*

HMS *Invincible* battle-cruiser lost at Jutland, 1916. (Author's collection)

engaging *Lutzow* in a fierce exchange of fire. Despite the *Lion* being hit three more times, it seemed that at last severe punishment was now being meted out to the German line.

It was now that a severe deficiency became apparent in the construction of the British projectiles. Despite the fact that British shells were falling accurately on their targets, they failed to penetrate the German armour, exploding prematurely and breaking up on impact, causing only minor damage. In the opinion of Admiral Hipper, this saved his ships from almost certain disaster at this stage of the battle.

At 4.17 p.m., the *Derfflinger* and *Seydlitz* shifted their fire to the *Queen Mary*, which had been making excellent practice on the German ships and which continued to respond with accurate fire, hitting both ships several times. At 4.26 p.m., to the horror of the observers on the *Tiger* and *New Zealand* next astern of her, three shells crashed home on the *Queen Mary*'s foredeck, followed by two further 12in shells from the next salvo. This caused a massive concussion as her magazines detonated in a colossal explosion that destroyed the forepart of the ship and flung a huge towering pillar of flame and writhing black smoke hundreds of feet into the air.

The *Tiger*, next astern, had to haul out of line to avoid hitting the wreckage, as debris from the doomed ship rained down on her decks. As *New Zealand* swept by she was shaken by further violent underwater detonations, as *Queen Mary* sank, taking 1,266 officers and men to the bottom of the North Sea.

As destroyers hurried to pick up the twenty or so survivors from the doomed ship, a shocked Admiral Beatty, contemplating the loss of two of his battle-cruisers within 22 minutes, was heard to remark on the bridge of the *Lion* to Captain Chatfield that, 'There seems to be something wrong with our bloody ships today'.

As the chase continued to the south-south-east, a fierce series of actions were being fought out between the British destroyers and the German torpedo boats, with HMS *Obdurate* and HMS *Nomad* being hit, while two German torpedo boats, *V29* and *V27*, were sunk. The destroyers HMS *Nestor* and HMS *Nicator* launched torpedoes at the German battle-cruisers at 6,000yd which, although they missed, caused the German ships to turn away. Their own torpedo boats fired torpedoes at the British line from 9,000yd without effect.

Suddenly, the whole situation changed dramatically, as at 4.38 p.m. Admiral Goodenough's 2nd Light Cruiser Squadron, scouting ahead, sighted from the *Southampton* the enemy battle fleet bearing 122° course 347° at a distance of 12 miles. Beatty waited until he saw the lead German battleship *Konig* emerging from the mist and, 7 minutes after the *Queen Mary* had been lost, at 4.33 p.m. he ordered his squadron to reverse course to the north-north-west, signalling the 5th Battle Squadron to follow suit. The battle now entered its second phase.

The German battle-cruisers had lured Beatty into their trap: the hunters had become the hunted.

The ships of the 5th Battle Squadron, *Barham, Valiant, Warspite* and *Malaya*, began their turn slightly later at 4.54 p.m., and were taken under fire from the High Seas Fleet at 19,000yd, with only *Barham* being hit, receiving only minor damage.

The destroyers HMS *Petard* and HMS *Turbulent* attacked the *Seydlitz* with torpedoes, striking her on the starboard side and causing damage and flooding in the forward boiler room, while the *Marksman* also fired torpedoes in pairs at the main German line without success. Later analysis showed that greater success could be achieved if attacks were made with groups of boats working together and launching multiple salvoes simultaneously.

The powerful *Queen Elizabeths* were now severely punishing the German battle-cruisers and at 4.55 p.m. both the already badly damaged *Seydlitz* and *Derfflinger* were hit by two 15in shells each.

Jellicoe and the battle squadrons of the Grand Fleet were now closing on the German fleet and had sent the 3rd Battle-Cruiser Squadron ahead to support Beatty's depleted squadron. Under the command of Admiral the Honourable Horace Hood, the squadron at 4.00 p.m. increased speed to 24 knots and steered for the reported position of Beatty's ships but, due to navigational errors, found the cruiser *Chester* on his starboard beam, which was being engaged by four German cruisers and had been hit seventeen times by 4.1in shells, receiving heavy damage and casualties, among whom was Boy First Class Jack Cornwall. He earned a posthumous Victoria Cross when, although mortally wounded, he remained at his gun awaiting orders when the rest of the crew were killed or wounded.

Admiral Hood's squadron in turn now opened fire on the enemy cruisers from 10,000yd, their shells disabling SMS *Wiesbaden* and severely damaging SMS *Pillau*, while the light forces of both sides continued to launch torpedo attacks on their opposite numbers.

As Jellicoe pounded southward, he was frustrated by the lack of accurate information regarding the position of the main body of the German fleet, as Beatty had failed to keep him informed, and what signals he had received were contradictory and inaccurate, with only sketchy information as to the last known bearings, position and speed of the High Seas Fleet.

Beatty's battle-cruisers were sighted at 6.00 p.m. where, with the onset of twilight, visibility had reduced to 7 miles and it was becoming imperative to have this information so that he could deploy the Grand Fleet from cruising formation of six lines of four ships in box formation into a single line 9 miles in length that would cross the enemy T, effectively trapping them.

At 6.01 p.m., Jellicoe signalled *Lion* 'Where is the enemy's battle fleet?' After an interval of 14 minutes, due to poor communications the reply came from Beatty, 'Have Enemy battle fleet in sight bearing south-west'.

This information arrived just in time, as the opposing fleets drew closer together and the flag signal 'Equal Speed Charlie London' broke from the masthead of the

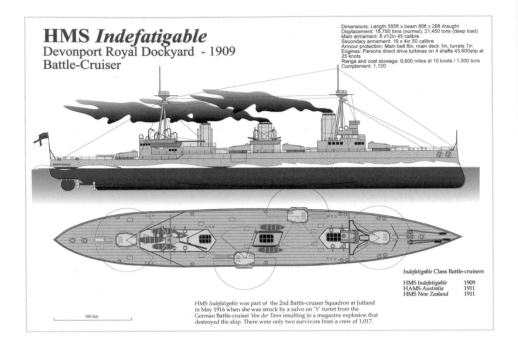

HMS *Indefatigable*
Devonport Royal Dockyard - 1909
Battle-Cruiser

Dimensions: Length 555ft x beam 80ft x 26ft draught
Displacement: 18,750 tons (normal), 21,450 tons (deep load)
Main armament: 8 x12in 45 calibre
Secondary armament: 16 x 4in 50 calibre
Armour protection: Main belt 6in, main deck 1in, turrets 7in
Engines: Parsons direct drive turbines on 4 shafts 43,600shp at 25 knots
Range and coal stowage: 6,600 miles at 10 knots / 1,300 tons
Complement: 1,120

Indefatigable Class Battle-cruisers

HMS *Indefatigable*	1909
HAMS *Australia*	1911
HMS *New Zealand*	1911

100 feet

HMS *Indefatigable* was part of the 2nd Battle-cruiser Squadron at Jutland in May 1916 when she was struck by a salvo on 'Y' turret from the German Battle-cruiser *Von der Tann* resulting in a magazine explosion that destroyed the ship. There were only two survivors from a crew of 1,017.

Iron Duke for the deployment of the port column of four ships, with the succeeding lines following in sequence, to form a single line on an east-south-easterly course. This manoeuvre was carried out not a moment too soon for, as the last of Jellicoe's ships formed into line, the High Seas Fleet appeared out of the mist, heading straight for the British line.

This must have seemed a moment of triumph for Jellicoe. After 2½ years of frustration and disappointment, here at last the German fleet had sailed into his trap. For Admiral Scheer this must have been his worst nightmare. As he pressed on at full speed he found himself confronted by a continuous line of great grey battleships fading into the mist at either end, an iron trap from which only a miracle could save him and his fleet from complete destruction.

At the rear of the British line on deployment the *Marlborough* was nearest to the enemy and opened fire at 9,000yd range, and although visibility was poor she and the other ships of the 5th and 6th divisions poured a withering storm of shells into the van of Scheer's battleships, wreaking terrible damage to the *Konig*, SMS *Grosser Kurfurst*, SMS *Kronprinz* and other ships of the 3rd Squadron of the High Seas Fleet.

At 6.20 p.m. the fleet flagship *Iron Duke* opened fire on a ship of the *Kaiser* class, scoring several hits and starting fierce fires.

The *Iron Duke* was a magnificent warship, 620ft in length, of 26,400 tons' displacement. Her turbines developed 29,000hp to deliver 21 knots, she mounted ten 13.5in 45 calibre Mk V guns that could hurl a 1,400lb high explosive shell to a range of 25,000yd at an elevation of 20°. She was also extremely well protected with a 12in main belt and 1.5in armour to the main deck.

As the Grand Fleet deployed, the 1st Cruiser Squadron – comprising the armoured cruisers *Defence, Warrior, Duke of Edinburgh* and *Black Prince* – were led by Rear Admiral Sir Robert Arbuthnot towards the enemy line, suddenly they found themselves emerging from the mist to within 9,000yd of the German dreadnoughts. Immediately, a storm of shells fell on the ships, with a 12in shell piercing the *Defence*'s thin armour, penetrating her aft 9.2 magazine and, as explosions ripped through her, she blew up, completely disintegrating with the loss of all her crew and the Rear Admiral himself.

The *Warrior* was in turn struck by over twenty shells, but miraculously survived the onslaught, though in a sinking condition. She was saved from almost certain destruction by the *Warspite* which, suffering from a jammed helm, steamed out of line in two complete circles to within 10,000yd of the German line, diverting their attention from the *Warrior*. *Warspite* was hit over twelve times by heavy shells but was saved from serious damage by her effective armour.

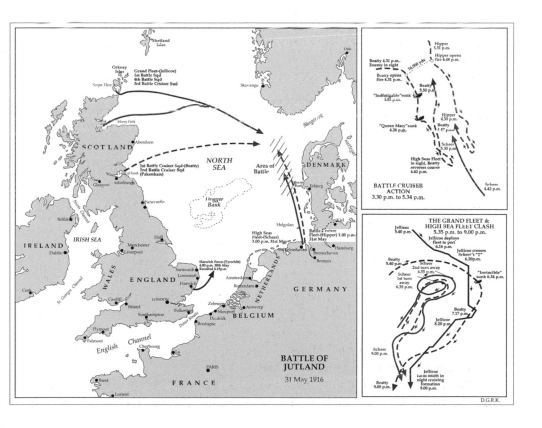

The *Warrior* and the two remaining ships turned away to safety. The *Warrior* was taken in tow by the seaplane carrier *Engadine* but, despite their best efforts, she sank the next day 160 miles east of Aberdeen.

At 6.00 p.m., Beatty steered his ships across the front of the Grand Fleet, masking their targets with his smoke and delaying Jellicoe from closing on the German fleet. Likewise, Vice-Admiral Hood turned his three battle-cruisers to starboard and opened an accurate fire on the German battle-cruisers, with *Invincible* and *Inflexible* scoring eight shell hits on Hipper's flagship *Lutzow* between 6.26 p.m. and 6.34 p.m., causing severe damage and flooding. *Derfflinger* received two hits from *Indomitable* while *Seydlitz* also took an armour-piercing shell.

As the duel continued, *Lutzow* and *Derfflinger* replied with accurate fire on HMS *Invincible*. At 6.34 p.m., a hit on the midships Q turret, penetrating the armour, started a fierce fire that quickly spread to the other magazines, and with a tremendous explosion the battle-cruiser blew apart, with the two halves sinking so that the bow and stern stood pointing to the sky like two steel tombstones. Of the crew of 1,028 there were only six survivors.

By 6.30 p.m., all the ships of the Grand Fleet were in action, pouring a continuous and rapid fire into the German line, with almost every ship being pounded mercilessly and tremendous damage being inflicted on them. If it were not for their exceptionally strong armour protection, watertight subdivision and superior methods of magazine protection to the British they would already have been sunk.

At this stage of the battle, despite the British losses, Jellicoe was in command and the German fleet were in danger of annihilation.

Hipper's battle-cruisers were battered wrecks, with both *Seydlitz and Defflinger* having most of their guns knocked out, and both down by the bows with thousands of tons of seawater on board, while *Lutzow* was in a sinking condition and falling out of the line.

At 6.33 p.m., in a desperate measure to save his ships, Admiral Scheer ordered the *Gefechtskehrtwendung*, or battle turn away, to be implemented, where the German battleships all individually turned through 180° on to a reverse course. This manoeuvre was covered by a mass attack by the 3rd Torpedo Boat Flotilla, whose torpedoes, fired at great range, did no harm.

By 6.45 p.m., the German ships had vanished as though by magic into the mist to the south-east, where Jellicoe was unwilling to follow because of the threat of torpedoes and mines. Accordingly, he turned the fleet to the south by divisions en echelon to stand between the German line of retreat and their bases to the east.

At this stage, Jellicoe was unaware that Scheer had in fact reversed his course and initially assumed the disappearance of the enemy was due to deteriorating visibility to the west. He therefore continued his southern course for a further 10 minutes before he realised that the High Seas Fleet had in fact turned away from him. Admiral Scheer, on the other hand, was fully aware that the combined might of the Grand Fleet now stood between him and the safety of Wilhelmshaven harbour.

At 6.54 p.m. the *Marlborough* at the rear of the line was struck by a torpedo, possibly fired by the 5,200-ton light cruiser *Wiesbaden* that had earlier been disabled and left as a stationary target by Admiral Beatty's battle-cruisers. She resolutely refused to sink, and continued to fire back at any ships that attacked her, despite being terribly damaged.

The *Marlborough* took on a 1,000 tons of seawater in her forward boiler room and developed a 7° list to starboard, but could still maintain its place in the line.

As the British ships began their cruise southward, the German fleet unexpectedly reappeared again at 7.00 p.m., once more on a north-easterly course.

Later, Admiral Scheer maintained that he had intended to re-engage Jellicoe's fleet, but more likely it was an attempt to break through behind the British fleet and reach the safety of their harbours.

Once again Scheer found that Jellicoe had crossed his T. The battered High Seas Fleet was now in the utmost peril; his attempt to escape had led him on to the waiting guns of the Grand Fleet.

At 7.00 p.m., with visibility favouring the British, while the Germans were starkly outlined against the setting sun, the *Ajax* opened fire from 18,000yd, followed by the other battleships, which smothered the van of the advancing German ships with a storm of shell-fire, causing them to suffer further heavy damage.

Scheer, alert to the possibility of the complete annihilation of his command, ordered his severely damaged battle-cruisers – now under the command of Captain Hartog of the *Derfflinger*, as the *Lutzow* had fallen out of the line in a sinking condition – to charge the British line and cover the withdrawal of the fleet.

The four battered battle-cruisers approached to within 7,800yd of the British battleships, where they received fearful punishment.

The *Derfflinger* was hit at 7.14 p.m. by a 15in HE shell from HMS *Revenge*, which penetrated the aftermost Y turret and exploded under the turret, killing the crew and starting a fierce cordite fire, which, thanks to good magazine protection, was contained.

A further hit from *Revenge* 3 minutes later penetrated the barbette of the aft X turret, starting another serious cordite fire, which also was brought under control.

Revenge scored two further hits on the boat deck and over the next 8 minutes *Derfflinger* took five 12in shells from HMS *Colossus* and one 12in HE from HMS *Collingwood*, with this shell exploding in the sick bay, wrecking a greater part of the superstructure.

Three further 15in shells from *Royal Oak* and a 12in shell from HMS *Bellerophon* also smashed into her around 7.20 p.m.

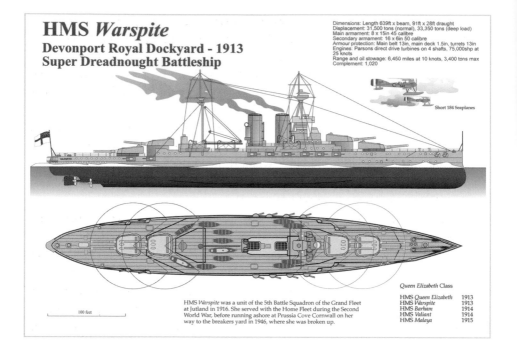

HMS *Warspite*
Devonport Royal Dockyard - 1913
Super Dreadnought Battleship

Dimensions: Length 639ft x beam, 91ft x 28ft draught
Displacement: 31,500 tons (normal), 33,350 tons (deep load)
Main armament: 8 x 15in 45 calibre
Secondary armament: 16 x 6in 50 calibre
Armour protection: Main belt 13in, main deck 1.5in, turrets 13in
Engines: Parsons direct drive turbines on 4 shafts, 75,000shp at 25 knots
Range and oil stowage: 6,450 miles at 10 knots, 3,400 tons max
Complement: 1,020

Short 184 Seaplanes

HMS *Warspite* was a unit of the 5th Battle Squadron of the Grand Fleet at Jutland in 1916. She served with the Home Fleet during the Second World War, before running ashore at Prussia Cove Cornwall on her way to the breakers yard in 1946, where she was broken up.

100 feet

Queen Elizabeth Class

HMS *Queen Elizabeth*	1913
HMS *Warspite*	1913
HMS *Barham*	1914
HMS *Valiant*	1914
HMS *Malaya*	1915

The *Seydlitz* received five hits between 7.14 p.m. and 7.20 p.m.: four 12in from HMS *Hercules* and HMS *St Vincent* and a 15in shell from the *Royal Oak*, these shells wrecking the aft superfiring turret and the 15in shell disabling the starboard 11in turret. At the back of the line *Von der Tann and Moltke* were hit several times. Finally, the battered hulks turned away, following the fleet into the smokescreens to the south. The death ride of the German battle-cruisers was at an end.

While this action was taking place, Scheer's battleships continued to take severe punishment, with the *Konig* being hit and the *Grosser Kurfurst* being hit seven times by 15in and 13.5in heavy shells from the ships of the 5th Battle Squadron, while the mighty *Agincourt* with her fourteen 12in guns hit SMS *Markgraf* and *Kaiser* with two shells each. SMS *Helgoland* received a 15in round that broke up on impact, causing only splinter damage.

At 7.18 p.m., Scheer ordered the second battle turn away, with his torpedo-boat flotillas covering the change of course with smokescreens and attacking the Grand Fleet. Jellicoe ordered the 4th Light Cruiser Squadron and destroyer flotillas to counter the move.

The German torpedo boats approached to within 7,500yd before discharging their torpedoes, where they were engaged by the battleships' secondary armament. The German torpedo boat *S35* was sunk by gunfire and others damaged. In all, about twenty-one torpedoes were fired, causing Jellicoe to order his ships to turn away to comb the tracks.

At this stage of the battle the German fleet were tactically beaten and there can be little doubt that, had Jellicoe turned towards instead of away from the German fleet, once contact had been re-established in the twilight, the ensuing action would have resulted in the annihilation of the High Seas Fleet. By turning away with half an hour of daylight left, the two fleets were moving away from each other at 20 knots.

At the same time Jellicoe was poorly served by his scouting cruisers, who failed to keep him informed of the enemy's movements. Equally, his subordinate captains in the line showed a lack of initiative when those at the rear of the line, who had clearly seen the German fleet reverse course, failed to inform their Commander-in-Chief of this vital information.

Even Goodenough's cruiser squadron, that up to now had been the most reliable source of information communicated to Jellicoe, saw at 7.30 p.m. the German battle fleet turning away to the south-west, but failed to communicate this urgent news to Jellicoe. At last realising that the German ships were on an opposing course at 7.35 p.m., Jellicoe turned to starboard in pursuit of the High Seas Fleet, expecting to come up with them again at 8.00 p.m., while at 7.45 p.m. Beatty's battle-cruisers, heading south-west across the path of the Grand Fleet, pressed on attracted by the sound of gunfire to the south.

Beatty regained contact with the German Fleet, which he duly reported to Jellicoe, but only supplied the bearing, again without indicating the ships' heading.

HMS *Colossus* GOVAN
Scotts Shipbuilding, Govern Clyde - 1910
Dreadnought Battleship

Dimensions: Length 541ft, Beam: , Draught:
Displacement: 20,000 tons (normal), 23,260 tons (deep load)
Main armament: 10 x 12in 50 calibre
Secondary armament: 16 x 4in 45 calibre
Armour protection: Main belt 11in, main deck 1.5in, turrets 10in
Engines: Parsons direct drive turbines on 4 shafts, 25,000shp at 21 knots
Coal stowage / Range: 1,000 tons 6,680 miles at 10 knots
Complement: 800

100 feet

Wing turrets bearing Green 090
Note port wing turret firing across

Colossus Class

HMS *Colossus*   1910
HMS *Hercules*   1910

Beatty once again fell on the four German battle-cruisers, causing more terrible damage to them. *Derfflinger* had lost six of her eight 12in guns, while *Seydlitz* and *Von der Tann* had four each out of action. Only *Moltke* had all ten of her guns fully operational.

Princess Royal opened fire at 8.19 p.m. at 12,000yd, scoring two hits with 13.5in armour-piercing shells, while *Lion* scored a hit on *Derfflinger* that jammed her sole remaining turret. At the same time she received three well-aimed shells from the *New Zealand* that, striking forward, burst under her armoured deck and increased the rate of flooding. The German ships attempted to make a reply but made no heavy-calibre hits, although *Lion* was hit by a 5.9in shell.

To the west of the German line, Beatty spotted the pre-dreadnoughts of the Second Squadron, the *Princess Royal* hitting SMS *Hannover* and *Tiger* straddling *Hessen*, while *New Zealand* hit SMS *Schleswig-Holstein* with two shells and fired on SMS *Schlesien*.

In turn, the *Indomitable* hit SMS *Pommern* with a 12in shell but was forced to cease fire at 8.33 p.m., as with the onset of darkness her gunlayers were unable to observe the fall of shot.

The British ships drew off and the action ended at 8.40 p.m. Five minutes later German battleships were spotted by the cruisers HMS *Royalist* and HMS *Caroline* of the 4th Light Cruiser Squadron, which moved to make an attack, but their commander, worried they might be British, stopped them. Eventually, however, he was persuaded to the contrary and the cruisers pressed home an attack, with torpedoes fired at a range of 7,000yd – all of which missed.

By now, at 9.15 p.m., it was too dark to consider further fleet action and at 9.17 p.m. Admiral Jellicoe ordered the fleet to assume night cruising order, with the intention of keeping between Scheer and his base and to renew action at first light. Admiral Beatty at the same time was positioned some 10 miles to the west of the battle fleet heading south-south-east, and took no further part in the night action.

On the German side at this time Admiral Hipper had transferred from the sinking *Lutzow* to the relatively undamaged *Moltke*, while Admiral Scheer in turn ordered his fleet to form line with the *Westfalen* at the head of the 1st Squadron and set course for Horns Reef.

The two fleets were now both steering SSE on gradually converging courses, although the slower cruising speed of the German fleet dictated that it would pass astern of the battle squadrons of the British fleet in the dark of the night.

The first skirmishes between the scouting flotillas began at 10.00 p.m. when Scheer's 7th Scouting Flotilla encountered the British 4th Flotilla stationed astern of the Grand Fleet.

The German torpedo boats *S14, S16, S18, and S24* launched torpedoes, to which the destroyers HMS *Garland*, *Constant* and *Fortune* replied with gunfire.

At 10.24 p.m. the light cruiser *Castor*, leading the 11th Flotilla, fought an action with the German light cruisers SMS *Hamburg*, *Elbing* and *Rostock*, with *Castor* hitting *Hamburg* with three 6in shells and who in turn was hit by ten 4.1in shells, which failed to penetrate the cruiser's armour.

Fifteen minutes later the German ships were joined by their 4th Scouting Group that included the light cruisers *Stettin*, *Frauenlob* and *Munchen*, which engaged Goodenough's 2nd Light Cruiser Squadron in a wild melee illuminated by searchlights, gun flashes and burning ships.

Stettin fired ninety-two 4.1in rounds at *Southampton*, knocking out a 6in gun, wrecking her wireless and causing many casualties.

Southampton responded by putting a torpedo into SMS *Frauenlob* and fatally damaging her with gunfire. She was set ablaze and capsized, with only nine survivors being picked up.

At 11.00 p.m., the Grand Fleet had unknowingly pulled ahead of the High Seas Fleet and Scheer altered course to port to break through the rear of the British line. The British destroyer flotillas began a series of confused actions, demonstrating the weakness in their training, and as a result these attacks were made piecemeal and in an uncoordinated manner, making them ineffectual.

At 11.30 p.m., the 4th Flotilla ran into the High Seas Fleet crossing its path. A challenge from *Tipperary* was answered with a blast of fire from the 5.9in guns of the *Westfalen*, followed by the *Nassau* opening up on the other destroyers.

The British ships fired torpedoes and, as the battleships turned away to avoid them, the battleship *Posen* rammed the cruiser *Elbing*, which later sank.

The *Spitfire*, after firing her torpedoes, rammed the *Nassau*, carrying off a section of the battleship's armour, and survived this close encounter to return to the Tyne next day.

As the *Broke* led the 4th Flotilla, she spotted the cruiser *Rostock*, torpedoing her in her boiler room. She was brought to a halt and later sank. The *Broke* was heavily damaged by the *Rostock's* 5.9in guns and the destroyer *Conquest* ran into *Sparrowhawk*, which was abandoned in a sinking condition.

Fortune was set on fire by *Westfalen*, while *Ardent* in a final brave attack at 12.25 a.m. on *Westfalen* was pounded into a blazing wreck and sank together with the badly damaged *Tipperary*.

The final loss of a major British heavy unit occurred at 10 minutes past midnight, when the armoured cruiser *Black Prince*, that earlier had been in action with the 1st Cruiser Squadron when the *Defence* had been blown up and the *Warrior* disabled, had for some reason been left behind by the fleet.

Now to the south-west, Captain Bonham closed on to a line of ships he assumed were British, when at 3,000yd range a German recognition signal flashed out in the darkness. Captain Bonham hauled round to port in an attempt to escape, but his fate was sealed.

Illuminating the *Black Prince* with searchlights, the *Thuringen* raked the cruiser with a storm of shells and she soon was ablaze from stem to stern.

As each succeeding ship swept past the wreck, they also added their quota of fire, leaving the *Black Prince* a blazing wreck, although she bravely attempted to fight back, hitting the *Rheinland* with two 6in shells. Eventually her magazines blew up in a colossal explosion and she vanished with all hands.

By an hour after midnight the German battle fleet had already broken through the destroyer screens and were crossing behind the Grand Fleet, while the sounds of firing and explosions were lighting the sky to the north of the British battle squadrons. As they headed south, they failed to inform their Commander-in-Chief aboard the *Iron Duke* of these startling developments, and minute by minute the opportunity to achieve what would have been the most comprehensive naval victory of all time slipped through his hands and evaporated with each mile further south that Jellicoe's ships sailed.

With the first streaks of dawn lighting the eastern sky at 2.10 a.m., the ships of the German Second Squadron broke through a final attack by the 11th Destroyer Flotilla, which delivered the heaviest combined torpedo attack on them, firing ten or so at a range of less than a mile, one of which struck the pre-dreadnought *Pommern*. This resulted in several internal explosions, followed by a tremendous explosion that blew the ship in two, after which it sank with all hands.

Earlier at 1.00 p.m., 90 miles off the Lyngwig lighthouse on the Danish coast, the foundering *Lutzow* lost its fight to stay afloat and her crew were taken off by torpedo boats as she sank bow first, with her screws lifting out of the water as she went down.

The *Seydlitz* was also struggling to keep afloat, having received one torpedo hit and twenty-one heavy and two medium-calibre shells. As dawn broke she was aground on a shoal off the Horns Reef with ninety-eight of her crew dead and fifty-five wounded, while *Derfflinger*, her decks a mass of twisted wreckage with 157 dead and twenty-one wounded, accompanied by the battered *Moltke* and the *Von der Tann*, crept eastwards into the dawn and slowly one by one the remnants of the High Seas Fleet returned to harbour.

Seydlitz was freed by the tugs sent to help her and, with pumps working at full pressure, she was towed off and stern first brought eventually safely into Wilhelmshaven on 2 June.

At 2.30 a.m., as the sky lightened into dawn, Admiral Jellicoe searched to the north-west for the expected signs of the High Seas Fleet, but to his great disappointment the horizon was empty. Beatty's battle-cruisers and the 5th Battle Squadron were out of sight some 16 miles to the south-west while his destroyer and cruiser flotillas were scattered far and wide.

Marlborough, having been hit by a torpedo, was being towed by the cruiser *Fearless* to the Humber, arriving on 2 June with her bows almost awash, but was repaired, rejoining the Fleet in September.

The *Warspite* was another casualty and, although extensively damaged in the battle, made her way back across the North Sea to Rosyth, being attacked by a U-boat on the way which she attempted to ram. After repair, she rejoined the fleet in July.

At 3.00 a.m., fearing that the German fleet had passed astern of him in the night, Jellicoe ordered a reversal of course to the north to try to regain contact with the High Seas Fleet and bring them under his guns once more, but he was too late.

Then at 3.55 a.m., Jellicoe received a wireless signal from the Admiralty informing him that at 2.30 a.m. the High Seas Fleet were in a position 16 nautical miles west of the Horns Reef, steering south-east at 16 knots.

This news came as a terrible shock to the Commander-in-Chief, as he realised that his chance to destroy the German fleet had been lost. Jellicoe turned his fleet for home at 7.30 p.m., collecting stragglers as they made their way across the North Sea. The great sea battle was over.

THE OUTCOME

The Germans had suffered considerable material damage to their fleet, but perhaps the greatest damage was to the morale of the officers and sailors of the German fleet. The battering they had received at Jutland left them with little appetite to meet the Grand Fleet again at sea.

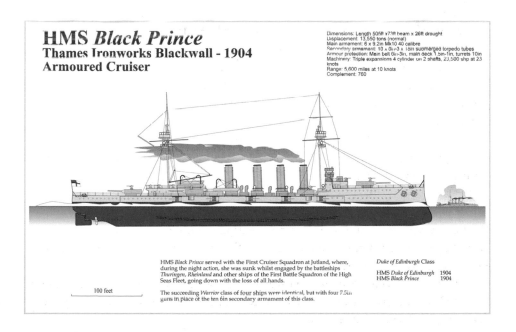

HMS *Black Prince*
Thames Ironworks Blackwall - 1904
Armoured Cruiser

Dimensions: Length 505ft x73ft beam x 26ft draught
Displacement: 13,550 tons (normal)
Main armament: 6 x 9.2in Mk10 40 calibre
Secondary armament: 10 x 6in-3 x 18in submerged torpedo tubes
Armour protection: Main belt 6in-3in, main deck 1.5in-1in, turrets 10in
Machinery: Triple expansions 4 cylinder on 2 shafts, 23,500 shp at 23 knots
Range: 5,600 miles at 10 knots
Complement: 760

HMS *Black Prince* served with the First Cruiser Squadron at Jutland, where, during the night action, she was sunk whilst engaged by the battleships *Thuringen, Rheinland* and other ships of the First Battle Squadron of the High Seas Fleet, going down with the loss of all hands.

Duke of Edinburgh Class

HMS *Duke of Edinburgh*   1904
HMS *Black Prince*   1904

100 feet

The succeeding *Warrior* class of four ships were identical, but with four 7.5in guns in place of the ten 6in secondary armament of this class.

On the German side they had lost 2,115 crewmen, the battleship *Pommern*, the battle-cruiser *Lutzow*, light cruisers *Elbing*, *Wiesbaden*, *Rostock* and *Frauenlob*, together with the torpedo boats *V4*, *V27*, *V29*, *S35* and *V28*.

British losses were altogether heavier, with 6,095 officers and men killed and the loss of three battle-cruisers – *Invincible*, *Indefatigable* and *Queen Mary* – together with three armoured cruisers – *Defence*, *Warrior* and *Black Prince*. Destroyer losses were *Tipperary*, *Ardent*, *Fortune*, *Nestor*, *Nomad*, HMS *Shark*, *Sparrowhawk* and *Turbulent*.

On balance it could be construed that, as the Germans claimed on reaching port before the British, that they had won a famous victory and this is how it appeared to the neutral nations. But the Grand Fleet had come within an ace of annihilating the High Seas Fleet, a fact that Admiral Scheer was only too conscious of, knowing that luck had been his greatest ally on that fateful day and that the Royal Navy still had command of the seas.

The day after the battle, Admiral Jellicoe could report that the Grand Fleet was ready for sea in 24 hours, as opposed to the several months required for the High Seas Fleet to repair their damage.

To say the British were disappointed with the results would be an understatement, and most of the odium for failing to destroy the German fleet fell on Jellicoe. By November 1916 he had been removed from command of the Grand Fleet and in a sideways promotion was appointed as First Sea Lord, while command of the fleet went to the more popular commander, at least in the public's opinion, the dashing Sir David Beatty.

16

SUBMARINES AND U-BOATS

In 1620 Cornelius van Drebbel, a Dutch doctor and inventor – who formerly had been in the employ of the Emperor Rudolf II in Prague in the role of chief alchemist to the court – constructed what could be considered the first practical underwater craft, which, according to contemporary accounts, achieved a degree of success in operation.

The completed submersible was constructed from two boats, with the upper boat inverted and attached to the gunwhale of the lower craft and the whole structure being covered with waxed and waterproof leather. Twelve oarsmen manning pairs of oars that projected through waterproof leather sleeves drove the craft at up to 4 knots.

The submersible is reported to have been tested on several occasions in the River Thames before King James I, where, thanks to the provision of air tubes attached to floats, it was able to remain submerged for up to 3 hours. However, it was viewed only as an interesting entertainment and was not developed further.

An altogether more warlike application of the submarine boat was provided in 1654 when the Council of Southern Holland commissioned the construction of a submersible Ram, specifically designed to attack and sink English ships, built to the design of a Frenchman called De Son. The craft had a cylindrical hull tapering to a cone at either end and mounting a heavy beam or ram on the central axis. Propulsion was provided by a clockwork spring mechanism that drove a centrally mounted paddle wheel. Despite the ingenuity of the design, it proved to be a failure.

During the American War of Independence in 1776 David Bushnell built a successful small submersible known as the Turtle, which again was operated by hand-cranked screw propellers, one for propulsion, the other for vertical movement, and towed a 150lb mine.

Early in the morning of 7 September 1776 the vessel made an attack on HMS *Eagle* in New York Harbour, where the pilot, Ezra Lee, was unable to attach the mine to the underside of the ship and had to abandon the attempt.

Later in 1800 Robert Fulton, an American inventor living in Paris, offered his design of an extremely well thought out submarine boat, propelled by a folding sail on the surface, and a hand-cranked screw propeller underwater, to Napoleon Bonaparte. On obtaining permission to build it from the Ministry of Marine, he demonstrated the craft on the River Seine, where it remained submerged for 17 minutes and reached a depth of 25ft. This craft in a later demonstration at Le Havre destroyed a small barque with a towed explosive mine.

During the Danish–Prussian War of 1848–51 over the Schleswig-Holstein question, the German North Sea coast was under blockade by the Danish Navy. In response to this a German engineer Wilhelm Bauer designed and built a hand-cranked propelled submarine, the *Brandtaucher*, which performed well in tests but had the misfortune on 1 February 1851 to become stuck on the bottom in Kiel Bay in 35ft of water.

As the water slowly began to fill the submarine through the damaged hull plates, Bauer persuaded his frightened crew to wait until the water pressure had risen sufficiently to equalise the outside water pressure, allowing them after a wait of 6 hours to escape safely through the main hatch, this being the first successful escape from a submarine.

In the American Civil War of 1860–65 the Confederate Navy built several semi-submersible, hand-propelled torpedo rams, and on 18 February 1864 the CSS *Hunley*, carrying a spar torpedo, attacked and sank the 1,240-ton steam sloop USS *Housatonic* in the blockaded Charlestown Harbour, but in the enterprise was herself sunk with the loss of her crew of eight.

Throughout the nineteenth century the French Navy took a particular interest in the development of a variety of experimental types, including *Le Plongeur* of 1863, a vessel of 420 tons submerged displacement, being 140ft in length and driven by compressed air – the first such craft driven by mechanical means rather than human effort.

It also carried an electrically fired spar torpedo and had a range of 5 nautical miles at 4 knots, carrying a crew of twelve, and was the inspiration for Jules Verne's classic *Twenty Thousand Leagues Under the Sea*.

In the years that followed, other experimental boats were launched including the *Gymnote* of 1889 and the later *Gustave Zédé*.

The *Gymnote*, originally planned by Dupuy de Lôme, was completed after his death by Arthur Krebs, who in 1884 co-operated with Captain Charles Reynard at the Chalais-Meudon aeronautical establishment to build a successful electrically propelled airship *La France*.

The *Gymnote*, completed in 1889, was 58ft in length, displacing 30 tons and was propelled by a 50hp electric motor, which gave a range of 65 nautical miles at a surface speed of 7.5 knots and 5 knots submerged with a crew of five. The boat carried three sets of hydroplanes along the hull and incorporated the first periscope and gyrocompass. After being used for experimental work, which included the fitting of two 14in torpedo tubes, the boat was scrapped in 1908.

In 1901 the Admiralty ordered five *Holland* class submarines built under licence by Vickers to the American Electric Boat Company's design, which had been developed by the American Irish nationalist J.P. Holland.

Holland as a Fenian had been experimenting for twenty-five years to design a boat that could be used to destroy what he saw as the oppressive power of the Royal Navy. These boats, carrying a crew of seven, had a surface displacement of 104 tons and 122 tons submerged, being 63ft overall with a beam of 11.5ft, and were propelled by a 160hp petrol engine, together with a 74hp electric motor for under water, imparting a speed of 8 and 5 knots respectively, with a useful range of 250 nautical miles. They were of single-hull construction, had internal ballast tanks and carried a single 14in torpedo tube and an armament of two torpedoes. Once in service, they were used for experimental work, and a great deal of practical experience was gained from their use, which aided in the design of the succeeding A class.

The Vickers shipbuilders of Barrow had an almost monopoly status in the building of submarines, and in the period from 1900 to 1914 of one hundred boats built, ninety were built by Vickers.

The thirteen A class boats of 180 tons, all completed between 1903 and 1905, were 100ft long on a beam of 11.5ft. Their electric motors were of 80hp, giving a speed of 7 knots submerged, while the twelve cylinder petrol engine of 450hp gave a surface speed of 11.5 knots. The last boat of this class A 13 was the first to be fitted with a diesel engine.

The succeeding B, C and D classes, constructed between 1905 and 1910, were progressively larger and incorporated all the advances made in the earlier boats, which included the conning tower, twin bow torpedo tubes in the B and C classes and with diesel engines now as the standard method of propulsion.

In the D class, tonnage had risen to 550 tons surface displacement and 600 tons submerged and they were the first British submarines to mount a deck gun, with two bow and one stern 18 torpedo tubes. They were larger, being 163ft in length, and had a wider beam of 20ft, with more powerful diesel engines of 1,200 combined hp and 550hp electric motors on two screws, which gave surface and submerged speeds of 16 and 9 knots respectively.

Ten of these boats were built and they were the first to incorporate wireless apparatus; they also introduced the external saddle ballast tanks. With a crew of twenty-five and a range of 2,500 nautical miles, they were the first true British ocean-going submarines. In the war they were employed of patrol duty in the North Sea and Heligoland Bight and were also deployed into the English Channel, where the D3 was bombed in error by a French airship in 1918. The approximate cost of a D class submarine was £90,000 each.

The definitive British submarine of the Great War is the E class, of which fifty-seven examples were built, including two for the Royal Australian Navy. They were active not only in the North Sea and Mediterranean, but also in the Baltic and the Dardanelles, while later they were also employed in operations against the Bolshevik forces in the Gulf of Finland during the Russian civil war of 1918–21.

The E class were of 660 tons surface and 800 tons submerged displacement, being 181ft in length by 22ft beam, driven by two eight cylinder diesel engines of 1,600 total hp and two 600hp electric motors on two screws, giving speeds of 16 knots surface and 19 knots submerged, with a range of 3,000 nautical miles at 10 knots. Improvements included transverse bulkheads which allowed greater diving depths to be achieved and beam torpedo tubes. The cost of these vessels had risen to £105,000.

The E class submarines led an active and exciting life in the Great War. The greater part of this activity involved operations in the North Sea where they were employed on patrol work, being sent into the German Bight close to the home of the High Seas Fleet.

A British submarine flotilla was sent into the Baltic Sea where the boats co-operated with the Russian Baltic Fleet, their task being to disrupt the iron ore trade between Sweden and Germany. The flotilla operated for some three years and successfully curtailed not only the transport of iron ore but also caused the German Baltic fleet to operate with greater circumspection.

The E class submarines entered the Baltic through the Kattegat and the shallow Great Belt and Little Belt, a route fraught with danger both from natural hazards and enemy action.

An early victim of the flotilla was the SMS *Undine*, a light cruiser of 3,130 tons that was sunk off Trelleborg on 7 November 1915 by the *E19*, commanded by Lieutenant-Commander Cromie with a salvo of two torpedoes. Cromie had also sunk four troop transports south of Oland on 11 October.

Another loss was the SMS *Prinz Adalbert*, an armoured cruiser of 9,550 tons, armed with four 8.2 and ten 4.1in guns; a powerful ship that was being employed to bombard the Russian port of Libau. On 1 July 1915 she was torpedoed by the *E9*, badly damaging her and causing her to take on several thousand tons of water, necessitating her return to Kiel. After repairs, the *Prinz Adalbert* returned to Libau on 23 October, escorted by two torpedo boats.

Here she was intercepted 20 miles south of the port by the *E8*, commanded by Lieutenant-Commander Francis Goodheart, who fired a spread of torpedoes at a range of 1,300yd, which struck the forward magazine. This resulted in a massive explosion that blew the ship apart, with the loss of 672 officers and men – the largest single loss of life in the war to the German Baltic Fleet. For this action Goodheart received the Cross of St George from Tsar Nicholas II.

The commander of the *E9* was Lieutenant-Commander Max Horton, who, in the Second World War as Commander-in-Chief Western Approaches, instituted the strategies that were eventually to defeat the U-boat. On 13 September 1914 the *E9* sank the light cruiser SMS *Hela* off Heligoland, with two torpedoes fired at 600yd range. A few days later it sank the torpedo boat *V116*. For these two actions Horton was awarded the DSO.

The E boats served in every theatre during the war, being part of the Anglo-French force in 1915 that attempted to force the Dardanelles during the Gallipoli campaign. Here they were highly successful in their operations, sinking over one hundred vessels, including troop transports, merchant ships and two Turkish battleships.

Submarines also landed parties to carry out acts of sabotage on rail communications, and in the case of the *E11* under the command of Lieutenant-Commander Martin Nasmith penetrated the Straits, avoiding the mine barriers and passing into the Sea of Marmara and on through the Bosporus to become the first enemy warship to enter the harbour of Constantinople for over one hundred years, underlining this bold venture by sinking a transport in broad daylight within sight of the Golden Horn.

Six E class submarines attached to the Allied Baltic Flotilla earlier mentioned, after sterling service against the Bolshevik forces, were eventually scuttled off Harmoya Light in the Gulf of Finland to avoid them falling into the hands of advancing enemy troops.

Two smaller classes of submarine followed the E class, the F class of 353 tons surface displacement of which only three were built and the successful H class of similar displacement of which fifty-two were constructed, with ten of these boats being built at the Fore River Yard in the USA in 1915, until the then neutral US Government clamped down on the building as violating their neutral status.

Two larger classes were also built – the G class of 700 tons – designed, as were the H boats, to supplement the war programme, and which proved to be handy little crafts more suited to coastal operations and harbour protection duties.

The larger J class of 1916 were of 1,200 tons surface displacement, powered with three diesel motors of 3,600 total hp, which gave a high surface speed of 19.5 knots. These were the fastest submarines in the world at that time.

These boats were built in response to reports that later proved inaccurate that the Germans were building large U-boats with a speed of 22 knots, but the need for a class of submarine that could operate with the fleet led in turn to the remarkable K class of steam submarines that were to follow.

Another interesting concept was represented by the R class of twelve small boats of only 450 tons surface displacement that were designed for high underwater speed, specially built to hunt U-boats and all built in 1918. They were 163ft in length, armed with six 20in bow torpedo tubes and powered by a single 240hp diesel engine and a 1,299hp electric motor, imparting surface and underwater speeds of 9.5 and 15 knots respectively, and carrying a complement of twenty-three.

Only one boat made an attack on an enemy U-boat, hitting it with a single torpedo that failed to detonate. The R boats had poor sea-keeping qualities and were difficult to control, while their low surface speed restricted their use. Two large experimental vessels, *Nautilus* and *Swordfish*, were built during 1916–17 to aid the development of ocean-going submarines that could fulfil the requirement for a fast fleet submarine that would accompany the Grand Fleet to sea at the required speed of an awesome 24 knots.

The *Nautilus* built by Vickers was 242ft in length, with 1,200 tons surface displacement and powered by diesel engines with a combined power of 3,700hp, giving a speed of 18 knots. Although the vessel did not reach operational status, due to various defects with machinery, she proved a useful test bed for later developments.

The *Swordfish*, on the other hand, proved more successful. Laid down for steam propulsion, she was 231ft in length and of 932 tons surface displacement. She was powered by two Parsons steam turbines of 3,750hp, together with electric motors producing 1,500hp on two shafts, giving 18 and 10 knots respectively.

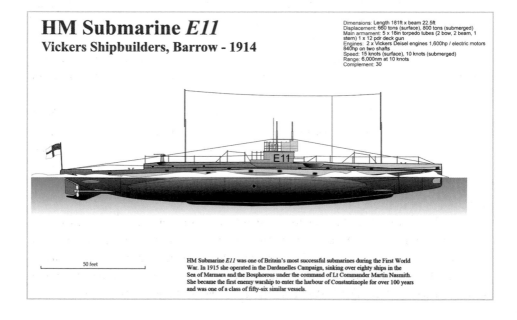

HM Submarine *E11*
Vickers Shipbuilders, Barrow - 1914

Dimensions: Length 181ft x beam 22.5ft
Displacement: 660 tons (surface), 800 tons (submerged)
Main armament: 5 x 18in torpedo tubes (2 bow, 2 beam, 1 stern) 1 x 12 pdr deck gun
Engines: 2 x Vickers Deisel engines 1,600hp / electric motors 840hp on two shafts
Speed: 15 knots (surface), 10 knots (submerged)
Range: 6,000nm at 10 knots
Complement: 30

50 feet

HM Submarine *E11* was one of Britain's most successful submarines during the First World War. In 1915 she operated in the Dardanelles Campaign, sinking over eighty ships in the Sea of Marmara and the Bosphorous under the command of Lt Commander Martin Nasmith. She became the first enemy warship to enter the harbour of Constantinople for over 100 years and was one of a class of fifty-six similar vessels.

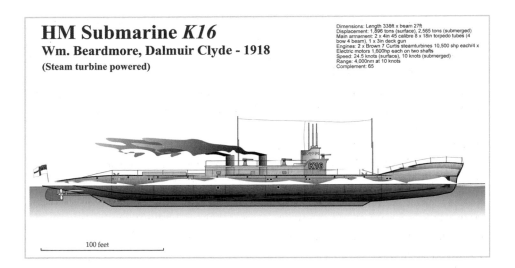

HM Submarine *K16*

Wm. Beardmore, Dalmuir Clyde - 1918

(Steam turbine powered)

Dimensions: Length 338ft x beam 27ft
Displacement: 1,896 tons (surface), 2,565 tons (submerged)
Main armament: 2 x 4in 45 calibre 8 x 18in torpedo tubes (4 bow 4 beam), 1 x 3in deck gun
Engines: 2 x Brown 7 Curtis steamturbines 10,500 shp each/4 x Electric motors 1,600hp each on two shafts
Speed: 24.5 knots (surface), 10 knots (submerged)
Range: 4,000nm at 10 knots
Complement: 65

100 feet

With this boat the obvious problems of employing steam propulsion in a vessel that was required to go under the sea were investigated, the most problematic issue being to effect the transition from steam propulsion to electric power as the boat submerged.

This, of course, involved shutting down the furnaces and boilers, sealing funnel outlets and air intakes and so on in the quickest possible time as the boat submerged and switching to electric motors.

During trials, serious problems were encountered during this transition process where, although efforts were made to vent the compartments prior to diving, steam condensing on the electrical switchgear could cause serious shorting of electrical circuits and fires and explosions on occasion.

Despite these drawbacks, the research programme continued and valuable lessons were learned from the *Swordfish* that were to be incorporated in the design of the following K class.

The origin of the K class dated back to 1913 and was a product of Admiral Jacky Fisher's fertile mind. The rationale behind these boats was that they would operate at the same speed or faster than the fleet and would be used in a fleet action where they could, thanks to their speed, position themselves in the rear of the line of the retreating enemy fleet, cutting them off from their base and attacking them with mass torpedo salvoes.

These boats were huge even by today's standards. With a length of 340ft and a beam of 26ft, they displaced 1,980 tons on the surface and 2,570 tons submerged. They were armed with four 18in bow torpedo tubes, four 18in tubes mounted on the beam and two 4in Q/F guns mounted on the superstructure and carried a complement of sixty officers and men. They also had a range of 12,500 nautical miles at 10 knots.

Originally as designed they also mounted an additional pair of 18in torpedo tubes on trainable mountings on the fore deck, intended for use during night actions, but these were removed as they were subject to damage in a seaway.

Engine power was provided by two 10,500shp heavy oil-fired Brown and Curtis or Parsons geared steam turbines for surface propulsion that imparted a speed of 24 knots – a speed that was not to be surpassed until the introduction of the nuclear submarines in the 1960s.

The four powerful 1,400hp electric motors that were required to drive the 2,570 ton bulk underwater gave a rather disappointing underwater speed of only 8 knots and an equally poor range of only 40 nautical miles at the lower speed of 4 knots, which would hardly be adequate if trying to carry out the task of attacking enemy warships while submerged.

Earlier it had been hoped that the diesel-engined J class boats would fulfil the specification but, as they failed to reach the necessary speed, the K class design was dusted off and an order for twenty-one boats was placed in August 1915 at a cost of £340,000 each.

The K boats were flush-decked, which made it possible under certain conditions for them to tend to go into an involuntary and uncontrolled dive in a seaway or even in calm weather, and most of them were accordingly modified with a bulbous bow to increase their sea-keeping qualities.

Unlike their predecessors, where the conning tower was protected by an inadequate canvas screen, the K boats were fitted with enclosed steel deckhouses offering better protection to the bridge crew.

Due to their great length, stability and depth-keeping problems were experienced in the boats where vertical motion was exacerbated by the fact that the safe diving depth was only 200ft. This meant that at a 10° angle of dive on a 339ft-long boat there would be a 60ft difference between bow and stern, while at a greater angle of dive the bow could be below the maximum safe depth while the stern was at the surface. The situation was made worse by the fact that the transverse bulkheads were only designed to withstand a pressure equal to a depth of 70ft.

A further problem experienced by the boats was the ingress of seawater into the boiler rooms through the funnels, sometimes even dowsing the furnaces.

The time required to prepare a K boat to dive was in the order of 5 minutes, with the fires drawn, funnels folded down and sealing covers locked.

The first of the class completed was the K3 in 1916 when during trials many problems were evident, particularly the excessive temperatures produced in the boiler rooms and the porpoising effect, driving the bow under, resulting from the boat's poor lateral stability – a problem that was to dog the class throughout their service. Of the seventeen K boats built, *K1, K4, K17* were lost due to collision, *K13* foundered in the North Sea and *K5* foundered in the Bay of Biscay after the war.

Only one engaged a German warship, when the *K12* attacked a U-boat with a torpedo that failed to explode.

The biggest disaster to befall the K boats was on the misty night of 31 December 1918 when four K boats of the 12th Submarine Flotilla, led by the cruiser HMS *Fearless* and five boats of the 13th Flotilla, accompanied the 5th Battle Squadron and other warships out of Rosyth for fleet exercises, showing only dimmed stern lights. On passing May Island, the *Fearless* saw lights dead ahead and altered course to port, where she collided with *K17*, slicing into her pressure hull, after which she sank in 8 minutes with the loss of all hands.

As the following submarines turned to avoid the wreckage, *K6* ran into *K4*, cutting her in half, where she was struck again by *K7* before she also sank with all hands. At the same time, the *K14*'s helm jammed, and in attempting to avoid both the cruiser and submarine, the *K22* also swung out of line, hitting the *K14*, seriously damaging both vessels.

Sweeping past 15 minutes later, the battle-cruiser *Inflexible* further damaged *K22*. Both boats struggled back to port and were later repaired. Another 15 minutes later in the mist the 5th Battle Squadron passed unaware over the scene of the tragedy, running down survivors still in the water.

In just over an hour two submarines had been sunk, a cruiser and three further K submarines had been badly damaged, and 270 crewmen were dead. The incident become known as the Battle of May Island.

On 29 January 1917 the *K13*, undergoing sea trials in the Gareloch with eighty persons on board, sank while diving when engine room ventilators were accidentally left open, flooding the engine room and aft torpedo compartment. After 2 hours the first rescue boat arrived and the captain of the *K13*, Commander Godfrey, escaped from a hatch in the conning tower.

As rescue attempts continued airlines were attached to the pressure hull, allowing the ballast tanks to be blown, where, after more than 40 hours, the bows were raised above the surface, here supported by two barges and hawsers around the hull. Holes were cut through the pressure hull and finally after 57 hours the last of forty-two survivors were rescued. The *K13* was later raised, repaired and recommissioned as *K22*.

On 18 November 1917, while on patrol off the Danish coast, the *K1* was in collision with the *K4* and badly damaged. After her crew had been taken off she was scuttled to avoid capture.

The final loss of a K boat was after the war when *K5* on exercises with the Atlantic Fleet in the Bay of Biscay on 20 January 1921 failed to surface after a dive. Later wreckage was recovered and it was assumed that *K5* had submerged beyond her safe pressure depth and was crushed.

The concept of the steam-propelled K class of submarine was a bold undertaking that failed to live up to its promise.

Perhaps the strangest class of submarine built for the Royal Navy were the four diesel electric M class that followed the Ks. These boats were marginally smaller at 303ft in length on a beam of 24.5ft, with a surface displacement of 1,600 tons and 1,950 tons submerged. They were ordered as replacements for four cancelled K class boats.

Two twelve cylinder 1,200hp diesel engines gave a speed of 15 knots on the surface, while four 800hp electric motors on two screws produced 9 knots submerged, with a range of 4,500 nautical miles, and tested to a pressure depth of 200ft. The armament was the most unusual feature of the boat, where, apart from four bow 18in torpedo tubes, there was a single Armstrong Whitworth 12in 40 calibre Mk IX model of an 1898 gun, firing an 850lb shell mounted in a turret on the casing forward of the conning tower.

The gun fired at a rate of one round per minute and was capable of being elevated to 20° and could traverse 15° either side of the boat's centre line, with a range of 15,000yd.

The muzzle end of the gun was sealed with a hinged scuttle to prevent the ingress of seawater when the boat was submerged. The gun could be fired either above or below the surface but it had to be loaded on the surface, which took around 3 minutes or so to accomplish.

Earlier in 1915 the submarine *E20* had carried a 6in howitzer mounted on the fore-casing and was briefly employed as a monitor, bombarding the seaward end of the German trenches on the Belgian coast, and may possibly have encouraged Admiral Lord Fisher to develop the idea of a submarine monitor.

As originally conceived, the M class was to be used in this role, with the gun being fired underwater at periscope depth, bombarding German coastal positions, but the rationale for their employment changed to being used to attack enemy merchant shipping, although they were never used in this capacity.

Three of the four boats were completed, with the fourth being cancelled before launch and, although they remained in service for several years after the war, they were an unsuccessful and flawed concept and very expensive to maintain in commission.

The *M1* entered service in 1918, under the command of Commander Max Horton, who had commanded the Baltic Flotilla, but was not to see action and subsequently was lost with all hands off Start Point on 12 November 1925 when she was in collision with the Swedish freighter SS *Vidar.*

The *M2* had its gun removed and was converted into a seaplane carrier with a single Parnell float plane carried with wings folded in a watertight hangar in place of the former gun turret.

A programme of aircraft launchings in cooperation with fleet manoeuvres were carried out with *M2*, until she was lost off Chesil Beach on 26 January 1930, when she failed to surface from a dive. It was thought that the hangar door had inadvertently been opened under water.

The *M3* was converted into a minelayer with a capacity for one hundred mines that were stored in the casing on a conveyor belt and laid via trapdoors at the stern. After performing valuable experimental work from which the later *Porpoise* class minelayers of the Second World War benefited, the *M3* was eventually sent to the breakers in 1932.

The last wartime British submarines built under the emergency war programme were seventy-one examples of the L class that were improved and enlarged versions of the famous E class.

The L boats were 231ft in length, with a 24ft beam, displacing 890 tons surface and 1,070 tons submerged, and had a range of 4,800 nautical miles with a crew of thirty-five. Diesel engines of 2,400hp and electric motors of 1,600hp gave 17.5 and 10.5 knots respectively. There were six 18in torpedo tubes, which in a later batch were replaced by six 21in tubes and either a 3in or 4in deck gun completed their armament.

The L class afforded greater crew comfort than earlier boats and gave good service in the Second World War and the inter-war period, with several boats being retained until 1946 for training purposes.

The German Navy was much slower in taking up the submarine, not launching their first *Unterseeboot* or U-boat until 1906, when, despite their late entry into submarine construction, the boats were of advanced design, being roughly comparable to our D class boats of 1910.

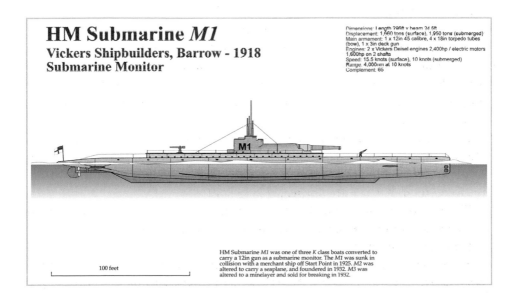

HM Submarine *M1*
Vickers Shipbuilders, Barrow - 1918
Submarine Monitor

Dimensions: Length 296ft x beam 24.5ft
Displacement: 1,660 tons (surface), 1,950 tons (submerged)
Main armament: 1 x 12in 45 calibre, 4 x 18in torpedo tubes (bow), 1 x 3in deck gun
Engines: 2 x Vickers Deisel engines 2,400hp / electric motors 1,600hp on 2 shafts
Speed: 15.5 knots (surface), 10 knots (submerged)
Range: 4,000nm at 10 knots
Complement: 65

100 feet

HM Submarine *M1* was one of three K class boats converted to carry a 12in gun as a submarine monitor. The *M1* was sunk in collision with a merchant ship off Start Point in 1925. *M2* was altered to carry a seaplane, and foundered in 1932. *M3* was altered to a minelayer and sold for breaking in 1932.

They were of double hull construction with twin screws and were tested to a pressure depth of 164ft, on occasion reaching 275ft in safety, a greater depth than British submarines operated at.

The *U19* of 1913, taken as an example of a pre-war boat, was 210ft in length on a 20ft beam, displacing 650 tons on the surface and 837 submerged. It was the first to be equipped with a diesel engine of 1,700hp, augmented by 1,200hp electric motors that gave 15.5 knots surface and 9.5 knots underwater. Armament consisted of four 19.7in torpedo tubes backed up by a highly effective 4.1in gun. Her complement numbered thirty-nine officers and men.

Prior to the war the submarine had not been considered a great threat to the faster dreadnoughts, being a weapon of marginal importance for coastal use defending harbours and so on. It was considered that they could only have a marginal effect on British maritime trade due to the complicated international prize laws that governed and protected the stopping, searching and sinking of merchant ships in time of war.

A fact unrealised by the Admiralty before the commencement of hostilities was the superior performance of the German U-boat over Britain's own craft, where a boat like the *U19* had a range of over 4,000 miles and could stay at sea for over three weeks 2,000 miles from her base, making her an extremely dangerous proposition.

In August 1914 Britain possessed fifty-five active submarines while Germany had only twenty-eight, which was soon to be augmented by a rapid building programme. A flotilla of ten U-boats were dispatched at the outbreak of war on 8 August on the first distant patrol by submarines, with the intention of attacking the Grand Fleet at sea in an effort to reduce their numerical advantage.

The patrol brought few results, with the only attack by torpedo on a British capital ship coming to nothing when it missed its target. One boat, *U15*, was rammed and sunk on the surface by HMS *Birmingham* off Fair Isle, with the loss of all hands, while a second went missing.

A second patrol on 12 August also resulted in the loss of a U-boat when *U13* failed to return, where it was thought she had been mined, which in turn shows how quickly defensive minefields were laid.

The first success for the U-boat arm came on 5 September 1914 when the 2,900 ton scout light cruiser HMS *Pathfinder* was hit by a single torpedo fired at 2,000yd range from the *U21* commanded by Leutnant zur See Otto Hersing. This struck under the bridge causing a massive blast as her magazine exploded, causing her to sink in minutes, carrying 250 of her crew to the bottom with only eighteen survivors.

Two weeks later, on 22 September, Leutnant zur See Otto von Weddigen patrolling the Broad Fourteens off the Dutch coast sank three 12,500-ton armoured cruisers in less than an hour. The HMS *Aboukir*, HMS *Hogue* and HMS *Cressy* were torpedoed one after the other at short range, killing 1,400 crew members (this incident is referred to in detail in Chapter 7).

Three weeks later von Weddigen on 15 October had a further success when he sank the protected cruiser HMS *Hawke* where again, following a magazine explosion, the ship sank with a heavy loss of life.

In November the *U18* even managed to penetrate the defences of Scapa Flow, although the British fleet was absent. On making her way back to sea she was rammed by a trawler, severely damaging her and causing her captain to scuttle his command.

A final and major success for the U-boats came on the last day of the year when the pre-dreadnought HMS *Formidable* was sunk by the *U21* off Berry Head in the English Channel, this being the second loss of a battleship, with the earlier sinking to a mine of the modern dreadnought *Audacious* having taken place in October 1914 off the Irish coast.

These losses came as a profound shock to the Admiralty, and a succession of measures were taken to remedy the situation, not least in withdrawing old and venerable warships from patrol duties near the enemy coast and ensuring that, while patrolling, ships followed irregular zigzag courses to confuse enemy submarines.

The first attacks on merchant shipping began in October 1914, when the SS *Glitra* on course for Stavanger in Norway was ordered to heave to and was searched for contraband by the *U17* commanded by Kapitanleutnant Feldkirker.

With the crew ordered into the lifeboats and no lives lost the action was conducted under the internationally agreed prize cruiser rules before the ship was scuttled by opening the seacocks, this being the first instance of a submarine sinking a merchant ship.

In contrast, a week later on 26 October 1914, the unarmed Belgian merchant ship *Admiral Ganteaume*, carrying 2,500 Belgian refugees, was torpedoed without warning. Although she made it back to port, this led to the deaths of forty passengers. The U-boat captain claimed he had mistaken her for a troop ship, which indicates the difficulties of trying to identify ships at almost sea level from the heaving deck of a submarine in poor weather.

By the end of 1914 the U-boat arm of the Imperial Navy had sunk nine warships, including two battleships and numerous merchant ships, for the loss of only five of their own submarines.

As early as January 1915 it had become apparent that a serious threat was posed to British merchant shipping by the depredations of German undersea craft operating along the North Sea coasts and the English Channel.

This threat was made all the more dangerous by the seizure by German forces of the harbours of Ostend and Zeebrugge in October 1914, which presented the enemy with well-equipped submarine bases in dangerous proximity to Britain's southern shores and from where they could threaten her maritime trade. As we have seen, the Admiralty seriously underestimated the potential danger posed by this novel form of warfare. Within a few short months of the outbreak of war the

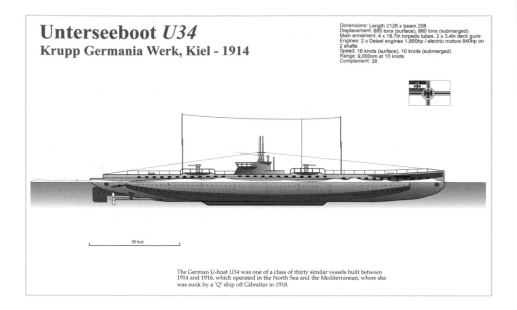

Unterseeboot *U34*
Krupp Germania Werk, Kiel - 1914

Dimensions: Length 212ft x beam 20ft
Displacement: 685 tons (surface), 880 tons (submerged)
Main armament: 4 x 19.7in torpedo tubes, 2 x 3.4in deck guns
Engines: 2 x Deisel engines 1,850hp / electric motors 840hp on 2 shafts
Speed: 16 knots (surface), 10 knots (submerged)
Range: 9,000nm at 10 knots
Complement: 38

50 feet

The German U-boat *U34* was one of a class of thirty similar vessels built between 1914 and 1916, which operated in the North Sea and the Mediterranean, where she was sunk by a 'Q' ship off Gibraltar in 1918.

U-boat had shown itself to be an efficient silent predator that could launch its attack unseen and was almost immune to counter attack, having the ability to slip away into the ocean depths undetected.

It soon became apparent that this unforeseen and aggressive deployment of the U-boat imperilled the passage of troops and munitions to the front and, most importantly, endangered the supply of foodstuffs and raw materials so vitally essential to the British Isles in time of war.

While the losses of merchant ships was a worrying development for Great Britain, Germany were facing a problem of altogether greater proportions, as the institution of the economic blockade on the German Empire by the Royal Navy on the first day of war exerted a stranglehold on their imports and was already having its effect, relying as they did to an even greater extent than Britain on the imports of food, fertilisers and the raw materials needed for the production of armaments.

The war was far from over by Christmas, as had been predicted by both sides when it started in August 1914, and as the land struggle settled into trench warfare from the Belgian coast to the Swiss border and began to expand into the Mediterranean and other parts of the globe, the realisation that the war could extend for years focused the attention of the British Government and the chancelleries of the Central Powers on how to react.

In the case of the British, it was how to defeat the U-boat threat, and in the case of Germany of how to break the British blockade. Ultimately, the British did defeat the U-boat, while Imperial Germany for its part devised a dangerous strategy that came within an ace of bringing Britain to the edge of starvation and to losing the war.

During January 1915, U-boats sank several merchant ships without warning in the North Sea, while in February the hospital ship *Asturias* was attacked with a torpedo that fortunately missed, despite being clearly painted as a hospital ship, with her white hull, broad green bands and red crosses.

The British blockade was not popular amongst the neutral countries, as it interfered with and restricted their trade, particularly the United States, who objected strongly to their ships being stopped and searched.

In response, Germany had, on 4 February 1915, declared the waters around the British Isles to be a war zone, where enemy merchant vessels would be destroyed and neutral vessels sailed at their own peril and could be sunk without warning. This declaration was as unpopular with the neutral nations as the announcement of the British blockade had been. The German Chancellor Bethmann-Hollweg did his best to modify the sink without warning clause, but was overruled by the requirements of the German Admiralty and War Council, which instituted the first phase of unrestricted submarine warfare that was to last from February to September 1915, at which time it was suspended for fear of the United States entering the war on the side of the Allies.

In the period before the declaration 43,500 tons of merchant shipping had been sunk by U-boats. This total rose steadily and in August 1915 168,000 tons were sunk. Once the unrestricted policy was in place losses rose to an average of 100,000 tons per month.

The most high-profile victim of the unrestricted submarine warfare policy, and one that was eventually to bring the United States into the war, was the sinking on 7 May 1915 of the 31,000-ton Cunard liner and Blue Riband holder *Lusitania*,

THE U-BOAT CAMPAIGN 1914 - 1918

TONNAGE OF MERCHANT SHIPPING SUNK EACH MONTH

THOUSANDS OF TONS

which was torpedoed by the *U20* commanded by Kapitanleutnant Schwieger 13 nautical miles off the Old Head of Kinsale in southern Ireland. Of the 1,960 souls on board, 1,198 were killed, of which 128 were American citizens, with the ship sinking in 18 minutes.

This incident caused a wave of outrage both in Britain and the United States where, but for the restraining hand of the US President Woodrow Wilson, the two countries were in grave danger of going to war.

This first phase of unrestricted warfare lasted until September 1915. Following further sinkings that involved the death of American citizens, such as that of the SS *Arabic* on 19 August, a further deterioration of German-American relations raised the real threat of the United States declaring war on Germany. The Imperial Government acted quickly and suspended the unrestricted policy for fear of antagonising the US Government further, leading to the spectre of a million or more fresh American troops joining the war on the Allies' side.

It is interesting here to note that the orders from the Chancellor Bethmann-Hollweg, stating that in future all passenger ships were only to be sunk after they had received a warning and that all passengers and crew should be safe or in lifeboats, were unacceptable to the German naval high command, who felt unable to prosecute the naval war on these terms.

A second period of unrestricted submarine warfare was conducted between March and May 1916, sinking over 200,000 tons of Allied shipping, which was again brought to a close when the activities of U-boats threatened to bring the United States into the war.

Finally, in January 1917 Germany threw caution to the wind and embarked on the final phase, even though it was to bring the United States into the war in April 1917. The German naval high command gambled that if they could sink Allied and British ships at a rate of 600,000 tons a month, Britain would be forced to the conference table and sue for peace.

This position was almost reached in April and May 1917 when over 900,000 tons of merchant shipping was sunk, leading to severe food shortages and riots in Britain. Had they been able to maintain this level of losses month after month, Britain could very well have been unable to continue the war. In order to counter the U-boat menace, more craft were made available, with trawlers, sloops and destroyers being equipped with depth charges and hydrophones that could be used to detect submarines underwater.

Other anti-submarine techniques included extensive mine barriers in the Dover Straits and the introduction of Q ships. These were ships masquerading as ordinary merchant ships but carrying an armament of concealed guns that would lure a U-boat to attack on the surface – a scheme that had modest success.

Many U-boats were sunk on the surface by merchant ships when under attack by running them down. One such event happened with the liner *Olympic* when off the Lizard on 12 May 1918, under the command of the splendidly named Captain Haddock, with 5,000 American troops on board, she rammed and sunk the *U103*.

Aircraft and airships were employed in increasing numbers, which also achieved considerable success, and forced U-boats to remain submerged in areas where their surface speed could gain them advantage in pursuing merchant ships.

The greatest advantage to reducing shipping losses was the surprisingly late introduction of the convoy system, which for various reasons had been rejected by their Lords of the Admiralty, until finally accepted as policy in April 1917, under the urging of Prime Minister Lloyd George, and which eventually caused British shipping losses to gradually decline.

In September 1917 losses had fallen to 316,000 tons and continued to reduce month after month. The German gamble had failed, Great Britain was not defeated and unrestricted submarine warfare had caused the United States to join the war in the Allied cause.

Although the U-boat war was to continue throughout 1918 with ever increasing severity and many more merchant ships lost, Allied countermeasures gradually gained the upper hand and losses, though still heavy, fell to 170,000 tons in January 1918 and continued to fall thereafter.

Of the later type of U-boat built during the war, the *U99* class of 1917 is typical, being of 750 tons surface and 952 tons submerged displacement, capable of 16.6 knots on the surface, armed with four 19.7in torpedo tubes with a range of 6,500 miles.

The Germans also built over one hundred submarine mine layers that were the most effective weapons, accounting for a large proportion of Allied vessels sunk The *UB* class of 1915 were small vessels of 168 tons surface and 183 tons submerged displacement that carried twelve mines in six vertical silos. While the later *UC111* class of 500 tons surface and 699 tons' displacement carried fourteen mines apiece. This form of warfare was equally dangerous to the perpetrators, as their intended victims and several of these boats were destroyed by the premature explosion of their own mines.

An unusual concept of the Germans was the submarine merchant ship. As their merchant surface fleet had been driven from the oceans by the Royal Navy, an underwater form of commerce as a blockade runner seemed to offer a solution.

The first of these was the mercantile cruiser *Deutschland*, a vessel of 1,500 tons surface and 1,850 tons submerged displacement and built as a private venture with funds from the North German Lloyd shipping company and commanded by a merchant captain. The *Deutschland* was 213ft in length and had a 30ft beam, displacing 2,770 tons submerged and powered by only a 800hp diesel engine and a 800hp electric motor. It could also manage 15 knots on the surface, where the majority of her voyages took pace. With a range of 12,000 miles, she could carry 700 tons of high value cargo.

Her first voyage from Bremerhaven to Baltimore took place in June 1916, where she carried a 750-ton cargo of valuable chemical dyes and medical drugs. On her return trip of 8,400 miles, she transported $17.5 million worth of nickel, tin and rubber, which paid for the cost of the submarine many times over.

A second voyage in November 1916 transported $10 million worth of cargo, but she was damaged in the harbour of New London by collision with a tug, necessitating repairs before departing with a cargo that included silver bullion. A third voyage was planned for January 1917 but, as relations with the United States worsened, it was cancelled.

The *Deutschland* was taken over by the Imperial Navy as the *U155* and armed with torpedo tubes and guns and was successfully operated until the end of the war, sinking over sixty Allied vessels.

The final class of U-boat based on the *Deutschland* were the submarine cruisers of similar displacement and length as the *Deutschland* but fitted with two 19.7in torpedo tubes and two large 5.9in guns, which were used to effect on Allied shipping.

British losses during the Great War amounted to 2,740 merchant ships totalling 7,750,000 tons, which represented 40 per cent of the pre-war fleet and cost the lives of 14,287 merchant seamen.

17

BALTIC OPERATIONS

At the outset of war in 1914 the Baltic Sea was effectively closed to the Royal Navy, with its only presence being affected by a British submarine flotilla of initially six E class boats that entered the Baltic covertly to co-operate with the Russian Baltic Fleet based at Kronstadt. The Russian Baltic Fleet at the beginning of the war was greatly inferior to the German High Seas Fleet, where the German commander Admiral Erhard Schmidt could call on modern dreadnought battleships and battle-cruisers that could be quickly transferred from their bases on the North Sea coast to the Baltic via the Kiel Canal, which could just as easily be returned to the North Sea should the tactical situation demand it.

In August 1915 the Russian fleet commander Admiral Vasily Kanin had at his disposal in the Gulf of Riga the 14,450 ton pre-dreadnought battleship *Slava*, with a main armament of only two 12in and twelve 6in guns – a *Borodino* class ship similar to the four battleships that had been sunk by the Japanese at the Battle of Tsushima in 1904. Also available to him were four small 1,700 ton gunboats, a minelayer and a flotilla of sixteen destroyers.

Early in August 1915, powerful units of the High Seas Fleet entered the Baltic with the intention of conducting a foray into the Gulf of Riga in support of German troops advancing from the south through Courland and to destroy the Russian naval forces stationed in the Gulf, including the *Slava*, and to capture the port of Riga.

On 8 August the German force comprising two dreadnoughts *Nassau* and SMS *Posen* of 18,600 tons, armed with twelve 11in guns and two pre-dreadnoughts, SMS *Braunschweig* and *Elsass*, mounting four 11in guns apiece and supported by four light cruisers and no less than fifty-six torpedo boats, attempted to break through the extensive minefields that protected the entrance to the Gulf.

At the same time the German fleet was further reinforced by the battle-cruisers *Moltke*, *Von der Tann* and *Seydlitz* commanded by Vice-Admiral von Hipper, who temporarily took over the command of the operation.

The two German pre-dreadnoughts engaged the Russian battleship *Slava* to allow the minesweepers to clear safe channels into the Gulf while the minelayer

Deutschland was sent to mine Moon Sound to the north between the mainland and the islands of Hiiumaa and Saaremaa.

Despite their overwhelming superiority, the German forces were unable to clear the minefields and retired, making a second attempt on 16 August, when they lost the minesweeper *T46* and the torpedo boat *V99*. But in return they managed to damage the *Slava* and successfully cleared the minefields by 19 August, which allowed the German ships into the Gulf to attack the shore installations.

However, before this could be accomplished, reports of British and Allied submarines operating in the restricted waters of the Gulf caused the German ships to withdraw, which demonstrates the influence a handful of British submarines could exert on naval operations in such enclosed waters.

Vice-Admiral von Hipper's battle-cruisers continued to operate in support of the army assault on Riga, when early on the morning of 20 August the *Seydlitz* was struck by a torpedo fired from the British submarine *E1* commanded by Lieutenant Noel Laurence.

The torpedo struck the forward torpedo flat at the bow, but failed to detonate the stored torpedoes. However, the ship was sufficiently badly damaged to need repair at the Blohm & Voss yards in Hamburg, lasting until the end of September.

The *E1* together with *E9*, commanded by Max Horton, had entered the Baltic on 15 October 1914 and based at Reval (modern Tallinn) in Estonia. The six E class submarines were joined by five of the earlier and smaller C class which had been shipped to the White Sea and transported by canal to Kronstadt where, as described earlier, they severely curtailed the iron ore trade between Sweden and Germany, as well as restricting German naval operations and training in the Baltic, which previously had been a German lake.

On the night of 18 October 1914 the *E1* penetrated Kiel Bay and attacked the armoured cruiser SMS *Victoria Louise*, firing a single torpedo, which ran too deep, passing under the ship's keel. This demonstration of British sea power reaching into the home of the German fleet in the Baltic caused the Kaiserliche Marine to be ever more cautious.

The *E13*, commanded by Lieutenant-Commander Geoffrey Layton, was accompanied by the *E8*, which safely made the passage, while *E13* transiting the Danish Straits on 13 August 1915 became stranded on Saltholm Island south of Copenhagen.

At first light, the stranded submarine was spotted by Danish naval forces, who sent torpedo boats to investigate; these were later reinforced by the coast defence ship *Peder Skram* to ascertain the nationality of the vessel.

At the same time German torpedo boats also had the *E13* under observation, as orders from the Danish naval Chief of Staff were received by the captain of the *Peder Skram* that he was to forestall any attempts by the Germans to seize or attack the British submarine. At 6.00 a.m. the Danish torpedo boat *Storen* reported two German torpedo boats passing close to the scene, followed by extensive wireless traffic.

Later, at 10.28 a.m., two German torpedo boats, *G132* and *G134*, approached at high speed while flying the international abandon ship flag signals, and when within range, the *G132* fired a single torpedo, which missed and exploded on the sea bed.

The Danish warships made no move to interfere and both German ships opened a rapid fire with deck guns on the helpless submarine that lasted less than 5 minutes, leaving the *E13* on fire, with poisonous chlorine gas spreading through the hull. Lieutenant Commander Layton ordered abandon ship and fourteen crew members including the commander were taken off by the torpedo boat *Storen*, leaving fifteen dead, whose bodies were later recovered and returned to England.

The failure of the Danish ships to protect the *E13* despite being ordered to protect her with all means at their disposal had allowed the Germans to carry out this attack.

The surviving crew were taken into internment for the duration, but Lieutenant Commander Layton and his first officer escaped to rejoin the fleet and the wreckage of *E13* was later raised and scrapped.

The *E18* and *E19* arrived safely at Reval on 15 September 1915. On 10 October the *E19* under the command of Lieutenant-Commander Francis Cromie, patrolling south of the Swedish island of Oland in the early hours of the morning, spotted a German steamer, the SS *Walther Leonhardt*, carrying iron ore which, after being ordered to heave to and the crew taking to the boats, was sunk by an explosive charge.

Later that morning a second steamer, the SS *Germania*, also carrying iron ore, was sighted and attempted to escape, being pursued by *E19* on the surface at 15 knots while firing her deck gun. The German ship eventually ran aground and a dynamite charge was laid which, although damaging the vessel, failed to sink it, and it was subsequently repaired.

After midday a third ship, the SS *Guntrune*, was boarded and, after the crew were in lifeboats, she was sunk by opening the seacocks. Immediately following this, another ship, the SS *Director Repperhagen*, was also sunk and finally at 5.30 p.m. the same day a fifth victim, the SS *Nicomedia* – whose crew, as they took to the boats, presented the British submariners with a barrel of beer – was sent to the bottom.

In a single day *E9* had sunk four ore carriers and wrecked another ashore without the expenditure of a single torpedo.

Later, on 7 November 1915, the *E19* patrolling off Cape Arkona on the Baltic island of Rugen fired two torpedoes at the light cruiser HMS *Undine* of 3,110 tons, causing her magazine to explode, but fortunately with the loss of only fourteen crew members.

This loss came only two weeks after the sinking of the 9,800-ton armoured cruiser SMS *Prinz Adalbert* off Libau on 23 October by the *E8*, resulting in a heavy loss of life. This, together with the loss of the 3,750 ton light cruiser SMS *Bremen* to a Russian mine in February 1915, served as a further demonstration of the positive effect the British submarine flotilla was having on the German ability to operate safely within the Baltic.

The *E18* under the command of Lieutenant-Commander R. Halahan, which had arrived at Reval on 18 June after being fired on by German cruisers during her passage, conducted four patrols, before being lost in June 1916, presumably to a mine in the eastern Baltic.

Much later in 1918 the *E1*, *E8*, *E9* and *E19* were scuttled outside Helsingfors in the civil war between the Bolsheviks and White Russian forces.

The four earlier C class submarines *C26*, *C27*, *C32* and *C35* of 290-ton surface displacement due to their short range were towed from Britain via the North Cape to Archangelsk in the White Sea. From there they were transported on barges through the White Sea canal, reaching St Petersburg in September 1916. But due to the lateness of the season and heavy ice they were not able to operate until the Spring of 1917.

The *C32* became stranded in the Gulf of Riga and had to be abandoned, while the remaining three C class boats were blown up at Helsingfors to avoid capture in 1918.

An incident of the greatest significance to the conduct of the war took place on 25 August 1914 when the German light cruiser SMS *Magdeburg* of 4,500 tons ran aground on the island of Oldensholm off the Estonian coast while conducting a sweep with other ships in the Gulf of Finland. This ship had previously fired the first shots of the Great War when on 2 August 1914 the *Magdeburg* shelled Russian positions in the port of Libau. Two Russian cruisers opened fire on the stranded ship, which was badly damaged, causing the crew to be evacuated, after giving up attempts to re-float the ship.

Subsequently, after the German forces had been driven off, Russian divers were able to recover German naval and merchant code books then in use, which also revealed the methods employed for constructing future codes, which once delivered to the Admiralty cryptographers in London enabled the Admiralty to decipher almost all of the German wireless traffic for the remainder of the war.

In the land war, unlike the trench warfare that had prevailed in the west from Nieuport on the coast of Belgium to the Swiss border for the past four years, on the Eastern Front the war was a more mobile affair.

Initially, the Russian troops enjoyed brief success, advancing into Austrian territory, but were heavily defeated by the Germans at the Battle of Tannenberg in late August 1914.

In early 1915 the Allies attempted to relive the pressure on the Russians by attacking Turkey with a landing at Gallipoli, which as we have seen was a costly failure, and did little to help the situation on the Eastern Front.

The strain on Russia, a poorly governed and bankrupt country, was made worse by further defeats in the field, mutinies in the army and strikes and food riots in a civilian population living on the verge of starvation.

Political agitators of all colours appealed to the masses and a disaffected army to withdraw from the crippling war – a situation that led to further mutinies, civil unrest and finally the revolution of February 1917, which forced Tsar Nicholas II to abdicate in March, allowing for the formation of a democratic provisional government.

This was a coalition under the leadership of Alexander Kerensky, who represented the moderate socialists, working together with the Soviet workers' councils or Bolsheviks. Once installed, the Duma or parliament, assured the Allied powers that it intended to continue to prosecute the war against Imperial Germany on the Eastern Front.

In return for this promise, the Allies, including the United States, which had just entered the war in April 1917, increased proportionally the supply of war materials and economic aid, with large convoys of merchant ships carrying thousands of tons of military supplies and munitions to the vast warehouses in Archangel and the ice-free port of Murmansk, where due to the complicated bureaucracy of army it piled up largely unused. Plagued by further mutinies and mass desertions, the major Russian offensive of June 1918 was a failure and was in turn crushed by the German counter-offensive.

Finally, in October 1917, following food riots in St Petersburg, the Kerensky Government was overthrown by the Bolsheviks, led by Vladimir Lenin, establishing a Communist government determined to end their part in the war. This was followed 5 months later in March 1918 by the Treaty of Brest-Litovsk, which was signed with Germany, formally ending the war on the Eastern Front.

With the treaty the Russians temporarily surrendered a vast swathe of territory, including the Crimea to the Germans.

The signing of the treaty allowed the Germans to withdraw a large number of troops and re-deploy them on the Western Front, where they launched their last great offensive, which was doomed to failure as the Allies strengthened by fresh American troops counter-attacked in July 1918, throwing the Germans back, breaking their line in September 1918. While in the south the Italian Army defeated the Austrians at the Battle of Vittorio Veneto and the war was almost at an end.

At home the civilian population were suffering terrible privation as a result of the British economic blockade and, following mutinies in the High Sea Fleet in October 1918 when they refused orders to put to sea to engage the Grand Fleet, hoping for a victory that would put Germany in a better negotiating position at the now inevitable cessation of hostilities, the German general Staff sued for peace, obtaining an armistice on 11 November 1918.

Before this, however, and worryingly for the Allies, in April 1918 a division of German troops had landed in southern Finland, this being part of the territories ceded to Germany under the terms of the Treaty of Brest-Litovsk, creating the fear that the Germans might seize the important railway between Petrograd (as St Petersburg had been renamed) and the strategic seaport of Murmansk, threatening the vast stores of stockpiled war materials.

Coincidentally, a civil war had broken out in Russia between the Bolsheviks (the Reds) and those still loyal to the Tsar and the monarchy (the White Russian forces or the Whites).

Into this confused situation the leaders of the British and French governments concluded that the western Allies should conduct a military intervention in north Russia with the three following objectives:

1. To prevent the large stockpile of Allied military materials from falling into the hands of either Bolshevik or German forces.
2. To rescue the Allied Czechoslovak Legion stranded along the Trans-Siberian Railroad, after being promised safe passage to the west from Vladivostok and later rescinded by the Bolsheviks.
3. To defeat the Bolshevik Army with the aid of the Czechoslovak Legion and thereafter with the assistance of White Russian forces continue the war against Germany on the Eastern Front.

Other Allied objectives included to contain and defeat the rise of Bolshevism and to encourage the independence of the Baltic states from Russia.

The North Russian Expeditionary Force constituted in July 1918 consisted of some 15,000 British, French, American and Canadian soldiers and artillery. They were landed at Archangelsk, with the Allied forces occupying the port supported by a Royal Naval flotilla of more than twenty ships, which included the seaplane carriers HMS *Pegasus and* HMS *Nairana*.

The Allied troops, including Polish and White guard units, advanced down the Vaga and northern Dvina rivers into territory held by Red forces, capturing key points up to 150 miles south of Archangel. In this offensive they were supported by a force of eleven river monitors, minesweepers and White Russian gunboats.

These ships varied in size and armament but were generally of 540 tons' displacement and mounted a single 9.2in and a 3in gun, performing valuable service on the navigable sections of the rivers. Nonetheless, Bolshevik gunboats, torpedo armed launches and mines took a steady toll on the Royal Naval flotilla.

On 18 September 1918, Bolshevik troops attacked the British Embassy in St Petersburg, sacking the building and killing the staff, including British Naval Attaché Captain Frances Crombie, whose body was mutilated by the attackers.

The initial Allied gains along the northern rivers and around Lake Onega were short-lived as the Bolsheviks gradually gained the upper hand, with more heavy artillery being used against Allied forces in the fierce fighting that caused the Allies to retreat from the Varga River during September, with the monitors making their final attack on the Red gunboats that month before withdrawing.

The final battles of the northern campaign were fought between March and April 1919 when, due to the inability of the Allies to hold the line and mutinies in the White Russian forces, the Allies withdrew from the northern theatre.

The last Royal Naval losses on the Dvina River was that of the monitors *M25* and *M27*, each of 540 tons. On 16 September, due to a fall in the river level, the two monitors were trapped, unable to join other ships of the Northern force, and they had to be blown up to avoid them falling into the hands of the Reds.

Earlier, in June and July 1919 respectively, the armed trawlers HMS *Sword Dance* and *Fandango* were lost to mines on the Dvina River.

In the south the Allied intervention commenced immediately following the armistice and now that the Royal Navy had access to the Baltic. A powerful squadron of C class cruisers, V and W class destroyers and seaplane carriers was dispatched, initially under the command of Rear Admiral Alexander-Sinclair, but replaced in January 1919 by Rear-Admiral Walter Cowan, with Tallinn as their base.

The British squadron used their guns to bombard Bolshevik positions while supporting Latvian and Estonian forces, who had declared their independence from Russia along with Lithuania in November 1918.

The British ships had also severely curtailed the activities of the Russian Bolshevik fleet, effectively trapping them in their base at Kronstadt. During the course of these actions the 4,100 ton cruiser HMS *Cassandra*, armed with five 6in guns, while on operations against enemy positions, was mined and lost in the Gulf of Finland, fortunately with a minimum loss of life.

On 26 December 1918 the cruisers HMS *Caradoc* and HMS *Calypso* and four destroyers were supporting Estonian troops off Tallinn when they fired on two Bolshevik destroyers, the *Avtroil* and the *Spartak*, that had been shelling the port, with the Russian ships surrendering without reply to the British salvoes. The two captured ships were handed over to the Estonian Provisional Government where they were incorporated into the nascent Estonian Navy.

The situation in the eastern Baltic following the armistice of 11 November 1918 was a confused one. German troops had earlier in 1917 taken Riga after much fierce fighting, and the German *Freikorps*, together with the ethnic Baltic German *Landeswehr* troops, were still fighting against the Russians and newly established local Estonian National Army units, who in turn were fighting against the Red Army, and, as mentioned earlier, German troops had occupied southern Finland in April 1918.

Throughout the summer of 1919, while the Royal Navy kept the Bolshevik fleet largely contained in Kronstadt harbour, occasional sallies were made by the Reds. One such attack was when the battleship *Petropavlovsk* (not to be confused with an earlier ship of the same name that was lost at Tsushima in 1904), a modern

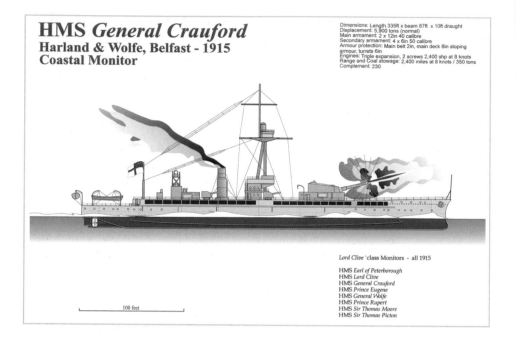

HMS *General Crauford*
Harland & Wolfe, Belfast - 1915
Coastal Monitor

Dimensions: Length 335ft x beam 87ft x 10ft draught
Displacement: 5,900 tons (normal)
Main armament: 2 x 12in 40 calibre
Secondary armament: 4 x 6in 50 calibre
Armour protection: Main belt 2in, main deck 6in sloping
armour, turrets 6in
Engines: Triple expansion, 2 screws 2,400 shp at 8 knots
Range and Coal stowage: 2,400 miles at 8 knots / 350 tons
Complement: 230

100 feet

Lord Clive class Monitors - all 1915

HMS *Earl of Peterborough*
HMS *Lord Clive*
HMS *General Crauford*
HMS *Prince Eugene*
HMS *General Wolfe*
HMS *Prince Rupert*
HMS *Sir Thomas Moore*
HMS *Sir Thomas Picton*

dreadnought of 24,000 tons mounting twelve 12in guns, probed the British base at Tallinn on 31 May, scoring a hit on the destroyer *Walker*, which perversely persuaded Admiral Cowan to move his base closer to Kronstadt.

From their new base at Vantaa on the coast of southern Finland on 17 June, a flotilla of fast Coastal Motor Boats (CMB) attacked the harbour of Kronstadt, where, for the loss of three CMBs, the flotilla sank the light cruiser *Oleg* and an accommodation ship, as well as damaging two battleships with torpedoes.

One of the battleships damaged was the dreadnought *Petropavlovsk*, which was struck by two torpedoes, causing her to sink. Due to the shallow water, she was later raised and repaired.

The British CMBs were in action both in the Baltic and in the northern Russian river systems and the Caspian, where they took a steady toll on Bolshevik shipping. They had originally been designed in secret with stepped hydroplane hulls, incorporating chine to reduce and deflect bow spray, and were to be employed in attacking enemy ships at anchor in their harbours, where their small size, speed and shallow draft would in turn make them difficult targets to hit and allow them to pass over defensive minefields to press home their attacks.

Of the four CMBs that took part in the action on Kronstadt naval base, the *CMB 88* is typical of the type. Built in the Thornycroft yard on the River Thames, she was 60ft overall, with a beam of 11ft, and displaced 11 tons. She was powered by two petrol engines with a combined 900hp on two screws, giving a speed of 40 to 42 knots.

She carried a complement of five and was armed with four Lewis machine guns and two 18in torpedoes. Once the CMB was heading at speed directly towards the target, the torpedo was launched with the engine running from a trough at the stern. As soon as the torpedo was running on course the CMB would turn aside to get out of its way.

Other Royal Naval ships were sent to the Baltic, including the aircraft carrier HMS *Vindictive*. This was a converted heavy cruiser of 9,340 tons' displacement, with a flying-off deck forward of the funnel superstructure and landing-on deck aft, similar to the much larger *Furious*.

She was equipped to carry six aircraft that were employed to carry out bombing and strafing attacks on gun and searchlight emplacements on the Kronstadt naval base. Also, in the Autumn, the force was further strengthened by the arrival of the monitor HMS *Erebus*, a powerful vessel of 8,000 tons' displacement and armed with two 15in guns that were used to effect in support of the White Russian Northern army's offensive against Petrograd.

On 16 July two British minesweepers, HMS *Myrtle* and HMS *Gentian*, were lost off the island of Saaremaa to mines. These two ships were *Flower* class sloops, of which seventy-two were built. Designed on merchant ship lines with no frills, they were completed within a six-month building period.

Initially designed as minesweepers, these handy vessels performed other duties, with thirty-nine being completed as Q ships. They were also employed on convoy protection and anti-submarine work, armed with depth charges.

HMS *Foxglove*
Barclay Curle, Glasgow - 1915
***Flower* Class Sloop**

Dimensions: Length 262ft x 33ft beam x 11ft draught
Displacement: 1,250 tons (normal)
Main armament: 2 x 4.7in Q/F guns - 12 depth charges
Armour protection: No special provision
Engines: Four cylinder triple expansion 2,200shp on one screw at 17 knots
Complement: 70 - 80

HMS *Foxglove* was one of the first group of seventy-two *Flower* class sloops, that were followed by an additional forty *Flower* class 'Q' ships, all built between 1915-17. *Foxglove* survived both World Wars, despite being dive bombed in Plymouth harbour in 1941. She was sent for breaking in 1946.

100 feet

The typical *Flower* class sloop was of 1,200 tons' displacement, with a length of 262ft on a beam of 33ft. Engine power was provided by a four cylinder triple expansion steam engine of 2,400hp on a single shaft, giving a speed of 15 to 17 knots.

Two other losses were those of the destroyer HMS *Verulam*, mined in the Gulf of Finland on 1 September 1919, and the destroyer HMS *Vittoria*, which was torpedoed by the Bolshevik submarine *Pantera* off the island of Seiskarin, this being the only success achieved by a Russian submarine in the conflict.

The Tsarist Russian Navy also conducted operations in the Black Sea against the Bolsheviks, without British assistance, while an even smaller group of British ships, supported with supplies and ammunition through Persia, operated on the land-locked Caspian Sea.

The Royal Navy put together an improvised flotilla of gunboats from commandeered local craft mounting 4in and 6in guns, which were active against the Red forces consisting of four old destroyers that had been sent from the Sea of Azov and the Black Sea via the Volga River into the Caspian, together with the fairly modern (1906) destroyer *Moskvitann* of 510 tons that carried two 12pdr guns and three torpedo tubes.

In an action between the Royal Navy scratch flotilla and the Bolshevik destroyers off Alexandrovsk, all the Russian Bolshevik ships and the *Moskvitann* were sunk or severely damaged.

At the beginning of the intervention in July 1918 some fourteen Allied countries including Japan, Italy and Portugal were involved. Britain and France, desperately short of soldiers for the Western Front, asked the United States to supply troops, which President Woodrow Wilson acceded to despite the misgivings of the State Department, who were very much against using American troops to support a despotic and undemocratic country such as Tsarist Russia, although at the same time they were alarmed by the equally ruthless alternative represented by the Bolsheviks, who threatened the capitalistic democracies through world revolution.

The long campaign was brought to an end by the White Russian forces being unable to contain or defeat the growing Bolshevik armies, who were gaining territory and forcing the White Russian armies to retreat into an ever smaller area of Russia that was under their control. Further defections and mutinies hastened the process and there were even minor incidences of refusal to obey orders on Royal Naval ships, including HMS *Vindictive* and the cruiser HMS *Delhi*. Here, poor conditions and war weariness amongst British sailors who had endured four years of war and were now involved in a seemingly unwinable war that lacked public support at home and was plagued by divided objectives and a positive plan to achieve a successful outcome, together with the imminent collapse of the White Russian forces against the Bolsheviks, caused the final withdrawal of the western interventionist forces in early 1920.

The Royal Navy's losses in the Baltic campaign amounted to the Light cruiser *Cassandra*, the destroyers *Verulam* and *Vittoria*, the submarine *L55* and the sloops *Gentain* and *Myrtle*, plus the loss of four CMBs. Four E class and three C class submarines at Helsingfors were blown up to avoid capture. The operations led to the deaths of 107 Royal Navy personnel.

In the North Russian campaign on the Dvina and Vaga rivers, British losses amounted to two monitors, *M25* and *M27*, and also the minesweepers *Sword Dance* and *Fandango*.

The monitor type of the Great War was a reworking of the coast defence ship, which it was realised could be effectively used for the bombardment of enemy shore positions. This type of ship being of shallow draught meant they were particularly useful on the Russian river systems. They could be built quickly and armed with whatever spare guns that were available, with the largest group of twenty-five or so built mounting either old 6in or 9.2in guns that gave sterling service not only in the Baltic but in the North Sea and the Mediterranean Sea.

Other larger monitors carried 12in and 15in guns and although, for reasons of economy after the war, the majority were scrapped, two of the largest – HMS *Erebus* and HMS *Terror*, each of 8,000 tons, both mounting two 15 guns – survived to serve in the Second World War.

The Allied intervention was an expensive operation that achieved little of any consequence and failed in its original purpose to crush the Bolshevik revolution and restore the Tsar, but was instrumental in allowing the Baltic states of Estonia, Latvia and Lithuania to achieve independence.

18

AIR POWER AT SEA

The Royal Navy in the shape of the Royal Naval Air Service had shown a great deal of interest in hydro-aviation before the outbreak of the war, actively fostering the development of seaplanes and flying boats, as this form of flying machine was seen as particularly suited to naval purposes.

The navy's approach to the acquisition of aircraft was to obtain them from diverse sources, in contrast to the army's almost sole reliance on the products of the Royal Aircraft Factory.

Short Brothers, in particular, and other private firms were encouraged in the development of seaplanes for naval use, with the navy trying out a wide variety of aircraft from the various manufacturers to determine those types most suitable for the particular demands of service at sea.

Early in 1908, in response to the success of the Zeppelin Company in Germany, the British Government in the form of the Committee of Imperial Defence – with the enthusiastic backing of both Prime Minister Asquith and the wily First Sea Lord Admiral Fisher – evaluated the threat posed by the advent of aerial navigation in time of war to Great Britain. They also considered what use aerial craft could be put to in the defence and came to the conclusion that a large rigid framed airship similar to a Zeppelin would be an indispensable asset to the Royal Navy in a scouting capacity.

At the time, the Admiralty was ahead of the Imperial German Navy in adopting the concept of the scouting airship working with the fleet; although it was widely believed in official circles that the German Navy were already building such craft.

In July 1908, Messrs Vickers Son & Maxim were given a contract to build what was described in the specification as an aerial scout, capable of 40 knots for 24 hours and able to rise to an altitude of 1,500ft, carrying wireless and other naval equipment. It had a crew of twenty officers and men, with a projected gross lift of 20 tons and a disposable (useful) lift of 3 tons. Such a vessel would be required to keep station with or scout ahead of the battle fleet, forming an extended patrol line to report the presence of enemy warships.

Built under conditions of the greatest secrecy, the airship *R1*, or *Mayfly* as she became known, was built at Barrow in Furness in a shed built out over the Cavendish dock, eventually emerging in May 1911 to be moored to a mast, where, floating on the water, she remained for three days riding out a storm. The finished vessel was 512ft in length with a beam of 48ft, but was adjudged to be too heavy and unable to fly.

On being returned to her shed, action was taken to lighten the ship by removing the equipment and the keel walkway structure but, as the airship was being taken out for further testing, a squall caused her to be crushed against the shed structure and she became a total loss, causing the Admiralty to temporarily abandon airship construction.

The first occasion on which an aircraft was to fly from the deck of a warship took place as early as November 1910 when a US Navy Curtis biplane was launched from a platform built over the forward 5in gun of the cruiser USS *Birmingham* in Hampton Roads.

Later, this feat was emulated by the Royal Navy when the dashing Lieutenant C.R. Samson flew a Short S27 off the foredeck of the battleship HMS *Africa*, moored in the Medway in December 1911. Later in May of the following year, he repeated the feat from a staging fixed over the bows of the battleship HMS *Hibernia* as the ship steamed at 15 knots in the English Channel.

The Royal Navy took the lead in the development of specialised ships for the carrying and launching of aircraft when, in early 1913, the old 5,500-ton cruiser HMS *Hermes* was converted to carry two seaplanes from a platform fitted forward. A rather precarious method of launching was accomplished by mounting the seaplane on a wheeled trolley, which was guided by rails during take-off to be jettisoned into the sea, with the aircraft being recovered from the sea by crane upon its return.

It is difficult for us today to realise just how revolutionary and extraordinary these developments appeared to be in 1910, when the aeroplane had literally only just emerged as a practical proposition and capable of being effectively controlled in the air.

After conducting trials, the *Hermes* was converted back to a cruiser, only to be reconverted to a seaplane carrier at the outbreak of war, where unfortunately she was torpedoed by the *U27* on 31 October off Dunkirk.

It says much for what was often considered to be a hidebound and inflexible organisation that the British Admiralty demonstrated considerable foresight in condoning these experiments at such an early date. Encouraged by these experiments, a collier was converted while building in 1914 to become the first purpose built seaplane carrier.

This ship, bearing the illustrious name *Ark Royal*, carried its aircraft in her holds, from where they were craned out for launching either from the short flying-off deck at the bows or by being lowered into the water when the ship was stationary for take-off and recovery. *Ark Royal* was 330ft in length with a beam of 50ft and powered by a 3,000hp vertical triple expansion engine that gave a speed of 11 knots. Her armament consisted of four 12pdr guns and accommodated eight seaplanes in her hold.

After the war she continued in a training role, being renamed *Pegasus* in 1934, and served through the Second World War as an aircraft transport and experimental catapult ship, finally going to the breakers in 1950.

Similar arrangements for the accommodation of aircraft and launching methods were employed in the second generation of carriers that were the faster Isle of Man steam packets and railway cross-Channel steamers, which had been impressed into service in 1914. These handy ships gave excellent service – their relatively high speed enabling them to keep station with the fleet – with the *Engadine* taking part in the Cuxhaven raid of December 1914, where her aircraft reconnoitred the German anchorages.

Later, at the Battle of Jutland the same ship, while attached to the battle-cruiser squadron, sent up an aeroplane that spotted the German High Seas Fleet – this being the only aircraft (as opposed to airship) reconnaissance made by either side during the engagement.

The *Engadine* was of 1,676 tons' displacement, 316ft in length, with a beam of 41ft. Her steam turbines were of 6,000hp, giving 21 knots, and her six Short 186 seaplanes, whose wings folded flat along the fuselage, were stored in a large hangar at the stern of the ship. At Jutland she also took in the heavily damaged armoured cruiser *Warrior*, which had to be abandoned the next day in a sinking condition.

After the war she was sold back to the South Eastern and Chatham Railway and later sold on to a US shipping company. She ended her days being mined off Corregidor in December 1941, with a large group of refugees aboard fleeing Japanese invasion of the Philippines.

Other actions involving these plucky railway ships included the Isle of Man steam packet *Ben-My-Chree* which, while in service during the Dardanelles campaign, launched the first successful air torpedo attack on a ship, before later being sunk by Turkish shore batteries.

The old Cunard record breaker HMS *Campania* of 20,000 tons built in 1893 was 622ft in length on a beam of 65ft, while her old engines of 28,000hp could still provide a speed of 19 knots.

She had been bought from the ship breakers at a nominal sum and converted in 1914–15 to carry ten aeroplanes. A 160-ft sloping flying-off deck was installed from her bow to her bridge. The forward funnel was split into two and the runway passed between them.

She was stationed with the Grand Fleet at Scapa Flow and often accompanied the fleet on sweeps of the North Sea, launching aircraft in favourable conditions on reconnaissance duties; although it was not until June 1916 that the first Short 184 torpedo bomber took off from her deck.

Campania was absent from Jutland due to an oversight when she did not receive the order to put to sea at her remote location in the anchorage. Thus, her aircraft were unavailable to Jellicoe at a critical time when their observations could have had a positive tactical influence on the outcome of the battle.

Between 1914 and 1917, other fast cross-Channel railway steamers, including the HMS *Empress*, HMS *Riviera*, HMS *Manxman*, *Pegasus*, and HMS *Narnia*, were added to the increasing number of ships that could launch aeroplanes.

Although the Royal Navy pioneered the development of the aircraft carrier in these early days, the main function of their aircraft was seen primarily to be in the role of a scouting adjunct to the battle fleet, with their offensive capability being regarded as a secondary consideration.

During the inter-war years this philosophy was maintained and, while torpedo-carrying aircraft were a part of the carrier's complement, the primary duty of the fleet's aircraft continued to be in the area of reconnaissance.

The United States and Japan, on the other hand, recognised and developed the offensive potential of carrier-borne aircraft that could strike at a distance far beyond the range of the guns of battleships. Extending this philosophy, some American and Japanese naval planners even foresaw the day when carrier-borne aircraft would launch massive attacks on an enemy fleet, while the opposing fleets were hundreds of miles apart, and could even deal a decisive blow without the fleets ever meeting.

In pursuit of these revolutionary ideas both the Americans and Japanese began building large fleet carriers, equipped with large squadrons of dive bombers, and torpedo-carrying planes to be used as long-range artillery; in both navies this policy was pursued with determination and employed with devastating effect during the Second World War.

The Royal Naval Air Service was particularly active in the early stages of the war in countering the Zeppelin threat, such as the incident in the early morning of 7 June 1915 when Flight Lieutenant R.A.W. Warneford, flying a Morane scout armed with six 20lb bombs, took off from Dunkirk to intercept the Zeppelin *LZ37* returning from a raid on England over Ghent. He destroyed her by dropping a string of bombs along her back, causing her to explode with great violence, falling on a convent in the suburbs of Ghent.

On the same morning fellow pilots, Flight Lieutenants Wilson and Mills flying Henri Farman bombers, attacked the Zeppelin sheds at Evere, near Brussels where the returning Zeppelin *LZ38* had just been berthed after the raid.

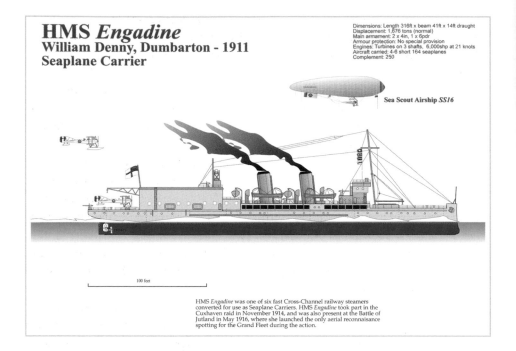

HMS Engadine
William Denny, Dumbarton - 1911
Seaplane Carrier

Dimensions: Length 316ft x beam 41ft x 14ft draught
Displacement: 1,676 tons (normal)
Main armament: 2 x 4in, 1 x 6pdr
Armour protection: No special provision
Engines: Turbines on 3 shafts, 6,000shp at 21 knots
Aircraft carried: 4-6 short 164 seaplanes
Complement: 250

Sea Scout Airship *SS16*

100 feet

HMS *Engadine* was one of six fast Cross-Channel railway steamers converted for use as Seaplane Carriers. HMS *Engadine* took part in the Cuxhaven raid in November 1914, and was also present at the Battle of Jutland in May 1916, where she launched the only aerial reconnaisance spotting for the Grand Fleet during the action.

On 9 October 1914, the Dunkirk squadron had earlier scored a success when Commander Spencer Grey and Flight Lieutenant Marix, flying Sopwith Tabloid biplanes, bombed the sheds at Dusseldorf, destroying the army Zeppelin *Z9* laying inside – the first success of its kind for the RNAS.

A further setback to German plans was dealt by a third and even more daring raid carried out from Belfort near the Alsace French border that was aimed at the very heart of the Zeppelin empire at Friedrichshafen. On the morning of 21 November 1914, three Avro 504s, each carrying four 25lb bombs, flew 125 miles through the mountains on a route designed to avoid Swiss territory. They emerged at sea level on the south side of Lake Constance, before climbing to attack the Zeppelin works, where the British airmen hit their target, damaging a Zeppelin under construction.

The serious threat posed to British merchant shipping by the depredations of German undersea craft operating along the North Sea coasts and the English Channel resulted not only in the loss of numerous merchant vessels, but the Royal Navy during the course of the war lost twelve capital ships and numerous smaller craft to mines and torpedoes. This encouraged the Admiralty to seek a remedy in the use of the aeroplane and the airship for mine-spotting and anti-submarine duties.

As a result of these alarming developments, an urgent conference was called at the Admiralty in February 1915, presided over by Lord Fisher, to address the problem and find an immediate solution to the submarine menace.

Following their Lordships' deliberations, proposals were made for the provision of faster CMBs and other patrol craft armed with depth charges and strengthening the light cruiser and destroyer flotillas based in the Channel and on the east coast, aided by patrols of seaplanes in coastal areas.

Lord Fisher also summoned Wing Commander Masterman and Commander Neville Usborne, two experts in the operation of airships, to the Admiralty to evaluate the possibilities of using small airships as submarine hunters and spotters to cooperate with the surface warships.

After receiving an assessment of the practicality of using such craft from the two officers, Fisher issued instructions for the immediate production of a number of small, fairly fast airships that could be handled after a minimum of instruction by a midshipman and two ratings, as well as being used for the purpose of hunting down and destroying enemy submarines within coastal waters.

It says much for Fisher's determination and organising ability that, within the space of three weeks of receiving the order, the first three SS or Sea Scout airships were ready for their trial flights.

Of the forty-nine Sea Scout airships built, the majority had long service lives working between 2 or even 3 years while operating under the most arduous conditions – proof of the rugged construction of the type. They were very successful within their limitations of performance, flying on average for over 1,000 hours and covering thousands of miles on vital convoy, patrol and mine-spotting work.

Later models with extended range included the larger *Coastal* and *North Sea* classes that could remain on continuous patrol for over 50 hours, the record being

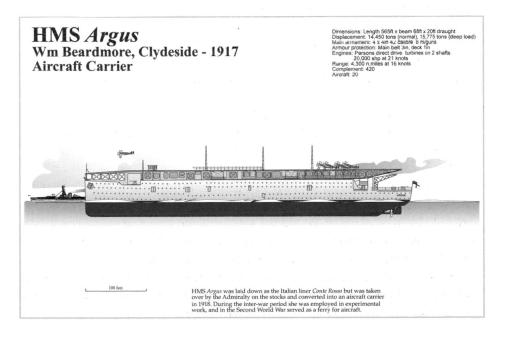

HMS *Argus*
Wm Beardmore, Clydeside - 1917
Aircraft Carrier

Dimensions: Length 565ft x beam 68ft x 20ft draught
Displacement: 14,450 tons (normal), 15,775 tons (deep load)
Main armament: 4 x 4in 42 calibre 6 in/guns
Armour protection: Main belt 3in, deck 1in
Engines: Parsons direct drive turbines on 2 shafts
20,000 shp at 21 knots
Range: 4,300 n.miles at 16 knots
Complement: 420
Aircraft: 20

100 feet

HMS *Argus* was laid down as the Italian liner *Conte Rosso* but was taken over by the Admiralty on the stocks and converted into an aircraft carrier in 1918. During the inter-war period she was employed in experimental work, and in the Second World War served as a ferry for aircraft.

set by the North Seas airship *NS11*, which in July 1919 made a continuous cruise of 101 hours, traversing 4,000 miles on mine patrol.

During the latter stages of the war, July 1917 to October 1918, RNAS airships flew in excess of 1,500,000 miles, escorted 2,200 convoys, flew 10,000 patrols, sighted fifty U-boats, attacking twenty-seven (the majority in concert with surface craft), and sighted 200 mines, destroying seventy-five from the air.

When favourable weather conditions allowed airships to operate with the fleet on their forays into the North Sea, they greatly extended the scouting line of the fleet's cruisers. Although by late 1917 the navy were coming to rely increasingly on the use of the first generation aircraft carriers or aircraft carried by cruisers and battleships for this form of reconnaissance.

By 1918 the earlier aircraft carriers had been joined by HMS *Argus*, the first flush-decked carrier, formerly an Italian liner, that had been appropriated by the Admiralty. It was equipped to carry twenty aircraft, which in design foreshadowed the Woolworth cargo ship conversions to light aircraft carriers of the Second World War.

Argus was of 14,450 tons' displacement, with an overall length of 565ft and a beam of 68ft. Her 20,000hp Parsons steam turbine on four shafts gave a top speed of 20 knots. She carried a crew of 495 and a complement of fifteen to twenty aircraft over a range of 6,500 miles. Being completely flush-decked without any superstructure or funnels, the smoke from the furnaces was ducted through vents on the sides aft in an effort to reduce the air disturbance over the deck to aircraft landing on.

Argus was joined by the massive HMS *Furious* in 1918, a converted large light battle-cruiser and equipped with a complement of twenty planes. *Furious* was of 19,500 tons' displacement and 786ft in length with a beam of 88ft. Her Brown & Curtis geared turbines of 90,000hp gave a speed of 31.5 knots.

Two sister cruisers, the *Glorious* and *Courageous*, were similarly converted to aircraft carriers after the war. These three ships had originally been designed to support a landing on the coast of Germany, being heavily armed with 15in guns and of shallow draught in order to operate in the waters off the Frisian Islands. Fortunately for all concerned the plan was not proceeded with.

Completed as an aircraft carrier, in her initial conversion *Furious* still sported her funnel and bridge superstructure on the centre line of the vessel, with separate landing-on and flying-off decks fore and aft connected by runways either side of the bridge structure to allow for transfer of aircraft between the decks. The aircraft were stored in holds fore and aft from where they were craned on to the deck for take-off.

On 19 July 1918 the *Furious* took part in the successful Tondern air raid, the first ever carrier strike from the sea on a land target, where two of the latest model Zeppelins, *L54* and *L60*, were destroyed.

The first ship to be designed as an aircraft carrier from the keel up was *Hermes* of 10,800 tons. It was launched in 1919 but not completed until 1923, equipped to carry twenty aircraft and the first to establish the now accepted design feature of setting the funnels and superstructure out on the starboard side to allow for a continuous, unobstructed flying-off deck.

The provision of aircraft for use by the fleet grew rapidly as the war progressed, so that by November 1918 the navy possessed over 130 aircraft operating at sea and were further supported by 104 patrol airships. In addition, many of the battleships were by that date fitted to carry a two-seat reconnaissance biplane over the forward gun turret, while twenty-two of the light cruisers were similarly equipped.

An advantage of this method of launching aircraft was that the turret could be turned into the wind, while the ship itself could maintain her course without the need to turn aside to face into the wind.

The Royal Naval Air Service were also very active in the Mediterranean theatre throughout the war, being involved at the outset with the Dardanelles campaign, where RNAS aircraft spotted for the guns of the battleships and located the mine barrages. They operated off the Syrian coast, the Gulf of Aqaba and the Red Sea against Ottoman Turkish positions.

During these operations the seaplane carrier *Ben-My-Chree*, a particular thorn in the Turkish side due to the activities of her aircraft, was sunk by a Turkish battery on the island of Kastellorizo off the coast of Asia Minor. Her place was taken by the seaplane carrier *Empress*, which continued to annoy the Turks.

Another first for the RNAS was on 12 August 1915 when a Short 184 seaplane from *Ben My-Chree* launched a 14in torpedo at a merchant ship in the Sea of Marmara, scoring a direct hit. This was the first time a ship had been attacked from the air in this fashion.

It transpired that the ship was already aground from an earlier attack by a British submarine, but this did not detract from the daring venture, particularly as five days later the feat was duplicated, sinking a troop transport in the same area.

As mentioned earlier (Chapter 14), the German cruiser *Konigsberg* was located in her place of refuge – the Rufiji Delta in East Africa – by a private exhibition pilot hastily commissioned into the RNAS and flying a leaky underpowered flying boat. She was eventually destroyed by two coastal monitors, *Mersey* and *Severn*, shooting on an unseen target hidden by jungle foliage 12 miles distant, thanks to the spotting reports supplied from RNAS aircraft.

Excellent though the seaplanes were, a larger and more robust type of aircraft capable of flying extended patrols deep into enemy controlled waters was required to counter the menace of the U-boat and to disrupt the reconnaissance activities of the scouting Zeppelins.

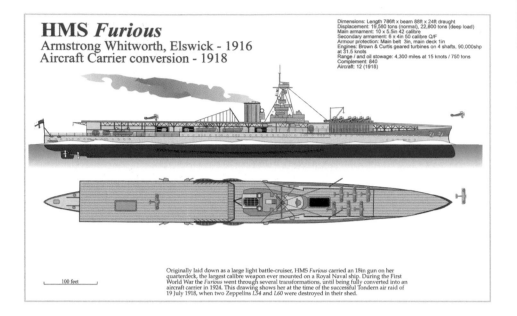

HMS *Furious*
Armstrong Whitworth, Elswick - 1916
Aircraft Carrier conversion - 1918

Dimensions: Length 786ft x beam 88ft x 24ft draught
Displacement: 19,580 tons (normal), 22,800 tons (deep load)
Main armament: 10 x 5.5in 42 calibre
Secondary armament: 6 x 4in 50 calibre Q/F
Armour protection: Main belt 3in, main deck 1in
Engines: Brown & Curtis geared turbines on 4 shafts, 90,000shp
at 31.5 knots
Range / and oil stowage: 4,300 miles at 15 knots / 750 tons
Complement: 840
Aircraft: 12 (1918)

100 feet

Originally laid down as a large light battle-cruiser, HMS *Furious* carried an 18in gun on her quarterdeck, the largest calibre weapon ever mounted on a Royal Naval ship. During the First World War the *Furious* went through several transformations, until being fully converted into an aircraft carrier in 1924. This drawing shows her at the time of the successful Tondern air raid of 19 July 1918, when two Zeppelins *L54* and *L60* were destroyed in their shed.

Following the sinking of the Cunard liner *Lusitania* in May 1915 and that of the White Star *Arabic* in August, the German Foreign Office were conscious that these acts had brought Germany and America to the verge of war.

The German Chancellor Bethmann-Hollweg prevailed on the High Command to suspend the policy of unrestricted submarine warfare, which had been introduced as a counter to the British economic blockade.

With the danger of war with the United States temporarily averted, a number of U-boats were transferred from their North Sea bases to the Mediterranean, where for a period they caused havoc among Allied merchant shipping and inflicted disastrous losses on the British and French warships in the Dardanelles.

By March 1916, overriding the misgivings of their own Foreign Office, the policy of unrestricted submarine warfare was again resumed by the Germans, only to be suspended once more in April following further strong protests from the United States.

This situation lasted until February 1917 when, throwing caution to the wind, the ultimate phase of the policy of unrestricted submarine warfare was implemented, regardless of the protests of both neutrals and the United States.

During this period the German Navy had some 112 U-Boats operational, with eighty stationed at the North Sea ports of Ostend and Zeebrugge and a further twenty-two operational in the Mediterranean and Adriatic based in the Austrian port of Pola. In a single week in February 1917, thirty-five ships were sunk in the English Channel and the Western Approaches by u-boats.

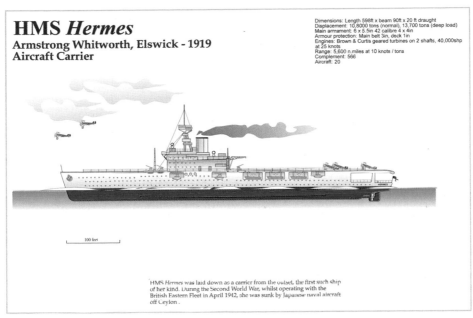

HMS *Hermes*
Armstrong Whitworth, Elswick - 1919
Aircraft Carrier

Dimensions: Length 598ft x beam 90ft x 20 ft draught
Displacement: 10,8000 tons (normal), 13,700 tons (deep load)
Main armament: 6 x 5.5in 42 calibre 4 x 4in
Armour protection: Main belt 3in, deck 1in
Engines: Brown & Curtis geared turbines on 2 shafts, 40,000shp at 25 knots
Range: 5,600 n.miles at 10 knots / tons
Complement: 566
Aircraft: 20

100 feet

HMS *Hermes* was laid down as a carrier from the outset, the first such ship of her kind. During the Second World War, whilst operating with the British Eastern Fleet in April 1942, she was sunk by Japanese naval aircraft off Ceylon.

Sopwith Pup aboard light cruiser *Yarmouth*. (Author's collection)

As a result of these mounting losses, severe food shortages were being experienced throughout the British Isles, with some areas seeing actual starvation being a real possibility. There was civil disorder and food riots in several major cities, requiring the authorities to suppress these outbreaks with force.

Remarkable as it may seem, despite the seriousness of the situation, the Government still allowed market forces and private suppliers to control the supply and distribution of food, the effect of which ensured that the poorer section of the community were those who suffered most.

Food shortages continued to be of concern throughout the war until belatedly the Government introduced food rationing in mid-1918, a measure long overdue, to finally ensure a fairer distribution of the nation's food resources.

At sea, intensive patrols were mounted by aeroplanes and airships, together with the provision of more surface patrol craft carrying depth charges and equipped with hydrophone detection equipment. These measures, along with the introduction of the convoy system, were ultimately to control the submarine menace.

The RNAS had acquired early in the war several examples of the Curtis H4 Small America flying boat which, although of limited range and performance, demonstrated the promise of further development.

These aircraft had been obtained through the efforts of a remarkable and dedicated reserve officer, Commander S.C. Porte, who in October 1915 was commanding the RNAS air station at Felixstowe.

Porte was well suited to the task in hand as he possessed considerable experience with flying boats, having earlier joined Glenn Curtis, the aviation pioneer at Hammondsport in the USA in 1913. In the US he assisted Curtis in the development of a twin-engined (later three-engined) flying boat that was being designed for the wealthy storeowner Rodman Wanamaker, specifically for a transatlantic flight attempt.

The attempt was scheduled for the autumn of 1914, with Porte as the pilot, the machine being delivered and tested before the outbreak of war, at which point the undertaking was abandoned.

Porte had previously held a commission in the Royal Navy from which he had been invalided in 1909 with tuberculosis, re-joining in 1914, where he argued the case forcefully for flying boats to be employed for anti-submarine and long-range reconnaissance work.

His proposals so impressed their Lordships that not only was he appointed to command the RNAS base at Felixstowe in September 1915, but he was also given a brief to develop the Curtis boats along the lines he had propounded.

The Admiralty had bought the original America along with several examples of the smaller Curtis H4 boats of two tons' displacement, powered by two 180hp Curtis engines, which were generally adjudged to be inferior in performance to the contemporary British seaplanes then in use.

Porte's first design was an enlarged and more powerful version of the Small America, the H12 or Large America. This was a much larger boat with a wing span of 90ft and powered by two Rolls Royce Eagle I engines of 275hp, giving a speed of 85mph, with the ability to climb to 11,000ft in 30 minutes and armed with four machine guns and four 100lb bombs.

These boats came into service in mid-1916 and, although the design of the planing hull displayed a structural weakness which required great caution during take-off and landing, the type proved to be a successful reconnaissance and anti-Zeppelin fighter. The first success against the latter by one of these machines took place on 14 April 1917 when Large America No. 8666 from Great Yarmouth air station under the command of Flight Lieutenant J.C. Galpin – with Flight Sub-Lieutenant R. Leckie as pilot, Chief Petty Officer V. Whatling as wireless operator and Air Mechanic O. Laycock as engineer – left to patrol the waters around the Terschelling lightship, observing radio silence to avoid detection by the enemy.

After 1 hour and 30 minutes, Galpin and his crew spotted a Zeppelin dead ahead and some 10 miles distant. No. 8666 was at that time flying at 6,000ft, some 3,000ft higher than the enemy airship. Their prey was the L22 commanded by Kapitan Dietrich-Bielefeld, which was just turning to the north-east, having reached the southern limit of her patrol line.

Dropping their bombs to lighten ship, Leckie opened the throttles and, using broken cloud as cover, put the flying boat's nose down, diving towards their quarry at over 100 knots, levelling out at her altitude at 75 knots and overhauling her on the starboard quarter.

From a range of 150ft, 8666 opened fire with the twin bow and midships guns, firing a complete tray of ZPT tracer from the forward gun and half a tray from the midships position before it jammed.

As the flying boat banked away to clear the gun, they saw a glow inside the envelope and within seconds the rear portion was in flames, quickly engulfing the entire framework, which fell stern first into the sea.

The cause of the loss of L22 was unknown to Strasser, as the Zeppelin had no time to send out a wireless message, so complete was the surprise of the attack. Strasser had to assume that the L22 had been lost to surface fire from British warships.

In his report Galpin stated that the L22 had been set alight before the German crew had realised the nature of the attack and the element of surprise together with their greater speed gave the flying boat the advantage. Galpin went on to say that, even under normal conditions, this type of flying boat should prove superior in every way to a Zeppelin, judging from the amount of power in reserve, and she proved an exceptionally steady gun platform.

The superior performance of these new flying boats forced the Naval Airship Division of the German Imperial Navy to abandon low Zeppelin patrol patterns in the German Bight and along the Dutch islands.

From now on, for safety, reconnaissance was to be conducted above 10,000ft, which lessened their ability to observe surface details effectively.

Further development of Porte's original concept followed with the introduction of the larger and more seaworthy F2a boats, built with a much stronger double-stepped hull.

The F2a spanned 98ft, with a loaded weight of 5 tons and two 350hp Rolls-Royce Eagle III engines producing a top speed of 90 knots. These formidable craft mounted no less than six .303 Lewis machine guns, plus bombs and with an endurance of 8 hours.

Carrying a crew of four, they were the first true long-distance over-water reconnaissance aircraft, with a range of 600 miles, enabling them to scout large areas of the North Sea with rapidity.

In the offensive role the F2as could more than hold their own against the nimble and equally effective Brandenburg sea monoplanes and biplanes that they encountered on their incursions into the German Bight and along the Frisian Islands. They would sometimes form an attacking squadron of four or five boats against the German seaplane bases. In the course of these forays, long-running aerial duels were often fought.

When attacked by the German aircraft, the F2as would form into line astern, flying straight and level to engage the enemy machines with intense combined broadsides of machine-gun fire from their superior armament of up to six machine guns, in the same manner as that employed by Nelson Wooden Walls a century earlier.

As a Zeppelin destroyer the F2a proved to be an efficient and steady gun platform, with a fair turn of speed and a respectable rate of climb, and able to bring its powerful armament to bear on a Zeppelin with every chance of success. F2as were responsible for the destruction of two Zeppelins and made several other attacks in which, although the airships managed to avoid their fiery fate, they were forced to abandon their patrol duties early or had to climb to altitudes where their observations were rendered ineffectual.

The F2a's greatest contribution possibly lay in its anti-submarine warfare role, together with its valuable contribution to mine-barrage spotting duties and the part it played in enforcing the blockade by reporting ships to the surface patrols on the lookout for blockade runners or contraband cargoes.

Alongside the numerous destroyers, mine hunters, CMBs and other patrol craft, airships and seaplanes, the F2as operating from Felixstowe, Great Yarmouth and other stations along the east coast were selected to fly the spider web patrols, starting in early 1917 and designed to counter the U-boat menace.

The central point of the patrolled area was based on the Nord Hinder light vessel, from where eight patrol lines radiated out for a distance of 30 miles, with concentric lines joining them at distances of 10, 20, and 30 miles from the centre, allowing 4,000 square miles of ocean to be systematically scoured with rapidity.

As the war progressed, the F2as and the earlier H12s became ever more active against the German seaplane bases along the Frisian Islands. They also flew long reconnaissance missions over the North Sea, attacking submarines and enemy merchant shipping and protecting the Allied convoys.

By mid-1917, the flying boat was able to perform all the duties with greater efficiency and reliability than those that had been attributed as the main role of the airship a few short years before.

Other devices designed to disrupt or destroy Zeppelins were also employed, including the towing of specially adapted lighters behind destroyers, carrying a single Sopwith Camel scout which could be rapidly brought to a suitable radius of action within enemy waters.

When a Zeppelin was sighted, the destroyer turned into the wind, working up to 30 knots, where the Camel after a run of 10ft was airborne.

By this method on 11 August 1918 Lieutenant S.D. Cully RN attacked and destroyed a patrolling Zeppelin, the L53, at the great height of 18,000ft off Terschelling, this being the last such airship destroyed in the war.

Only six days prior to this incident the leader of naval airships, the redoubtable Fregattenkapitan Peter Strasser, had been killed when the L70, the most modern airship of the fleet, had fallen in flames off the Norfolk coast with the loss of all her crew.

These losses marked the end of the Imperial Navy's Airship Service as a fighting force, and by these actions in the last year of the war the aeroplane had proved its undoubted ascendancy over the airship in all aspects of operation, apart from that of endurance.

Another successful method by the fleet to warn of the presence of U-boats or minefields, was the use of kite balloons that were eventually carried in the ratio of one balloon at the rear of each division of four ships of the Grand Fleet when in cruising formation on North Sea sweeps.

These balloons, with a capacity of 30,000 cubic feet of hydrogen, were towed by a battleship at a height of 1,500ft, capable of being towed at the ship's maximum speed. The observer in the basket would be in telephone communication with the battleship, from where he could, in suitable conditions, identify U-boats or minefields, and allow the divisional commander to call up destroyers or other light forces to deal with the situation.

Admiral Beatty also equipped six destroyers with kite balloons to accompany and scout ahead of the battle-cruiser fleet to perform similar duties and, more particularly, to extend the radius of his scouting line.

In August 1914 the Royal Naval Air Service was composed of fifty officers and 500 men flying thrity landplanes and fifty-eight seaplanes of indifferent performance.

By 1 April 1918 the service had expanded to 5,000 officers and 50,000 men, operating from forty-four aerodromes, fourteen airship stations and seven kite balloon stations.

Their equipment included 1,850 aircraft, including almost 1,000 seaplanes and flying boats, together with over 100 aircraft carried by the ships of the Fleet and even more at the time of the armistice.

THE ZEEBRUGGE AND OSTEND RAIDS

Not all of the Royal Navy's actions were confined to ship-to-ship or fleet actions. The need often arose to either support the army in landings on enemy controlled territory or using their own marines to raid enemy harbours, settlements or fortresses. An early example of a successful raid was the expedition against Cadiz in 1587 led by Sir Francis Drake.

In the reign of Queen Elizabeth I, the continuing raids by English privateers against the Spanish possessions in the Americas and the seizing of their treasure fleets that supplied the gold so necessary to the economy of the Spanish Empire created tensions between England and Spain, whose king, Philip II, had resolved to overthrow the heretical Protestant monarch and impose Catholicism on England. Finally in 1585, war broke out between the two countries. England was supported by the Dutch United Provinces, who were waging their own war for independence against Spain in the Spanish Netherlands.

Philip II ordered a great fleet to be assembled and armed at Cadiz and Lisbon that would sail to the Netherlands to embark the army of the Duke of Medina-Sidonia and invade England, in what was known as the Enterprise of England.

Queen Elizabeth, who had over the years managed to avoid war through her diplomatic skills could now see the inevitability of conflict. On learning of the Spanish plans of conquest from her spies, she took pre-emptive action by ordering her favourite, Sir Francis Drake, to lead an expedition against the Invincible Armada, as the Spanish described it. The Queen supplied Drake with four Royal ships – the *Elizabeth Bonaventure*, *Golden Lion*, *Rainbow* and *Dreadnought* – together with twenty armed merchantmen and pinnaces.

Off the coast of Galicia the fleet fell in with two Dutch merchantmen, who informed them that a fleet was being assembled in Cadiz and would soon be ready to sail.

In the early morning of 29 April 1587, Drake and his fleet entered the harbour of Cadiz, penetrating the inner harbour, where over eighty ships lay against minimal resistance.

Over the next two days the English fleet destroyed forty of the ships present and equally importantly burnt the warehouses containing naval stores, which included the destruction of over 1,500 tons of barrel staves and hoops. This last action was of particular importance, as the completed barrels, made from well-seasoned wood, could hold 25,000 tons of supplies and fresh water.

Not only did this daring raid delay the launching of the Armada for another year, but when they did sail their provisions and water had to be stored in unseasoned wood. This allowed the meat and other supplies to rot and the water to turn brackish and undrinkable; circumstances which during the attempted invasion of 1588 did more damage to the Spanish ships than the English cannon.

Drake next raided the fortress of Sagres and intercepted the Spanish treasure ship *San Felipe*, from which he removed gold, silver and silk to the value of £108,000, of which Drake's share was 10 per cent. The fleet returned to England in June 1587, the whole expedition having been a complete success that had achieved its planned objectives.

Other examples of a successful naval landing was that of General Wolfe and his troops during the siege of Quebec in 1759, in what would now be referred to as combined operations.

The ports of Zeebrugge and Ostend had been seized by German forces in October 1914 and were immediately used by the German Navy as bases of operations for their U-boat flotillas, giving them more immediate access to the Straits of Dover and the English Channel.

The British Admiralty ordered the creation of a series of mine barrages in early 1915 to be laid between the Belgian coast and Dover, consisting of mines laid in conjunction with light steel indicator nets of up to 12 miles in length, anchored to the seabed and set at varying depths. A second similar barrage was positioned further south between Folkestone and Cap Gris Nez, with the intention of entangling enemy U-boats.

Sir Roger Keyes was appointed head of the Mine Barrage Committee, where he liaised with the Dover Patrol of fast destroyers and patrol boats under the command of Sir Reginald Bacon.

The first success by this passive defensive system came on 4 March 1915 when the *U8* was caught and sunk after running into the nets. On learning of the method employed to sink the *U8*, the German Admiralty forbade the use of the Strait of Dover to U-boats for almost a year.

By March 1916, with U-boats fitted with net cutters, they once again risked passing through the Dover Straits, with some making the faster passage on the surface at night.

The earlier British mines had proved ineffective until replaced with the H2 model later in the war that produced better results, with twelve U-boats being sunk in the barrage.

The barrage become so successful that it eventually caused the German Navy to finally abandon the use of the Dover Straits in August 1918.

The harbours of Zeebrugge and Ostend were both linked by canals capable of allowing for the passage of large ocean-going ships to the inland port of Bruges, some 7 miles from the coast, which was an ideal port as a base for U-boats and torpedo craft.

The first operations of the Flanders Flotilla, commanded by Kapitanleutnant Bertenbach, took place on 11 November 1914 when the gunboat *Niger* was sunk by a Flanders U-boat off the Deal light vessel. Its first loss occurred on 26 November when the *U11* was lost to a mine in the straits.

Early in 1915, plans were in hand to turn the Flemish harbours into impregnable war bases, with 14,000 construction workers drafted in from the Kaiserliche Werft organisation, who set about building protected submarine pens, workshops, storehouses and dry docks, together with floating docks and magazines. These new constructional facilities received attention initially from the Royal Naval Air Service and later Royal Flying Corps bombing squadrons based at Dunkirk and Nieuport. However, such attacks were largely ineffective and more damage was done to the Belgian civilian population – with over 700 houses being destroyed over the war period – than to the submarine bases.

Efforts were made by the Royal Navy to bombard the locks at both Zeebrugge and Ostend using monitors and the 12in guns of the old pre-dreadnoughts HMS *Venerable* of 1899 and the even older *Revenge* built in 1892, which had been struck from the navy list in 1911 but recommissioned with her four old 13.5in guns re-lined to 12 calibre and anti-torpedo bulges fitted. In order to allow her name to be used for a new *Royal Sovereign* class battleship, she was renamed HMS *Redoubtable*.

Positioned off the Belgian coast with her protecting ships from the Dover Force, her bilge tanks were counter flooded to heel the ship over by 15° and increase the range of her guns. While the two old battleships and the monitors performed excellent work in bombarding the seaward end of the German trenches, their attempts to destroy the lock gates on the Bruges canals met with little success.

April 1915 found the first of the small but very effective *UC* class mine-laying submarines operating out of Ostend, creating a very worrying situation, as they could lay mines undetected off British harbours and in coastwise shipping lanes.

The first success was that of the *UC11* operating out of Ostend and laying her mines south of the Goodwin Sands, where within 24 hours its first victim, the destroyer HMS *Mohawk*, was sunk, puzzling the Admiralty as to how the mines had been laid.

These boats were quite small, the first of them being of 168 tons surface and 183 tons submerged displacement. They were 111ft long with a beam of only 10.5ft and a crew of fourteen; a diesel engine of 90hp gave a surface speed of 6.5 knots, while the electric motor of 175hp imparted an underwater speed of 5 knots.

In place of torpedo tubes, six vertically inclined mine silos carried a total of twelve mines, carrying a crew of fourteen. Later models built during 1916–17 were much larger. They had a corresponding increase in range, with a displacement of 500 tons surface and 580 tons submerged, carrying up to fourteen mines apiece. About 115 of this type were built during the war.

The range of these submarine minelayers came as an unpleasant surprise to the Admiralty, highlighted by the sinking of *Hampshire* off the Orkney Isles in 1916, with Lord Kitchener en route to Russia on board. This was attributed to a mine laid by a UC boat.

Over the next three months, twenty-three merchant ships, sixteen fishing boats and a further two British destroyers were sunk due to their activities. Only when the *UC2* was sunk by accident and subsequently raised by the Royal Navy were they made aware of this new type of vessel.

By October 1915, sixteen U-boats were operational from Zeebrugge and Ostend, while throughout 1916 the Flanders Flotilla were very active in the southern North Sea and further afield. More UC boats continued to join the Flotilla during the winter months, with twenty-two at its disposal in January 1916, rising to thirty boats by March, which were now causing havoc among British merchant shipping. By April 1917, over 621,800 tons of shipping had been sunk by U-boats, a great proportion of which had fallen victim to the Flanders Flotilla.

The port of Bruges, as described earlier, had rapidly developed during 1915–16 as a major submarine and torpedo boat base, with concrete U-boat shelters, barracks, storehouses and repair facilities to support the ships of the Flanders Flotilla. This concentration of German naval power so close to the British coast saved the U-boats almost 300 miles of dangerous open sea passage. It was only 11 miles from Ostend and 7 miles from the nearest coastline and it soon received the attention of the Royal Navy.

On 7 September 1915, four monitors of the Dover Patrol led by Admiral Bacon – HMS *Lord Clyde, HMS Marshal Ney*, HMS *Prince Rupert* and HMS *Sir John Moore* – and escorted by sixteen destroyers, with up to forty drifters towing explosive anti-submarine nets to protect the monitors, bombarded Bruges, taking station 10 miles out to sea off Ostend.

The *Lord Clyde* was of 5,900 tons' displacement, 335ft in length and with a beam of 87ft. It was powered by triple expansion engines of 2,500hp on two screws, which gave a speed of only 8 knots. Her armament consisted of two 12in 40 calibre guns that had previously seen service in the *Majestic* class pre-dreadnought battleships.

During the bombardment, in which only fourteen rounds were fired, part of the dockyard in Bruges was set on fire and the *Lord Clyde* was herself hit by long range coastal batteries four times due to her slow speed, but made it safely back to port, while the monitors failed to hit the important lock gates either in this or subsequent operations. An initial plan to attack the harbours of Zeebrugge and Ostend directly had been considered by Vice-Admiral Sir Reginald Bacon, who in 1915 commanded the Dover Patrol in the early days of the war in order to deny the ports to enemy submarines and torpedo boats, but it failed to receive official authorisation. Finally in 1917, the scheme was resurrected by First Sea Lord Sir John Jellicoe and Vice-Admiral Sir Roger Keyes, who took over command of the Dover Patrol in 1918. The plan for a raid on the two ports, as formally approved by the Admiralty in late Autumn 1917, involved the sealing of the entrances to the canals with blockships and destroying the lock gates.

For the operation against Zeebrugge, three old cruisers dating from the 1890s, HMS *Iphiginia*, HMS *Thetis* and HMS *Intrepid*, were chosen as the blockships. The cruiser *Vindictive*, a 5,750-ton, three funnelled protected cruiser launched in 1897, was to carry the main assault party, together with two Mersey ferries, the *Iris* and *Daffodil*. These ferries were to carry additional troops, along with over seventy other vessels, including two C class submarines that were to be involved in the raid.

The blockships were stripped of all unnecessary equipment and loaded with concrete, while the *Vindictive* was similarly modified, with her masts removed, additional armour plate added and most of her existing guns removed, to be replaced with 7.5in army howitzers and flame throwers, complete with boarding ramps and ladders fixed to her main deck.

The entrance to the harbour at Zeebrugge was protected by a mile long curving mole, 200ft at its widest point, with a parapet 30ft above sea level at high tide on the seaward side and connected to the mainland by a 1,500ft-long iron viaduct. Along the mole and on the shore was an extensive system of trenches and included batteries of artillery in excess of 200 guns, of which 130 were of 6in to 12in calibre with a range of 36,000yd, which defended the entrance and lock gates. This formidable system of defence in April 1918 protected thirty-five torpedo boats and thirty submarines further up the canal in the port of Bruges – a seemingly impregnable fortress, from where they could sail out at will to menace British sea communications and trade.

On 22 April 1918 at 4.50 p.m., the assault force assembled off Clacton and began the 7-hour trip. Promptly at 11.20 a.m. on the morning of the 23rd – St George's Day – monitors began a bombardment of Zeebrugge and Ostend, this being a diversionary tactic that had been carried out over several nights previously in order to deceive the defences.

Towards midnight, motor launches began to lay smokescreens to cover the advance of the cruiser *Vindictive* as it steamed towards the end of the mole accompanied by HMS *Iris* and HMS *Daffodil*.

The Zeebrugge Raid, 23 April 1918

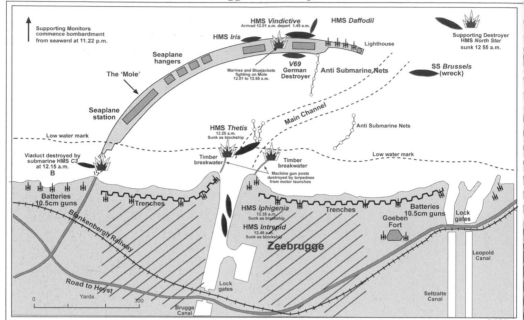

All seemed to be going well and Captain Gardener was confident he could lay his cruiser alongside the end of the mole, where his guns could be used in defence of the landing party and to create a diversion to allow the blockships an uncontested passage into the canal.

This was not to be. The German gunners, alerted to the sounds of the ships approaching under the cover of darkness and smokescreens, opened fire, guided by the sound. At that moment the wind changed direction, revealing the attacking squadron to the gun crews. Immediately, the *Vindictive* came under a heavy and sustained fire at point blank range, causing casualties and severe damage to her upperworks and bridge.

Due to the fierce fire being directed at the ship and the strong tide that was running, *Vindictive*, instead of docking at the end by the lighthouse, was forced to moor 1,000ft further down the mole; a position where her guns were practically useless against the defences.

The *Iris* came alongside astern of the *Vindictive*, managing to secure herself with grapnels, and laid her storming ladders and ramps to the mole, allowing her marines to engage the troops and gun positions.

The *Vindictive* was unable to secure herself to the mole and, in order to prevent her drifting further in the strong tide, the *Daffodil* held her against the mole, holding her in position. This allowed *Vindictive* to land her storming parties, who made their way up the ramps on to the mole to engage the defenders. Without the support of her heavy howitzers, however, they made little progress.

It had been anticipated that in addition to the fire from the shore batteries, the attacking force would be counter-attacked by a large torpedo boat flotilla, but in the event, for some reason, they had earlier been withdrawn to Bruges harbour. Only one German torpedo boat was alongside the mole – this was attacked by *Coastal Motor Boat No. 5* that scored a hit with a torpedo.

Of the two C class submarines involved, the *C1* had parted her tow en route and arrived too late to take part in the operation.

Meanwhile, the submarine *C3* had successfully passed round the mole, and at 12.20 a.m. succeeded in ramming into the steelwork of the viaduct, where Captain Sandford primed the charges. Shortly after the crew of five had been taken off by motor launch, the 5 tons of Amatol exploded, completely destroying the viaduct and cutting off any further German reinforcements from reaching the fighting at the end of the mole.

At 12.50 a.m. the cruiser *Thetis* under the command of Captain Ralph Sneyd rounded the mole and headed for the canal entrance. Captain Sneyd's orders were to steam three quarters of a mile up the canal to ram the lock gates. Under heavy gunfire, the *Thetis* was repeatedly hit, causing severe damage. Her propellers became entangled in anti-submarine nets, bringing her to a halt less than 100yd from the entrance.

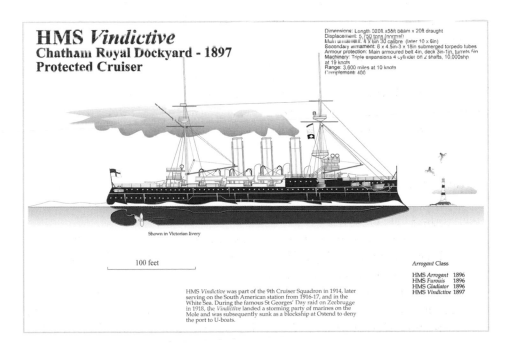

HMS *Vindictive*
Chatham Royal Dockyard - 1897
Protected Cruiser

Dimensions: Length 320ft x 58ft beam x 20ft draught
Displacement: 5,750 tons (normal)
Main armament: 4 x 6in 30 calibre (later 10 x 6in)
Secondary armament: 6 x 4.5in-3 x 18in submerged torpedo tubes
Armour protection: Main armoured belt 4in, deck 3in-1in, turrets 6in
Machinery: Triple expansions 4 cylinder on 2 shafts, 10,000shp at 19 knots
Range: 3,600 miles at 10 knots
Complement: 400

Shown in Victorian livery

100 feet

Arrogant Class

HMS *Arrogant* 1896
HMS *Furious* 1896
HMS *Gladiator* 1896
HMS *Vindictive* 1897

HMS *Vindictive* was part of the 9th Cruiser Squadron in 1914, later serving on the South American station from 1916-17, and in the White Sea. During the famous St Georges' Day raid on Zeebrugge in 1918, the *Vindictive* landed a storming party of marines on the Mole and was subsequently sunk as a blockship at Ostend to deny the port to U-boats.

Unable to proceed further, her captain set charges and scuttled her across the fairway, with the crew being taken off by the brave work of the motor launch crews, who risked a storm of shell and machine-gun fire to rescue their comrades.

Benefiting from her having cleared away the anti-submarine nets, the captain of the *Intrepid*, Lieutenant Stuart Bonham-Carter, followed the *Thetis* in and steamed into the harbour entrance under fierce and heavy fire, placing his ship across the canal entrance in the planned position at its narrowest point, before setting off the scuttling charges.

The third cruiser *Iphigenia* also made it, with Lieutenant Billyard-Leake positioning his ship across the entrance close to the *Intrepid*. It seemed that at last the canal entrance was sealed.

During this stage of the operation the destroyer *North Star*, which with two others had been engaging the shore batteries in support of the blockships, took the wrong course in the smoke screen, and on emerging close to shore came under sustained fire at close range and was sunk. Once again, most of her crew were taken off by the sterling work of the motor launches.

In the fierce fighting taking place at the end of the mole, casualties among the British sailors and marines were extremely heavy and, without the supporting fire from *Vindictive*'s howitzers, most of the primary objectives were not taken. By 12.50 a.m., after heavy losses, the storming party was withdrawn, re-embarking the survivors. By 1.10 a.m. the *Vindictive* and her consorts had departed the mole and were standing out to sea. The raid was at an end.

As the battered fleet returned to their ports, the first reports represented the action as a great and triumphal feat of arms, a bold blow against the enemy. This view that the raid had achieved its planned objectives was confirmed by aerial reconnaissance photographs taken the next morning that showed the blockships across the canal entrance, effectively rendering it unusable to the passage of enemy submarines and torpedo boats.

It was estimated that at least twenty-three torpedo boats and twelve submarines were effectively sealed up in Bruges harbour and unable to access the open sea. Yet, these successes had been achieved at considerable cost, with 230 of the attackers killed, 360 wounded and 40 taken prisoner, together with the loss of two motor launches and a destroyer. German casualties on the other hand were limited to eight dead and sixteen wounded, indicative of the secure concrete gun emplacements and trench systems from which they repelled the attack on the mole.

The news of the raid gave a tremendous boost to the morale of the Navy and the general public at a time when news from the Western Front was anything but good. The whole operation was presented to the public as a great and successful feat of arms that had completely frustrated the Germans' ability to launch attacks from the harbour of Bruges. It had also been conducted with great heroism and skill, with eleven Victoria Crosses and other gallantry medals being awarded. Nonetheless, this did not change the fact that it was a badly conceived plan, relying on élan and British pluck to carry the day and too much being left to chance. It was the naval equivalent of the frontal assault that was being practised daily by soldiers, with horrifying results, on the Western Front.

In reality, the raid achieved only a temporary inconvenience to the Flanders Flotilla, as within a few days smaller craft were able to squeeze past the blockships. By the end of May dredgers had excavated a new channel around the sunken ships, allowing the U-boats once again to use the entrance, leaving the sunken ships in place. The wrecks were finally raised to clear the channel after the war in 1920.

Further up the coast a simultaneous attack was taking place at Ostend. As at Zeebrugge, an initial bombardment by monitors preceded the attack. As there was not a mole at this port, no diversionary tactics were employed. A direct assault commenced at midnight, with the approach of the blockships to be covered, as at Zeebrugge, by a smokescreen laid by motor launches.

Unfortunately, as at the other port, a shift in the wind revealed their approach at the vital moment and both the cruisers, HMS *Brilliant* and HMS *Sirius*, destined to be sunk as blockships came under a storm of well-directed shellfire that battered both ships, causing many casualties.

Unknown to Commander A. Goodsal of the *Brilliant* or Lieutenant-Commander Henry Hardy of the *Sirius*, the buoys at the entrance of Ostend harbour that marked the fairway had been moved shortly before the attack 2,300yd to the east. This was due to the fact that the Germans had captured a British motor launch that had partial information on board indicating the possible nature of such a raid.

The *Brilliant* and *Sirius* steamed at high speed amid the shell splashes, then turned to starboard, lining up the buoys towards the canal entrance. Within minutes both ships had run on to shoal banks and were hard aground hundreds of yards short of their proposed objective. Their captains had no option but to set scuttling charges and, still under fierce artillery fire, evacuate the crews into the motor launches, while taking severe casualties.

The raid on Ostend had been a complete failure. With the canal exit undamaged, no amount of patriotic propaganda describing the derring-do of our ships could change the fact that the German U-boats could still pass into the North Sea with impunity.

During a later bombardment by monitors on 22 September 1917 came a degree of success when the lock gate at Bruges was hit by twelve shells, which caused the lock basin to empty, resulting in temporary closing of the canal. A further attempt to close the canal at Ostend was put in hand by Commodore Keyes almost immediately following the 23 April raid, with the intention of trapping the U-boats and torpedo craft at Bruges.

For what seemed, in the light of previous experience, a suicide mission, volunteers were called for from the survivors of the earlier raid.

Among those who came forward were Lieutenant Commander Henry Hardy of the *Sirius* and Commander Alfred Godsal of the *Brilliant*. These two officers proposed a revised plan to Commodore Keyes to attack the mouth of the canal, which the authors of the plan claimed would have every chance of success, although in outline it was generally similar to the earlier plan.

HMS *Sappho*, a 3,500-ton protected cruiser built in 1891, and the battered survivor of the Zeebrugge raid *Vindictive* were selected for the task and fitted out with additional armour. Their ballast tanks and forward flats were filled with concrete in order to protect the bows and to create a more difficult obstacle to remove when sunk in position.

The *Vindictive* was under the command of Commander Godsal, together with six officers and forty-eight crew, who, as with the crew of the *Sappho* under Lieutenant-Commander Harvey, were all volunteers and veterans of the earlier raid. As in the earlier raid, the attack would be supported by the four Lord Clyde monitors some distance off the coast that were to engage the heavy coastal batteries, supported closer in by eight destroyers. The plan was that under the cover of a smokescreen the two cruisers would head directly for the canal entrance, turn to block the channel and scuttle the ships in the narrowest part.

It was hoped that by closing the exit, together with the ships sunk at Zeebrugge, which at that time the British believed had been a complete success, it would deny the use of Bruges to the enemy for some considerable time.

The British ships assembled at Dunkirk on 9 May 1918, sailing after dark. Unfortunately, just after midnight *Sappho* had a boiler explosion, causing her to lose power and she had to be towed back to Dunkirk.

Commander Lynes leading in the *Faulknor* decided to continue the operation and at 1.30 a.m. the attacking force closed the port in foggy weather, with the CMBs launching torpedoes at the gun emplacements at the end of the two piers, destroying them. At the same time heavy bombers of the RAF dropped incendiary bombs on the German shore batteries, but without significant results, while further assistance was offered from Royal Marine Artillery long-range guns from positions around Ypres.

The fog that had suddenly developed hid the harbour from view and caused Commander Godsal to have to search for the entrance, as the German shore batteries carried on a duel with the monitors offshore. Two German torpedo boats put to sea to attack the British cruiser, but in the fog came into collision with each other, damaging both ships and causing them to return to harbour. At last Godsal located the canal entrance and, led by a motor launch *ML254* dropping flares, the *Vindictive* headed in at full speed, while drawing heavy fire from the German batteries that smashed in to the old cruiser from point-blank range. One shell destroyed the bridge killing Commander Godsal and killing or wounding most of the bridge crew.

With the burning and battered ship now within the entrance to the canal, First Lieutenant Victor Crutchley, although wounded, took the wheel in an attempt to bring the ship about and place her across the fairway. Unfortunately, a shell had destroyed the port propeller and Crutchley was unable to manoeuvre the ship and she drifted onto a sandbank. Cruchley ordered the demolition charges to be detonated, settling the ship on the edge of the channel, partially blocking it.

Under intense machine-gun fire from the shore, Lieutenant Crutchley ordered the remaining crew to take to the boats on the protected side, which consisted of a single launch, ML254, which in turn had come under machine-gun fire, wounding her captain Lieutenant Drummond.

The ML254 took off thirty-eight survivors from the Vindictive's crew of fifty-five and, as she proceeded seaward, she encountered the motor launch ML276. Drummond informed its captain that he believed survivors from the Vindictive were still in the water. Immediately, Lieutenant Rowley Bourke of the ML276 entered the harbour to search for the missing men under continuous and heavy machine-gun and artillery fire. After visiting the wreck on four occasions he picked up two sailors and the badly wounded navigation officer. However, as the ML276 headed out to sea she was struck by two 6in shells. Miraculously, this did not destroy the little boat, and she was fortunate to be taken in tow by another motor launch.

Meanwhile, ML254, in a sinking condition, had reached the destroyer HMS Warwick, which took her survivors on board, only shortly after to have the ship run on to a defensive mine that left her in danger of sinking. The destroyer HMS Velox came alongside, lashing herself to the damaged ship, with the survivors from the damaged vessels taken aboard the Velox as the two ships limped off to Dover, arriving on the morning of 10 May. British casualties were reported as eight dead, twenty-nine wounded and ten missing, while German losses were three killed and eight wounded. For this action a further three Victoria Crosses and other decorations were awarded.

The effect of this last raid was possibly more damaging to the Germans as, although the Vindictive had failed in its attempt to completely block the channel, it was partially successful in trapping some of the larger vessels in the harbour at Bruges, although smaller boats such as the dangerous UC minelayers could still use the channel.

In October 1918 British and Belgian forces finally recaptured Ostend, and after 4 years the threat it had posed was at an end. The wreck of the Vindictive was raised in August 1920, with the bow section of the famous ship being preserved on the seafront at Ostend as a memorial to the raid.

'THE GERMAN FLAG WILL BE HAULED DOWN AT SUNSET ...'

By August 1916 a sufficient number of warships had been repaired following the damage inflicted on the High Seas Fleet at Jutland for Admiral Scheer to plan another raid on the English coast, with the target being Sunderland. The battle plan followed that of earlier raids, with the battle-cruisers *Moltke* and *Von der Tann*, the dreadnoughts *Markgraf*, *Grosser Kurfürst* and the newly commissioned SMS *Bayern* detailed for the task of making the assault, with the rest of the High Seas Fleet comprising sixteen battleships following some 20 miles behind.

From their experience at Jutland, and recognising the need for effective reconnaissance, Admiral Scheer ordered four Zeppelins to scout far out in the North Sea to warn of the approach of British ships, plus four further Zeppelins to scout directly ahead of the fleet itself. Additionally, twenty-four U-boats were positioned in the southern North Sea with the intention of ambushing the Grand Fleet, with the fleet setting sail from the Jade Basin at 9.00 p.m. on 18 August.

News of the German intentions had already been received via wireless intercepts that had been swiftly decoded in Room 40, who in turn alerted Fleet HQ that evening. On receipt of this information, the Grand Fleet at Scapa was led to sea in the early afternoon by Admiral Burney, later to be joined by Admiral Jellicoe, who, having been on leave, joined the fleet from the cruiser HMS *Royalist* later in the day at sea.

Vice-Admiral Beatty departed the Firth of Forth with six battle-cruisers and five battleships of the 5th Battle Squadron to join the main fleet of twenty-nine battleships off the Long Forties. In addition, the Harwich Force, comprising five light cruisers and twenty destroyers, had also put to sea, making best speed to a position off the western side of the Dogger Bank.

An early loss was that of the light cruiser *Nottingham* attached to Beatty's force, which was hit by three torpedoes from the U-boat *U52* at 6.00 a.m. on the morning of 19 August. It sank after an hour with minimal loss of life.

At 6.15 a.m., the Admiralty informed Jellicoe that the enemy was 200 miles to the south-east and later the same source informed him that the battle-cruiser fleet would be within 40 miles of the German fleet by 2.00 p.m. Jellicoe increased the speed of the fleet to maximum and, with good visibility and weather conditions, he felt confident of intercepting the German fleet before dark.

The High Seas Fleet in turn received a report from a patrolling Zeppelin that had sighted the Grand Fleet temporarily heading north, away from Scheer, to avoid a minefield. A further report from another airship, the *L13*, which had spotted the Harwich Force heading north-east, but mistakenly identified the cruisers as battleships, fortuitously caused Hipper to change course at 12.10 p.m. to the south-east, away from the approaching British fleet.

Unsure of the position of the British Fleet or their strength, Scheer prudently turned for home at 2.35 p.m. and aborted the raid on Sunderland. By 4.00 p.m. Jellicoe had received information that the German fleet had turned back to port and abandoned the undertaking, ordering his ships back to their bases.

At 4.52 p.m., the light cruiser *Falmouth* was hit by two torpedoes from the *U52* and sank the following day while under tow, after being hit by two further torpedoes from the *U66*.

The Harwich Force sighted the German ships at 5.45 p.m. as they made for home, but were too far behind to attack them before nightfall and gave up the chase.

A final success for British forces came when the German battleship *Westfalen* was torpedoed at 5.05 a.m on the morning of 19 August by the submarine *E23*, commanded by Lieutenant Commander R. Turne, patrolling off the Jade Basin. The German ship, although damaged, managed to make it home.

This operation was the last occasion on which the High Seas Fleet approached British shores for the rest of the war and on 6 October the resumption of the policy of unrestricted submarine warfare meant that U-boats would not be available to the fleet to participate in any further raiding operations with them.

At the same time in September 1916 at a conference aboard the *Iron Duke*, it was decided that in the light of recent events it would in future put the fleet at unnecessary risk to undertake fleet operations below 55° North latitude – that is to say no further south than the latitude of Newcastle, unless some extreme emergency such as an invasion was undertaken by German forces.

A further German fleet operation took place on 18–19 October 1916 off the coast of Norway, and, although Admiral Jellicoe was made aware of the sortie through naval intelligence, he chose to leave his ships in port with steam up, as it was judged that the risks did not justify the possible results.

The Germans in turn failed to find the reported warships and abandoned the sortie after the SMS *Munchen* was struck by a torpedo fired by the British submarine *E38*, but made it back to port.

In November, Admiral Scheer ordered a division of dreadnoughts to aid two U-boats, *U20* and *U30*, that had become stranded in fog on the Danish coast. The *U30* was towed off and survived the war, but the *U20* was stuck fast and had to be abandoned and blown up.

On the return trip, lying in wait off the Horns Reef was the British submarine *J1* of 1,200 tons surface displacement and which was propelled by three 1,200hp diesel engines that delivered 19.5 knots, making them the fastest class of submarines in existence at that time.

The *J1* successfully managed to torpedo two battleships of the squadron, the *Grosser Kurfurst* and the *Kronprinz* which, although seriously damaged, made it to port for subsequent repair. Commander Laurence of the *J1* was awarded a bar to his Distinguished Service Order for his actions.

Since the Battle of Jutland, the High Seas Fleet had been largely restricted to its bases, rarely venturing into the North Sea in any force. But the fleet was employed in the Baltic against Russian forces in Operation Albion when, after eventually taking the port of Riga, the Naval High Command planned to seize the island of Osel and its gun batteries that controlled the entrance to the Gulf of Finland and the Russian naval base at Kronstadt.

For the operation beginning in September 1917 the German Navy deployed no less than twelve dreadnoughts, accompanied by nine light cruisers, and sixty torpedo boats. Against this formidable force the Russians attempted to defend the island with two battleships, an armoured cruiser and nine destroyers. Needless to say, the Germans prevailed and took the island, taking 100,000 prisoners and 100 guns.

It may come as a surprise to the reader that the convoy system that had been employed by the Royal Navy since the Dutch Wars, and that played such an important part of the war effort during the Second World War, was not instituted fully until 1917 in the Great War. The Admiralty's main objection was that they lacked the necessary escort vessels and that a convoy presented a larger target to U-boats.

After much opposition from the Admiralty, the advantages were eventually accepted and in July 1916 the Harwich to Hook of Holland convoy, which had suffered from the attentions of the Flanders U-boat flotilla, was instituted. This was followed in February 1917 by similar protection being offered to the Humber to Bergen convoys and the trans-Atlantic convoys later in the year. But it was only at the War Council's insistence, following the loss of 860,000 tons of shipping in March 1917, that the Admiralty finally consented to fully embrace the universal concept of the convoy.

In a change of policy, the new Commander-in-Chief of the Grand Fleet, Sir David Beatty, moved the battle fleet permanently from Scapa Flow down to Rosyth on the Firth of Forth from April 1918, bringing the fleet closer to the enemy, in order to more rapidly intercept any further incursions of the German Fleet, while still observing the principle of not risking the fleet further south than 55° N. The change from the lonely windswept Orkney Isles to the home comforts of shore leave in Rosyth or Edinburgh must have been very much welcomed by the crews, who could now enjoy the everyday pleasures of a sailor at liberty in port.

Fearful of exposing his ships on further raids on the English coast, Admiral Scheer next turned his attentions to the British convoys to Norway that were essential to the British war effort for its supplies of timber.

Using his light surface forces, two lightly protected convoys were intercepted and several merchant ships sunk in mid-1917, which persuaded the Admiralty to detail a squadron of battleships based at Invergordon to protect the convoys. Admiral Scheer saw this move as an opportunity he had been waiting for – to destroy a detached squadron of the Grand Fleet.

After several small-scale attempts to disrupt the Norwegian convoys throughout 1917, on 23 April 1918 Admiral Scheer organised a major operation to fall on the Norwegian eastbound and westbound convoys simultaneously, based on information communicated by Naval Intelligence.

Hipper's battle-cruisers left the Schillig Roads heading northward to the Skagerrak, with the battleships of the High Seas Fleet leaving later to follow 20 miles behind Hipper's Squadron in support. Unfortunately, although the battle-cruisers reached the rendezvous point undetected and on time, faulty intelligence meant that they had missed both the east and westbound convoys, each having sailed the day before.

Admiral Beatty had sortied with a force of thirty-one battleships and four battle-cruisers, but he was too late to catch the retreating German ships, highlighting the disadvantage the Grand Fleet was at and had been at for the past four years when the High Seas Fleet chose to conduct operations off the Norwegian or Danish coasts that were relatively near to their home bases.

A further disaster befell the Germans when the battle-cruiser *Moltke*, while steaming at high speed, cast a propeller, causing the turbine to race to destruction, damaging other machinery and flooding the engine room. The battle-cruiser was towed back to port by the battleship SMS *Oldenburg*.

On returning through the defensive minefields off Helgoland, the *Moltke* was torpedoed by the submarine *E42*, but despite this was able to reach port safely. The *Moltke* was subsequently repaired and conducted training programmes in the Baltic in September and October 1918, which effectively was the only relatively safe place for ships of the High Seas Fleet to operate in, so dominant was the Royal Navy's control of the North Sea.

The German Army had launched an offensive in March 1918 on the Western Front as a final effort to defeat the Allies before the more than one million men of the United States Army could be deployed on the battlefield.

At this stage the Germans had the advantage of transferring almost fifty divisions of battle-hardened troops from the Russian front thanks to the cessation of hostilities with that country following the Treaty of Brest-Litovsk.

Initially, the Allies were taken by surprise by the offensive, which was very successful, with advances of up to 60 miles being made on the Somme and Aisne fronts – a scale of advance that had not been seen since 1914 – but rather less on the Belgium border and in the south on the Champagne and Marne sector. However, the Germans were unable to maintain the advance and ultimately, after suffering heavy casualties and plagued with logistical problems, lack of rations and supplies thanks to the British blockade, the offensive stalled.

In August 1918, an Allied counter-attack threw back the exhausted German troops, causing them to lose all the ground they had taken in the last five months, allowing the Allies to advance and break through the vaunted Hindenburg Line.

As the war drew to its now inevitable close in the latter months of 1918, Germany's allies were crumbling one by one, with first Bulgaria seeking an armistice in late September and then Turkey entering negotiations for peace, which was eventually signed aboard *Agamemnon* on 30 October.

The High Seas Fleet were being increasingly troubled by a collapse of morale and discontent among the crews, who were concerned with a lack of rations and their conditions on board ships and in the barracks, even though they were better off than the soldiers fighting on the Western Front.

A general war weariness and political agitation was rife on the ships, which was related to the conduct of the war and a growing sense that Germany was doomed to lose the struggle.

Through the long months of inactivity as the ships of the High Seas Fleet remained swinging idly at their anchors at Kiel and Wilhelmshaven, the crews seethed with dissent that proved a fertile ground for political agitators to inflame the injustices real or imagined held by the sailors.

The effects of the punishment they had received at Jutland from the guns of British battleships had undermined the morale of the Navy as a whole and the majority of those officers and men who had experienced the battle were under no illusions about how close the High Seas Fleet had come to total annihilation and had no wish to be exposed to the guns of the Grand Fleet again.

By August the situation on the Western Front was desperate and General Ludendorff, while telling his army to hold their current positions, advised the Kaiser the war was lost and that a negotiated armistice was necessary.

On 24 October, with the German Army falling back to the frontier, Admiral von Hipper, now commanding the High Seas Fleet, planned a sortie. He took to sea the majority of the High Seas Fleet to confront the Grand Fleet in a final battle that it was thought would improve the German Government's negotiating position at the armistice talks. However, the sailors of the High Seas Fleet had no intention of sacrificing themselves in an already lost cause and rose in rebellion against their officers.

On 29 October when the orders for the fleet to sail from Wilhelmshaven were issued, the sailors in three of the dreadnoughts of the 3rd Squadron mutinied and refused to weigh anchor. This was followed by sailors of the 1st Squadron on the battleships *Thuringen* and *Helgoland*, who also rebelled and sabotaged the ships' engines to stop them putting to sea, while the officers had all but lost control over their crews.

Initially, a group of the mutineers were arrested, but by 4 November they were freed by thousands of their colleagues as the Soldiers' and Sailors' Revolutionary Councils took over first the port of Kiel and then two days later Wilhelmshaven, with each warship being controlled by a sailors' council. Under the influence of the Soldiers' and Sailors' Revolutionary Councils, the revolution spread rapidly throughout Germany and on 10 November 1918 the Kaiser abdicated and crossed the border into exile in the Netherlands.

There followed a period of civil war between varying left-and-right wing political factions until in August 1919 a new constitution was adopted by the Weimar Republic, composed largely of social democrats and the Army, that became the legitimate government of Germany.

During the negotiations to settle the details of the armistice, the Allies insisted that the High Seas Fleet should be surrendered, but this was rejected by the German Government representatives, claiming that as the fleet had not been defeated it was unacceptable to them. The Allies reluctantly agreed on internment in a neutral port and approached Spain and Norway to take the ships, but both refused. It was then suggested by Britain that the German ships should be interned at Scapa Flow, and on 12 November the terms were delivered to the German Government, instructing them to have the High Seas Fleet ready for sea on 18 November.

The German representative crossed the North Sea on 15 November in a light cruiser to meet with Sir David Beatty on the *Queen Elizabeth* in the Firth of Forth, where the terms were presented to the German Government. Under these terms all the U-boats were ordered to proceed to Harwich where they were to surrender to Rear Admiral Tyrwhitt and the Harwich Force. For the U-boat, the weapon that had almost brought Britain to her knees, there was to be no question of mere internment.

The surface ships were ordered to sail to the Firth of Forth and to surrender to Admiral Beatty, from where they would be led to Scapa Flow to be interned pending the outcome of peace negotiations. Having no room for manoeuvre, Rear Admiral Meurer signed the document at midnight on the same day.

At Harwich, the first submarines began to arrive on 20 November, being escorted in by destroyers, with no show of emotion or cheering from the waiting British sailors, on the strict orders of Rear Admiral Tyrwhitt, to be anchored in long lines in the River Stour. Eventually 176 U-boats were brought into captivity, with several foundering, possibly deliberately, during the crossing. Under the terms of the surrender the German ships were to be demilitarised by removing the breech mechanisms of their main armament and the emptying of their shell rooms before departure.

In revolutionary Germany, rail transport disruptions and general shortages meant that the coal stocks necessary to carry the ships across the North Sea were so low that the scrapings of the coal dumps, including the dust, were required to provide sufficient bunkerage for the fleet.

The once proud ships of the High Seas Fleet posed a sorry sight as they prepared for sea; the long neglect during the months of inactivity spent in their harbours was evident in their peeling paintwork, rust-stained sides, dull brass-work and weed-covered bottoms. Admiral Hipper could not bring himself to face the humiliation of the surrender and the sad duty devolved onto Vice-Admiral Ludwig von Reuter, who in turn had been instructed by the chief of naval staff, Admiral Adolf von Trotha, that under no circumstances was he to allow the Allies to seize the ships, as they were still the property of the German Government, who expected them to be returned to Germany at the conclusion of peace negotiations.

On 21 November the ships of the High Seas Fleet, comprising nine (eventually eleven) battleships, five battle-cruisers, eight light cruisers and forty-nine torpedo boats, left the Jade Basin to a position 100 miles west of the Firth of Forth. The cruiser *Cardiff*, flying the flag of Rear Admiral Alexander-Sinclair, sailed out alone to meet the German fleet and led it to the rendezvous with the Grand Fleet 40 miles east of the Isle of May.

Admiral Beatty took the combined Grand Fleet and Allied warships, including nine American dreadnoughts and French warships, to sea shortly after the departure of the *Cardiff* in an assemblage of more than over 365 ships. This mighty array of sea power, their crews at action stations and with gun crews in anti-flash gear and gas masks closed up for action at their guns, headed eastwards to meet their enemies of the four-year war.

In the morning light in near perfect weather for the North Sea, with naval airships flying overhead, Admiral Beatty, on sighting the *Cardiff* approaching, formed the fleet into two long lines 6 miles apart, allowing the *Cardiff* to lead the German ships between the lines. At the correct moment Beatty ordered both lines to turn inward through 180° to bring *Lion* abeam of the German flagship of von Reuter, with the ship's guns trained inward on the German fleet. The three columns of warships, friend and foe together, then shaped course for the Firth of Forth, with the Grand Fleet anchoring above and the German fleet below the Forth rail bridge.

The *Queen Elizabeth*, with Beatty on board, pulled out of line below the bridge to see the German ships pass to their anchorages. There was no cheering and little sense of elation among the officers and men of the Grand Fleet as their enemies, who over the past four years they had only seen briefly as vague fleeting shapes that disappeared into the mists, passed closely by.

There remained one final act to carry out, and at 11.00 a.m. Admiral Beatty transmitted a signal to Vice-Admiral von Reuter that the German flag would be hauled down at sunset and not be hoisted again without permission.

Over the next five days the German ships were escorted to Scapa Flow, with the move being completed on 27 November. The ships were anchored in lines on the west side of the Flow in Gutter Sound and off the island of Hoy.

In mid-December the majority of the ships' crews were repatriated to Germany. Their numbers were now reduced from the 20,000 who had brought the ships into internment to 4,800, leaving only small skeleton crews to maintain the ships, awaiting the outcome of the Paris peace talks being held at Versailles that would determine the fate of the ships.

The peace talks continued for seven months. While it was in progress the British blockade was still in force, cutting off the supply of much needed foodstuffs to a starving populace, needlessly extending their sufferings. In the end, despite the harsh terms and the unrealistic reparations imposed on Germany, the German plenipotentiaries had no option but to sign the document.

At Scapa Flow during internment, the conditions on the German ships deteriorated under the Sailors' Councils, which effectively controlled them. The lack of discipline and poor food, which had to be supplied from Germany, delivered once a fortnight together with the post. The crews were confined to their ships, and with little recreation or outside communication this led to the further demoralisation of the crews.

The living conditions quickly deteriorated, with the ships infested with rats, cockroaches and other vermin, and although a doctor was available to the fleet, there was no dentist and the British refused to supply one. The crews augmented their meagre diet by fishing and catching seagulls to eat, while Admiral von Reuter transferred from the *Friedrich der Grosse* to the cruiser *Emden*, as the Sailors' Council on the flagship proved too difficult for him to deal with.

In the negotiations to decide the disposal or otherwise of the German fleet, France and Italy had hoped to receive 25 per cent each of the ships in reparations, while the British wanted to see all the ships destroyed, recognising that any redistribution would be detrimental to British interests.

On learning of the possible terms of the treaty in May 1919, von Reuter prepared plans for the possible scuttling of his ships in accordance with the instructions given to him by Admiral von Trotha in November.

At the same time, the British were aware that such action could be taken and, while keeping an eye on the situation, planned in turn to seize the ships by force immediately after the signing of the peace treaty.

The 1st Battle Squadron that was guarding the interned ships was under the command of Admiral Fremantle. Having been informed that the armistice that was to run out on 21 June had been extended until 23 June to allow the complex negotiations to be completed, he took the majority to sea for exercises on 20 June, leaving only a handful of destroyers and armed drifters on guard.

Believing hostilities were about to recommence on the morning of 21 June, Admiral von Reuter sent the signal 'Paragraph 11 today acknowledge' at 11.20 a.m. on that day to all ships and, in accordance with previously issued instructions, the crews opened sea cocks and flood valves, allowing the sea into the ships where all watertight doors and portholes were fixed open. By noon, watchers on shore noticed that the *Friedrich der Grosse* was listing to port and that all ships had hoisted the imperial battle flag.

Admiral Fremantle's squadron was recalled to port, but only the battleship *Baden* and a handful of destroyers and one cruiser were saved or beached in shallow water. By 5.00 p.m. the bulk of the High Seas Fleet lay on the bottom of Scapa Flow. Ten battleships, four light cruisers and thirty-two destroyers were sunk. Nine German sailors were shot and killed, with nineteen wounded, while 1,700 others picked up from boats were sent as prisoners of war to the POW camp at Nigg.

Although the French and Italians were furious at the loss of ships they had hoped to acquire, the British, in the shape of the First Sea Lord Admiral Sir Rosslyn Wemyss, viewed it as a blessing in disguise, as it disposed of the contentious question of the redistribution of the ships among the Allies.

A salvage company was formed in 1923 that raised and scrapped four destroyers. This was followed by a larger company founded by Ernest Cox, who bought the rights to raise the German fleet for a nominal sum from the Admiralty in 1924, and with the aid of an ex-German floating dock raised twenty-four destroyers in eighteen months.

Cox next went on to raise the battle-cruisers SMS *Hindenburg* and *Seydlitz*, eventually raising five battleships, battle-cruisers and cruisers before the outbreak of the Second World War.

The battleships *Konig, Kronprinz Wilhelm*, and *Markgraf*, plus four cruisers still lie in deep water, protected under the Ancient Monuments & Archaeological Areas Act 1979. However, small-scale salvage was still carried out to recover small pieces of steel known as Low background steel (still used in research and by industry because it has not been contaminated with radio isotopes, as it antedates nuclear contamination from the mid-twentieth century).

In April 1919, the Admiral Sir David Beatty hauled down his flag: the Grand Fleet, having served the purpose for which it had been created, ceased to exist. They were reorganised into the Home, Atlantic and Mediterranean fleets, which were composed as follows:

Home Fleet – Admiral Sir Henry Oliver
King George V, Orion, Monarch, Conqueror, Thunderer and *Erin*

Atlantic Fleet – Admiral Sir Charles Madden
Royal Sovereign and *Queen Elizabeth* classes, battle-cruisers, *Repulse, Renown, Lion* and *Princess Royal*

Mediterranean Fleet – Admiral Sir John de Robeck
Iron Duke class *Ajax* and *Centurion*

With the war over, substantial reductions in personnel and ships had to be urgently made on the grounds of economy. At the time of the armistice in November 1918, the strength of the Royal Navy was 415,000 officers and men. By December 1919 this figure had been reduced to 162,000 officers and men. Similarly with ships, all of the older battleships, including the original *Dreadnought* and the battle-cruiser *Indomitable* went to the breakers between 1920 and 1922, together with ten of the earlier dreadnoughts and all of the old pre-dreadnoughts. All the old protected cruisers, armoured cruisers and the majority of the light cruisers, together with hundreds of destroyers, sloops, corvettes and other naval craft, were sold or went to the scrapyards in the early 1920s, their job done.

One final job remained for the Royal Navy to perform and that was the clearance of mines. During the war the Germans had laid an estimated 1,360 individual minefields in the proximity of the British coastline and harbours, comprising an estimated 20,000 mines, 90 per cent of which had been laid by the *UC* class submarine minelayers. British minelayers had laid 65,000 mines in barrages designed to control the exit through the Dover Straits, the Northern Barrage and mines laid in German home waters. Additionally, a further 11,000 mines were deposited in the Mediterranean Sea by the Royal Navy. The Admiralty undertook to clear these mines by the end of November 1919 and engaged officers and men who had previously been employed in minesweepers to volunteer for this specialised duty for a period of three months on extra pay.

This work was given the utmost priority in order to make the approaches to British harbours and shipping lanes safe for merchant traffic once again, where, thanks to the large number of minesweepers involved in an intensive programme of clearance, the greater part of the work was completed by December 1919 as planned, although individual drifting mines posed a hazard for many years to come. During this work they were assisted by the flying boats and airships of the Royal Naval Air Service in spotting minefields and individual floating mines from the air, either by destroying them by machine-gun fire from the air or calling up surface craft to deal with them.

In this task the RNAS airships were particularly useful, due to their long duration, as demonstrated by the cruise of the North Seas class airship *NS11* with a Hydrogen capacity of 360,000 cubic feet giving a gross lift of 10 tons and powered by two 240hp. Fiat engines giving a speed of 70mph that made a continuous cruise of 101 hours, traversing 4,000 nautical miles on mine patrol over the North Sea in July 1919.

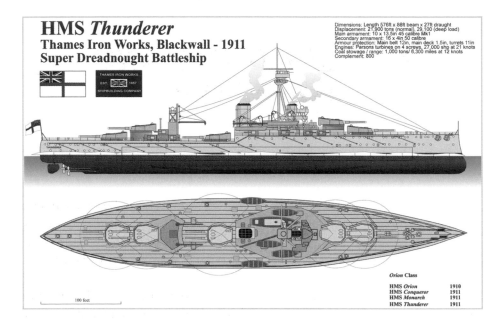

HMS *Thunderer*
Thames Iron Works, Blackwall - 1911
Super Dreadnought Battleship

Dimensions: Length 576ft x 88ft beam x 27ft draught
Displacement: 27,900 tons (normal), 29,100 (deep load)
Main armament: 10 x 13.5in 45 calibre Mk1
Secondary armament: 16 x 4in 50 calibre
Armour protection: Main belt 12in, main deck 1.5in, turrets 11in
Engines: Parsons turbines on 4 screws, 27,000 shp at 21 knots
Coal stowage / range: 1,000 tons/ 6,300 miles at 12 knots
Complement: 800

100 feet

Orion Class

HMS *Orion*	1910
HMS *Conqueror*	1911
HMS *Monarch*	1911
HMS *Thunderer*	1911

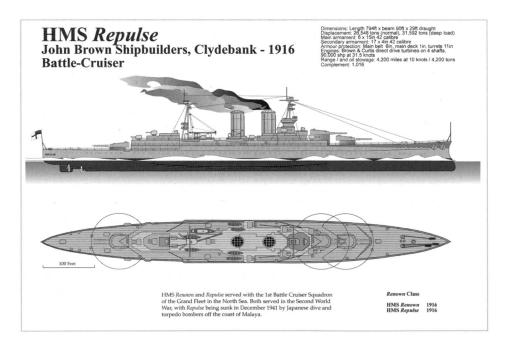

HMS *Repulse*
John Brown Shipbuilders, Clydebank - 1916
Battle-Cruiser

Dimensions: Length 794ft x beam 90ft x 29ft draught
Displacement: 26,548 tons (normal), 31,592 tons (deep load)
Main armament: 6 x 15in 42 calibre
Secondary armament: 17 x 4in 42 calibre
Armour protection: Main belt 6in, main deck 1in, turrets 11in
Engines: Brown & Curtis direct drive turbines on 4 shafts,
90,000 shp at 31.5 knots
Range / and oil stowage: 4,200 miles at 10 knots / 4,200 tons
Complement: 1,016

100 Feet

HMS *Renown* and *Repulse* served with the 1st Battle Cruiser Squadron of the Grand Fleet in the North Sea. Both served in the Second World War, with *Repulse* being sunk in December 1941 by Japanese dive and torpedo bombers off the coast of Malaya.

Renown Class

| HMS *Renown* | 1916 |
| HMS *Repulse* | 1916 |

EPILOGUE

THE CAPTAINS AND
THE KINGS

With the signing of the peace treaty on 28 June 1919, along with the rapid running down of the fleet on the grounds of economy and in the light of experience so painfully learnt during the war, a new direction was required for the principles on which the next generation of warships should be built, and, indeed, how the war at sea should be fought in future.

Not only were the ships to be affected by these changes, but the war had highlighted serious deficiencies in all areas of training, particularly in the area of communications between individual ships, squadrons and the Admiralty.

The lack of effective reporting of intelligence from scouting squadrons to their Commander-in-Chief during fleet operations in the North Sea, where particularly at Jutland Admiral Jellicoe had been starved of the vital knowledge by his subordinate commanders regarding the position of the German ships, robbed Jellicoe of the opportunity to annihilate the High Seas Fleet which, had there been an extra hour of daylight and better visibility, he undoubtedly would have accomplished.

The First Sea Lord Earl Beatty and others at the Admiralty considered that, to maintain the pre-eminent position of the Royal Navy, more and bigger battleships needed to be built.

In this, he was opposed by more forward-thinking officers like Sir Percy Scott, who argued for smaller capital ships limited in displacement to 10,000 tons, both on the terms of cost and of the rapid development of air power, whose destructive potential had been ably demonstrated during the war, along with the development of the aircraft carrier.

Also, the rise of the U-boat and the torpedo had been so successfully employed by the Germans that they almost brought Britain to edge the of defeat and augured for the changes in sea warfare that were to come.

In the end, Beatty's view prevailed and after the war two large battleships, HMS *Rodney* and HMS *Nelson*, both of 35,000 tons' displacement and each mounting nine 16in guns, were laid down, together with the battle-cruiser HMS *Hood*. At 41,200 tons and carrying eight 15in guns, this was the largest ship in the Royal Navy and it perpetuated the same errors of poor armour protection that had caused the British to lose three battle-cruisers at Jutland. Ultimately, it was to be the cause of the loss of the *Hood* herself in 1941.

These were followed by what were to be the last generation of battleships, with the *King George V* class built under the terms of the Washington Treaty that attempted by agreement to limit the size of all nations' battleships to 35,000 tons, and postponed their building for five years.

Five of this class, HMS *King George V*, HMS *Prince of Wales*, HMS *Duke of York*, HMS *Anson* and HMS *Howe*, were laid down in 1937, with all taking an active part in the Second World War. The *Prince of Wales*, after having been damaged in the action in the North Atlantic against the German battleship SMS *Bismarck* when the *Hood* was sunk, was herself sunk along with the battle-cruiser HMS *Repulse* by Japanese aircraft off the Malayan coast on 10 December 1941, demonstrating the vulnerability of battleships to air attack.

The final expression of the British battleship was HMS *Vanguard* of 44,500 tons, laid down in 1941, but not completed until April 1946, at a cost of £9,000,000. She was built too late to take part in the war and was already outmoded by the startling developments in air power, as well as being out of step with post-war naval development. She was soon reduced to the reserve fleet, before going to the breakers in 1960.

On the positive side, the material shortcomings highlighted by the First World War were being addressed, with more attention being given to effective communication and methods of the rapid reporting of information, thanks to better training and improved wireless communications.

The standard of gunnery was also greatly improved with the adoption of the concentration of fire technique, where salvoes from a group of ships were directed jointly onto an individual target, with the fall of shot being adjusted from the analysis of the individual ship's ranging information. This group firing was most effective and hits could be registered after three salvoes, in marked contrast to poor shooting at Jutland, where at one stage the battle-cruisers took almost an hour to secure a hit on their opposite numbers.

Later developments in the 1940s brought in the era of radar-aimed and -laid guns, where enemy ships could be ranged and fired on from great range with pinpoint accuracy in the most appalling weather conditions or the depths of night, as was the *Scharnhorst* when she was engaged and sunk by the *Duke of York* in December 1943 – this being the last surface action between capital ships.

The quality of British projectiles had also been a cause for great concern, when it was revealed that many of their heavy armour-piercing shells failed to penetrate the German armour, but broke up on impact, causing only superficial damage.

This shortcoming was addressed during the inter-war period, with the quality of British gunnery and the penetrating power of shells being greatly improved, with improvements in metallurgy, more effective fuses and better training. The protection of magazines was also improved, with the installation of more effective double closing interlocking anti-flash doors to the shell rooms and hoists and the storage of ready-use ammunition in closed boxes to prevent the flash in the case of a hit on a turret spreading to the magazines, as at Jutland. Although great improvements were made, the problems of protecting magazines were never completely solved.

Of the main characters involved in the drama of the war at sea in the Great War, four men (two British and two Germans) had held the fate of their respective nations in their hands.

The British Commander-in-Chief from 1914 to 1916, Admiral Sir John Jellicoe (1859–1935), who many held responsible for the failure to destroy the High Seas Fleet at Jutland, was relieved of command of the Grand Fleet in November 1916 to become First Sea Lord, where, during his term of office, the German U-boat campaign almost brought Britain to the edge of starvation. Jellicoe was once again blamed for his lack of commitment to overcoming the menace, and he was dismissed by the First Lord of the Admiralty Sir Eric Geddes in December 1917. He was created Viscount Jellicoe of Scapa in January 1918 and promoted to Admiral of the Fleet in mid-1918.

Having been replaced by the more popular Sir David Beatty, this promotion bore all the aspects of a bowler hatting, as he bore the odium of losing tactically at Jutland, although he importantly retained the command of the seas in a strategic sense. It is sad to relate that neither the Admiralty nor his successor as Commander of the Grand Fleet, Sir David Beatty, saw fit to invite him to attend the surrender of the High Seas Fleet in November 1918.

Jellicoe became Governor General of New Zealand from 1920 until 1925. On his return to England, he was created the Earl Jellicoe of Scapa in June 1925 and wrote his critical account of the Battle of Jutland and the operations of the Grand Fleet in the Great War. After living in quiet retirement, he died from pneumonia on 20 November 1935 at the age of 75.

Vice-Admiral Sir David Beatty (1871–1936) succeeded Admiral Jellicoe as Commander-in-Chief of the Grand Fleet in November 1916, being promoted to full Admiral in January 1919, and even more rapidly to Admiral of the Fleet in May 1919. He was a participant in the Washington Naval Treaty of 1922, leaving the Navy in 1927, retiring to a quiet life in Leicestershire, where he died on 11 March 1936 at the age of 65. He was buried, as was Jellicoe, in Westminster Abbey.

On the German side, Admiral Reinhard Scheer (1863–1928) became commander of the High Seas Fleet in January 1914 and in August 1916 was promoted to Chief of Naval Staff. Retiring from the navy after the war, he wrote his memoirs in 1919. In 1920 an intruder broke into his home and murdered his wife and maid and injured his daughter. After this incident he retired from public life, but accepted an invitation from Earl Jellicoe to visit him in England, but died before he could make the trip on 26 November 1928 at the age of 65. He was buried at Weimar outside of Berlin.

The great commander of the German battle-cruisers Admiral Franz von Hipper (1863–1932), who took over command of the High Seas Fleet from Admiral Scheer in August 1916, retired from the Navy in December 1918 and did not involve himself in politics or write his memoirs. Instead, he retired completely from public life and lived quietly in Altona, a suburb of Hamburg, until his death at the age of 68 in May 1932. He was buried at his home village of Othmarschen in Bavaria.

Of the kings and emperors who had played such an influential part in world affairs before the outbreak of the war, Franz Joseph of Austria had died in 1916 of natural causes, the German leader Kaiser William II fled into exile in the Netherlands following the revolution in November 1918, and the Russian Tsar Nicholas II and his family were executed by Bolshevik revolutionaries at Yekaterinburg in July 1918.

In the east, the Ottoman Empire had crumbled away, whilst throughout Europe and the Balkans other dynasties had fallen or were transformed into new democratic states. Only Great Britain's King George V remained secure in his throne, from where he could speculate on the massive changes of fortune he had witnessed in the fate of nations.

Following the end of the war, the Grand Fleet was rapidly run down on the grounds of economy and ceased to exist as a unit in April 1919. The remaining ships were assigned to the new Home Fleet that, as the name suggests, took over its duties in home waters, while other ships formed the Atlantic and Mediterranean fleets.

In the ultimate analysis, the great fleets of battleships built by Great Britain and Germany at such enormous cost did little to directly affect the outcome of the war, which by its nature was chiefly determined on the fields of Flanders, the Balkans, Russia and the Middle East.

However, by its very presence, the Grand Fleet nullified the German High Seas Fleet and allowed Great Britain and her Allies to command the seas and continue the trade that was essential to the winning of the war, despite the determined efforts of German undersea craft to bring Britain and her Allies to their knees.

Once again the old maxim applied:'It is upon the Navy, under the good Providence of God, that the safety, honour and welfare of this realm do chiefly depend.'

APPENDIX 1

ORDER OF BATTLE OF THE GRAND FLEET
AS IT PUT TO SEA, 30 May 1916

BATTLE FLEET
Fleet Flagship HMS *Iron Duke* – Flying the flag of the Commander-in-Chief
ADMIRAL SIR JOHN JELLICOE

SECOND BATTLE SQUADRON
First Division
VICE-ADMIRAL SIR MARTYN JERRAM – *King George V* (Flag) *Ajax, Centurion, Erin*

Second Division
REAR ADMIRAL A.C. LEVINSON – *Orion* (Flag), *Monarch, Conqueror, Thunderer*

FOURTH BATTLE SQUADRON
Third Division
ADMIRAL SIR JOHN JELLICOE – *Iron Duke* (Fleet Flagship), *Royal Oak, Superb, Canada*

Fourth Division
VICE-ADMIRAL SIR DOVETON STURDEE – *Benbow* (Flag), *Bellerophon, Temeraire, Vanguard*

FIRST BATTLE SQUADRON
Sixth Division
VICE-ADMIRAL SIR CECIL BURNEY – *Marlborough* (Flag), *Revenge, Hercules, Agincourt*

Fifth Division
REAR ADMIRAL E.F. GAUNT – *Colossus* (Flag), *Collingwood, Neptune, St Vincent*

ATTACHED BATTLE-CRUISERS
Third Battle-Cruiser Squadron
REAR ADMIRAL THE HON. H.L.A. HOOD – *Invincible* (Flag), *Inflexible, Indomitable*

First Cruiser Squadron
Rear Admiral Sir Robert Arbuthnot – *Defence* (Flag), *Warrior, Duke of Edinburgh, Black Prince*

Second Cruiser Squadron
Rear Admiral H.L. Heath – *Minotaur* (Flag), *Hampshire, Cochrane, Shannon*

Fourth Light Cruiser Squadron
Commodore E. Le Mesurier – *Calliope* (Flag), *Constance, Caroline, Royalist, Comus, Boadicea, Blanche, Bellona, Active, Canterbury, Chester*

Eleventh Destroyer Flotilla
Commodore J.R.P. Hawksley – *Castor* (Flag Lieutenant Cruiser), *Kempenfelt, Ossory, Mystic, Moon, Morning Star, Magic, Mounsey, Mandate, Marne, Minion, Manners, Michael, Mons, Martial, Milbrook*

Twelfth Destroyer Flotilla
Captain A.J.B. Stirling – *Faulknor* (Flag), *Marksman, Obedient, Maenad, Opal, Mary Rose, Marvel, Menace, Nessus, Narwhal, Mindful, Onslaught, Munster, Nonsuch, Noble, Mischief*

Fourth Destroyer Flotilla
Captain C.J. Wintour – *Tipperary* (Flag), *Broke, Achates, Porpoise, Spitfire, Unity, Garland, Ambuscade, Ardent, Fortune, Sparrowhawk, Contest, Shark, Acasta, Ophelia, Christopher, Owl, Hardy, Midge*

Attached to Battle Fleet
Oak (Destroyer), *Abdiel* (Minelayer)

BATTLE-CRUISER FLEET
Fleet Flagship HMS *Lion*
Vice-Admiral Sir David Beatty

FIRST BATTLE-CRUISER SQUADRON
Rear Admiral O. de Brock – *Lion* (Flag), *Princess Royal, Queen Mary, Tiger*

SECOND BATTLE-CRUISER SQUADRON
Rear Admiral W.C. Pakenham – *New Zealand, Indefatigable*

FIFTH BATTLE SQUADRON
Rear Admiral H. Evan-Thomas – *Barham* (Flag), *Valiant, Warspite, Malaya*

FIRST LIGHT CRUISER SQUADRON
COMMODORE E.S. ALEXANDER-SINCLAIR – *Galatea* (Flag), *Phaeton, Inconstant, Cordelia*

SECOND LIGHT CRUISER SQUADRON
COMMODORE W.E. GOODENOUGH – *Southampton* (Flag), *Birmingham, Nottingham, Dublin*

THIRD LIGHT CRUISER SQUADRON
REAR ADMIRAL T.D. NAPIER – *Falmouth* (Flag), *Yarmouth, Birkenhead, Gloucester*

FIRST DESTROYER FLOTILLA
CAPTAIN C.D. ROPER – *Fearless* (Flag Lieutenant Cruiser), *Acheron, Ariel, Attack, Hydra, Badger, Goshawk, Defender, Lizard, Lapwing*

THIRTEENTH DESTROYER FLOTILLA
CAPTAIN J.U. FARIE – *Champion* (Flag Lieutenant Cruiser), *Nestor, Nomad, Narborough, Obdurate, Petard, Pelican, Nerissa, Onslow, Moresby, Nicator*

COMBINED NINTH & TENTH FLOTILLAS
COMMANDER M.L. GOLDSMITH – *Lydiard* (Flag), *Liberty, Landrail, Laurel, Moorsom, Morris, Turbulent, Termagant*

Attached to Battle-cruiser Fleet
Engadine (Seaplane Carrier)

APPENDIX 2

ORDER OF BATTLE OF THE HIGH SEAS FLEET
AS IT PUT TO SEA, 31 May 1916

BATTLE FLEET
Fleet Flagship SMS *Friedrich der Grosse* Flying the flag of the Commander-in-Chief
VICE-ADMIRAL REINHARD SCHEER

FIRST SQUADRON
VICE-ADMIRAL REINHARD SCHEER – *Friedrich der Grosse* (Flag), *Ostfriesland*,
Thuringen, Helgoland, Oldenburg, Posen, Rheinland, Nassau, Westfalen

SECOND SQUADRON
REAR ADMIRAL MEURER – *Deutschland* (Flag), *Hessen, Pommern, Hannover, Schlesien,
Schleswig-Holstein*

THIRD SQUADRON
REAR ADMIRAL BENCKE – *Konig* (Flag), *Grosser Kurfurst, Kronprinz, Markgraf, Kaiser,
Kaiserin, Prinzregent Leopold*

LIGHT CRUISER SQUADRONS
COMMODORE VON REUTER – *Stettin* (Flag), *Munchen, Hamburg, Frauenlob, Stuttgart*

TORPEDO BOAT FLOTILLAS
COMMODORE MICHELSEN – *Rostock* (Flag, Light Cruiser)

First Flotilla
KAPITAN-LEUTNANT C. ALBRECHT – *G39, G40, G38, S3*

Third Flotilla
KORVETTENKAPITAN HOLLMAN – *S53, V71, V73, G88, S54, V48, G42*

Fifth Flotilla

KORVETTENKAPITAN HEINECKE – *G11*, *V2*, *V4*, *V6*, *V1*, *V3*, *G7*, *G8*, *G5*, *G9*, *G10*

Seventh Flotilla

KORVETTENKAPITAN VON KOCH – *S24*, *S15*, *S17*, *S20*, *S16*, *S18*, *S19*, *S23*, *V186*, *V189*

BATTLE-CRUISER FLEET

Battle-cruiser Fleet Flagship SMS *Lutzow*

VICE ADMIRAL VON HIPPER – *Lutzow* (Flag), *Derfflinger*, *Seydlitz*, *Moltke*, *Von der Tann*

LIGHT CRUISER SQUADRON

REAR ADMIRAL BODICKER – *Frankfurt* (Flag), *Wiesbaden*, *Pillau*, *Elbing*

TORPEDO BOAT FLOTILLAS

KORVETTENKAPITAN HEINRICH – *Regensburg* (Flag)

Second Flotilla

KAPITAN ZUR SEE SCHUUR – *B98*, *G101*, *G102*, *B112*, *B97*, *B109*, *B110*, *B111*, *G103*, *G104*

Sixth Flotilla

KORVETTENKAPITAN M. SCHULTZ – *G41*, *V44*, *G87*, *G88*, *V69*, *V45*, *V46*, *S50*, *G37*

Ninth Flotilla

KORVETTENKAPITAN GOEHLE – *V27*, *V28*, *S36*, *S51*, *S52*, *V10*, *S34*, *S33*, *V99*, *S35*

BIBLIOGRAPHY

Archibald, E.H.H., *The Fighting Ship in the Royal Navy* (Blandford Press, 1984)

Bacon, Admiral Sir Reginald, *Life of Lord Fisher of Kilverstone* (Hodder & Stoughton, 1929)

Bassett, Ronald, *Battle-Cruisers: A History 1908–1948*, (Macmillan, 1947)

Buttlar-Brandenfels, T. von, *Zeppeline Gegen England* (v Hasse & Koeler, 1925)

Brown, D.K., *The Grand Fleet: Warship Design & Development 1906–1922* (Chatham Publishing, 1999)

Burt, R.A., *Battleships of the Grand Fleet* (Arms and Armour Press, 1982)

Churchill, Winston Spencer, *My Early Life* (Odhams Press, 1958)

Corbett, J.S., *Principles of Maritime Strategy* (Longmans Green, 1911)

Cousins, Geoffrey, *The Story of Scapa Flow* (Frederick Muller, 1965)

Fleming, H.M. le, *Warships of World War 1* (Ian Allan, 1961)

Gagen, Ernst von, *Der Krieg zur See 1914–1918* (E.G. Mittler & Son, 1964)

Grove, Eric, *Big Fleet Actions* (Brockhampton Press, 1991,)

Hough, Richard, *The Great War at Sea 1914–1918* (Oxford University Press, 1983)

James, Admiral Sir William, *Code Breakers of Room 40* (St Martin's Press, 1956)

Jane, F.T., *Jane's Fighting Ships of World War 1* (Random House, 1990)

Macintyre, Captain Donald *Jutland* (Evans Brothers, 1957)

Marriott, L, *Battleships* (Igloo Books, 2010)

Massie, R.K. *Castles of Steel* (Jonathan Cape, 2004)

Miller, J., *Scapa* (Birlinn Books Ltd, 2001)

Pardoe, J., *The Cruise of the Sea Eagle* (Cressy Press, 2005)

Pears, R., *British Battleships 1892–1957* (Putnam, 1957)

Rhodes, J.R., *Gallipoli* (Macmillan, 1965)

Ridley-Kitts, Daniel, *Military, Naval & Civil Airships Since 1783* (History Press, 2012)

Saunders, Hilary St George, *Per Ardua* (Oxford University Press, 1944)

Simpson, Colin, *Lusitania* (Penguin Books, 1972)

Staff, G., *Battle of the Baltic Islands 1917* (Pen and Sword, 2008)

Trotter, W.P., *The Royal Navy in Old Photographs* (J.M. Dent & Sons, 1975)

Wingate, J., *Warship Profile H.M.S. Dreadnought* (Profile Publications, 1970)

Warner, George, *The Groundwork of British History* (Blackie and Son, 1912)

Wells, Capt. J. R.N., *The Immortal Warrior* (Kenneth Mason, 1987)

INDEX